Optimization Models
and Applications

Optimization Models and Applications

Editors

Siamak Pedrammehr
Mohammad Reza Chalak Qazani

Basel • Beijing • Wuhan • Barcelona • Belgrade • Novi Sad • Cluj • Manchester

Editors
Siamak Pedrammehr
Faculty of Design
Tabriz Islamic Art University
Tabriz
Iran

Mohammad Reza Chalak Qazani
Faculty of Computing and
Information Technology (FoCIT)
Sohar University
Sohar
Oman

Editorial Office
MDPI
St. Alban-Anlage 66
4052 Basel, Switzerland

This is a reprint of articles from the Special Issue published online in the open access journal *Axioms* (ISSN 2075-1680) (available at: www.mdpi.com/journal/axioms/special_issues/HIP0152SM0).

For citation purposes, cite each article independently as indicated on the article page online and as indicated below:

Lastname, A.A.; Lastname, B.B. Article Title. *Journal Name* **Year**, *Volume Number*, Page Range.

ISBN 978-3-7258-0138-1 (Hbk)
ISBN 978-3-7258-0137-4 (PDF)
doi.org/10.3390/books978-3-7258-0137-4

© 2024 by the authors. Articles in this book are Open Access and distributed under the Creative Commons Attribution (CC BY) license. The book as a whole is distributed by MDPI under the terms and conditions of the Creative Commons Attribution-NonCommercial-NoDerivs (CC BY-NC-ND) license.

Contents

About the Editors vii

Preface ix

Siamak Pedrammehr and Mohammad Reza Chalak Qazani
Special Issue "Optimisation Models and Applications"
Reprinted from: *Axioms* **2024**, *13*, 45, doi:10.3390/axioms13010045 1

Mohammad Rasouli, Assef Zare, Majid Hallaji and Roohallah Alizadehsani
The Synchronization of a Class of Time-Delayed Chaotic Systems Using Sliding Mode Control Based on a Fractional-Order Nonlinear PID Sliding Surface and Its Application in Secure Communication
Reprinted from: *Axioms* **2022**, *11*, 738, doi:10.3390/axioms11120738 4

Xing-Xing Ma and Yang-Dong Xu
Robust Multi-Criteria Traffic Network Equilibrium Problems with Path Capacity Constraints
Reprinted from: *Axioms* **2023**, *12*, 662, doi:10.3390/axioms12070662 21

Sofia Giuffrè
A Nonconstant Gradient Constrained Problem for Nonlinear Monotone Operators
Reprinted from: *Axioms* **2023**, *12*, 605, doi:10.3390/axioms12060605 37

Chetan Swarup, Ramesh Kumar, Ramu Dubey and Dowlath Fathima
New Class of K-G-Type Symmetric Second Order Vector Optimization Problem
Reprinted from: *Axioms* **2023**, *12*, 571, doi:10.3390/axioms12060571 50

Sarra Gismelseed, Amur Al-Yahmedi, Riadh Zaier, Hassen Ouakad and Issam Bahadur
Predicting Sit-to-Stand Body Adaptation Using a Simple Model
Reprinted from: *Axioms* **2023**, *12*, 559, doi:10.3390/axioms12060559 77

Juan Rafael Acosta-Portilla, Carlos González-Flores, Raquiel Rufino López-Martínez and Armando Sánchez-Nungaray
Efficient Method to Solve the Monge–Kantorovich Problem Using Wavelet Analysis
Reprinted from: *Axioms* **2023**, *12*, 555, doi:10.3390/axioms12060555 99

Saman Rajebi, Siamak Pedrammehr and Reza Mohajerpoor
A License Plate Recognition System with Robustness against Adverse Environmental Conditions Using Hopfield's Neural Network
Reprinted from: *Axioms* **2023**, *12*, 424, doi:10.3390/axioms12050424 128

Vahid Pourmostaghimi, Farshad Heidari, Saman Khalilpourazary and Mohammad Reza Chalak Qazani
Application of Evolutionary Optimization Techniques in Reverse Engineering of Helical Gears: An Applied Study
Reprinted from: *Axioms* **2023**, *12*, 252, doi:10.3390/axioms12030252 140

Mohammad Rasouli, Assef Zare, Hassan Yaghoubi and Roohallah Alizadehsani
Designing a Secure Mechanism for Image Transferring System Based on Uncertain Fractional Order Chaotic Systems and NLFPID Sliding Mode Controller
Reprinted from: *Axioms* **2023**, *12*, 828, doi:10.3390/axioms12090828 159

Hassan Yaghoubi, Assef Zare and Roohallah Alizadehsani
Analysis and Design of Robust Controller for Polynomial Fractional Differential Systems Using Sum of Squares
Reprinted from: *Axioms* **2022**, *11*, 623, doi:10.3390/axioms11110623 . . . . **180**

Xiaole Guo
On Mond–Weir-Type Robust Duality for a Class of Uncertain Fractional Optimization Problems
Reprinted from: *Axioms* **2023**, *12*, 1029, doi:10.3390/axioms12111029 . . . . **193**

About the Editors

Siamak Pedrammehr

Siamak Pedrammehr earned his Bachelor's and Master's degrees in Mechanical Engineering from the University of Tabriz in Iran. He further advanced his academic credentials by obtaining a Ph.D. in Engineering from Deakin University in Australia, where he subsequently received the prestigious Alfred Deakin Postdoctoral Research Fellowship in 2019. Following his Ph.D., he was appointed as a postdoctoral research fellow by Iran's National Elites Foundation at the University of Tabriz, a role he fulfilled for two years.

Currently, Dr. Pedrammehr holds a position as an Assistant Professor at the Faculty of Design at Tabriz Islamic Art University. He maintains an active research partnership with Deakin University. His research interests are diverse and include modeling and simulation, manufacturing processes, applied AI and socio-industrial studies.

Mohammad Reza Chalak Qazani

Mohammad Reza Chalak Qazani commenced his academic journey in manufacturing and production engineering, obtaining his Bachelor's degree from the University of Tabriz, Iran. He continued his studies in robotic and mechanical engineering, earning a master's degree from Tarbiat Modares University, Iran. Furthering his scholarly pursuit, he achieved his Ph.D. from the Institute for Intelligent Systems Research and Innovation (IISRI) at Deakin University, Australia. Upon completion of his doctorate, Dr. Qazani was granted the esteemed Alfred Deakin Postdoctoral Research Fellowship at the IISRI, dedicating two years to the advancement of model predictive control, motion cueing algorithms and soft computing controllers.

Currently, Dr. Qazani serves as an Assistant Professor within the Faculty of Computing and Information Technology (FoCIT) at Sohar University in Oman. His instructional expertise encompasses a spectrum of subjects, including data structures and algorithms, enterprise resource planning modeling and implementation, modeling and visualization, computer architecture, introductory artificial intelligence and advanced machine learning.

Preface

With its roots in diverse fields, optimization has evolved into an indispensable tool shaping the landscapes of engineering, economics, the environment, health, systems, businesses and more. It has become a guiding light, leading us toward optimal solutions in the intricate web of scientific challenges. In the celestial expanse of optimization, this book explores the convergence of theory and practice, shedding light on the transformative applications across various domains. Furthermore, it serves as a platform bridging theoretical rigor with practical significance, addressing scientific challenges across disciplines such as functional analysis, critical point theory, bifurcation theory, set-valued analysis, calculus of variations, etc. The convergence of theory and reality within this realm aims to advance optimization solutions and provide insights into the fundamental scientific challenges of our time. We extend our heartfelt gratitude to the authors for their outstanding contributions and to the diligent reviewers whose valuable comments have enhanced the quality of the articles. Special thanks to the Editorial Board and the Editorial Office of *Axioms* for their invaluable support and guidance throughout the publication process. We trust that our readers will find the articles in this journal to be informative, insightful and rich sources of new and valuable information on optimization models and their practical applications.

We wish you a happy reading!

Siamak Pedrammehr and Mohammad Reza Chalak Qazani
Editors

Editorial
Special Issue "Optimisation Models and Applications"

Siamak Pedrammehr [1,2,*] and Mohammad Reza Chalak Qazani [1,3]

1. IISRI, Deakin University, Waurn Ponds, VIC 3216, Australia; m.r.chalakqazani@gmail.com
2. Faculty of Design, Tabriz Islamic Art University, Tabriz 5164736931, Iran
3. FoCIT, Sohar University, Sohar 311, Oman
* Correspondence: s.pedrammehr@tabriziau.ac.ir

Citation: Pedrammehr, S.; Qazani, M.R.C. Special Issue "Optimisation Models and Applications". *Axioms* 2024, *13*, 45. https://doi.org/10.3390/axioms13010045

Received: 3 January 2024
Accepted: 5 January 2024
Published: 11 January 2024

Copyright: © 2024 by the authors. Licensee MDPI, Basel, Switzerland. This article is an open access article distributed under the terms and conditions of the Creative Commons Attribution (CC BY) license (https://creativecommons.org/licenses/by/4.0/).

Optimisation models have transcended their origins to become indispensable tools across many fields, including engineering, economics, the environment, health, systems of systems, businesses, and beyond. These models serve as guiding lights, illuminating the path toward optimal solutions. Within the optimisation realm, the following four distinct categories emerge, akin to constellations in the scientific cosmos: physics-based optimisation algorithms, swarm-based optimisation algorithms, game-based optimisation algorithms, and evolutionary-based optimisation algorithms. Over the past half-century, the optimisation domain has been a crucible where theory meets practice, generating solutions that have left indelible marks on diverse applications. In this Special Issue, our study takes us to the heart of the intricate interplay between optimisation models and their practical applications. In this realm, theory and reality merge to address fundamental scientific challenges. We earnestly invite researchers, akin to celestial navigators, to contribute their original, high-quality research papers. Let us explore the celestial expanse of optimisation and its transformative applications.

This Special Issue explores the intersection of optimisation models and real-world applications, encompassing diverse disciplines such as functional analysis, the critical point theory, bifurcation theory, set-valued analysis, calculus of variations, partial differential equations, variational and topological methods, fixed-point theory, game theory, convex analysis, matrix theory, control theory, and data mining. As a platform for researchers, it aims to bridge theoretical rigour with practical significance in addressing scientific challenges and advancing optimisation solutions across domains.

Rasouli et al. (Contribution 1) devised an adaptive sliding mode control for fractional-order chaotic systems, addressing an unknown time delay, uncertainty, and disturbances. Utilising a nonlinear fractional order PID sliding surface, stability is ensured using the Lyapunov theory and validated through MATLAB simulations. This approach extends to secure image communication, showcasing positive outcomes in correlation with NPCR, PSNR, and information entropy, even under uncertain parameters.

Ma and Xu (Contribution 2) introduced a method tackling robust multi-criteria traffic network equilibrium problems with path-capacity constraints. This study formulates an equivalent min-max optimisation problem, deploying a direct search algorithm and a smoothing optimisation approach based on a ReLU activation function variant for efficient solutions. Numerical examples highlight algorithm efficiency, particularly in small-scale traffic networks.

Giuffrè (Contribution 3) explored a nonconstant gradient-constrained problem, establishing a connection with a double obstacle problem. This study fulfils a constraint qualification condition, enabling the application of solid duality theory. It provides evidence for the existence of Lagrange multipliers, suggesting potential avenues for future research within this framework.

Swarup et al. (Contribution 4) delved into K-bonvexity/K-pseudo convexity concepts, establishing duality theorems for a K-Wolfe multi-objective second-order symmetric duality model. This work broadens mathematical perspectives, potentially contributing to applications in higher-order symmetric fractional programming problems and variational control problems over cones.

Gismelseed et al. (Contribution 5) employed a mathematical model to investigate factors influencing the sit-to-stand (STS) motion, formulating an optimisation problem to minimise joint torques. The model successfully predicted key STS motion characteristics, considering the motion speed, reduced joint strength, and seat height. These results align with experimental findings, providing insights into STS biomechanics for clinical investigations and daily activities related to human mobility.

Acosta-Portilla et al. (Contribution 6) introduced a methodology for solving the Monge–Kantorovich mass transfer problem, utilising Haar multiresolution analysis and wavelet transform. This approach significantly reduces computational operations, achieving efficient solutions at different resolution levels. Comparative results demonstrate consistent improvement over previous resolution levels, with exact solutions in some cases. This work offers valuable insights and suggests research opportunities for different discretisation techniques and cost function characteristics.

Rajebi et al. (Contribution 7) presented a robust license plate recognition system that is effective in adverse environmental conditions. Unlike prior approaches, this method evaluates and recognises license plates from various sources, handling environmental challenges by removing image artifacts before recognition. Utilising Hopfield's neural network for recognition reduces the execution time. It enhances accuracy compared to traditional methods, contributing significantly to automated surveillance systems.

Pourmostaghimi et al. (Contribution 8) introduced a helical gear reverse engineering methodology employing swarm-based optimisation, specifically the Grey Wolf Optimisation and Particle Swarm Optimisation. Results showcase superior performance in accuracy, convergence speed, and stability. This study suggests diverse gear applications and explores the impact of algorithm tuners on convergence speed.

Rasouli et al. (Contribution 9) proposed a robust synchronisation method for chaotic systems amid uncertainty. Combining the sliding mode control with adaptive rules ensures the convergence of unknown parameters and time delays to zero. Simulations show the robust synchronisation of uncertain, jerk-crusty systems, and the control strategy is applied successfully to secure communication.

Yaghoubi et al. (Contribution 10) present a novel approach for robust stability in polynomial fractional differential (PFD) systems using Caputo derivatives. Employing the sum of squares (SOSs) method, this research addresses stability challenges beyond linear matrix inequalities. Demonstrating robust Mittag–Leffler stability conditions, this study introduces a robust controller for PFD systems with unknown parameters and a polynomial state feedback controller for PFD-controlled systems, validated through simulations, offering innovative solutions for stability and control challenges.

Guo (Contribution 11) investigated a Mond–Weir-type robust duality for uncertain semi-infinite multi-objective fractional optimisation problems. It establishes a robust dual problem, incorporating a new subdifferential constraint qualification and a generalised convex-inclusion assumption. This study unveils robust #-quasi-weak, strong duality properties, extending previous results. These findings contribute to understanding uncertain fractional optimisation and suggest the future exploration of mixed-type robust approximate dual problems. Specific research funding sources for this work are not provided in the article.

We extend our heartfelt gratitude to the authors for their outstanding contributions to this journal in the field of 'Optimisation Models and Applications'. Our sincere appreciation goes to the diligent reviewers whose valuable comments and feedback have significantly enhanced the quality of the articles. We also acknowledge the invaluable support and guidance provided by the editorial board and the editorial office of *Axioms* throughout the publication process. We trust that our readers will find the articles in this journal to be informative, insightful, and rich sources of new and valuable information on optimization models and their practical applications.

Author Contributions: All authors contributed equally to writing, editing, and reviewing the manuscript. All authors have read and agreed to the published version of the manuscript.

Conflicts of Interest: The authors declare no conflicts of interest.

List of Contributions

1. Rasouli, M.; Zare, A.; Yaghoubi, H.; Alizadehsani, R. Designing a Secure Mechanism for Image Transferring System Based on Uncertain Fractional Order Chaotic Systems and NLFPID Sliding Mode Controller. *Axioms* **2023**, *12*, 828.
2. Ma, X.-X.; Xu, Y.-D. Robust Multi-Criteria Traffic Network Equilibrium Problems with Path Capacity Constraints. *Axioms* **2023**, *12*, 662.
3. Giuffrè, S. A Nonconstant Gradient Constrained Problem for Nonlinear Monotone Operators. *Axioms* **2023**, *12*, 605.
4. Swarup, C.; Kumar, R.; Dubey, R.; Fathima, D. New Class of KG-Type Symmetric Second Order Vector Optimization Problem. *Axioms* **2023**, *12*, 571.
5. Gismelseed, S.; Al-Yahmedi, A.; Zaier, R.; Ouakad, H.; Bahadur, I. Predicting Sit-to-Stand Body Adaptation Using a Simple Model. *Axioms* **2023**, *12*, 559.
6. Acosta-Portilla, J.R.; González-Flores, C.; López-Martínez, R.R.; Sánchez-Nungaray, A. Efficient Method to Solve the Monge–Kantarovich Problem Using Wavelet Analysis. *Axioms* **2023**, *12*, 555.
7. Rajebi, S.; Pedrammehr, S.; Mohajerpoor, R. A License Plate Recognition System with Robustness against Adverse Environmental Conditions Using Hopfield's Neural Network. *Axioms* **2023**, *12*, 424.
8. Pourmostaghimi, V.; Heidari, F.; Khalilpourazary, S.; Qazani, M.R.C. Application of Evolutionary Optimisation Techniques in Reverse Engineering of Helical Gears: An Applied Study. *Axioms* **2023**, *12*, 252.
9. Rasouli, M.; Zare, A.; Hallaji, M.; Alizadehsani, R. The synchronisation of a class of time-delayed chaotic systems using sliding mode control based on a fractional-order nonlinear PID sliding surface and its application in secure communication. *Axioms* **2022**, *11*, 738.
10. Yaghoubi, H.; Zare, A.; Alizadehsani, R. Analysis and Design of Robust Controller for Polynomial Fractional Differential Systems Using Sum of Squares. *Axioms* **2022**, *11*, 623.
11. Guo, X. On Mond–Weir-Type Robust Duality for a Class of Uncertain Fractional Optimisation Problems. *Axioms* **2023**, *12*, 1029.

Disclaimer/Publisher's Note: The statements, opinions and data contained in all publications are solely those of the individual author(s) and contributor(s) and not of MDPI and/or the editor(s). MDPI and/or the editor(s) disclaim responsibility for any injury to people or property resulting from any ideas, methods, instructions or products referred to in the content.

Article

The Synchronization of a Class of Time-Delayed Chaotic Systems Using Sliding Mode Control Based on a Fractional-Order Nonlinear PID Sliding Surface and Its Application in Secure Communication

Mohammad Rasouli [1], Assef Zare [1,*], Majid Hallaji [2] and Roohallah Alizadehsani [3]

1. Faculty of Electrical Engineering, Gonabad Branch, Islamic Azad University, Gonabad 6518115743, Iran
2. Faculty of Electrical Engineering, Neyshabure Branch, Islamic Azad University, Neyshabure 6518115743, Iran
3. Institute for Intelligent Systems Research and Innovation (IISRI), Deakin University, Geelong, VIC 3216, Australia

* Correspondence: assefzare@gmail.com

Citation: Rasouli, M.; Zare, A.; Hallaji, M.; Alizadehsani, R. The Synchronization of a Class of Time-Delayed Chaotic Systems Using Sliding Mode Control Based on a Fractional-Order Nonlinear PID Sliding Surface and Its Application in Secure Communication. *Axioms* **2022**, *11*, 738. https://doi.org/10.3390/axioms11120738

Academic Editor: Jose Manoel Balthazar

Received: 21 November 2022
Accepted: 12 December 2022
Published: 16 December 2022

Publisher's Note: MDPI stays neutral with regard to jurisdictional claims in published maps and institutional affiliations.

Copyright: © 2022 by the authors. Licensee MDPI, Basel, Switzerland. This article is an open access article distributed under the terms and conditions of the Creative Commons Attribution (CC BY) license (https://creativecommons.org/licenses/by/4.0/).

Abstract: A novel approach for the synchronization of a class of chaotic systems with uncertainty, unknown time delays, and external disturbances is presented. The control method given here is expressed by combining sliding mode control approaches with adaptive rules. A sliding surface of fractional order has been developed to construct the control strategy of the abovementioned sliding mode by employing the structure of nonlinear fractional PID (NLPID) controllers. The suggested control mechanism using Lyapunov's theorem developed robust adaptive rules in such a way that the estimation error of the system's unknown parameters and time delays tends to be zero. Furthermore, the proposed robust control approach's stability has been demonstrated using Lyapunov stability criteria and Lipschitz conditions. Then, in order to assess the performance of the proposed mechanism, the presented control approach was used to simulate the synchronization of two chaotic jerk systems with uncertainty, unknown time delays, and external distortion. The results of the simulation confirm the robust and desirable synchronization performance. Finally, a secure communications mechanism based on the proposed technique is shown as a practical implementation of the introduced control strategy, in which the message signal is disguised in the transmitter with high security and well recovered in the receiver with high quality, according to the mean squared error (MES) criteria.

Keywords: chaotic synchronization; sliding mode control; adaptive control; uncertainty; unknown time-delay; secure communication

MSC: 93D09; 93B51

1. Introduction

Chaos is a phenomenon that occurs in nonlinear dynamic systems. The dynamic behavior of these systems is fully dependent on the initial conditions; therefore, even the tiniest change in these parameters generates big changes in their behavior. Many domains of study, including economics [1,2], chemistry [3,4], biology [5,6], and engineering [7,8], have discovered chaotic systems. Many scientists from numerous domains have been interested in the synchronization of chaotic systems in recent years [5]. Pecora and Carroll proposed chaos synchronization in 1990 [6].

Fractional order (FO) controllers were developed by combining fractional calculation with existing controllers. The increased number of configurable parameters in this type of controller creates more flexibility in the control process, which improves the performance of the controlled system. In this regard, the fractional PI controller [7,8], the fractional PD controller [9], the fractional lag–lead controller [10], the fractional CRONE controller [11,12], the adaptive FO PID controller [13], the reference adaptive control [14], the fractional model [15,16], and the fractional sliding mode control [17–19] have all been mentioned.

Adaptive sliding mode controllers have been shown to exhibit robust performance against system parameter changes and system uncertainties [20,21], with their greatest advantage being stability against system disturbances.

Adaptive control [22–24] is used to achieve control objectives when there is uncertainty in the system. Because of the benefits of stability against system parameter uncertainties, adaptive control has a faster convergence speed.

Sliding mode control, on the other hand, is a popular and successful strategy that is simple to implement [25,26]. The sliding mode controller is a variable structure controller that works well for nonlinear systems with model uncertainty. The primary aspect of sliding mode control is that it directs the system's states from the initial states to a suitable sliding surface that is provided and then maintains the states at the mentioned sliding surface for all subsequent iterations. Several articles have been provided in this area for the synchronization of chaotic systems utilizing sliding mode control. Qamati et al. [27] successfully synchronized identical Genesio–Tesi chaotic systems using adaptive sliding mode control. The integrated sliding mode control method was used to examine the control and synchronization of extremely chaotic Zhou systems, as discussed in [28].

The authors of [29] proposed a hybrid fractional-order sliding mode control method for finite-time synchronization of a chaotic class using the direct Lyapunov method. Synchronization of fractional order chaotic systems is introduced in [30]. In this design, a sliding surface based on non-linear fractional order PID is presented. In [31], Khan et al. have proposed an adaptive sliding mode control approach for synchronizing complicated chaotic systems with uncertainty and disturbance. The authors of [32] have investigated an adaptive sliding control with fuzzy logic for the synchronization of chaotic fractional order systems with uncertainty and exogenous shocks. In [33], a class of complicated fractional order systems with non-uniform order has been explored, and an adaptive sliding control has been proposed for synchronizing this class of systems. An adaptive controller has been devised in [34] for integer-order synchronization with uncertainty and unknown time delays.

The time delays in the system being unknown is one of the factors to consider for uncertain systems with time delays. This issue can provide significant challenges in the controller design process for a variety of purposes, including synchronization. The amount of time delays in the system is unknown which, on the other hand, increases the complexity of the system model, which can be considered in enhancing the security level of data transmission in the field of secure telecommunications. A sliding surface based on NLFPID is proposed to direct and keep all the states of the system to the sliding surface in order to synchronize a class of chaotic systems with uncertainty and unknown time delays.

A sliding surface based on NLFPID is proposed to direct and keep all the states of the system on the sliding surface in order to synchronize a class of chaotic systems with uncertainty and unknown time delays. Then, for robust synchronization of uncertain chaotic systems with unknown time delays, a fractional order adaptive control is adopted. Following that, updating and estimating laws for uncertain parameters are determined using an appropriate Lyapunov function and Lipschitz condition to ensure the system's stability. Finally, the synchronization of two chaotic jerk systems with uncertain and unknown time delays, as well as uncertainty and distortion, are examined and simulated in order to evaluate the performance of the proposed approach. The simulation results demonstrate the efficacy of the proposed adaptive-sliding control mechanism for synchronization that is robust against uncertainty, external distortions, and unknown time delays. Furthermore, based on the obtained results, the proposed control approach is effective in estimating uncertain parameters and unknown delays.

To implement the proposed control strategy, a secure telecommunication mechanism based on chaos masking is presented at the end, indicating optimal security in sending and high quality in retrieving information despite the presence of various uncertainties and uncertain parameters in the system structure.

The following innovations have been presented in the study that was carried out in order to synchronize two uncertain chaotic systems.

1. Using the NLFOPID sliding surface instead of conventional sliding surfaces.
2. The existence of unknown time delays.
3. The limits of uncertainty and disturbance are unknown.

Accordingly, based on the above concepts, using the appropriate Lyapunov function and update rules, a control mechanism has been proposed, which can overcome the problem of unknown time delays, uncertain uncertainty, and uncertain disturbances by properly adjusting the controller parameters.

This article is structured as follows. Section 2 presents the basic definitions used in the article. Section 3 describes the description of chaotic systems with uncertainty and unknown time delays. Section 4 presents an NLFPID-based sliding surface for directing and maintaining system states on the sliding surface. The adaptive robust control technique for the synchronization of uncertain chaotic systems with finite and uncertain time delays is detailed in Section 5. Section 6 investigates and simulates the synchronization of two chaotic jerk systems with unknown time delays, as well as uncertainty and distortion, and Section 7 presents results based on the stated ideas.

2. Basic Definitions of the Fractional-Order Derivative

Definition 1. *The fractional order integral and derivative are defined as follows [27]*:

$$D_t^\alpha = \begin{cases} \frac{d^\alpha}{dt^\alpha} & \alpha > 0 \\ 1 & \alpha = 0 \\ \int_a^t (d\tau)^{-\alpha} & \alpha < 0 \end{cases} \tag{1}$$

where D_t^α is the fractional order operator.

Definition 2. *The Riemann–Liouville fractional order integral order α of the function $f(t)$ is defined as follows [28]*:

$$_{t_0}I_t^\alpha f(t) = \frac{1}{\Gamma(\alpha)} \int_{t_0}^t \frac{f(\tau)}{(t-\tau)^{1-\alpha}} d\tau \tag{2}$$

where t_0 is the initial time and $\Gamma(\alpha)$ is the Gamma function, which is defined as follows:

$$\Gamma(\alpha) = \int_0^\infty e^{-t} t^{\alpha-1} dt \tag{3}$$

where is the Gamma function operator.

Definition 3. *Suppose $n-1 < \alpha \leq n$. $n \in N$. The fractional Riemann–Liouville derivative of order α is defined for the function $f(t)$ as follows [26]*:

$$_{t_0}D_t^\alpha f(t) = \frac{d^\alpha f(t)}{dt^\alpha} = \frac{1}{\Gamma(n-\alpha)} \frac{d^n}{dt^n} \int_{t_0}^t \frac{f(\tau)}{(t-\tau)^{\alpha-n+1}} d\tau \tag{4}$$

Remark 1. *The Riemann–Liouville fractional order derivative in Equation (4) is first integrated and then derived. Therefore, the derivative of a constant number in this definition is not equal to zero.*

Definition 4. *The Caputo fractional order derivative of order α in the continuous function $f(t)$ is defined as follows [29]:*

$$_{t_0}D_t^\alpha f(t) = \begin{cases} \frac{1}{\Gamma(m-\alpha)} \int_{t_0}^t \frac{f^{(m)}(\tau)}{(t-\tau)^{\alpha-m+1}} d\tau & m-1 < \alpha < m \\ \frac{d^m f(t)}{dt^m} & \alpha = m \end{cases} \quad (5)$$

where m is the first integer after α.

Definition 5. *If the function $f(x,t)$ is piecewise linear and satisfies the Lipschitz conditions, then [34]:*

$$|f(t,x) - f(t,\hat{x})| \leq \gamma_f |x - \hat{x}| \qquad \forall\, x, \hat{x} \in R^n \quad (6)$$

where $f(x,t)$ is Lipschitz at x and the positive constant γ_f, is called the Lipschitz constant.

3. The System Descriptor Equations

The equations characterizing a class of master–slave chaotic systems with uncertainty and unknown time delays in the presence of an unknown disturbance will be introduced in this section; the canonical form dynamics of the master system are as follows:

$$\begin{cases} \dot{x}_i = x_{i+1}. & 1 \leq i \leq n-1 \\ \dot{x}_n = \sigma_0^T x + f(x(t-\tau_1),t) + \Delta f(x(t),t) + d_1(t). \end{cases} \quad (7)$$

Equations of the slave system are as follows:

$$\begin{cases} \dot{y}_i = y_{i+1}. & 1 \leq i \leq n-1 \\ \dot{y}_n = \sigma_0^T y + g(y(t-\tau_2),t) + \Delta g(y(t),t) + d_2(t) + u(t). \end{cases} \quad (8)$$

The differential equations are expressed in the forms corresponding to a number of well-known chaotic systems, such as the Van der Pol oscillator, Duffing's oscillator, Genesio–Tesi's system, Arneodo's system, etc. [35], where $x(t), y(t) \in R^n$ describes the dynamic states of the master and slave systems, σ_0^T represents the constant coefficients in linear states of the system, and $f(x(t-\tau_1),t) \cdot g(y(t-\tau_2),t) \in R$ are the terms of nonlinear functions with unknown time delays with a τ_1, τ_2 delay, and $\Delta f(x(t),t)$, $\Delta g(x(t),t)$ describes nonlinear bounded uncertainties of the master and slave systems. Additionally, $d_1(t), d_2(t)$ describes the external disturbances of the master and slave systems, and $u(t)$ is the control law applied to the slave system.

Definition 6. *If the following criterion is met for the systems given in Equations (1) and (2) for all conditions influencing the system, including all initial conditions, uncertainties, and unknown time delays, as well as external disturbance, the system has robust synchronization:*

$$\lim_{t \to \infty} |y_i(t) - x_i(t)| = \lim_{t \to \infty} |e_i(t)| = 0.\ i = 1, \ldots, n, \quad (9)$$

where $e_i(t)$ introduces synchronization errors in the master and slave systems.

As a result, the following are the dynamic equations proposing the synchronization error for the uncertain chaotic master and slave systems with unknown time delays, as specified in Equations (1) and (2):

$$\begin{cases} \dot{e}_i = e_{i+1}. & 1 \leq i \leq n-1 \\ \dot{e}_n = \sigma_0^T E + g(y(t-\tau_2),t) + \Delta g(x(t),t) + d_2(t) \\ \quad -f(x(t-\tau_1),t) - \Delta f(x(t),t) - d_1(t) + u(t). \end{cases} \quad (10)$$

where $E = (e_1 \cdot e_2 \cdots e_n)^T$. As a result, by initially introducing a PI sliding surface and a fractional order non-linear derivative, all states of the system should be directed to and held on the sliding surface. The system's uncertainty bounds and unknown parameters should then be estimated and updated by creating an adaptive controller. In the continuation of the robust synchronization of chaotic systems (7) and (8) in the presence of external disturbances, bounded nonlinear uncertainties, and unknown time delays, it should be performed such that the dynamics of the slave system state in a finite time conforms to the dynamic behavior. The estimation error of the unknown parameters in both chaotic systems tend to zero in any state, and the robust stability of the system in finite time is guaranteed.

Assumption 1. *The unknown external disturbances $d_1(t), d_2(t)$ and unknown bounded nonlinear uncertainties $\Delta f(x(t),t)$ and $\Delta g(x(t),t)$ in the master and slave systems (7) and (8) satisfy the following conditions:*

$$|\Delta f(x(t),t)| \leq \beta_1 \omega_1(x).$$
$$|\Delta g(y(t),t)| \leq \beta_2 \omega_2(y).$$
$$|d_1(t)| \leq \rho_1.$$
$$|d_2(t)| \leq \rho_2.$$
(11)

where $|\cdot|$ describes l_1 norm and $\beta_2, \beta_1, \rho_2, \rho_1$ are unknown real positive constants, and $\omega_2(\cdot), \omega_1(\cdot)$ are known functions.

Assumption 2. *Unknown time delays introduced by non-linear functions $f(x(t-\tau_1),t)$, $g(y(t-\tau_2),t) \in R$ are represented in the general forms of (7) and (8) in the master and slave systems, for each $x(t), y(t) \in R$ and, according to (6), they satisfy the following Lipschitz condition:*

$$\begin{aligned} & |f(x(t-\tau_1)) - f(x(t-\hat{\tau}_1))| \leq k_1 |x(t-\tau_1) - x(t-\hat{\tau}_1)| \\ & |x(t-\tau_1) - x(t-\hat{\tau}_1)| \leq m_1 |(t-\tau_1) - (t-\hat{\tau}_1)| = m_1 |\tilde{\tau}_1| \\ & \Rightarrow |f(x(t-\tau_1)) - f(x(t-\hat{\tau}_1))| \leq l_1 |\tau_1 - \hat{\tau}_1| = l_1 |\tilde{\tau}_1|, \; l_1 = k_1 m_1 \\ & |g(y(t-\tau_2)) - g(y(t-\hat{\tau}_2))| \leq k_2 |y(t-\tau_2) - y(t-\hat{\tau}_2)| \\ & |y(t-\tau_2) - y(t-\hat{\tau}_2)| \leq m_1 |(t-\tau_2) - (t-\hat{\tau}_2)| = m_2 |\tilde{\tau}_2| \\ & \Rightarrow |g(y(t-\tau_2)) - g(y(t-\hat{\tau}_2))| \leq l_2 |\tau_2 - \hat{\tau}_2| = l_2 |\tilde{\tau}_2|, \; l_2 = k_2 m_2 \end{aligned}$$
(12)

where $\tau_1, \tau_2 \in R$ expresses unknown time delays, $\hat{\tau}_1, \hat{\tau}_2 \in R$ estimates unknown time delays, and l_1 and l_2 are positive and uncertain constants.

4. The Sliding Mode Control Approach Based on NLFPID Controllers

We will provide an NLFPID-based sliding surface to synchronize the chaotic system with unknown uncertainty and time delays presented in (7) and (8). The novel NLF sliding surface is presented in accordance with the NLFPID controller structure established in [35], which enhances tracking:

$$s(t) = h(e) \cdot \left[k_p e_n(t) + T_I D^{-\lambda} \sum_{i=1}^{n} k_{1i} e_i + T_d D^{\delta} \sum_{i=1}^{n} k_{2i} e_i(t) \right]. \quad (13)$$

where $h(e)$ is a nonlinear function, defined as follows:

$$h(e) = k_0 + (1 - k_0)\|E(t)\|. \quad k_0 \in (0,1) \tag{14}$$

where $\|E\|$ is the first norm of the dynamic state of the system error, expressed as $\|E(t)\| = \sum_{i=1}^{n}|e_i|$. T_I and T_d are the time constants of integral and derivative phrases. The parameters k_{1i} and k_{2i} are positive constant values of the sliding surface that fulfill the intended system's stability. The following conditions must be met if the system is in sliding mode:

$$s(t) = 0 \quad , \quad \dot{s}(t) = 0. \tag{15}$$

Therefore, the fractional order derivative of the sliding surface in Equation (13) is as follows:

$$\begin{aligned}\dot{s}(t) &= k_0 k_p \dot{e}_n(t) + k_0 T_i D^{1-\lambda} \sum_{i=1}^{n} k_{1i} e_i(t) + k_0 T_d D^{1+\delta} \sum_{i=1}^{n} k_{2i} e_i(t) \\ &+ (1-k_0)\Big[k_p \tfrac{d}{dt}(\|E(t)\|e_n(t)) \\ &+ T_I \tfrac{d}{dt}\big(\|E(t)\| D^{-\lambda} \sum_{i=1}^{n} k_{1i} e_i(t)\big) \\ &+ T_d \tfrac{d}{dt}\big(\|E(t)\| D^{\delta} \sum_{i=1}^{n} k_{2i} e_i(t)\big)\Big] = 0.\end{aligned} \tag{16}$$

In this scenario, we will substitute the final dynamic of the system's integer order error specified in Equation (10) in Equation (16), yielding:

$$\begin{aligned}\dot{s}(t) &= k_0 k_p (g(y(t-\tau_2),t) + \Delta g(x(t),t) + d_2(t) - f(x(t-\tau_1),t) \\ &- \Delta f(x(t),t) - d_1(t) + \sigma_0^T \cdot E(t) + u(t)) \\ &+ k_0 T_i D^{1-\lambda} \sum_{i=1}^{n} k_{1i} e_i(t) + k_0 T_d D^{1+\delta} \sum_{i=1}^{n} k_{2i} e_i(t) \\ &+ (1-k_0)\Big[k_p \tfrac{d}{dt}(\|E(t)\|e_n(t)) \\ &+ T_I \tfrac{d}{dt}\big(\|E(t)\| D^{-\lambda} \sum_{i=1}^{n} k_{1i} e_i(t)\big) \\ &+ T_d \tfrac{d}{dt}\big(\|E(t)\| D^{\delta} \sum_{i=1}^{n} k_{2i} e_i(t)\big)\Big] = 0.\end{aligned} \tag{17}$$

The control signal in this scenario is as follows:

$$\begin{aligned}u(t) &= \tfrac{-1}{k_0 k_p}\big(k_0 T_i D^{1-\lambda} \sum_{i=1}^{n} k_{1i} e_i(t) + k_0 T_d D^{1+\delta} \sum_{i=1}^{n} k_{2i} e_i(t) \\ &+ (1-k_0)\Big[k_p \tfrac{d}{dt}(\|E(t)\|e_n(t)) \\ &+ T_I \tfrac{d}{dt}\big(\|E(t)\| D^{-\lambda} \sum_{i=1}^{n} k_{1i} e_i(t)\big) \\ &+ T_d \tfrac{d}{dt}\big(\|E(t)\| D^{\delta} \sum_{i=1}^{n} k_{2i} e_i(t)\big)\Big]\big) \\ &+ f(x(t-\hat{\tau}_1),t) - g(y(t-\hat{\tau}_2),t) - \sigma_0^T \cdot E(t) - bs + \overline{u}(t).\end{aligned} \tag{18}$$

In Equation (18), the phrase $\overline{u}(t)$ comprises the sentences arising from estimating the bounds of the system's uncertainties and disturbances, which are specified as follows:

$$\overline{u}(t) = -\text{sgn}(s)[\hat{\beta}_2 \omega_2(y) + \hat{\beta}_1 \omega_1(x) + \hat{\rho}_2 + \hat{\rho}_1]. \tag{19}$$

5. Stability Analysis of the Proposed Mechanism

In this section, the robust adaptive controller is designed using the sliding surface based on NLFPID such that the synchronization of chaotic systems is guaranteed by the proposed control approach.

Theorem 1. *Synchronization of systems (6) and (7) is guaranteed by the definition of the controller $u(t)$ in spite of disturbances d_1 and d_2 and uncertainties Δf and Δg along with unknown time delays τ_1 and τ_2:*

$$\begin{aligned}
u(t) = & -g(y(t - \hat{\tau}_1)) + f(x(t - \hat{\tau}_2)) \\
& - \tfrac{1}{k_0 k_p}(k_0 T_l D^{1-\lambda} \textstyle\sum_{i=1}^n k_{1i} e_i(t) + k_0 T_d D^{1+\delta} \sum_{i=1}^n k_{2i} e_i(t)) \\
& + (1 - k_0)\left[k_p \tfrac{d}{dt}(\|E(t)\| e_n(t))\right. \\
& + T_l \tfrac{d}{dt}(\|E(t)\| D^{-\lambda} \textstyle\sum_{i=1}^n k_{1i} e_i(t)) \\
& \left. + T_d \tfrac{d}{dt}(\|E(t)\| D^{\delta} \textstyle\sum_{i=1}^n k_{2i} e_i(t))\right] - \sigma_0^T \cdot E(t) - bs \\
& - \mathrm{sgn}(s)(\hat{\beta}_2 \omega_2(y) + \hat{\beta}_1 \omega_1(x) + \hat{\rho}_2 + \hat{\rho}_1).
\end{aligned} \quad (20)$$

where $\hat{\rho}_1$ and $\hat{\rho}_2$ are the estimations of input disturbances, $\hat{\tau}_1$ and $\hat{\tau}_2$ are estimates of time delays, and $\hat{\beta}_1 \omega_1$ and $\hat{\beta}_2 \omega_2$ are estimates of uncertainty in the master and slave systems. Therefore, in order to guarantee the stability of the system, we use the update laws to estimate the mentioned parameters as follows:

$$\begin{aligned}
\tilde{\tau}_i &= \tau_i - \hat{\tau}_i. \quad \tilde{\beta}_i = \beta_i - \hat{\beta}_i. \quad \tilde{\rho}_i = \rho_i - \hat{\rho}_i. \\
\dot{\hat{\tau}}_i &= -\dot{\tilde{\tau}}_i = |s| \mathrm{sgn}(\tilde{\tau}_i) + b \tilde{\tau}_i. \\
\dot{\hat{\rho}}_i &= -\dot{\tilde{\rho}}_i = k_0 k_p |s| + b \tilde{\rho}_i. \\
\dot{\hat{\beta}}_2 &= -\dot{\tilde{\beta}}_2 = k_0 k_p |s| \omega_2(y) + b \tilde{\beta}_2. \\
\dot{\hat{\beta}}_1 &= -\dot{\tilde{\beta}}_1 = k_0 k_p |s| \omega_1(x) + b \tilde{\beta}_1.
\end{aligned} \quad (21)$$

Proof. The following Lyapunov function is defined as follows:

$$v(t) = \tfrac{1}{2}[s^2(t) + \tilde{\beta}_1^2 + \tilde{\beta}_2^2 + l_1 \tilde{\tau}_1^2 + l_2 \tilde{\tau}_2^2 + \tilde{\rho}_1^2 + \tilde{\rho}_2^2]. \quad (22)$$

According to Equation (22), the derivative of the Lyapunov function is as follows:

$$\begin{aligned}
\Rightarrow \dot{v}(t) &= \tfrac{1}{2}\tfrac{d}{dt}(s^2 + \tilde{\beta}_1^2 + \tilde{\beta}_2^2 + l_1 \tilde{\tau}_1^2 + l_2 \tilde{\tau}_2^2 + \tilde{\rho}_1^2 + \tilde{\rho}_2^2) \\
&= s\dot{s} + \sum_{i=1}^{2}\left(\tilde{\beta}_i \dot{\tilde{\beta}}_i + l_i \tilde{\tau}_i \dot{\tilde{\tau}}_i + \tilde{\rho}_i \dot{\tilde{\rho}}_i\right).
\end{aligned} \quad (23)$$

By substituting (17) in (23), Equation (24) is obtained:

$$\begin{aligned}
\dot{v}(t) = s \cdot \big[& k_0 k_p (g(y(t-\tau_2),t) + \Delta g(x(t),t) + d_2(t) \\
& -(f(x(t-\tau_1),t) + \Delta f(x(t),t) + d_1(t)) + \sigma_0^T \cdot E(t) + u(t)) \\
& + k_0 T_i D^{1-\lambda} \sum_{i=1}^n k_{1i} e_i(t) + k_0 T_d D^{1+\delta} \sum_{i=1}^n k_{2i} e_i(t) \\
& + (1-k_0) \big[k_p \tfrac{d}{dt} (\|E(t)\| e_n(t)) \\
& + T_I \tfrac{d}{dt} (\|E(t)\| D^{-\lambda} \sum_{i=1}^n k_{1i} e_i(t)) \\
& + T_d \tfrac{d}{dt} (\|E(t)\| D^{\delta} \sum_{i=1}^n k_{2i} e_i(t)) \big] \big] + \sum_{i=1}^{2} \left(\tilde{\beta}_i \dot{\tilde{\beta}}_i + l_i \tilde{\tau}_i \dot{\tilde{\tau}}_i + \tilde{\rho}_i \dot{\tilde{\rho}}_i \right).
\end{aligned} \quad (24)$$

By substituting (20) in (24), Equation (25) is obtained:

$$\begin{aligned}
\dot{v}(t) = s \cdot k_0 k_p (& g(y(t-\tau_2),t) - g(y(t-\hat{\tau}_2),t) + \Delta g(x(t),t) + d_2(t) \\
& + f(x(t-\hat{\tau}_1),t) - f(x(t-\tau_1),t) - \Delta f(x(t),t) - d_1(t) - bs \\
& - sgn(s)[\hat{\beta}_2 \omega_2(y) + \hat{\beta}_1 \omega_1(x) + \hat{\rho}_2 + \hat{\rho}_1]) \\
& + \sum_{i=1}^{2} \left(\tilde{\beta}_i \dot{\tilde{\beta}}_i + l_i \tilde{\tau}_i \dot{\tilde{\tau}}_i + \tilde{\rho}_i \dot{\tilde{\rho}}_i \right).
\end{aligned} \quad (25)$$

Thus, we have:

$$\begin{aligned}
\dot{v}(t) \leq |s| \cdot \big[& k_0 k_p (|g(y(t-\tau_2),t) - g(y(t-\hat{\tau}_2),t)| + |\Delta g(x(t),t)| \\
& + |f(x(t-\hat{\tau}_1),t) - f(x(t-\tau_1),t)| - |\Delta f(x(t),t)| \\
& + |d_2(t) - d_1(t)|) \big] - k_0 k_p b s^2 \\
& + k_0 k_p s(-sgn(s)[\hat{\beta}_2 \omega_2(y) + \hat{\beta}_1 \omega_1(x) + \hat{\rho}_2 + \hat{\rho}_1]) \\
& + \sum_{i=1}^{2} \left(\tilde{\beta}_i \dot{\tilde{\beta}}_i + l_i \tilde{\tau}_i \dot{\tilde{\tau}}_i + \tilde{\rho}_i \dot{\tilde{\rho}}_i \right).
\end{aligned} \quad (26)$$

By substituting (11) and (12) in (26), Equation (27) is obtained:

$$\begin{aligned}
\dot{v}(t) \leq |s| \cdot \big[& k_0 k_p (l_2 |\tau_2 - \hat{\tau}_2| + \beta_2 \omega_2(y) + l_1 |\tau_1 - \hat{\tau}_1| + \beta_1 \omega_1(x) + \rho_1 - \rho_2) \big] \\
& - k_0 k_p b s^2 \\
& + k_0 k_p s((-sgn(s)[\hat{\beta}_2 \omega_2(y) + \hat{\beta}_1 \omega_1(x) + \hat{\rho}_2 + \hat{\rho}_1])) \\
& + \sum_{i=1}^{2} \left(\tilde{\beta}_i \dot{\tilde{\beta}}_i + l_i \tilde{\tau}_i \dot{\tilde{\tau}}_i + \tilde{\rho}_i \dot{\tilde{\rho}}_i \right).
\end{aligned} \quad (27)$$

The derivative of the Lyapunov function would be as follows:

$$\dot{v}(t) \leq |s| [k_0 k_p (l_1 |\tilde{\tau}_1| + \tilde{\beta}_2 \omega_2(y) + l_2 |\tilde{\tau}_2| + \tilde{\beta}_1 \omega_1(y) + \hat{\rho}_2 + \hat{\rho}_1)] - b s^2 \\
+ \sum_{i=1}^{2} \left(\tilde{\beta}_i \dot{\tilde{\beta}}_i + l_i \tilde{\tau}_i \dot{\tilde{\tau}}_i + \tilde{\rho}_i \dot{\tilde{\rho}}_i \right). \quad (28)$$

Using the update laws (21) and substituting them in (28), Equation (29) is obtained:

$$\Rightarrow \dot{v}(t) \leq -b(s^2 + \tilde{\beta}_1^2 + \tilde{\beta}_2^2 + \tilde{\tau}_1^2 + \tilde{\tau}_2^2 + \tilde{\rho}_1^2 + \tilde{\rho}_2^2) = -bv(t). \tag{29}$$

Thus, the stability of the proposed method for synchronization of the chaotic system with uncertainty, disturbance, and unknown time delays is proved. □

6. Simulation Results

This section evaluates the accuracy of synchronizing uncertain chaotic systems with unknown time delays using the proposed control mechanism based on an NLF sliding surface, adaptive controller, and update rules that estimate the system's parameters. Two modified jerk chaotic systems with the aforementioned properties were used for this purpose. The equations governing the master system in the canonical form are as follows [33]:

$$\begin{cases} \dot{x}_1 = x_2 \\ \dot{x}_2 = x_3 \\ \dot{x}_3 = -\varepsilon_1 x_1(t) - x_2(t) - \varepsilon_2 x_3(t) + f_3(x_1(t-\tau_1), t). \end{cases} \tag{30}$$

where $\varepsilon_1 = \frac{3}{2}$, $\varepsilon_2 = 0.35$, and $f_3(x_1(t-\tau_1), t)$ is a piecewise linear function:

$$f_3(x_1(t-\tau_1), t) = \tfrac{1}{2}(v_0 - v_1)[|x_1(t-\tau_1)+1| - |x_1(t-\tau_1)-1|] \\ + v_1 x_1(t-\tau_1). \tag{31}$$

where $v_0 < -1 < v_1 < 0$ and $v_0 = -2.5$, $v_1 = -0.5$.

When the initial conditions are selected as $(x_1(0); x_2(0); x_3(0))^T = (-0.52; 0.52; 0.87)^T$, the system's chaotic behavior would be as shown in Figure 1.

$$\begin{cases} \dot{x}_1 = x_2 \\ \dot{x}_2 = x_3 \\ \dot{x}_3 = -\varepsilon_1 x_1(t) - x_2(t) - \varepsilon_2 x_3(t) + f_3(x_1(t-\tau_1), t) + \Delta f(x(t), t) + d_1(t). \end{cases} \tag{32}$$

The dynamic of the slave system follows the equations below:

$$\begin{cases} \dot{y}_1 = y_2 \\ \dot{y}_2 = y_3 \\ \dot{y}_3 = -\varepsilon_1 y_1(t) - y_2(t) - \varepsilon_2 y_3(t) + g_3(y_1(t-\tau_2), t) + \Delta g(y(t), t) + d_2(t) + u(t). \end{cases} \tag{33}$$

where the nonlinear terms of the slave system are as follows:

$$g_3(y_1(t-\tau_2), t) = \tfrac{1}{2}(v_0 - v_1)[|y_1(t-\tau_2)+1| - |y_1(t-\tau_2)-1|] \\ + v_1 y_1(t-\tau_2). \tag{34}$$

Accordingly, the dynamic of the synchronization error for the chaotic jerk master and slave systems would be as follows:

$$\begin{cases} \dot{e}_1 = e_2 \\ \dot{e}_2 = e_3 \\ \dot{e}_3 = -\varepsilon_1 e_1(t) - e_2(t) - \varepsilon_2 e_3(t) - g(y_1(t-\tau_2)) + f(x_1(t-\tau_1)) \\ \quad + \Delta g(y(t), t) - \Delta f(x(t), t) + d_2(t) - d_1(t) + u(t). \end{cases} \tag{35}$$

In this step, we apply the robust adaptive control signal, which is designed by combining the sliding surface based on the NLFPID controllers and described in Equation (20), to the slave system.

The following figures show the behavior of the chaotic system synchronized with the above dynamic equations before and after applying the proposed control signal. Figures 1 and 2 respectively show the phase diagram and the behavior of the jerk system without applying the controller.

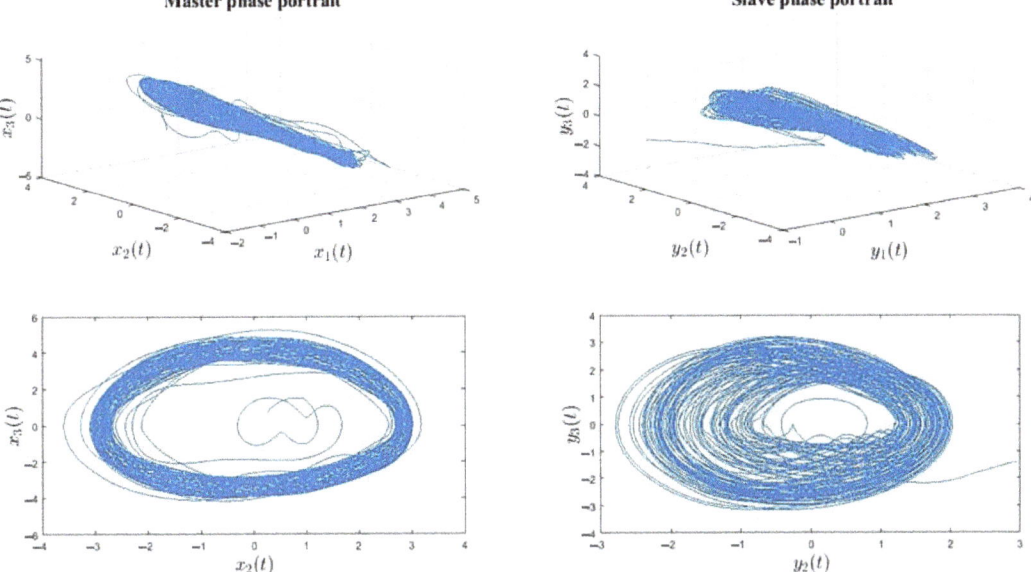

Figure 1. Phase diagram of the jerk master and slave systems without applying the controller.

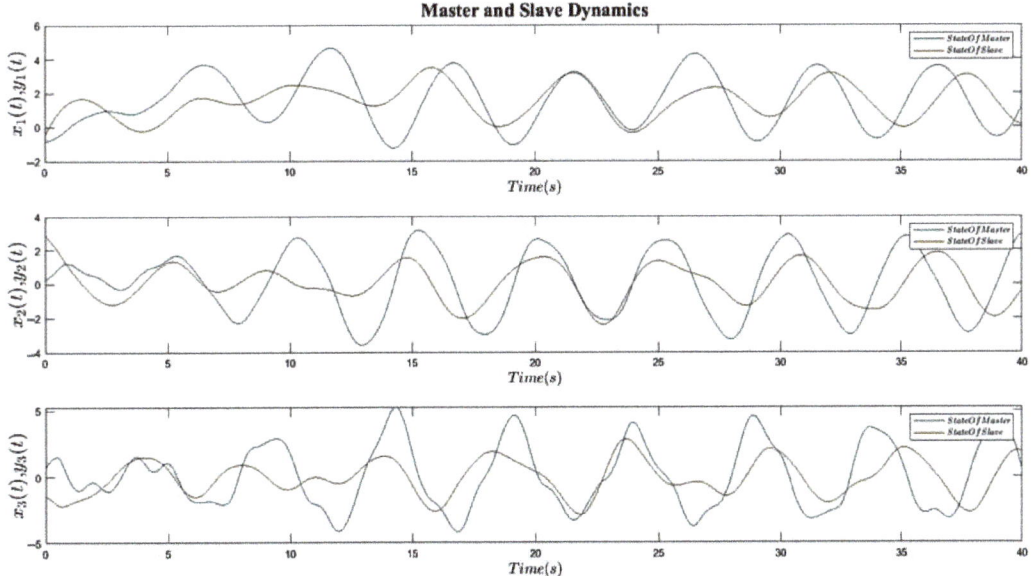

Figure 2. Behavior of master and slave system states without applying the control signal.

Figure 3 shows the behavior of the synchronized system. The synchronization error of the jerk system is shown in Figure 4. The control signal based on the proposed mechanism is shown in Figure 5. The estimation of the system parameters is shown in Figure 6. The disturbance and uncertainty of the master and slave system are shown in Figure 7.

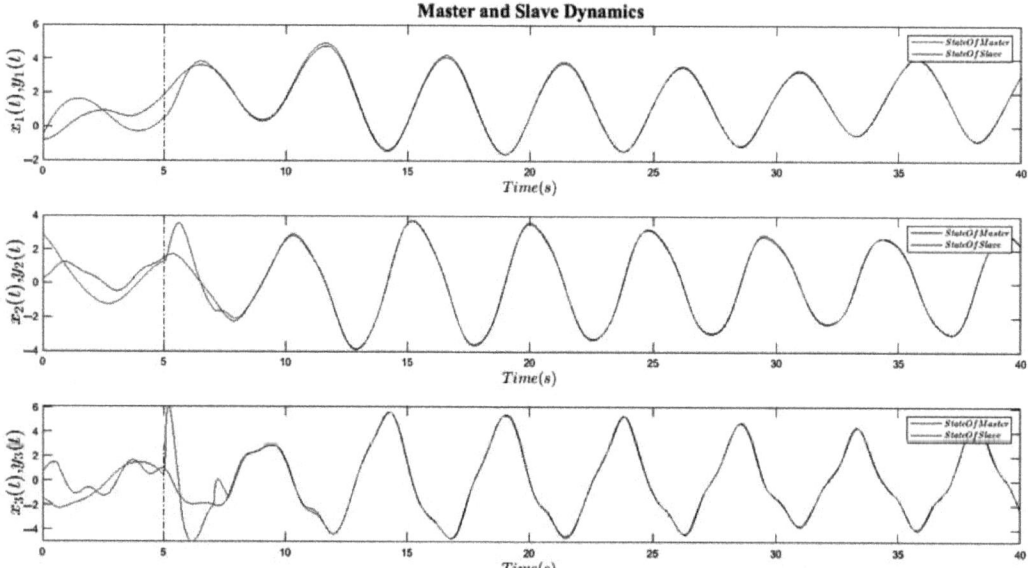

Figure 3. Synchronization of jerk systems using the proposed mechanism and applying the control signal at t = 5 s.

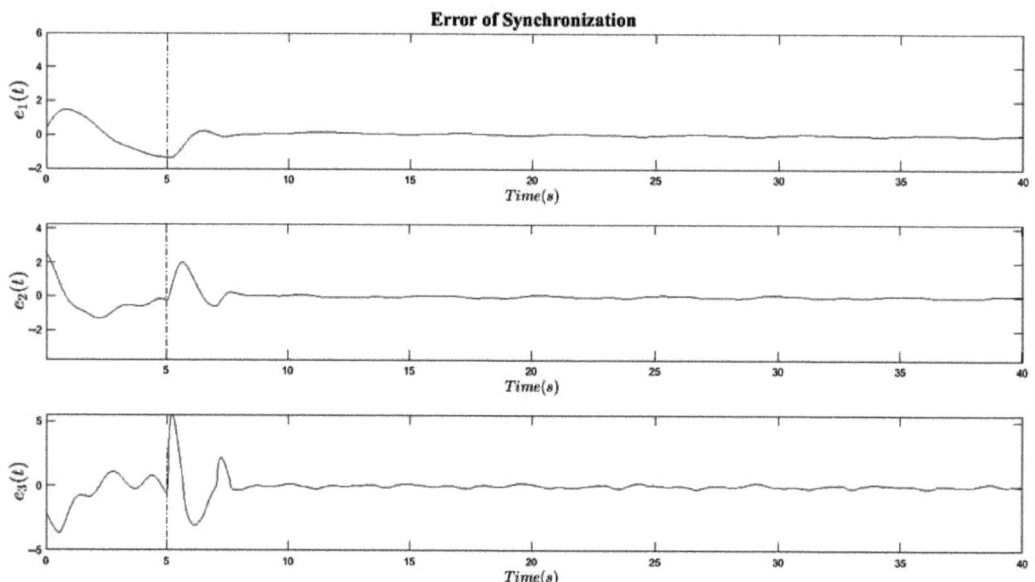

Figure 4. Synchronization error of the master and slave systems.

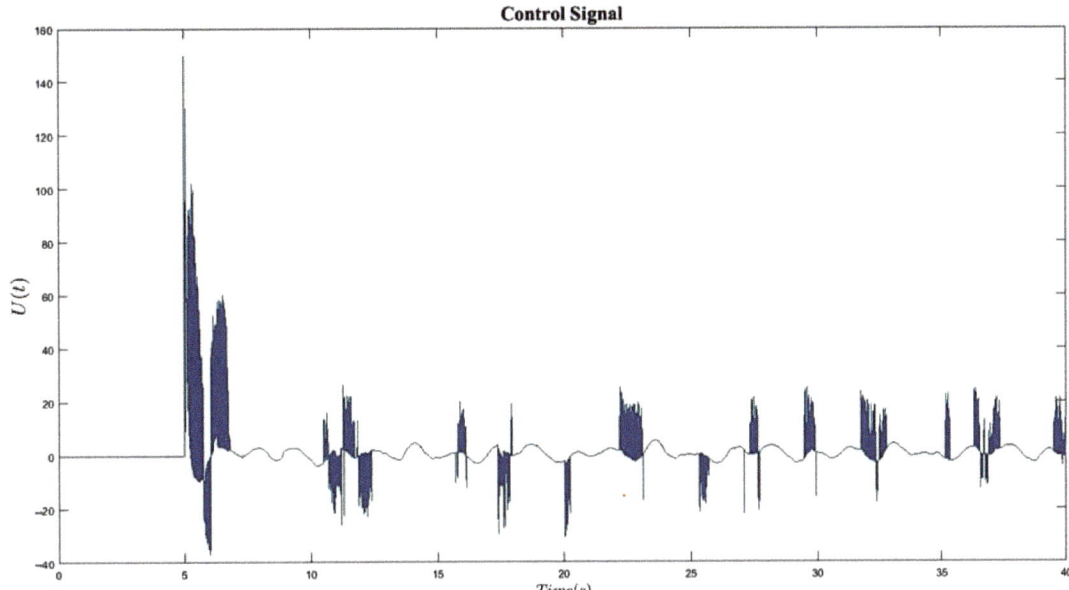

Figure 5. The control signal based on the proposed adaptive sliding mode control.

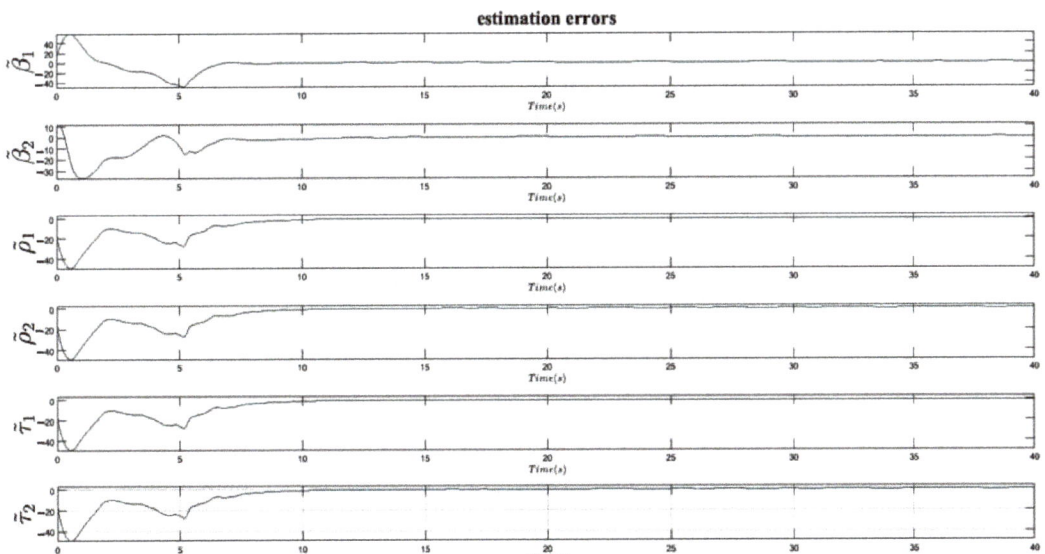

Figure 6. Estimation error of the system parameters.

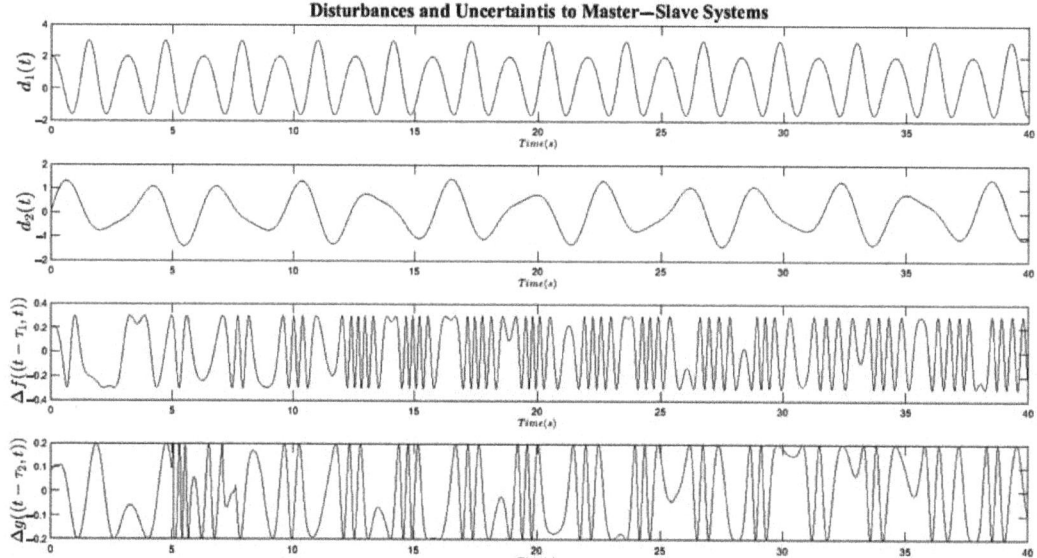

Figure 7. Uncertainty and disturbances of the master and slave systems.

In this article, simulations have been performed for $t = 40$ S, where $k_{11} = k_{22} = 10$ and $k_{12} = k_{21} = 20$ have been selected. Additionally, the gain and time constants of the non-linear fractional order PID sliding surface are $k_p = 1.5$, $T_i = 0.75$ and $T_d = 0.5$. The fractional order of the integral and derivative part of the sliding surface is defined as $\delta = 0.4$ and $\lambda = 0.75$. The parameters of the proposed robust controller are $b = 2$. The uncertain time delays of the system are $\tau_1 = 0.65$ and $\tau_2 = 0.35$. Unknown disturbances applied to both systems are as follows:

$$d_1(t) = sin^2 3t + 2cos4t, \quad d_2(t) = sin2t + 0.4sin\pi t$$

7. Application in Secure Communication

The synchronization of the chaotic system with uncertainty and unknown time delays was discussed in the preceding section. The proposed robust control strategy is placed in the framework of a secure communication mechanism in this part such that the message signal is sent by the master system after the encryption process. The chaotic masking method was utilized for this aim. Figure 8 depicts how to convey the primary message signal using the proposed mechanism. A wireless communication channel is employed in this block diagram. The communication channel might be either wired or wireless.

If $M(t)$ is the original message signal that is coupled with the master system and $S(t)$ is the sent message, then [36]:

$$S(t) = M(t) + \sum_{j=1}^{n} \gamma_j x_j. \tag{36}$$

where x_j is the state of the chaotic system and γ_j is the constant number. $S(t)$ is the masked chaotic signal that is sent by the created communication channel. Using the proposed chaotic synchronization mechanism, the system states are integrated with the message signal in a weighted manner to perform the masking process. The receiver side can receive the message signal as follows:

$$R(t) = S(t) - \sum_{j=1}^{n} \gamma_j y_j. \tag{37}$$

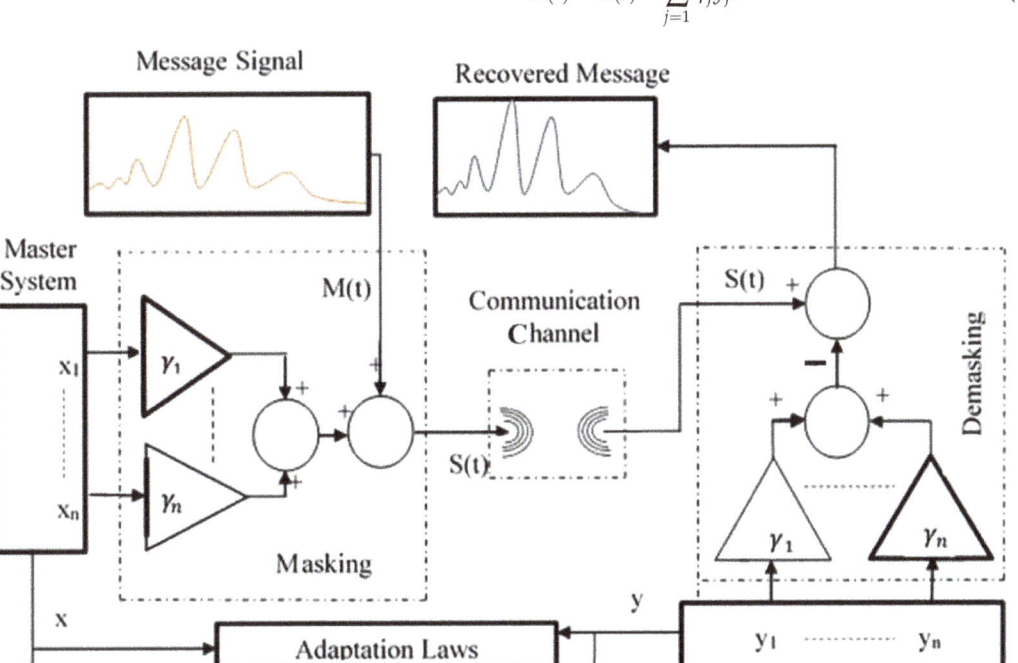

Figure 8. Chaotic secure communication structure based on the proposed approach.

Using the concept of synchronization, the following signal can be reconstructed in the receiver as follows:

$$R(t) = M(t) + \sum_{j=1}^{n} \gamma_j x_j - \sum_{j=1}^{n} \gamma_j y_j = M(t) + \sum_{j=1}^{n} \gamma_j (x_j - y_j) \tag{38}$$

$$\Rightarrow x_j - y_j = e_j \cong 0 \Rightarrow R(t) \to M(t).$$

In this step, two message signals are generated, which are applied to the synchronized system via the chaotic masking mechanism mentioned above. In this phase, the control signal is applied to the slave system, and the message signal is applied to the synchronized system after achieving the established time to reduce the mean square error. The transition time in the simulations ends at $t = 4.5$ s. At this point, the encrypted message's signal is applied, and the signal $S(t)$ is received on the receiver's side and decoded to extract the signal $R(t)$. The simulation results in the Figures 9 and 10 demonstrate a good performance of the proposed system.

Table 1 shows the mean square error of the original message signal and the recovered signal.

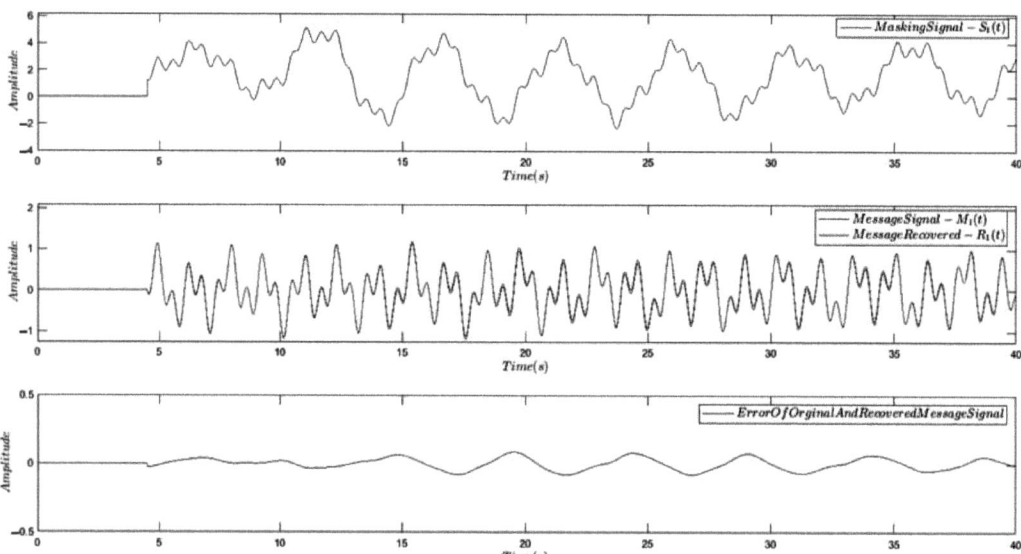

Figure 9. Message 1, masked and retrieved, and the error between these two signals.

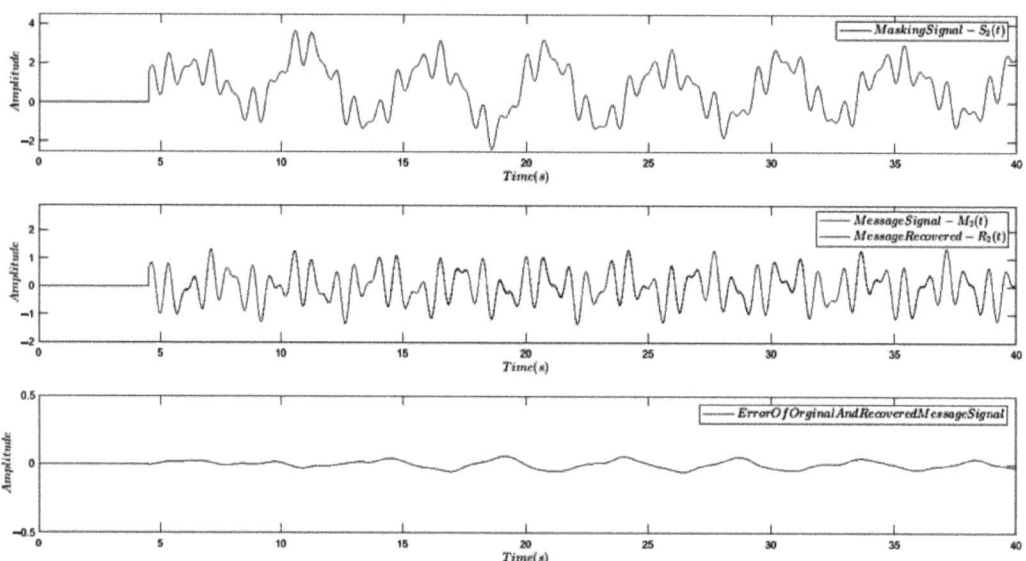

Figure 10. Message 2, masked and retrieved, and the error between these two signals.

Table 1. Represents the mean square error of the main message signal and the retrieved signal.

Root Mean Squre Error	
M_1 and R_1	M_2 and R_2
0.041544	0.025857

The following are the message signals:

$$M_1(t) = 1.8sin(1.7t) + 4.5cos(10.2t) + 5.4sin(1.33\pi t).$$

$$M_2(t) = 2.25sin(1.9t) + 2.88cos(10.66t) + 4.05sin(2.33\pi t).$$

The masked parameters of the message signal are $\gamma_1 = 1$, $\gamma_2 = 0.5$, and $\gamma_3 = 0.33$. Thus, encoding is as follows:

$$S_1(t) = M_1 + \gamma_1 x_1$$

$$S_2(t) = M_2 + \gamma_2 x_1 + \gamma_3 x_2$$

8. Conclusions

This study investigates the robust synchronization of a class of chaotic systems with uncertainty, external disturbances, and unknown parameters, such as unknown time delays, by introducing a new adaptive sliding mode control technique. First, an NLFPID-based sliding surface is proposed in the suggested robust control mechanism. The adaptive laws are then defined in order to estimate the uncertain parameters of the system using Lyapunov theory and Lipschitz conditions in chaotic systems, and ultimately the stability of the proposed robust control system is proven. The synchronization of two uncertain jerk chaotic systems with unknown time delays based on the proposed controller is simulated using MATLAB, and the results express the capability and desired performance of the proposed approach in the robust synchronization of the mentioned systems. Finally, the proposed adaptive sliding mode control approach has been used in a robust secure chaotic communication mechanism, and the simulation results indicate favorable quality in the secure transmission and reception of information despite uncertain parameters in the master and slave systems of the communication mechanism.

Author Contributions: Conceptualization, M.R. and A.Z.; methodology, M.R., A.Z. and M.H.; software, M.R., A.Z., R.A. and M.H.; validation, M.R., A.Z. and M.H.; formal analysis, M.R., A.Z. and R.A.; investigation, M.R., A.Z. and M.H.; resources, M.R. and M.H.; data curation, M.R., A.Z. and M.H.; writing—original draft preparation, M.R., A.Z., R.A. and M.H.; writing—review and editing, M.R., A.Z., R.A. and M.H.; visualization, M.R., A.Z. and R.A.; supervision, A.Z. and M.H.; project administration, A.Z. and M.H. All authors have read and agreed to the published version of the manuscript.

Funding: This research received no external funding.

Data Availability Statement: Not applicable.

Conflicts of Interest: The authors declare no conflict of interest.

References

1. Peters, E.E. *Fractal Market Analysis: Applying Chaos Theory to Investment and Economics*; John Wiley & Sons: Hoboken, NJ, USA, 1994.
2. Rössler, O.E. Chaos and chemistry. In *Nonlinear Phenomena in Chemical Dynamics*; Springer: Berlin/Heidelberg, Germany, 1981; pp. 79–87.
3. Rapp, P.E. Chaos in the neurosciences: Cautionary tales from the frontier. *Biologist* **1993**, *40*, 89–94.
4. Chen, Y.; Leung, A.Y. *Bifurcation and Chaos in Engineering*; Spfinge-Vereag: London, UK, 1998; pp. 169–180.
5. Nijmeijer, H. Control of Chaos and Synchronization. Available online: https://www.sciencedirect.com/science/article/abs/pii/S016769119700042X?via%3Dihub (accessed on 1 December 2022).
6. Pecora, L.M.; Thomas, L.; Carroll, T.L. Synchronization in chaotic systems. *Phys. Rev. Lett.* **1990**, *64*, 821. [CrossRef] [PubMed]
7. Maheswari, C.; Priyanka, E.; Meenakshipriya, B. Fractional order $PI^\lambda D^\mu$ controller tuned by coefficient diagram method and particle swarm optimization algorithms for SO_2 emission control process. *Proc. Inst. Mech. Eng. Part I J. Syst. Control. Eng.* **2017**, *231*, 587–599.
8. Podlubny, I. Fractional-order systems and PI/sup/spl lambda//D/sup/spl mu//-controllers. *IEEE Trans. Autom. Control.* **1999**, *44*, 208–214. [CrossRef]
9. Rahimian, M.; Tavazoei, M. Stabilizing fractional-order PI and PD controllers: An integer-order implemented system approach. *Proc. Inst. Mech. Eng. Part I J. Syst. Control. Eng.* **2010**, *224*, 893–903. [CrossRef]

10. Luo, Y.; Chen, Y. Fractional order [proportional derivative] controller for a class of fractional order systems. *Automatica* **2009**, *45*, 2446–2450. [CrossRef]
11. Monje, C.A.; Calderon, A.J.; Vinagre, B.M.; Feliu, V. The fractional order lead compensator. In Proceedings of the Second IEEE International Conference on Computational Cybernetics, 2004. ICCC 2004, Vienna, Austria, 30 August–1 September 2004; pp. 347–352.
12. Monje, C.A.; Vinagre, B.M.; Calderón, A.J.; Feliu, V.; Chen, Y.Q. Auto-tuning of fractional lead-lag compensators. *IFAC Proc. Vol.* **2005**, *38*, 319–324. [CrossRef]
13. Oustaloup, A.; Sabatier, J.; Moreau, X. From fractal robustness to the CRONE approach. *ESAIM Proc.* **1998**, *5*, 177–192. [CrossRef]
14. Yaghooti, B.; Salarieh, H. Robust adaptive fractional order proportional integral derivative controller design for uncertain fractional order nonlinear systems using sliding mode control. *Proc. Inst. Mech. Eng. Part I J. Syst. Control. Eng.* **2018**, *232*, 550–557. [CrossRef]
15. Abedini, M.; Nojoumian, M.A.; Salarieh, H.; Meghdari, A. Model reference adaptive control in fractional order systems using discrete-time approximation methods. *Commun. Nonlinear Sci. Numer. Simul.* **2015**, *25*, 27–40. [CrossRef]
16. Shi, B.; Yuan, J.; Dong, C. On fractional model reference adaptive control. *Sci. World J.* **2014**, *2014*, 521625. [CrossRef] [PubMed]
17. Dumlu, A. Design of a fractional-order adaptive integral sliding mode controller for the trajectory tracking control of robot manipulators. *Proc. Inst. Mech. Eng. Part I J. Syst. Control. Eng.* **2018**, *232*, 1212–1229. [CrossRef]
18. Binazadeh, T.; Shafiei, M. Output tracking of uncertain fractional-order nonlinear systems via a novel fractional-order sliding mode approach. *Mechatronics* **2013**, *23*, 888–892–892. [CrossRef]
19. Chen, D.; Liu, Y.; Ma, X.; Zhang, R. Control of a class of fractional-order chaotic systems via sliding mode. *Nonlinear Dyn.* **2012**, *67*, 893–901. [CrossRef]
20. Yahyazadeh, M.; Noei, A.R.; Ghaderi, R. Synchronization of chaotic systems with known and unknown parameters using a modified active sliding mode control. *ISA Trans.* **2011**, *50*, 262–267. [CrossRef]
21. Wang, X.; Zhang, X.; Ma, C. Modified projective synchronization of fractional-order chaotic systems via active sliding mode control. *Nonlinear Dyn.* **2012**, *69*, 511–517. [CrossRef]
22. Yuan, W.; Zhou, J.; Nadal, I.; Boccaletti, S.; Wang, Z. Adaptive control of dynamical synchronization on evolving networks with noise disturbances. *Phys. Rev. E* **2018**, *97*, 022211. [CrossRef]
23. Jajarmi, A.; Hajipour, M.; Baleanu, D. New aspects of the adaptive synchronization and hyperchaos suppression of a financial model. *Chaos Solitons Fractals* **2017**, *99*, 285–296.
24. Cho, S.; Baek, J.; Han, S. Adaptive control using time delay control for synchronization of chaotic systems. In Proceedings of the 2016 16th International Conference on Control, Automation and Systems (ICCAS), Gyeongju, Republic of Korea, 16–19 October 2016; pp. 763–766.
25. Li, W.; Liang, W.; Chang, K. Adaptive sliding mode control for synchronization of unified hyperchaotic systems. In Proceedings of the 2019 24th International Conference on Methods and Models in Automation and Robotics (MMAR), Międzyzdroje, Poland, 26–29 August 2019; pp. 93–98.
26. Luo, J.; Qu, S.; Xiong, Z. Finite-time increased order chaotic synchronization using an adaptive terminal sliding mode control. In Proceedings of the 2019 Chinese Control and Decision Conference (CCDC), Nanchang, China, 3–5 June 2019; pp. 1258–1263.
27. Ghamati, M.; Balochian, S. Design of adaptive sliding mode control for synchronization Genesio–Tesi chaotic system. *Chaos Solitons Fractals* **2015**, *75*, 111–117. [CrossRef]
28. Toopchi, Y.; Wang, J. Chaos control and synchronization of a hyperchaotic Zhou system by integral sliding mode control. *Entropy* **2014**, *16*, 6539–6552. [CrossRef]
29. Mohadeszadeh, M.; Pariz, N. Hybrid control of synchronization of fractional order nonlinear systems. *Asian J. Control.* **2021**, *23*, 412–422. [CrossRef]
30. Mirrezapour, S.Z.; Zare, A.; Hallaji, M. A new fractional sliding mode controller based on nonlinear fractional-order proportional integral derivative controller structure to synchronize fractional-order chaotic systems with uncertainty and disturbances. *J. Vib. Control* **2022**, *28*, 773–785. [CrossRef]
31. Mahmoud, M.S. Disturbance observer-based robust control and its applications: 35th anniversary overview. *IEEE Trans. Ind. Electron.* **2019**, *67*, 2042–2053.
32. Khan, A.; Nasreen; Jahanzaib, L.S. Synchronization on the adaptive sliding mode controller for fractional order complex chaotic systems with uncertainty and disturbances. *Int. J. Dyn. Control.* **2019**, *7*, 1419–1433. [CrossRef]
33. Shirkavand, M.; Pourgholi, M. Robust fixed-time synchronization of fractional order chaotic using free chattering nonsingular adaptive fractional sliding mode controller design. *Chaos Solitons Fractals* **2018**, *113*, 135–147. [CrossRef]
34. Sun, Z. Synchronization of fractional-order chaotic systems with non-identical orders, unknown parameters and disturbances via sliding mode control. *Chin. J. Phys.* **2018**, *56*, 2553–2559. [CrossRef]
35. Zare, A.; Mirrezapour, S.Z.; Hallaji, M.; Shoeibi, A.; Jafari, M.; Ghassemi, N.; Alizadehsani, R.; Mosavi, A. Robust adaptive synchronization of a class of uncertain chaotic systems with unknown time-delay. *Appl. Sci.* **2020**, *10*, 8875. [CrossRef]
36. Petráš, I. *Fractional-Order Nonlinear Systems: Modeling, Analysis and Simulation*, 1st ed.; Springer Science & Business Media: London, UK, 2011.

Article

Robust Multi-Criteria Traffic Network Equilibrium Problems with Path Capacity Constraints

Xing-Xing Ma and Yang-Dong Xu *

Department of Mathematics, Chongqing University of Posts and Telecommunications, Chongqing 400065, China; maxx0205@126.com
* Correspondence: xyd04010241@126.com

Abstract: With the progress of society and the diversification of transportation modes, people are faced with more and more complicated travel choices, and thus, multi-criteria route choosing optimization problems have drawn increased attention in recent years. A number of multi-criteria traffic network equilibrium problems have been proposed, but most of them do not involve data uncertainty nor computational methods. This paper focuses on the methods for solving robust multi-criteria traffic network equilibrium problems with path capacity constraints. The concepts of the robust vector equilibrium and the robust vector equilibrium with respect to the worst case are introduced, respectively. For the robust vector equilibrium, an equivalent min–max optimization problem is constructed. A direct search algorithm, in which the step size without derivatives and redundant parameters, is proposed for solving this min–max problem. In addition, we construct a smoothing optimization problem based on a variant version of ReLU activation function to compute the robust weak vector equilibrium flows with respect to the worst case and then find robust vector equilibrium flows with respect to the worst case by using the heaviside step function. Finally, extensive numerical examples are given to illustrate the excellence of our algorithms compared with existing algorithms. It is shown that the proposed min–max algorithm may take less time to find the robust vector equilibrium flows and the smoothing method can more effectively generate a subset of the robust vector equilibrium with respect to the worst case.

Keywords: multi-criteria traffic network; robust vector equilibrium; min–max method; smoothing method

Citation: Ma, X.-X.; Xu, Y.-D. Robust Multi-Criteria Traffic Network Equilibrium Problems with Path Capacity Constraints. *Axioms* **2023**, *12*, 662. https://doi.org/10.3390/axioms12070662

Academic Editors: Siamak Pedrammehr and Mohammad Reza Chalak Qazani

Received: 5 June 2023
Revised: 24 June 2023
Accepted: 29 June 2023
Published: 3 July 2023

Copyright: © 2023 by the authors. Licensee MDPI, Basel, Switzerland. This article is an open access article distributed under the terms and conditions of the Creative Commons Attribution (CC BY) license (https://creativecommons.org/licenses/by/4.0/).

1. Introduction

Traveling is necessary for everyday human life. However, with the progress of society and the diversification of transportation modes, people also expect to find the most efficient route. Traffic network equilibrium problem can describe the distributions of traffic flows in the logistics industry and transportation network, which is expected to provide an effective method for travelers to choose an optimization route. The fundamental principle in the model is the concept of equilibrium that was initially introduced by Wardrop [1]. The principle asserts that travelers will choose the path only if the cost for this path is the minimum possible among all the paths joining the same O-D pair.

1.1. Literature Reviews

It has been shown that the Wardrop equilibrium concept is a powerful principle which is widely used in supply and demand networks, traffic assignment, optimization of traffic control, and other fields (see, e.g., Athanasenas [2]; Nagurney [3]; Ji and Chu [4]; Xu et al. [5]; Wang et al. [6]; Ma et al. [7]). It is worth noting that most of these equilibrium models in the above references are based on a single criterion. Travelers (in this paper, we use the terms 'user' and 'traveler' interchangeably) will naturally consider multi-criteria when choosing travel paths, including travel time, distance, cost, weather, safety, and other relevant factors. The equilibrium model with multi-criteria was first put forward by Chen and Yen [8], which was an extension of the classical Wardrop user equilibrium principle. Regarding the theoretical analysis for multi-criteria traffic equilibrium models, we refer the reader to Yang and Goh [9], Li et al. [10], Luc et al. [11], and Raith and Ehrgott [12].

Recently, Phuong and Luc [13] established the equivalent relationship between strong vector equilibrium flows and the solutions of variational inequality problems in terms of a kind of increasing functions. Moreover, they presented a modified projection method to handle multi-criteria traffic network equilibrium problems. Subsequently, Luc and Phuong [14] introduced two optimization problems to show that the optimal solutions are exactly the equilibrium of the traffic network and then put forward a modified Frank–Wolfe gradient algorithm for multi-criteria traffic network equilibrium problems. However, this method may lead to the non-differentiability of the objective functions of the two optimization problems. After that, Phuong [15] proposed a smoothing method to solve multi-criteria network equilibrium problems. Although this method solves the defects existing in [14], it does not take into account the data uncertainty.

In the actual traffic network, there are various uncertain factors, such as traveler preferences, weather, traffic congestion, and holidays. Hence, uncertainty in the logistics industry and transportation has received more and more attention. In recent years, some related works with uncertain demands or uncertain parameters in traffic network or ecological networks have been investigated in [16–21]. Daniele and Giuffré [16] investigated a general random traffic equilibrium problem and characterize the random Wardrop equilibrium distribution by means of a random variational inequality. Dragicevic and Gurtoo [17] modeled the maintenance of ecological networks in forest environments based on random processes, such as extreme natural events. However, the two above papers do not consider the multi-criteria. Recently, Ehrgott and Wang [18] presented alternative approaches for combining the principles of multi-objective decision-making with a stochastic user equilibrium model based on random utility theory. However, since uncertain parameters in [18] need to know probabilistic information, this may be inconsistent with the reality because the probabilistic information of related data are usually known. Cao et al. [19] and Wei et al. [20] only discussed relationships between and the solutions of variational inequality and robust equilibrium flows but not give the computational methods. Minh and Phuong [21] paid attention to a modified Frank–Wolfe gradient algorithm for robust equilibrium flows. The uncertain data in the model proposed in [21] are in a parameter set that does not need probability information. However, the computational efficiency of the algorithm is not good, due to the non-differentiability of the objective functions. In all, there are some research gaps on computational methods for robust multi-criteria traffic network equilibrium problems with path capacity constraint. This prompts us to continuously investigate this topic.

1.2. Contributions

To overcome computational inefficiency for the robust vector equilibrium flows in existing methods, this paper proposes two new computational methods for the robust vector equilibrium principle and the robust vector equilibrium principle with respect to the worst case, respectively. Firstly, an equivalent min–max optimization problem is constructed, in which the solution is equivalent to the robust vector equilibrium flow. A direct search algorithm with constraints for solving this problem is proposed. For the robust vector equilibrium with respect to the worst case, we transform it into an deterministic vector equilibrium problem based on a variant version of ReLU activation function. Then, we give an algorithm to solve the robust vector equilibrium with respect to the worst case.

In summary, the contributions of the manuscript are ranked in ascending gathered as follows:

(1) The robust vector equilibrium and the robust vector equilibrium with respect to the worst case principles are introduced.
(2) An equivalent min–max optimization problem is established and then a direct search algorithm is proposed to generate a subset of robust vector equilibrium flows.

(3) To generate a subset of the robust vector equilibrium with respect to the worst case, a two-step strategy is implemented. More specifically, a smoothing optimization problem is constructed based on a variant version of ReLU activation function to compute the robust weak vector equilibrium flows with respect to the worst case, and then, the robust vector equilibrium flows are found with respect to the worst case by using the heaviside step function.

This paper is divided into the following parts. Section 2 mainly introduces the robust vector equilibrium principle and robust vector equilibrium principle with respect to the worst case. Section 3 gives a min–max method to generate the subset of robust vector equilibrium flows. Section 4 presents a smoothing algorithm to find the subset of the robust vector equilibrium principle with respect to the worst case. Finally, conclusions of this paper and discussions for future research are provided in Section 5.

2. Definitions and Main Derivations

We review some fundamental definitions and properties that are relevant to this study. Throughout this paper, let $\mathbb{R}^*$ ($* = n, m$) denote the $*$-dimensional Euclidean space. Let $\mathbb{R}_+^m := \{x \in \mathbb{R}^m : x_i \geq 0, \ i = 1, \cdots, m\}$ and $\mathbb{R}_{++}^m := \{x \in \mathbb{R}^m : x_i > 0, \ i = 1, \cdots, m\}$. The superscript $\top$ denotes transpose. The partial order in $\mathbb{R}^m$ is induced by $\mathbb{R}_+^m$, defined by:

$$x \geqq y \text{ if } x_i \geq y_i \text{ for all } i = 1, \ldots, m,$$

$$x \succeq y \text{ if } x_i \geq y_i \text{ for all } i = 1, \ldots, m \text{ and there exists } i_0 \text{ such that } x_{i_0} > y_{i_0}.$$

and the following stronger relation is given by:

$$x \succ y \text{ if } x_i > y_i \text{ for all } i = 1, \ldots, m.$$

Next, we will denote by e the vector of all ones. Given $X \subseteq \mathbb{R}^m$, the set of minimal elements of X is denoted by $\text{Min}(X)$, consists of vectors $x \in X$ such that there is no $x' \in X, x' \preceq x$.

Definition 1. *Given $f : \mathbb{R} \times \mathbb{R} \to \mathbb{R}$, we say that a point (x^*, y^*) is a saddle-point of the function f, if*

$$f(x^*, y) \leq f(x^*, y^*) \leq f(x, y^*), \ \forall (x, y) \in \mathbb{R} \times \mathbb{R}.$$

2.1. Robust Multi-Criteria Traffic Network

For a traffic network, $\mathcal{N}$ denotes the set of the nodes and $\mathcal{E}$ denotes the set of directed arcs. Let $\mathcal{W}$ be the set of origin–destination (O-D) pairs and $\mathcal{D} = (d_\omega)_{\omega \in \mathcal{W}}$ be the demand vector, where $d_\omega > 0$ is the flow demand on O-D pair ω. Thus, a traffic network is always denoted by $G = \{\mathcal{N}, \mathcal{E}, \mathcal{W}, \mathcal{D}\}$. For $\omega \in \mathcal{W}$, P_ω is the set of available paths on the O-D pair ω and $P = \cup_{\omega \in \mathcal{W}} P_\omega$ is the set of all available paths of the network. Let $n = \sum_{\omega \in \mathcal{W}} |p_\omega|$. For a given $p_k \in P_\omega$, y_{p_k} is the traffic flow on this path and $y = (y_1, y_2, \cdots, y_n)^\top \in \mathbb{R}^n$ is called a path flow. For given $p_k \in P_\omega$, suppose $l_{p_k} \in \mathbb{R}_+$, $u_{p_k} \in \mathbb{R}_+$ with $l_{p_k} < u_{p_k}$; the path flow y_{p_k} needs to satisfy the capacity constraint $l_{p_k} \leq y_{p_k} \leq u_{p_k}$. The traffic load is always presented by arc flows z_α, $\alpha \in \mathcal{E}$, or path flows y_{p_k}, $p_k \in P$. Given a path flow, the arc flow can be obtained by the following formula:

$$z_\alpha = \sum_{p_k \in P} y_{p_k} \delta_{\alpha p_k},$$

where

$$\delta_{\alpha p_k} = \begin{cases} 1, & \text{if } \alpha \text{ belongs to path } p_k, \\ 0, & \text{otherwise.} \end{cases}$$

The arc flow is denoted by $z := (z_\alpha)_{\alpha \in \mathcal{E}}$. A path flow y is said to be feasible flow if it satisfies:

$$\Omega = \{y \in \mathbb{R}_+ : \forall \omega \in W, \forall p_k \in P_\omega, l_{p_k} \leq y_{p_k} \leq u_{p_k}, \sum_{p_k \in P_\omega} y_{p_k} = d_\omega\}.$$

Let $t_\alpha : \mathbb{R}^n \to \mathbb{R}^m$ be a vector-valued cost function along with arc $\alpha \in \mathcal{E}$. Let $c_{p_k} : \mathbb{R}^n \to \mathbb{R}^m$ be a vector-valued cost function on the path p_k. Thus, we have that the cost function c_{p_k} for path p_k is the sum of cost functions for arcs belonging to path p_k, namely:

$$c_{p_k}(y) = \sum_{\alpha \in \mathcal{E}} \delta_{\alpha p_k} t_\alpha(y). \tag{1}$$

However, the path cost functions may be perturbed in reality. This means that it not only depends on the path flow y but also on parameters of $\xi \in U := U_1 \times U_2 \times \cdots \times U_n$. Throughout this paper, the cost function $c_{p_k}(y, \xi)$ is often given in the form $c_{p_k}(y, \xi) = c_{p_k}(y) + \xi_{p_k}$.

2.2. Robust Vector Equilibrium and Related Concepts

Now, we give the following definitions on a robust vector equilibrium and a robust (weak) vector equilibrium with respect to the worst case.

Definition 2. *A feasible flow $\bar{y} \in \Omega$ is said to be a robust vector equilibrium, if for each O-D $\omega \in W$, path $p_k, p_j \in P_\omega$, one has:*

$$c_{p_k}(\bar{y}, \xi) - c_{p_j}(\bar{y}, \xi) \succeq 0_{\mathbb{R}^m}, \forall \xi \in U \Rightarrow \text{ either } \bar{y}_{p_k} = l_{p_k} \text{ or } \bar{y}_{p_j} = u_{p_j}.$$

The worst case of the cost function on the path p_k under all possible scenarios is defined as follows:

$$C_{p_k}(y) = \begin{pmatrix} \sup_{\xi \in U} c_{1p_k}(y, \xi) \\ \vdots \\ \sup_{\xi \in U} c_{mp_k}(y, \xi) \end{pmatrix}, C_{p_j}(y) = \begin{pmatrix} \sup_{\xi \in U} c_{1p_j}(y, \xi) \\ \vdots \\ \sup_{\xi \in U} c_{mp_j}(y, \xi) \end{pmatrix}$$

The following definitions are given based on the worst case of path costs, which is called the robust vector equilibrium with respect to the worst case and the robust weak vector equilibrium with respect to the worst case.

Definition 3. *A feasible flow $\bar{y} \in \Omega$ is a robust vector equilibrium with respect to the worst case, if for $\forall \omega \in W, \forall p_k, p_j \in P_\omega$, one has:*

$$C_{p_k}(\bar{y}) - C_{p_j}(\bar{y}) \succeq 0_{\mathbb{R}^m} \Rightarrow \text{ either } \bar{y}_{p_k} = l_{p_k} \text{ or } \bar{y}_{p_j} = u_{p_j}.$$

Definition 4. *A feasible flow $\bar{y} \in \Omega$ is in robust weak vector equilibrium with respect to the worst case, if for $\omega \in W, p_k, p_j \in P_\omega$, one has:*

$$C_{p_k}(\bar{y}) - C_{p_j}(\bar{y}) \succ 0_{\mathbb{R}^m} \Rightarrow \text{ either } \bar{y}_{p_k} = l_{p_k} \text{ or } \bar{y}_{p_j} = u_{p_j}.$$

Remark 1. *What should be noteworthy is that a robust vector equilibrium with respect to the worst case is also a robust vector equilibrium when U is a compact set. Conversely, it is not necessarily true. Although there is no parameter in the concept of the robust vector equilibrium with respect to the worst case, it still depends on the values of the parameter or sensitive to parameters. Now, we give the following example to illustrate the above cases.*

Example 1. *Consider a network problem with one O-D pair $\omega = (x, x')$. Two criteria, i.e., travel time and travel cost, and two available paths, i.e., $P_\omega = \{p_1, p_2\}$, with the travel demand $d_\omega = 30$.*

Assume that the path capacity constraints and cost function on the paths p_1 and p_2 are, respectively, given as follows:
$$l_{p_1} = 0, \ l_{p_2} = 0; \ u_{p_1} = 30, \ u_{p_2} = 30.$$
$$c_{p_1}(y, \xi_1) = \begin{pmatrix} y_1 + 2y_2 + \xi_1 \\ 6y_1 + 2y_2 + \xi_1 \end{pmatrix}, \ c_{p_2}(y, \xi_2) = \begin{pmatrix} y_1 + 6y_2 \\ 6y_1 + 2y_2 - \xi_2 \end{pmatrix}.$$

with $\xi_1 \in [-1, 2]$ and $\xi_2 \in [0, 1]$.

Direct computation shows that $\bar{y} = (30, 0)$ is the robust vector equilibrium. However, it is not the robust vector equilibrium with respect to the worst case since we have:
$$C_{p_1}(\bar{y}) = \begin{pmatrix} 32 \\ 182 \end{pmatrix}, \ C_{p_2}(\bar{y}) = \begin{pmatrix} 30 \\ 180 \end{pmatrix},$$

but $y_{p_1} \neq l_{p_1}$ and $y_{p_2} \neq u_{p_2}$.

If $\xi_1 \in [-1, 0]$ and $\xi_2 \in [-2, 0]$, then we have $C_{p_2}(\bar{y}) - C_{p_1}(\bar{y}) \succeq 0_{\mathbb{R}^m}$, $y_{p_1} = u_{p_1}$ and $y_{p_2} = l_{p_2}$. Hence, $\bar{y} = (30, 0)$ is the robust vector equilibrium with respect to the worst case. It can be seen that the robust vector equilibrium with respect to the worst case is sensitive to parameter perturbations.

3. Min–Max Method for Robust Vector Equilibrium

In this section, a min–max algorithm is proposed to look for a subset of the robust vector equilibrium flows.

3.1. Description of the Algorithm

In this subsection, we construct an optimization problem whose solution is equivalent to the the robust vector equilibrium flow. For $(y, \xi) \in \Omega \times U$, we define:

$$\psi(y, \xi) := \sum_{p_k, p_j \in P_\omega, \omega \in W} (y_{p_k} - l_{p_k})(u_{p_j} - y_{p_j})[c_{p_k}(y, \xi) - c_{p_j}(y, \xi)]^\top H_+[c_{p_k}(y, \xi) - c_{p_j}(y, \xi)].$$

Proposition 1. *Let $\bar{y}$ be a feasible flow. The following statements are equivalent.*

(i) $\bar{y}$ is a robust vector equilibrium;
(ii) There exists $(\bar{y}, \bar{\xi})$ such that it is a saddle-point of the problem, denoted as follows:

$$\min_{y \in \Omega} \max_{\xi \in U} \psi(y, \xi) \quad (2)$$
$$s.t. \ y \in \Omega.$$

and $\psi(\bar{y}, \bar{\xi})$ is equal to zero.

Proof. Firstly, we prove the implication $(i) \Rightarrow (ii)$. Since $\psi(y, \xi) \geq 0$, it suffices to prove $\psi(\bar{y}, \xi) = 0$ for all $\xi \in U$, i.e., $0 = \psi(\bar{y}, \xi) = \psi(\bar{y}, \bar{\xi}) \leq \psi(y, \xi)$. Hence, for every $\xi \in U$, $p_k \in P_\omega$, $\omega \in W$, we consider the following term:

$$O_{p_k} = \sum_{p_j \in P_\omega} (y_{p_k} - l_{p_k})(u_{p_j} - y_{p_j})[c_{p_k}(y, \xi) - c_{p_j}(y, \xi)]^\top H_+[c_{p_k}(y, \xi) - c_{p_j}(y, \xi)].$$

If $c_{p_k}(\bar{y}, \xi) - c_{p_j}(\bar{y}, \xi) \succeq 0_{\mathbb{R}^m}$ for some $p_j \in P_\omega$, then by Definition 2, one has $\bar{y}_{p_k} = l_{p_k}$ or $\bar{y}_{p_j} = u_{p_j}$ and so $O_{p_k} = 0$. If $c_{p_k}(\bar{y}, \xi) - c_{p_j}(\bar{y}, \xi) \prec 0_{\mathbb{R}^m}$, for some $p_j \in P_\omega$, $H_+[c_{p_k}(\bar{y}, \xi) - c_{p_j}(\bar{y}, \xi)] = 0_{\mathbb{R}^m}$, and hence, $O_{p_k} = 0$. By the above cases, one has $\psi(\bar{y}, \xi) = 0$ for all $\xi \in U$.

Conversely, if (ii) is satisfied, $(\bar{y}, \bar{\xi})$ is a saddle-point and $O_{p_k} = 0$. If for every $\xi \in U$, some p_k, $p_j \in P_\omega$, $\omega \in W$ one has $c_{p_k}(\bar{y}, \xi) - c_{p_j}(\bar{y}, \xi) \succeq 0_{\mathbb{R}^m}$, then $[c_{p_k}(\bar{y}, \xi) - c_{p_j}(\bar{y}, \xi)]^\top H_+[c_{p_k}(\bar{y}, \xi) - c_{p_j}(\bar{y}, \xi)] > 0$ and so $\bar{y}_{p_k} = l_{p_k}$ or $\bar{y}_{p_j} = u_{p_j}$. Consequently, $\bar{y}$ is a robust vector equilibrium. □

Now, a min–max algorithm is proposed to solve problem (2). In our algorithm, we select different steps for the two variables y and ξ, which is different from one proposed in [22]. In addition, we extend the search directions of the algorithm to make the search faster and more suitable for different needs. Thus, our algorithm is an improvement of that in [22].

Direction set: The set D consist of finite unit vectors which can span $\mathbb{R}^n$. Here, in order to reduce the computational cost, we only consider some directions in D. For example, when $n = 2$, in this paper, let $D = \left\{ (1,0), (\frac{\sqrt{3}}{2}, \frac{1}{2}), (1,1), (\frac{1}{2}, \frac{\sqrt{3}}{2}), (0,1), (-\frac{1}{2}, \frac{\sqrt{3}}{2}), (-1,1), (-\frac{\sqrt{3}}{2}, \frac{1}{2}), (-1,0), (-\frac{\sqrt{3}}{2}, -\frac{1}{2}), (-1,-1), (-\frac{1}{2}, -\frac{\sqrt{3}}{2}), (0,-1), (\frac{1}{2}, -\frac{\sqrt{3}}{2}), (1,-1), (\frac{\sqrt{3}}{2}, -\frac{1}{2}) \right\}$.

Step length: Let initial step $t_0 = 1$ and $d_k = \arg\min_{y_i} \psi_k(y_k + t_k d, \xi_k)$, $d \in D$. Let $\tilde{y}_k = y_k + t_k d_k$. If iteration is successful, i.e., $\psi_k(\tilde{y}_k, \xi_k)) < \psi_k(y_k + t_k d, \xi_k) - c t_k^2$ for all $d \in D$ ($c > 0$), then the next step length value $t_{k+1} = 1$; if the iteration is unsuccessful, then $t_{k+1} = \|\tilde{y} - y_k\|/2$.

Remark 2. *It is worth noting that computations for y_t and ξ_t in Algorithm 1 are based on Algorithm 2.*

Algorithm 1: Min–max algorithm (Algorithm 1).

input : ψ: objective function; c: forcing function constant $c > 0$;
T: maximum number of iterations; t_0: initialize step size;
(y_0, ξ_0): initial iteration point; $S = \emptyset$, $SE = \emptyset$.

1 **for** $t = 1, \cdots, T$ **do**
2 $\quad$ $\xi_t = \mathbf{A1}(-\psi(y_{t-1}, .), \xi_{t-1})$
3 $\quad$ $y_t = \mathbf{A1}(\psi(., \xi_t), y_{t-1})$
4 $\quad$ return (y_T, ξ_T), store it in S.
5 Choose a (y_T, ξ_T) from S, compute $\psi(y_T, \xi_T)$.
6 If $\psi(y_T, \xi_T) \leq \epsilon$, store y_T in SE and return to **Step 5** until no element of S left.

Algorithm 2: Algorithm 2 $(\psi(), y_0)$.

input : ψ: objective function; c: forcing function constant $c > 0$;
T: maximum number of iterations; t_0: initialize step size value;
y_0: initial iteration point.

1 **for** $k = 0, \cdots, T-1$ **do**
2 $\quad$ 1. Generate direction set
$\quad\quad D = \{d^i : \text{any one unit direction of a certain point}\}$.
3 $\quad$ 2. Generate the points
$$y = y_k + t_k d \subset \Omega, \ \forall d \in D.$$
$\quad$ 3. Choose $d_k = \arg\min_d \psi(y, \xi_k)$ and let $\tilde{y}_k = y_k + t_k d_k$.
4 $\quad$ 4. **if** $\psi(\tilde{y}, \xi_k) < \psi(y_k, \xi_k) - c t_k^2$ **then**
5 $\quad\quad$ (Iteration is successful)
6 $\quad\quad$ $y_{k+1} = \tilde{y}, t_{k+1} = 1;$
7 $\quad$ **else**
8 $\quad\quad$ (Iteration is unsuccessful)
9 $\quad\quad$ $y_{k+1} = y_k, t_{k+1} = \|\tilde{y} - y_k\|/2$.
10 return y_T

3.2. Comparison with Other Methods

In this subsection, we will give three numerical examples to show the comparison with that of [22]. In these numerical examples, both Algorithm 1 and the algorithm proposed in [22] start from the same set of initial points. To make a fair comparison, all test problems are run five times to reduce the impact of randomness.

Remark 3. *There is a step calculation method in reference [22]—if the iteration is successful: $t_{k+1} = \min(t_{max}, \gamma t_k)$, $\gamma > 1$, where t_{max} is the largest step size; if iteration is unsuccessful: $t_{k+1} = \frac{1}{\gamma} t_k$. Compared with the step calculation method in reference [22], the step calculation method presented in Algorithm 1 has better performance, since Algorithm 1 selects different step size for different variables and extends the search directions. What is more, Algorithm 1 requires neither gradient information nor redundant parameters.*

Example 2. Consider a network problem depicted in Figure 1, where $\mathcal{N} = \{1, 2\}$, $\mathcal{W} = \{\omega\} = \{(1,2)\}$, $\mathcal{E} = \{\alpha_1, \alpha_2\}$, $\mathcal{D} = d_\omega = 30$. There are two criteria: travel time and travel cost. The cost functions of arcs and constraints of paths are given as below: $t_{1,\alpha_1}(y, \xi) = y_1^2 + 2y_1y_2 + y_2 - \xi_1$, $t_{2,\alpha_1}(y, \xi) = y_1 + y_2^2$; $t_{1,\alpha_2}(y, \xi) = y_1^2 + 10y_2y_2$, $t_{2,\alpha_2}(y, \xi) = 7y_1 + 6y_2^2 - 6\xi_2$.

$$l_{p_1} = 0, \ l_{p_2} = 0; \ u_{p_1} = 30, \ u_{p_2} = 30.$$

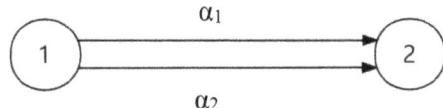

Figure 1. Network topology for Example 2.

Then, we have:

$$c_{p_1}(y, \xi) = \begin{pmatrix} y_1^2 + 2y_1y_2 + y_2 - \xi_1 \\ y_1 + y_2^2 \end{pmatrix}, \quad c_{p_2}(y, \xi) = \begin{pmatrix} y_1^2 + 10y_2y_2 \\ 7y_1 + 6y_2^2 - 6\xi_2 \end{pmatrix}.$$

where $\xi_1 \in [0, 1]$ and $\xi_2 \in [0, 1]$. Initial feasible flows and a subset of the robust vector equilibrium flows are obtained in 23.82s. The results are shown in Table 1. However, if we use step calculational method in [22], then it takes 25.68 s and the obtain the same robust vector equilibrium flows with our algorithm.

Table 1. Computational results of Algorithm 1.

Initial Feasible Flows	Robust Vector Equilibrium Flows
(0.00, 30.00) (3.75, 26.25)	(25.00, 5.00) (25.75, 4.25)
(11.25, 18.75) (11.25, 18.75)	(25.50, 4.50) (25.25, 4.75)
(15.00, 15.00) (18.75, 11.25)	(25.00, 5.00) (25.75, 4.25)
(22.50, 7.50) (26.25, 3.75)	(25.50, 4.50) (26.25, 3.75)
(30.00, 0.00)	(30.00, 0.00)

Example 3. Consider the network problem depicted in Figure 2, where $\mathcal{N} = \{1, 2, 3, 4\}$, $\mathcal{W} = \{(1,4), (2,4)\}$, and there are two O-D pairs, ω_1, ω_2. $\mathcal{E} = \{\alpha_1, \alpha_2, \alpha_3, \alpha_4, \alpha_5\}$, $p_1 = (\alpha_1\alpha_5)$, $p_2 = (\alpha_2)$, $p_3 = (\alpha_3\alpha_5)$, $p_4 = (\alpha_4)$, $\mathcal{D} = \{d_{\omega_1}, d_{\omega_2}\} = \{55, 35\}$. There are two criteria: travel time and travel cost. Constrains of paths are given as follows:

$$l_{p_1} = 0, \ l_{p_2} = 0, \ l_{p_3} = 0, \ l_{p_4} = 0;$$
$$u_{p_1} = 55, \ u_{p_2} = 55, \ u_{p_3} = 35, \ u_{p_4} = 35.$$

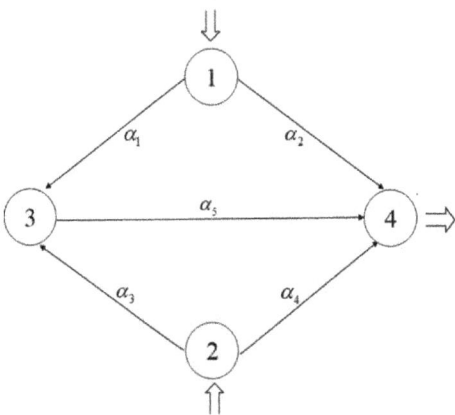

Figure 2. Network topology for Example 3.

The cost functions of arcs are defined as follows:

$$t_{\alpha_1}(y,\xi) = \begin{pmatrix} y_1^2 + 2y_2 + y_3^2 + y_4^2 + 1 \\ 2y_1 + y_2^2 + 2y_3 + y_4 + \frac{3}{2} - 6\xi_1 \end{pmatrix}, \quad t_{\alpha_2}(y,\xi) = \begin{pmatrix} 2y_1 + 3y_2 + 5y_3 + y_4 + 1 + \xi_2 \\ 2y_1 y_2 + y_2 + y_3^2 + y_4 + \frac{1}{2} \end{pmatrix},$$

$$t_{\alpha_3}(y,\xi) = \begin{pmatrix} 2y_1 + y_2 + y_3^2 + y_4 + \frac{3}{2} + 3\xi_3 \\ y_3^2 + 5y_4 + 1 \end{pmatrix}, \quad t_{\alpha_4}(y,\xi) = \begin{pmatrix} 2y_2 + 3y_3 y_4 + y_4^2 + 1 \\ y_1^2 + y_2 + y_4 + \frac{1}{2} - 8\xi_4 \end{pmatrix}, \quad t_{\alpha_5}(y,\xi) = \begin{pmatrix} y_1 + y_2 \\ y_3 + y_4 \end{pmatrix}.$$

Then, we have:

$$c_{p_1}(y,\xi) = \begin{pmatrix} y_1^2 + y_1 + 3y_2 + y_3^2 + y_4^2 + 1 \\ 2y_1 + y_2^2 + 3y_3 + 2y_4 + 1.5 - 6\xi_1 \end{pmatrix}, \quad c_{p_2}(y,\xi) = \begin{pmatrix} 2y_1 + 3y_2 + 5y_3 + y_4 + 1 + \xi_2 \\ 2y_1 y_2 + y_2 + y_3^2 + y_4 + 0.5 \end{pmatrix}$$

$$c_{p_3}(y,\xi) = \begin{pmatrix} 3y_1 + 2y_2 + y_3^2 + y_4 + 1.5 + 3\xi_3 \\ y_3^2 + y_3 + 6y_4 + 1 \end{pmatrix}, \quad c_{p_4}(y,\xi) = \begin{pmatrix} 2y_2 + 3y_3 y_4 + y_4^2 + 1 \\ y_1^2 + y_2 + 8y_4 + 0.5 - 8\xi_4 \end{pmatrix}$$

where $\xi_i \in [0,1], i = 1,2,3,4$. Initial feasible flows and a subset of the robust vector equilibrium flows are obtained in 40.56 s. The results are shown in Table 2. The time cost of Algorithm 1 is 4% lower than that of the step calculation method in [22].

Table 2. Computational results of Algorithm 1.

Initial Feasible Flows	Robust Vector Equilibrium Flows
(0.00, 55.00, 0.00, 35.00)	(27.00, 28.00, 27.00, 8.00)
(5.00, 50.00, 5.00, 30.00)	(27.00, 28.00, 27.00, 8.00)
(10.00, 45.00, 10.00, 25.00)	(27.00, 28.00, 27.00, 8.00)
(15.00, 40.00, 15.00, 20.00)	(27.00, 28.00, 27.00, 8.00)
(20.00, 35.00, 20.00, 15.00)	(27.00, 28.00, 27.00, 8.00)
(25.00, 30.00, 25.00, 10.00)	(29.00, 26.00, 29.00, 6.00)
(30.00, 25.00, 30.00, 5.00)	(29.00, 26.00, 29.00, 6.00)
(35.00, 20.00, 35.00, 0.00)	

Example 4. *Consider the network problem depicted in Figure 3, where* $\mathcal{N} = \{1,2,3,4,5,6\}$, $\mathcal{W} = \{\omega_1, \omega_2\} = \{(1,5),(2,6)\}$, $\mathcal{E} = \{\alpha_1, \alpha_2, \alpha_3, \alpha_4, \alpha_5, \alpha_6, \alpha_7, \alpha_8, \alpha_9\}$, $\mathcal{D} = \{d_{\omega_1}, d_{\omega_2}\}$, $d_{\omega_1} = 25$, $d_{\omega_2} = 20$, *with two criteria: travel time and travel cost.* $P_\omega = \{p_1, p_2, p_3, p_4, p_5, p_6, p_7\}$, *where* $P_{\omega_1} = \{p_1, p_2, p_3, p_4\}$, $P_{\omega_2} = \{p_5, p_6, p_7\}$, $p_1 = (\alpha_3)$, $p_2 = (\alpha_2 \alpha_5 \alpha_8)$, $p_3 = (\alpha_1 \alpha_4 \alpha_5 \alpha_8)$, $p_4 = (\alpha_1 \alpha_6 \alpha_8)$, $p_5 = (\alpha_7)$, $p_6 = (\alpha_6 \alpha_9)$, *and* $p_7 = (\alpha_4 \alpha_5 \alpha_9)$.

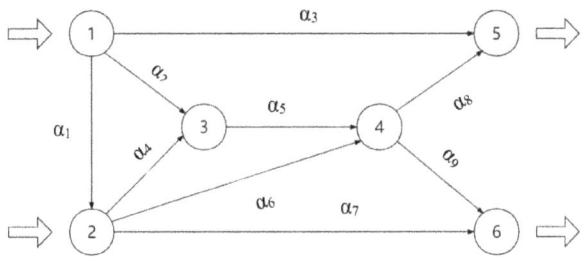

Figure 3. Network topology for Example 4.

The constrains of paths and cost functions are given as follows:

$$l_{p_1} = 0,\ l_{p_2} = 0,\ l_{p_3} = 0,\ l_{p_4} = 0,\ l_{p_5} = 0,\ l_{p_6} = 0,\ l_{p_7} = 0;$$

$$u_{p_1} = 25,\ u_{p_2} = 25,\ u_{p_3} = 25,\ u_{p_4} = 25,\ u_{p_5} = 20,\ u_{p_6} = 20,\ u_{p_7} = 20.$$

$$t_{1,\alpha_1}(y,\xi) = 4(y_6 + y_7) + 50 - 2\xi_3,\ t_{2,\alpha_1}(y,\xi) = (y_6 + y_7)^2 + 90 - 2\xi_3;$$

$$t_{1,\alpha_2}(y,\xi) = 2y_2 + 20 - \xi_2 + 4\xi_6,\ t_{2,\alpha_2}(y,\xi) = 3y_2^2 + 10;$$

$$t_{1,\alpha_3}(y,\xi) = 4y_1^2 + 100 + \xi_1,\ t_{2,\alpha_3}(y,\xi) = 2y_1^2 + 110 + 6\xi_1;$$

$$t_{1,\alpha_4}(y,\xi) = 2(y_4 + y_7) + 10 + \xi_2,\ t_{2,\alpha_4}(y,\xi) = (y_4 + y_7)^2 + 30 - \xi_2 + \xi_3;$$

$$t_{1,\alpha_5}(y,\xi) = 2(y_3 + y_4 + y_7)^2 + 10 - \xi_2,\ t_{2,\alpha_5}(y,\xi) = (y_3 + y_4 + y_7)^2 + 20 + \xi_2;$$

$$t_{1,\alpha_6}(y,\xi) = 5(y_4 + y_5)^2 + 430 + 2\xi_3 + \xi_4,\ t_{2,\alpha_6}(y,\xi) = 2(y_4 + y_5) + 530 + 2\xi_3 - \xi_4;$$

$$t_{1,\alpha_7}(y,\xi) = 2y_2^2 + 100 + 5\xi_5,\ t_{2,\alpha_7}(y,\xi) = 3y_5 + 300;$$

$$t_{1,\alpha_8}(y,\xi) = (y_3 + y_6 + y_7)^2 + 20,\ t_{2,\alpha_8}(y,\xi) = 2(y_3 + y_6 + y_7) + 10;$$

$$t_{1,\alpha_9}(y,\xi) = (y_5 + y_6)^2 + 30 - 4\xi_6,\ t_{2,\alpha_9}(y,\xi) = 2(y_5 + y_6) + 10 + 2\xi_7 - \xi_3;$$

where $z_{\alpha_i}(i = 1, 2, \ldots, 9)$ denotes the flow on arc α_i. Then we have

$$c_{p_1}(y,\xi) = \begin{pmatrix} 4y_1^2 + 100 + \xi_1 \\ 2y_1^2 + 110 + 6\xi_1 \end{pmatrix},\ c_{p_2}(y,\xi) = \begin{pmatrix} 2y_2 + 2(y_3 + y_4 + y_7)^2 + (y_3 + y_6 + y_7)^2 + 50 - 2\xi_2 \\ 3y_2^2 + (y_3 + y_4 + y_7)^2 + 2(y_3 + y_6 + y_7)^2 + 40 + \xi_2 \end{pmatrix}$$

$$c_{p_3}(y,\xi) = \begin{pmatrix} 4(y_6 + y_7) + 2(y_4 + y_7) + 2(y_3 + y_4 + y_7)^2 + (y_3 + y_6 + y_7)^2 + 90 - 2\xi_3 \\ (y_6 + y_7)^2 + (y_4 + y_7)^2 + (y_3 + y_4 + y_7)^2 + 2(y_3 + y_6 + y_7)^2 + 150 - \xi_3 \end{pmatrix}$$

$$c_{p_4}(y,\xi) = \begin{pmatrix} 4(y_6 + y_7) + 5(y_4 + y_5)^2 + (y_3 + y_6 + y_7)^2 + 500 + \xi_4 \\ (y_6 + y_7)^2 + 2(y_4 + y_5) + 2(y_3 + y_6 + y_7)^2 + 630 - \xi_4 \end{pmatrix}$$

$$c_{p_5}(y,\xi) = \begin{pmatrix} 2y_2^2 + 100 + 5\xi_5 \\ 3y_5 + 300 \end{pmatrix},\ c_{p_6}(y,\xi) = \begin{pmatrix} 5(y_4 + y_5)^2 + (y_5 + y_6)^2 + 460 - 4\xi_6 \\ 2(y_4 + y_5) + 2(y_5 + y_6) + 540 \end{pmatrix}$$

$$c_{p_7}(y,\xi) = \begin{pmatrix} 2(y_4 + y_7) + 2(y_3 + y_4 + y_7)^2 + (y_5 + y_6)^2 + 50 \\ (y_4 + y_7)^2 + (y_3 + y_4 + y_7)^2 + 2(y_5 + y_6)^2 + 60 + 2\xi_7 \end{pmatrix}$$

where $\xi_i \in [0,1], i = 1,2,3,4,5,6,7$. Initial feasible flows and a subset of the robust vector equilibrium flows are obtained in 538.47 s. The results are shown in Table 3. The algorithm proposed in [22] obtains the same robust vector equilibrium flows, but its time cost is 548.32 s.

Table 3. Computational results of Algorithm 1.

Initial Feasible Flows		Robust Vector Equilibrium Flows	
$(0,0,0,25,0,0,20)$	$(0,0,0,25,0,0,0,20)$	$(9,7,9,0,19,0,1)$	$(12,13,0,0,8,0,12)$
$(0,25,0,0,0,0,20)$	$(25,0,0,0,0,0,20)$	$(15,10,0,0,9,0,11)$	$(15,10,0,0,9,0,11)$
$(0,0,0,25,0,20,0)$	$(0,0,0,25,0,0,20,0)$	$(12,8,5,0,15,0,5)$	$(15,10,0,0,9,0,11)$
$(0,25,0,0,0,20,0)$	$(25,0,0,0,0,20,0)$	$(9,7,9,0,19,0,1)$	$(12,13,0,0,8,0,12)$
$(0,0,0,25,20,0,0)$	$(0,0,0,25,0,20,0,0)$	$(11,7,7,0,18,0,2)$	
$(0,25,0,0,20,0,0)$	$(25,0,0,0,20,0,0)$		

4. Smoothing Method for the Robust Vector Equilibrium with the Worst Case

It is worth noting that the algorithm in [21] needs to solve a non-smoothing optimization problem. This results in its computational inefficiency. This prompts us to continuously investigate algorithm for solving robust equilibrium flows. In this section, we propose a smoothing method to calculate a subset of the robust vector equilibrium with respect to the worst case. The algorithm is denoted Algorithm 3. To generalize a subset of the robust vector equilibrium flows with respect to the worst case, we use a two-step strategy. The first step is to construct an equivalent optimization problem with the help of a variant version of ReLU activation function for finding the robust weak vector equilibrium flows with respect to the worst case. The second step is to judge whether or not the robust weak vector equilibrium flows with respect to the worst case are equal to the robust vector equilibrium flows with respect to the worst case by an equivalent optimization problem using the vector version of heaviside step function.

Algorithm 3: Robust vector equilibrium algorithm (denoted Algorithm 3).

1. Choose a positive integer q and a tolerance level $\epsilon \geq 0$.
2. Enter $l = (l_{p_k})_{p_k \in P}$ and $u = (u_{p_k})_{p_k \in P}$. Set $\delta_j = d_{\omega_j}/(q|P_{\omega_j}|)$, $j = 1, \cdots, \tilde{l}$.
3. Choose $(k_1, \cdots, k_n)^\top \in \mathbb{N}^n$ satisfying

$$\sum_{i \in I_j} k_i = q|P_{\omega_j}|, \text{ and } l_{p_i} \leq k_i \delta_j \leq u_{p_i}, \ i \in I_j, \ j = 1, \cdots, \tilde{l}.$$

4. Store $y = (y_{p_1}, \cdots, y_{p_n})^\top$ in S^0 where

$$y_{p_i} = k_i \delta_j, \ i \in I_j, \ j = 1, \cdots, \tilde{l}$$

   and return to **Step 3** for other vectors $(k_1, \cdots, k_n)$ unless no one left.
5. Choose a feasible flow y^0 from S^0 to start. Set $k = 0$, $S^0 = S^0 \setminus \{y^0\}$ and $WE = \emptyset$.
6. For every $i, j \in \{1, \cdots, n\}$, solve

$$\text{minimize } \phi(y)$$
$$\text{subject to } y \in \Omega$$
$$\left| y_{p_i} - y_{p_i}^0 \right| \leq \delta_{\omega(i)}, \ i = 1, \cdots, n.$$

   If $\phi(y) \leqq \epsilon$, store y in WE and return to **Step 5** until no element of S^0 left.
7. Choose a feasible flow $y \in WE$, $WE = WE \setminus \{y\}$.
8. Compute

$$\varphi(y) = \sum_{\omega \in W} \sum_{p_k, p_j \in P_\omega} (y_{p_k} - l_{p_k})(u_{p_j} - y_{p_j})(C_{p_k}(y) - C_{p_j}(y))^\top H_+ [C_{p_k}(y) - C_{p_j}(y)]$$

9. If $\varphi(y) \leqq \epsilon$, store y in E and return to **Step 7** until no element of WE left.

Define a function $r : \mathbb{R} \to \mathbb{R}$ and give its vector version function $\mathcal{R} : \mathbb{R}^n \to \mathbb{R}^m$ as follows:

$$r(a) = \left(\max\{0, a\}\right)^2.$$

$$\mathcal{R}(x) = (\prod_{i=1}^{n} r(x_i))e,$$

In addition, the heaviside step function $h_+ : \mathbb{R} \to \mathbb{R}$ and its vector version function $H_+ : \mathbb{R}^n \to \mathbb{R}^m$ are also given below:

$$h_+(a) = \begin{cases} 1, & \text{if } a \geq 0, \\ 0, & \text{otherwise.} \end{cases}$$

$$H_+(x) = (\prod_{i=1}^{n} h_+(x_i))e, \ \forall x \in \mathbb{R}^m.$$

4.1. Description of the Algorithm

In this subsection, we construct an optimization problem whose solution is equivalent to a robust weak vector equilibrium flow with respect to the worst case. For $y \in \Omega$, we define:

$$\phi(y) := \sum_{\omega \in W} \sum_{p_k, p_j \in P_\omega} (y_{p_k} - l_{p_k})(u_{p_j} - y_{p_j})(C_{p_k}(y) - C_{p_j}(y))^\top \mathcal{R}[C_{p_k}(y) - C_{p_j}(y)].$$

Proposition 2. *Let $\bar{y}$ be a feasible flow. The following statements are equivalent.*
(i) $\bar{y}$ is a robust weak vector equilibrium with respect to the worst case;
(ii) $\bar{y}$ is an optimal solution of the problem, denoted:

$$\min \phi(\bar{y}) \quad \text{s.t.} \ y \in \Omega. \tag{3}$$

and the optimal value $\phi(\bar{y})$ is equal to zero.

Proof. We first prove the implication (i) $\Rightarrow$ (ii). It is not hard to see $\phi(y) \geq 0$ for every $y \in \Omega$. Thus, if $\bar{y}$ is a robust weak vector equilibrium with respect to the worst case, in order to deduce (ii), it suffices to prove $\phi(\bar{y}) = 0$. In addition, for every $p_k \in p_\omega$, $\omega \in W$, consider the term:

$$Q_p = \sum_{\omega \in W} \sum_{p_k, p_j \in P_\omega} (y_{p_k} - l_{p_k})(u_{p_j} - y_{p_j})(C_{p_k}(y) - C_{p_j}(y))^\top \mathcal{R}[C_{p_k}(y) - C_{p_j}(y)].$$

If $C_{p_k}(\bar{y}) - C_{p_j}(\bar{y}) \succ 0_{\mathbb{R}^m}$, for some $p_j \in P_\omega$, then by Definition 4, either $\bar{y}_{p_k} = l_{p_k}$ or $\bar{y}_{p_j} = u_{p_j}$; if $C_{p_k}(\bar{y}) - C_{p_j}(\bar{y}) = 0_{\mathbb{R}^m}$, for some $p_j \in P_\omega$, we also get $Q_p = 0$; if $C_{p_k}(\bar{y}) - C_{p_j}(\bar{y}) \prec 0_{\mathbb{R}^m}$, then $\mathcal{R}[C_{p_k}(y) - C_{p_j}(y)] = 0_{\mathbb{R}^m}$, and thus, $Q_p = 0$. As a result, one has $\phi(\bar{y}) = 0$.

Conversely, assume that $\bar{y}$ is an optimal solution of Problem (3) and $\phi(\bar{y}) = 0$. Then, we have $Q_p = 0$ for all $p \in P$. If there exists some $p_k, p_j \in p_\omega$, $\omega \in W$ such that $C_{p_k}(\bar{y}) - C_{p_j}(\bar{y}) \succ 0_{\mathbb{R}^m}$, then $(C_{p_k}(y) - C_{p_j}(y))' \mathcal{R}[C_{p_k}(y) - C_{p_j}(y)] \succ 0_{\mathbb{R}^m}$, and thus, either $\bar{y}_{p_k} = l_{p_k}$ or $\bar{y}_{p_j} = u_{p_j}$ by $Q_p = 0$. Consequently, we deduce that $\bar{y}$ is a robust weak vector equilibrium with respect to the worst case. □

For $y \in \Omega$, we define

$$\varphi(y) = \sum_{\omega \in W} \sum_{p_k, p_j \in P_\omega} (y_{p_k} - l_{p_k})(u_{p_j} - y_{p_j})(C_{p_k}(y) - C_{p_j}(y))^\top H_+[C_{p_k}(y) - C_{p_j}(y)].$$

Then, by using a similar method of proof, we may establish the following result for the robust vector equilibrium with respect to the worst case.

Proposition 3. *Let $\bar{y}$ be a feasible flow. The following statements are equivalent.*
(i) $\bar{y}$ *is a robust vector equilibrium with respect to the worst case.*
(ii) $\bar{y}$ *is an optimal solution of the problem, denoted as follows:*

$$\min \varphi(y)$$
$$s.t.\ y \in \Omega.$$
(4)

and the optimal value $\varphi(\bar{y})$ is equal to zero.

Algorithm 3 is mainly based on ideas of Propositions 2 and 3. **Steps 1–4** create a subset of feasible flows with the initial conditions, denoted as S^0, with which **Steps 4–6** will start. **Steps 5–6** are aimed at solving Problem (3) given in Proposition 2 by using first-order optimization methods, and then a subset of the robust weak vector equilibrium flows with respect to the worst case is gained. **Steps 7–9** focus on solving Problem (4) given in Proposition 3, and then a subset of the robust vector equilibrium flows with respect to the worst case is generated.

Assume that $\mathcal{W}$ consists of $\tilde{l}$ elements $\omega_1, \ldots, \omega_{\tilde{l}}$ in the network and for each pair ω_j. Let $I_j = \{i \in \{1, \ldots, n\} : p_i \in P_{\omega_j}\}$. Denote WE by the subset of the robust weak vector equilibrium flows with respect to the worst case and E by the subset of the robust vector equilibrium flows with respect to worst case.

4.2. Comparison with Other Methods

In this subsection, we will give two numerical examples to show the comparison with that of [21]. In these numerical examples, both Algorithm 3 and the algorithm proposed in [21] start from the same set of initial points. To make a fair comparison, all test problems are run five times to reduce the impact of randomness.

Example 5. *Consider the network problem depicted in Figure 4, where $\mathcal{N} = \{1, 2, 3, 4, 5\}$, $\mathcal{W} = \{\omega_1, \omega_2\} = \{(1,4), (1,5)\}, \mathcal{E} = \{\alpha_1, \alpha_2, \alpha_3, \alpha_4, \alpha_5, \alpha_6, \alpha_7, \alpha_8, \alpha_9\}, \mathcal{D} = \{d_{\omega_1}, d_{\omega_2}\}, d_{\omega_1} = 25, d_{\omega_2} = 20$, with two criteria: travel time and travel cost, $P_\omega = \{p_1, p_2, p_3, p_4, p_5, p_6, p_7\}$, where $P_{\omega_1} = \{p_1, p_2, p_3, p_4\}, P_{\omega_2} = \{p_5, p_6, p_7\}$.*

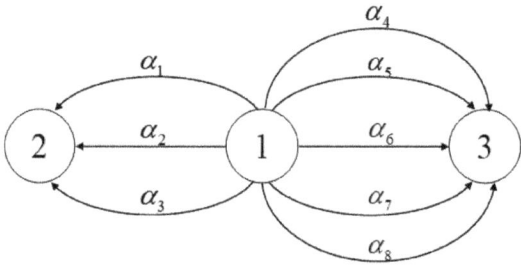

Figure 4. Network topology for Example 5.

Assume that:

$$l_{p_1} = l_{p_2} = l_{p_3} = l_{p_4} = l_{p_5} = l_{p_6} = l_{p_7} = l_{p_8} = 0;$$

$$u_{p_1} = 100,\ u_{p_2} = 100, u_{p_3} = 100, u_{p_4} = 200,\ u_{p_5} = 100, u_{p_6} = 120, u_{p_7} = 150, u_{p_8} = 100;$$

$$t_{1,\alpha_1}(y,\xi) = y_1^2 + y_2^2 + y_3^3 + \xi_1, \; t_{2,\alpha_1}(y,\xi) = 2y_1 + 5y_2 + 3y_3 + y_4 - 2\xi_1;$$
$$t_{1,\alpha_2}(y,\xi) = 8y_1y_2 + y_2^2 + y_7 + y_8 + 4\xi_2, \; t_{2,\alpha_2}(y,\xi) = y_2 + 10y_3 + 2y_7 + y_8 + 2\xi_2;$$
$$t_{1,\alpha_3}(y,\xi) = y_1 + y_2^2 + y_3^3 + y_5 + y_6 - 3\xi_3, \; t_{2,\alpha_3}(y,\xi) = 10y_3^3 + 2y_5 + \xi_3;$$
$$t_{1,\alpha_4}(y,\xi) = y_1 + y_2 + y_4^3 + y_5^2 + y_8^3 + \xi_4, \; t_{2,\alpha_4}(y,\xi) = y_1 + 2y_4 + y_6y_5 + 15y_8;$$
$$t_{1,\alpha_5}(y,\xi) = y_1 + y_3 + y_4^3 + y_5^2 + y_6^2, \; t_{2,\alpha_5}(y,\xi) = y_1 + 5y_3 + 5y_5 + 3y_6 + 12y_7 + 4\xi_5;$$
$$t_{1,\alpha_6}(y,\xi) = y_3 + y_4 + y_5 + y_6^3 - 3\xi_6, \; t_{2,\alpha_6}(y,\xi) = 3y_3 + 10y_5 + y_6 + 2y_8 - 2\xi_6;$$
$$t_{1,\alpha_7}(y,\xi) = y_2 + 8y_4^2 + y_5 + y_7^3 + 2\xi_7, \; t_{2,\alpha_7}(y,\xi) = y_1 + y_2 + 5y_4 + 3y_7;$$
$$t_{1,\alpha_8}(y,\xi) = y_1 + y_3 + 8y_6y_7 + y_8^2 + \xi_8, \; t_{2,\alpha_8}(y,\xi) = y_1 + y_3 + 10y_5^3 + y_8 - \xi_8,$$

where $\xi_i \in [0,1], i = 1,2,3,4,5,6,7,8$. Then, we have

$$C_{p_1}(y) = \begin{pmatrix} y_1^2 + y_2^2 + y_3^3 + 1 \\ 2y_1 + 5y_2 + 3y_3 + y_4 \end{pmatrix}, \; C_{p_2}(y) = \begin{pmatrix} 8y_1y_2 + y_2^2 + y_7 + y_8 + 4 \\ y_2 + 10y_3 + 2y_7 + y_8 + 2 \end{pmatrix}$$

$$C_{p_3}(y) = \begin{pmatrix} y_1 + y_2^2 + y_3^3 + y_5 + y_6 \\ 10y_3^3 + 2y_5 + 1 \end{pmatrix}, \; C_{p_4}(y) = \begin{pmatrix} y_1 + y_2 + y_4^3 + y_5^2 + y_8^3 + 1 \\ y_1 + 2y_4 + y_6y_5 + 15y_8 \end{pmatrix}$$

$$C_{p_5}(y) = \begin{pmatrix} y_1 + y_3 + y_4^3 + y_5^2 + y_6^2 \\ y_1 + 5y_3 + 5y_5 + 3y_6 + 12y_7 + 4 \end{pmatrix}, \; C_{p_6}(y) = \begin{pmatrix} y_3 + y_4 + y_5 + y_6^3 \\ 3y_3 + 10y_5 + y_6 + 2y_8 \end{pmatrix}$$

$$C_{p_7}(y) = \begin{pmatrix} y_2 + 8y_4^2 + y_5 + y_7^3 + 2 \\ y_1 + y_2 + 5y_4 + 3y_7 \end{pmatrix}, \; C_{p_8}(y) = \begin{pmatrix} y_1 + y_3 + 8y_6y_7 + y_8^2 + 1 \\ y_1 + y_3 + 10y_5^3 + y_8 \end{pmatrix}$$

Choosing $q = 2$, we have 32 feasible flows and 2 robust (weak) vector equilibrium flows with respect to the worst case, which are obtained in 0.18 s. Robust (weak) vector equilibrium flows with respect to the worst case are shown in Table 4. However, using the algorithm proposed in [21], it will take 13.826 s to obtain five robust vector equilibrium flows with respect to the worst case, which are shown in Table 5.

Table 4. Computational results of Algorithm 3.

Robust Weak Vector Equilibrium Flows (Worst Case)	Robust Vector Equilibrium Flows (Worst Case)
(100, 100, 100, 145.125, 0, 120, 134.875, 100)	(100, 100, 100, 145.125, 0, 120, 134.875, 100)
(100, 100, 100, 150, 0, 120, 130, 100)	(100, 100, 100, 150, 0, 120, 130, 100)

Table 5. Computational results of algorithm in [21].

Robust Vector Equilibrium Flows (Worst Case)
(100, 100, 100, 30, 100, 120, 150, 100)
(100, 100, 100, 50, 100, 120, 130, 100)
(100, 100, 100, 100, 100, 120, 80, 100)
(100, 100, 100, 150, 100, 120, 30, 100)
(100, 100, 100, 200, 100, 100, 100, 0)

Example 6. *Consider the network problem depicted in Figure 5, where* $\mathcal{N} = \{1,2,3,4,5\}$, $\mathcal{W} = \{\omega_1, \omega_2\} = \{(1,4),(1,5)\}, \mathcal{E} = \{\alpha_1, \alpha_2, \alpha_3, \alpha_4, \alpha_5, \alpha_6, \alpha_7, \alpha_8, \alpha_9\}, \mathcal{D} = \{d_{\omega_1}, d_{\omega_2}\}$ *with* $d_{\omega_1} = 25, d_{\omega_2} = 20$, *with two criteria: travel time and travel cost,* $P_\omega = \{p_1, p_2, p_3, p_4, p_5, p_6, p_7\}$,

where $P_{\omega_1} = \{p_1, p_2, p_3, p_4\}$, $P_{\omega_2} = \{p_5, p_6, p_7\}$. $p_1 = (\alpha_4)$, $p_2 = (\alpha_2 \alpha_8)$, $p_3 = (\alpha_2 \alpha_6 \alpha_3)$, $p_4 = (\alpha_1 \alpha_3)$, $p_5 = (\alpha_5)$, $p_6 = (\alpha_2 \alpha_9)$, $p_7 = (\alpha_1 \alpha_7)$. Let:

$$l_1 = 0,\ l_2 = 0,\ l_3 = 0,\ l_4 = 0,\ l_5 = 0,\ l_6 = 0,\ l_7 = 0;$$

$$u_1 = 15,\ u_2 = 20,\ u_3 = 15,\ u_4 = 10,\ u_5 = 15,\ u_6 = 10,\ u_7 = 15.$$

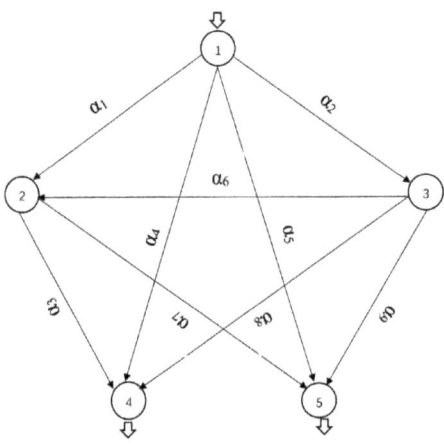

Figure 5. Network topology for Example 6.

Now, we give the cost function of arcs as follows:

$$t_{\alpha_1}(y,\xi) = \begin{pmatrix} 4(y_6 + y_7) + 2(y_3 + y_4 + y_7)^2 + 300 - 2\xi_1 \\ (y_6 + y_7)^2 + (y_3 + y_4 + y_7)^2 + 330 - \xi_1 \end{pmatrix},\ t_{\alpha_2}(y,\xi) = \begin{pmatrix} 2(y_3 + y_4 + y_7)^2 + 50 + \xi_2 \\ (y_3 + y_4 + y_7)^2 \end{pmatrix}$$

$$t_{\alpha_3}(y,\xi) = \begin{pmatrix} 2(y_3 + y_7) + 2(y_4 + y_7)^2 + 300 + 2\xi_1 + \xi_6 \\ (y_3 + y_7)^2 + 2(y_4 + y_7) + 100 + \xi_1 - \xi_3 \end{pmatrix},\ t_{\alpha_4}(y,\xi) = \begin{pmatrix} 4y_1^2 + 100 + \xi_4 \\ 2y_1^2 + 110 + 6\xi_4 \end{pmatrix}$$

$$t_{\alpha_5}(y,\xi) = \begin{pmatrix} 2y_2^2 + 100 + 5\xi_5 \\ 3y_2 + y_5 + 300 \end{pmatrix},\ t_{\alpha_6}(y,\xi) = \begin{pmatrix} (y_3 + y_6 + y_7)^2 - 260 - \xi_6 - \xi_2 \\ 2(y_3 + y_6 + y_7)^2 + 50 - \xi_1 \end{pmatrix}$$

$$t_{\alpha_7}(y,\xi) = \begin{pmatrix} 2(y_3 + y_7) + 2(y_4 + y_7)^2 - 150 + 3\xi_1 - \xi_7 \\ (y_3 + y_7)^2 + (y_4 + y_7)^2 - 310 + \xi_1 \end{pmatrix},\ t_{\alpha_8}(y,\xi) = \begin{pmatrix} 2y_2 + (y_3 + y_6 + y_7)^2 - \xi_2 \\ 3y_2^2 + 2(y_3 + y_6 + y_7)^2 + 40 - \xi_8 \end{pmatrix}$$

$$t_{\alpha_9}(y,\xi) = \begin{pmatrix} 5(y_5 + y_6)^2 + 410 + \xi_2 \\ 2(y_5 + y_6)^2 + 540 - \xi_9 \end{pmatrix}$$

where $\xi_i \in [0,1], i = 1,2,3,4,5,6,7,8,9$. Then, we have:

$$C_{p_1}(y) = \begin{pmatrix} 4y_1^2 + 101 \\ 2y_1^2 + 116 \end{pmatrix},\ C_{p_2}(y) = \begin{pmatrix} 2y_2 + 2(y_3 + y_4 + y_7)^2 + (y_3 + y_6 + y_7)^2 + 50 \\ 3y_2^2 + (y_3 + y_4 + y_7)^2 + 2(y_3 + y_6 + y_7)^2 + 41 \end{pmatrix},$$

$$C_{p_3}(y) = \begin{pmatrix} 4(y_3 + y_7) + 2(y_4 + y_7)^2 + 2(y_3 + y_4 + y_7)^2 + (y_3 + y_6 + y_7)^2 + 90 \\ (y_3 + y_7)^2 + 2(y_4 + y_7) + (y_3 + y_4 + y_7)^2 + 2(y_3 + y_6 + y_7)^2 + 150 \end{pmatrix},$$

$$C_{p_4}(y) = \begin{pmatrix} 4(y_3 + y_7) + 2(y_4 + y_7)^2 + 4(y_6 + y_7) + 2(y_3 + y_4 + y_7)^2 + 601 \\ (y_3 + y_7)^2 + 2(y_4 + y_7) + (y_6 + y_7)^2 + (y_3 + y_4 + y_7)^2 + 430 \end{pmatrix},$$

$$C_{p_5}(y) = \begin{pmatrix} 2y_2^2 + 105 \\ 3y_2 + y_5 + 300 \end{pmatrix}, \quad C_{p_6}(y) = \begin{pmatrix} 5(y_5 + y_6)^2 + 2(y_3 + y_4 + y_7)^2 + 460 \\ 2(y_5 + y_6) + (y_3 + y_4 + y_7)^2 + 540 \end{pmatrix},$$

$$C_{p_7}(y) = \begin{pmatrix} 4(y_6 + y_7) + 2(y_4 + y_7)^2 + 2(y_3 + y_4 + y_7)^2 + 2(y_3 + y_7) + 152 \\ (y_6 + y_7)^2 + (y_4 + y_7)^2 + (y_3 + y_4 + y_7)^2 + (y_3 + y_7)^2 + 20 \end{pmatrix}.$$

Choosing $q = 1$, 80 feasible flows are created and a subset of robust vector equilibrium flows with respect to the worst case (displayed in Tables 6) are obtained. This takes about 0.62 s. However, using the algorithm presented in [21], it spends 579 s to obtain a subset of robust vector equilibrium flows with respect to the worst case, which are shown in Table 7.

Table 6. Computational results of Algorithm 3.

Robust Weak Vector Equilibrium Flows (Worst Case)	Robust Vector Equilibrium Flows (Worst Case)
$(11.88, 11.29, 1.83, 0, 13.23, 0, 6.77)$	$(11.88, 11.29, 1.83, 0, 13.23, 0, 6.77)$
$(10.56, 12.5, 1.94, 0, 13.33, 0, 6.67)$	$(10.56, 12.5, 1.94, 0, 13.33, 0, 6.67)$
$(10.04, 14.92, 0.04, 0, 11.89, 0, 8.11)$	$(10.04, 14.92, 0.04, 0, 11.89, 0, 8.11)$
$(11.03, 12.4, 1.57, 0, 13.33, 0, 6.67)$	$(11.03, 12.4, 1.57, 0, 13.33, 0, 6.67)$
$(11.42, 13.58, 0, 0, 11.93, 0, 8.07)$	$(11.42, 13.58, 0, 0, 11.93, 0, 8.07)$
$(10.45, 12.5, 2.05, 0, 13.33, 0, 6.67)$	$(10.45, 12.5, 2.05, 0, 13.33, 0, 6.67)$
$(11.12, 10, 3.88, 0, 15, 0, 5)$	$(11.12, 10, 3.88, 0, 15, 0, 5)$

Table 7. Computational results of algorithm in [21].

Robust Vector Equilibrium Flows (Worst Case)
$(10.94, 12.5, 1.56, 0, 12.29, 0, 7.71)$
$(10.94, 13.28, 0.78, 0, 12.29, 0, 7.71)$
$(12.66, 10.78, 1.56, 0, 12.29, 0, 7.71)$
$(10.94, 12.5, 1.56, 0, 12.5, 0, 7.5)$

5. Conclusions

In this paper, we mainly consider a robust multi-criteria traffic network equilibrium problem with path capacity constraints. Firstly, the robust vector equilibrium principle and the robust vector equilibrium principle with respect to the worst case are given. We pay attention to constructing an equivalent min–max optimization problem for the robust vector equilibrium, in which the solution is equivalent to a robust vector equilibrium. Then, a direct search algorithm is proposed for solving the corresponding min–max optimization problem. The step size in the algorithm requires neither gradient information nor redundant parameters. What is more, we select different step sizes for different variables and extend the search directions. The results of three numerical experiments show that it takes less time than the method in [22] to find the robust vector equilibrium flows.

To generate a subset of the robust vector equilibrium with respect to the worst case, we employ a two-step strategy. The first step is to construct a smoothing optimization problem based on a variant version of the ReLU activation function to compute the robust weak vector equilibrium flows with respect to the worst case. The second step is to judge whether or not the robust weak vector equilibrium flows with respect to the worst case are equal to the robust vector equilibrium flows with respect to the worst case. Compared with the algorithm in [21], the results of two numerical experiments show that our algorithm can greatly reduce the computational cost.

Recently, robust vector optimization based on set orders is widely used in the uncertain optimization environment [23,24]. It is noteworthy that the robust vector equilibrium principles considered in this paper are all based on vector order. In addition, our method can only be applied to small-scale traffic networks. Therefore, an interesting topic for future research is to investigate large-scale, multi-criteria traffic networks based on set orders.

Author Contributions: Conceptualization, X.-X.M. and Y.-D.X.; Writing—original draft preparation, X.-X.M. and Y.-D.X.; Writing—review and editing, X.-X.M. and Y.-D.X. All authors have read and agreed to the published version of the manuscript.

Funding: This research was supported by the National Natural Science Foundation of China (Grant number: 11801051) and the Natural Science Foundation of Chongqing (Grant number: cstc2019jcyj-msxmX0075).

Data Availability Statement: The data that support the findings of this study are available from the corresponding author upon reasonable request.

Conflicts of Interest: The authors declare no conflict of interest.

References

1. Wardrop, J. Some theoretical aspects of road traffic research. *Proc. Inst. Civil Eng. Part II* **1952**, *1*, 325–362. [CrossRef]
2. Athanasenas, A. Traffic simulation model for rural road network management. *Trans. Res. Part E* **1997**, *33*, 233–243. [CrossRef]
3. Nagurney, A. On the relationship between supply chain and transportation network equilibria: A super network equivalence with computations. *Trans. Res. Part E* **2006**, *42*, 293–316. [CrossRef]
4. Ji, X.F.; Chu, Y.Y. A target-oriented bi-attribute user equilibrium model with travelers perception errors on the tolled traffic network. *Trans. Res. Part E* **2020**, *144*, 102–150. [CrossRef]
5. Xu, Z.T.; Chen, Z.B.; Yin, Y.F.; Ye, J.P. Equilibrium analysis of urban traffic networks with ride-sourcing services. *Trans. Sci.* **2021**, *55*, 1227–1458. [CrossRef]
6. Wang, J.; Du, M.Q.; Lu, L.L.; He, X.Z. Maximizing network throughput under stochastic user equilibrium with elastic demand. *Netw. Spat. Econ.* **2018**, *18*, 115–143. [CrossRef]
7. Ma, J.; Meng, Q.; Cheng, L.; Liu, Z.Y. General stochastic ridesharing user equilibrium problem with elastic demand. *Trans. Res. Part B* **2022**, *162*, 162–194. [CrossRef]
8. Chen, G.Y.; Yen, N.D. *On the Variational Inequality Model for Network Equilibrium*; Internal Report 3; Department of Mathematics, University of Pisa: Pisa, Italy, 1993; Volume 196.
9. Yang, X.Q.; Goh, C.J. On vector variational inequalities: Application to vector equilibria. *J. Optim. Theory Appl.* **1997**, *95*, 431–443. [CrossRef]
10. Li, S.J.; Teo, K.L.; Yang, X.Q. A remark on a standard and linear vector network equilibrium problem with capacity constraints. *Eur. J. Oper. Res.* **2008**, *184*, 13–23. [CrossRef]
11. Luc, D.T.; Rocca, M.; Papalia, M. Equilibrium in a vector supply demand network with capacity. *Appl. Anal.* **2011**, *90*, 1029–1045. [CrossRef]
12. Raith, A.; Ehrgott, A. On vector equilibria, vector optimization and vector variational inequalities. *J. Multi-Crit. Decis. Anal.* **2011**, *18*, 39–54. [CrossRef]
13. Phuong, T.T.T.; Luc, D.T. Equilibrium in multi-criteria supply and demand networks with capacity constraints. *Math. Methods Oper. Res.* **2015**, *81*, 83–107.
14. Luc, D.T.; Phuong, T.T.T. Equilibrium in multi-criteria transportation networks. *J. Optim. Theory Appl.* **2016**, *169*, 116–147. [CrossRef]
15. Phuong, T.T.T. Smoothing method in multi-criteria transportation network equilibrium problem. *Optimization* **2019**, *68*, 1577–1598. [CrossRef]
16. Daniele, P.; Giuffré, S. Random variational inequalities and the random traffic equilibrium problem. *J. Optim. Theory Appl.* **2015**, *167*, 363–381. [CrossRef]
17. Dragicevic, A.; Gurtoo, A. Stochastic Control of Ecological Networks. *J. Math. Biol.* **2022**, *85*, 7. [CrossRef]
18. Ehrgott, M.; Wang, J.Y.T.; Watling, D.P. On multi-objective stochastic user equilibrium. *Trans. Res. Part B* **2015**, *81*, 704–717. [CrossRef]
19. Cao, J.D.; Li, R.X.; Huang, W.; Guo, J.H.; Wei, Y. Traffic network equilibrium problems with demands uncertainty and capacity constraints of arcs by scalarization approaches. *Sci. China Technol. Sci.* **2018**, *61*, 1642–1653. [CrossRef]
20. Wei, H.Z.; Chen, C.R.; Wu, B.W. Vector network equilibrium problems with uncertain demands and capacity constraints of arcs. *Optim. Lett.* **2021**, *15*, 1113–1131. [CrossRef]
21. Minh, N.B.; Phuong, T.T.T. Robust equilibrium in transportation networks. *Acta Math. Vietnam.* **2020**, *45*, 635–650. [CrossRef]
22. Dzahini, K.J. Expected complexity analysis of stochastic direct-search. *Comput. Optim. Appl.* **2022**, *81*, 1–22. [CrossRef]
23. Bouza, G.; Quintana, E.; Tammer, C. A steepest descent method for set optimization problems with set-valued mappings of finite cardinality. *J. Optim. Theory Appl.* **2021**, *190*, 711–743. [CrossRef]
24. Eichfelder, G.; Quintana, E.; Rocktäschel, S. A vectorization scheme for nonconvex set optimization problems. *SIAM J. Optim.* **2022**, *32*, 1184–1209. [CrossRef]

Disclaimer/Publisher's Note: The statements, opinions and data contained in all publications are solely those of the individual author(s) and contributor(s) and not of MDPI and/or the editor(s). MDPI and/or the editor(s) disclaim responsibility for any injury to people or property resulting from any ideas, methods, instructions or products referred to in the content.

Article

A Nonconstant Gradient Constrained Problem for Nonlinear Monotone Operators

Sofia Giuffrè

Department of Information Engineering, Infrastructure and Sustainable Energy (DIIES) Mediterranea University of Reggio Calabria, Loc. Feo di Vito, 89122 Reggio Calabria, Italy; sofia.giuffre@unirc.it

Abstract: The purpose of the research is the study of a nonconstant gradient constrained problem for nonlinear monotone operators. In particular, we study a stationary variational inequality, defined by a strongly monotone operator, in a convex set of gradient-type constraints. We investigate the relationship between the nonconstant gradient constrained problem and a suitable double obstacle problem, where the obstacles are the viscosity solutions to a Hamilton–Jacobi equation, and we show the equivalence between the two variational problems. To obtain the equivalence, we prove that a suitable constraint qualification condition, Assumption S, is fulfilled at the solution of the double obstacle problem. It allows us to apply a strong duality theory, holding under Assumption S. Then, we also provide the proof of existence of Lagrange multipliers. The elements in question can be not only functions in L^2, but also measures.

Keywords: variational inequalities; non-constant gradient constraints; obstacle problem; nonlinear monotone operators; Lagrange multipliers

MSC: 35J87; 65K10; 49N15

Citation: Giuffrè, S. A Nonconstant Gradient Constrained Problem for Nonlinear Monotone Operators. *Axioms* **2023**, *12*, 605. https://doi.org/10.3390/axioms12060605

Academic Editors: Siamak Pedrammehr and Mohammad Reza Chalak Qazani

Received: 18 May 2023
Revised: 15 June 2023
Accepted: 16 June 2023
Published: 18 June 2023

Copyright: © 2023 by the author. Licensee MDPI, Basel, Switzerland. This article is an open access article distributed under the terms and conditions of the Creative Commons Attribution (CC BY) license (https://creativecommons.org/licenses/by/4.0/).

1. Introduction

A very interesting problem, which has attracted much interest for many decades because of its simple formulation in terms of differential equations, is the elastic–plastic torsion problem, namely, the problem of minimizing the functional

$$\frac{1}{2}\int_\Omega (|Dv|^2 - hv)dx \qquad (1)$$

on the class of functions $\{v \in H_0^1(\Omega) \,:\, |Dv| \leq 1\}$.

The elastic–plastic torsion problem arises when a long elastic bar with cross section Ω is twisted by an angle. In particular, the formulation due to R. von Mises (see [1]) of the elastic–plastic torsion problem of a cylindrical bar is the following one:

"Find a function $u(x)$, which vanishes on $\partial\Omega$ and is continuous, together with its first derivatives on Ω; on Ω the gradient of u, Du, must have an absolute value less than or equal to a given positive constant t; whenever, in Ω, $|Du| < t$, the function u must satisfy the differential equation $\Delta u = -2\nu\alpha$, where the positive constants ν and α denote the shearing modulus and the angle of twist per unit length respectively".

The plastic region, P, refers to the range of deformation in which the material exhibits significant plastic or irreversible behavior. It is the region beyond the elastic limit where the material undergoes permanent changes in shape, and the deformation is not recoverable. When a material is loaded within its elastic limit, it deforms elastically, meaning that it can return to its original shape once the load is removed. However, beyond the elastic limit, the material enters the plastic region, and plastic deformation occurs. In particular, the set

$$E = \{x \in \Omega : |Du(x)| < t\}$$

is the set of points where the cross section still remains elastic, namely the elastic set, and the set
$$P = \{x \in \Omega : |Du(x)| = t\},$$
is the set of points where the material has become plastic due to the torsion, namely the plastic set.

The ridge R of Ω is, by definition, the set of points in Ω where $dist(x, \partial\Omega)$ is not $C^{1,1}$, whereas the part of ∂E, which is contained in Ω, is called the free boundary (see [2]).

For the derivation of the variational inequality from the physical problem see [3].

Ting [4] investigated problem (1) for $n = 2$, whereas the existence of a Lagrange multiplier formulation for (1) (and hence of a corresponding system of partial differential equations) was proved for constant h in [5] by Brézis.

Glowinski et al. [6] studied the numerical aspects; for results on the elastic and plastic sets E and P and on the free boundary we refer to Caffarelli and Friedman [2]. In [7] Brezis and Sibony proved that the elastic–plastic torsion problem is equivalent to an obstacle-type problem, in which the distance function represents the obstacle. Moreover, they proposed two numerical methods for the obstacle problem.

In [8] Chiadò Piat and Percivale proved the existence of measure-type Lagrange multipliers under more general assumptions on the operator and on h.

Daniele et al. [9] obtained similar results, solving a problem unsolved for a long time by using a new infinite dimensional duality theory. They show, for a class of problems including Problem (1), the existence of an L^∞ Lagrange multiplier, if the problem admits solution and a constraint qualification condition is fulfilled at this solution (see Section 3). The Lagrange multiplier is the solution to a dual problem (see also [10–12] for other results related to linear and nonlinear monotone operators).

Many other studies in the past years are related to the problem when the gradient constraints are no longer constant, since it models many interesting physical and biological phenomena (see [13] for an overview of constrained and unconstrained free boundary problems).

Studying variational problems with gradient constraints involves techniques from the calculus of variations and constrained optimization. Some common methods include: Lagrange multipliers, penalty methods, augmented Lagrangian methods, and projection methods. As is well known, Lagrange multipliers introduce additional unknowns and allow the constraints to be incorporated into the objective function through a modified Lagrangian. The resulting problem can then be solved using variational methods or numerical optimization techniques.

Relevant issues related to the problem with gradient constraints are existence and regularity of the solution, existence of Lagrange multipliers, connection with double obstacle problem, and numerical aspects.

Regarding the existence and regularity of the solution, we refer to L. Evans in [14], who studied general linear elliptic equations with a non-constant gradient constraint $g(x) \in C^2(\overline{\Omega})$, and proved that there exists a unique solution in the space $W^{2,p}_{loc}(\Omega) \cap W^{1,\infty}_0(\Omega)$, with $1 < p < \infty$ (see also [15–18] for other regularity results).

The conditions required for the existence of a Lagrange multiplier are typically related to the regularity of the problem, such as the smoothness of the objective function and constraints.

One of the important conditions for the existence of a Lagrange multiplier is the constraint qualification. There are different types of constraint qualifications, such as the linear independence constraint qualification (LICQ), the Mangasarian–Fromovitz constraint qualification (MFCQ), and Slater's condition (see Theorem 4).

If the qualification condition is satisfied, then according to the Lagrange multiplier theorem, there exists a Lagrange multiplier associated with the optimal solution. The Lagrange multiplier, generally, provides information about the sensitivity of the objective function to changes in the constraints.

However, let us stress that the existence of a Lagrange multiplier does not guarantee a unique solution to the optimization problem. It only indicates the existence of a necessary condition for an optimum.

A very interesting property of variational problems with gradient constraints is the relationship with double obstacle problems. Let us remark that the equivalence is not always true, as observed in [14] (see also [19,20]). Equivalence results between the two problems associated to the Laplacian or to a linear operator are contained in [19–21] (see also [22]).

The equivalence also holds for the problem associated to a nonlinear strongly monotone operator $a(Du)$ with nonconstant gradient constraint of type $G(Du) \leq M$, where G is a strictly convex function (see [23]).

Let us note that monotone operators play a fundamental role in various branches of mathematics, including optimization theory, to analyze several mathematical problems involving nonlinear operators. Monotone operators are extensively used in the study of variational inequalities too (see [24]).

The paper adds to the literature on nonconstant gradient constrained problem further results related to the relationship with double obstacle problem and the existence of Lagrange multipliers. Here we investigate the problem associated to a nonlinear strongly monotone operator as in [23], but we consider the nonconstant gradient constraint of type $|Du| \leq g(x)$, with $g(x) \in C^2(\overline{\Omega})$, $g(x) > 0$. We also prove the existence of L^2 Lagrange multipliers and, under less restrictive assumptions, an existence result of measure-type Lagrange multipliers. Let us note that the existence of Lagrange multipliers as measures is not proved for gradient contraints of type $G(Du) \leq M$.

In particular, the problem under consideration is

$$\text{Find } u \in K_g = \left\{ v \in H_0^{1,2}(\Omega) : |Dv|^2 = \sum_{i=1}^n (D_i v)^2 \leq g(x), \text{ a.e. in } \Omega \right\} \text{ such that:}$$

$$\int_\Omega \sum_{i=1}^n a_i(Du)(D_i v - D_i u)\, dx \geq \int_\Omega f(v-u)\, dx, \quad \forall v \in K_g, \qquad (2)$$

where $a(p) : \mathbb{R}^n \to \mathbb{R}^n$ is a strongly monotone operator of class C^2 (see (6)).

Let us note that it follows from classical results in the literature that there exists a unique solution to problem (2) (see [25]).

In the first result of the paper (Theorem 1) we show that, under a condition on the gradient constraint g, problem (2) is equivalent to the following double obstacle problem

Find $u \in K$ such that:

$$\int_\Omega \sum_{i=1}^n a_i(Du)(D_i v - D_i u)\, dx \geq \int_\Omega f(v-u)\, dx, \quad \forall v \in K, \qquad (3)$$

where $K = \left\{ v \in H_0^{1,2}(\Omega) : w_1(x) \leq v(x) \leq w_2(x) \text{ a.e. in } \Omega \right\}$, and

$$w_1 = \inf_{v \in K} v(x), \quad w_2 = \sup_{v \in K} v(x).$$

From Theorem 5.1 in [26] (see also [20]), $w_2 \in H^{1,\infty}(\Omega)$ is the viscosity solution to the Hamilton–Jacobi equation

$$\begin{cases} |Du| = \sqrt{g(x)} & \text{a.e. in } \Omega \\ u = 0 & \text{on } \partial\Omega \end{cases} \qquad (4)$$

and

$$w_2(x) = \inf_{x_0 \in \partial\Omega} L(x, x_0) \qquad (5)$$

where

$$L(x, x_0) =$$
$$inf\left\{\int_0^{T_0} \sqrt{g(\xi(s))}ds : \xi : [0, T_0] \to \overline{\Omega},\ \xi(0) = x,\ \xi(T_0) = x_0,\ |\xi'(s)| \leq 1 \text{ a.e. in } [0, T_0]\right\}$$

w_1 can be calculated analagously.

It is important to note that the regularity of these obstacles follows from the theory of the viscosity solutions to Hamilton–Jacobi equations (see [17], p. 31), even if the solutions to the Hamilton–Jacobi equations are, in general, not smooth.

As already recalled, the problems are, generally, not equivalent, but a condition on the sign of the second derivatives of g is required.

Before proving the equivalence, in Section 3 we achieve a regularity result for solutions to (3) (Theorem 8), that we need in the sequel.

Then, thanks to the equivalence, it is possible to prove that Lagrange multipliers exist in L^2 (Theorem 2).

Finally, an existence result of Lagrange multipliers as Radon measures holds, under less restrictive assumptions (Theorem 3).

The results are obtained following variational arguments and the strong duality theory.

Let us remark, that, during the past several decades, the variational methods have played a key role in solving many problems arising in nonlinear analysis and optimization theory such as differential hemivariational inequalities systems (see [27]), monotone bilevel equilibrium problems, generalized global fractional-order composite dynamical systems, generalized time-dependent hemivariational inequalities systems, optimal control of feedback control system, and so on.

Moreover, let us emphasize that real-life applications have been investigated on the basis of the theory of variational inequalities with operators of monotone type (see [28–30] for mathematical models describing flows of Bingham-type fluids and flows of an Oldroyd type by means of a variational inequality approach).

Finally, let us stress that the problem under consideration is strictly connected to the Monge–Kantorovich mass transfer problem. In particular, in [31] the authors study the integrability of the Lagrange multiplier, assuming that f belongs to $L^p(\Omega)$ in the case of constant gradient constraint (see also [32] for variable constraint g). The Monge–Kantorovich mass transfer problem has applications in diverse fields such as economics, image processing, computer vision, transportation planning, and statistical physics. It provides a mathematical framework for studying the optimal flow of mass, resources, or information between different distributions or regions.

The paper is organized as follows: in Section 2 we state our main results of equivalence between the variational problems and existence of Lagrange multipliers, in Section 3 we provide a preliminary regularity result and some results of the theory of strong duality are recalled. In Section 4 we prove Theorem 1 and Section 5 is devoted to the proofs of Theorems 2 and 3. Finally, in Section 6 we provide our conclusions and suggest new problems that may be of interest for future research.

2. Results

The main results of the paper are presented in this section.

In what follows we assume that Ω is an open bounded convex subset of $\mathbb{R}^n$ and the boundary $\partial\Omega$ is of class C^2.

Moreover, the operator a is of class C^2, with $a(0) = 0$.

In the first two results, we assume that a is a strongly monotone operator, that is, there exists $\lambda > 0$, such that

$$(a(p) - a(q), p - q) \geq \lambda \|p - q\|^2 \quad \forall p, q \in \mathbb{R}^n, p \neq q. \tag{6}$$

Theorem 1. *Assuming that a satisfies assumption (6), $f \equiv \text{constant} > 0$, and the following condition is fulfilled*

$$-\sum_{i,j=1}^{n} \frac{\partial}{\partial x_i}\left(\frac{\partial a_i}{\partial p_j}\frac{\partial g}{\partial x_j}\right) \geq 0 \quad \text{in } \Omega, \tag{7}$$

then, the solution u to problem (2) is also the solution to problem (3).

Moreover, the following coincidence of sets holds:

$$P = \{x \in \Omega : |Du|^2 = g(x)\} = I = \{x \in \Omega : u(x) = w_1(x) \text{ or } u(x) = w_2(x)\}.$$

Regarding the Lagrange multipliers, we prove the existence in two different cases. In the first one, the Lagrange multipliers are L^2 functions, whereas, in the second one, under less restrictive assumptions, they are measures.

Let us stress that the second result (Theorem 3) holds under assumption of strictly monotonicity on the operator a, namely

$$(a(P) - a(Q), P - Q) > 0 \quad \forall P, Q \in \mathbb{R}^n, P \neq Q. \tag{8}$$

Theorem 2. *Under the same assumptions as in Theorem 1, if $u \in K_g \cap W^{2,p}(\Omega)$ solves problem (2), then, there exists a Lagrange multiplier $v \in L^2(\Omega)$, $v \geq 0$ a.e. in Ω, that is*

$$\begin{cases} v\left(\sum_{i=1}^{n}(D_i u)^2 - g(x)\right) = 0 \quad \text{a.e. in } \Omega \\ \sum_{i=1}^{n} \frac{\partial a_i(Du)}{\partial x_i} + f = v \quad \text{a.e. in } \Omega. \end{cases} \tag{9}$$

Theorem 3. *Assume that a satisfies assumption (8) and $f \in L^p(\Omega)$, $p > 1$. If $u \in K_g$ solves problem (2), then there exists a Lagrange multiplier $\mu^* \in (L^\infty(\Omega))^*$, that is*

$$\begin{cases} \langle \mu^*, y \rangle \geq 0 \quad \forall y \in L^\infty(\Omega), \ y \geq 0 \quad \text{a.e. in } \Omega; \\ \langle \mu^*, \sum_{i=1}^{n}(D_i u)^2 - g(x)\rangle = 0; \\ \int_\Omega \left\{\sum_{i=1}^{n} a_i(Du)\frac{\partial \varphi}{\partial x_i} - f\varphi\right\} dx = \langle \mu^*, -2\sum_{i=1}^{n} \frac{\partial u}{\partial x_i}\frac{\partial \varphi}{\partial x_i}\rangle \quad \forall \varphi \in H_0^{1,\infty}(\Omega). \end{cases} \tag{10}$$

3. Preliminary Results

This section is devoted to some preliminary results that we need to prove our theorems.

In particular, first we recall the strong duality theory and, then, we prove a regularity result for the solution to the double obstacle problem (3) that we need to apply in Section 4 a maximum principle.

For the sake of clarity, here we provide the main results of classical strong duality theory and a new strong duality theory, obtained using new separation theorems based on the notion of quasi-relative interior.

For the classical results of strong duality theory we refer to ([33], Theorems 6.7 and 6.11).

It is important to note that strong duality has important implications in optimization theory. It allows us to obtain lower bounds on the optimal value of the primal problem by solving the dual problem. It also provides a way to assess optimality and obtain dual solutions that can provide additional information about the primal problem, such as shadow prices or sensitivity analysis.

The framework, in which the classical theory works, is the following one: X is a real linear space and $S \subset X$ is a nonempty subset; $(Y, \|\cdot\|)$ is a partially ordered real normed space with ordering cone C, and $C^* = \{\lambda \in Y^* : \langle \lambda, y \rangle \geq 0 \ \forall y \in C\}$ is the dual cone of C, whereas Y^* is the topological dual of Y. Moreover, $F : S \to \mathbb{R}$ is a given objective functional, $G : S \to Y$ is a given constraint mapping and the constraint set is given as $\mathbb{K} := \{v \in S : G(v) \in -C\}$.

We consider the primal problem

$$\min_{\substack{G(v) \in -C \\ v \in S}} F(v) \tag{11}$$

and the dual problem

$$\max_{\lambda \in C^*} \inf_{v \in S}[F(v) + \lambda(G(v))], \tag{12}$$

where λ is the Lagrange multiplier associated with the sign constraints.

As is well known (see [33]), the weak duality always holds, namely,

$$\max_{\lambda \in C^*} \inf_{v \in S}[F(v) + \lambda(G(v))] \leq \min_{\substack{G(v) \in -C \\ v \in S}} F(v) \tag{13}$$

Moerover, if problem (11) is solvable and in (13) the equality holds, the strong duality between the primal problem (11) and the dual problem (12) holds.

Theorem 4 (classical strong duality property [33]). *Assume that the composite mapping $(F, G) : S \to \mathbb{R} \times Y$ is convex-like with respect to product cone $\mathbb{R}_+ \times C$ in $\mathbb{R} \times Y$, $\mathbb{K}$ is nonempty and the ordering cone C has a nonempty interior $int(C)$. If the primal problem (11) is solvable and the generalized Slater condition is satisfied, namely there is a vector $\bar{v} \in S$ with $G(\bar{v}) \in -int(C)$, then the dual problem (12) is also solvable and the extremal values of the two problems are equal. Moreover, if u is the optimal solution to problem (11) and $\bar{v} \in C^*$ is a solution to problem (12), it follows that*

$$\bar{v}(G(u)) = 0. \tag{14}$$

Moreover, if

$$\mathcal{L}(v, \nu) = F(v) + \nu(G(v)),$$

is the Lagrange functional, then the following relationship with the saddle points of $\mathcal{L}(v, \nu)$ holds.

Theorem 5 (see [33]). *Under the same assumptions as in Theorem 4, if the ordering cone C is closed, then a point $(u, \bar{v}) \in S \times C^*$ is a saddle point of the Lagrange functional $\mathcal{L}(v, \nu)$, namely*

$$\mathcal{L}(u, \nu) \leq \mathcal{L}(u, \bar{v}) \leq \mathcal{L}(v, \bar{v}), \ \forall v \in S, \forall \nu \in C^*,$$

if and only if u is a solution to the primal problem (11), $\bar{v}$ is a solution to the dual problem (12) and the extremal values of the two problems are equal.

Let us stress that we apply classical strong duality theory to prove Theorem 3, whereas we need a new theory (see [9]) to obtain the other results. Indeed, in our framework, as in many applications in infinite dimensional settings, the classical theory does not work, since the assumption of nonemptiness of the ordering cone is not fulfilled.

Here, we recall the new strong duality theory in its complete version, namely in the case of inequality and equality constraints.

The assumptions read as follows:

Let $(X, \|\cdot\|_X)$, $(Y, \|\cdot\|_Y)$, $(Z, \|\cdot\|_Z)$ be real normed spaces with Y^*, Z^* topological dual of Y and Z, respectively; Y is partially ordered by a convex cone C, $C^* = \{\mu \in Y^* : \langle \mu, y \rangle \geq 0 \ \forall y \in C\}$ is the dual cone of C. S is a nonempty subset of X, and $F : S \to \mathbb{R}$, $G : S \to Y$, $H : S \to Z$ are three functions.

Moreover, we define the feasible set

$$\mathbb{K} = \{v \in S : \ G(v) \in -C, \ H(v) = \theta_Z\}.$$

We recall the definition of tangent cone to $S^* \subset X$ at a point $v \in X$:

$$T_{S^*}(v) := \left\{ l \in X : l = \lim_n \mu_n(v_n - v), \mu_n > 0, v_n \in S^* \; \forall n \in N, \lim_n v_n = v \right\}$$

We introduce the following constraint qualification assumption: we say that Assumption S is satisfied at a point $v_0 \in \mathbb{K}$ if

$$T_{\widetilde{N}}(0, \theta_Y, \theta_Z) \cap \left( ]-\infty, 0[\times \{\theta_Y\} \times \{\theta_Z\} \right) = \emptyset, \tag{15}$$

where

$$\widetilde{N} = \{(F(v) - F(v_0) + \alpha, G(v) + w, H(v)) : v \in S \setminus \mathbb{K}, \alpha \geq 0, w \in C\}.$$

Under Assumption S the following strong duality property holds (see [9]).

Theorem 6. *Let us assume that F and G are convex functions, H is an affine-linear mapping and $v_0 \in \mathbb{K}$ is a solution to the primal problem*

$$\min_{v \in \mathbb{K}} F(v). \tag{16}$$

Then, if Assumption S is fulfilled at v_0, the dual problem

$$\max_{\substack{\lambda \in C^* \\ \mu \in Z^*}} \inf_{v \in S} \{F(v) + \langle \lambda, G(v) \rangle + \langle \mu, H(v) \rangle\} \tag{17}$$

is also solvable and the extreme values of the primal problem and of the dual problem coincide. Moreover, if $(v_0, \lambda^*, \mu^*) \in \mathbb{K} \times C^* \times Z^*$ solves problem (17), then $\langle \lambda^*, G(v_0) \rangle = 0$.

Moreover, if

$$\mathcal{L}(v, \lambda, \mu) = F(v) + \langle \lambda, G(v) \rangle + \langle \mu, H(v) \rangle$$

is the Lagrange functional, then the following result on the saddle points of the Lagrange functional holds.

Theorem 7 ([9]). *Under the same assumptions as in Theorem 6, $v_0 \in \mathbb{K}$ solves problem (16) if and only if there exist $\lambda^* \in C^*$ and $\mu^* \in Z^*$ such that (x_0, λ^*, μ^*) is a saddle point of the Lagrange functional, namely*

$$\mathcal{L}(v_0, \lambda, \mu) \leq \mathcal{L}(v_0, \lambda^*, \mu^*) \leq \mathcal{L}(v, \lambda^*, \mu^*), \quad \forall v \in S, \lambda \in C^*, \mu \in Z^*.$$

Now, we prove the following regularity result, that we will use in Section 4.

Theorem 8. *Let the assumptions of Theorem 1 be satisfied and u be the solution to problem (3). Then, $u \in W^{2,p}(\Omega)$. In particular, if $p > n$, $Du \in C^{0,\alpha}(\Omega)$.*

Proof. The first goal is an estimate for

$$|u|_1 = \sup\left\{ \frac{|u(x) - u(y)|}{|x - y|} : x, y, \in \overline{\Omega}, x \neq y \right\},$$

obtained using similar arguments as in [34].

Let u be the solution to (3), we set $\tilde{u}$ the extension by zero of u to $\mathbb{R}^n$ and

$$u^h(x) = \max\{\tilde{u}(x+h) - \tilde{u}(x) - M|h|, 0\} \quad \forall x, h \in R^n, \tag{18}$$

where $M = \max\{|w_1|_1, |w_2|_1\}$.

Defining

$$u_1(x) = \max\{\tilde{u}(x), \tilde{u}(x+h) - M|h|\} = \tilde{u}(x) + u^h(x),$$

$$u_2(x) = \min\{\tilde{u}(x), \tilde{u}(x-h) + M|h|\} = \tilde{u}(x) - u^h(x-h).$$

as in [19,23], we have $u_{1/\Omega}, u_{2/\Omega} \in K$ and

$$\tilde{w}_1(x) \leq u_2(x) \leq u_1(x) \leq \tilde{w}_2(x) \text{ a.e. in } \Omega.$$

Following the same arguments as in [12], we get

$$\int_{\mathbb{R}^n} \sum_{i=1}^n (a_i(D\tilde{u}(x+h)) - a_i(D\tilde{u}(x)))D_i u^h(x) dx \leq 0. \tag{19}$$

Setting $X_h^+ = \{x \in R^n : \tilde{u}(x+h) - \tilde{u}(x) - M|h| \geq 0\}$, from (18) and (19) it follows that

$$\int_{X_h^+} \sum_{i=1}^n (a_i(D\tilde{u}(x+h)) - a_i(D\tilde{u}(x)))(D_i \tilde{u}(x+h) - D_i\tilde{u}(x)) dx \leq 0. \tag{20}$$

Thanks to strong monotonicity assumption (6) and to inequality (20), we may conclude that $u^h = 0$ in X_h^+ and then

$$\tilde{u}(x+h) - \tilde{u}(x) - M|h| \leq 0 \quad \forall x, h \in \mathbb{R}^n,$$

namely,
$$|u|_1 \leq M$$

and
$$|Du| \leq M \quad \text{a.e. in } \Omega. \tag{21}$$

To conclude, we consider the following elastic–plastic torsion problem
Find $w \in K_M = K \cap \{v \in H_0^1 : |Dv| \leq M \text{ a.e. in } \Omega\}$ such that:

$$\int_\Omega \sum_{i=1}^n a_i(Dw)(D_i v - D_i w) \, dx \geq \int_\Omega f(v-w) dx, \quad \forall v \in K_M. \tag{22}$$

Since the feasible set K_M is a bounded, closed, and convex set, from classical results (see [35]), the unique solution $u \in K_M$ to the variational inequality (22) belongs to $W^{2,p}(\Omega)$. Then, the thesis is achieved. □

4. The Equivalence of the Two Variational Problems

Now, we may prove Theorem 1.
Obviously,
$$K_g \subseteq K. \tag{23}$$

Then, to prove the equivalence of the two problems, we have to show that if $u \in K$ is the solution to (3), then u belongs to K_g.

To this aim, setting

$$F(v) = \int_\Omega \left\{ \sum_{i=1}^n a_i(Du)(D_i v - D_i u) - f(v-u) \right\} dx$$

we note that problem (3) may be rewritten as the optimization problem

$$\min_{v \in K} F(v), \tag{24}$$

which satisfies Assumption S.

Indeed, if we set

$$X = S = L^2(\Omega), \; Y = L^2(\Omega) \times L^2(\Omega),$$
$$C = C^* = \{(a(x), b(x)) \in L^2(\Omega) \times L^2(\Omega) : a(x), b(x) \geq 0 \text{ a.e. in } \Omega\},$$
$$G(v) = (G_1(v), G_2(v)) = (w_1 - v, v - w_2),$$

we have

$$\tilde{N} = \{(F(v) + \alpha, w_1 - v + a, v - w_2 + b), v \in L^2 \setminus K, \alpha \geq 0, y = (a,b) \in C\}.$$

Following similar arguments as in [23,36] we may show that, if

$$\left(l, \theta_{L^2(\Omega)}, \theta_{L^2(\Omega)}\right) = \lim_n [\mu_n(F(v_n) + \alpha_n, w_1 - v_n + a_n, v_n - w_2 + b_n)],$$

with $\mu_n > 0$, $\lim_n (F(v_n) + \alpha_n) = 0$, $\alpha_n \geq 0$, $v_n \in L^2(\Omega) \setminus K$, $\lim_n \mu_n(w_1 - v_n + a_n) = \theta_{L^2(\Omega)}$, $\lim_n \mu_n(v_n - w_2 + b_n) = \theta_{L^2(\Omega)}$, $y_n = (a_n, b_n) \in C$, then

$$l \geq 0,$$

namely, Assumption S is fulfilled at the solution to problem (24).

Then, if we consider the Lagrange functional

$$\mathcal{L}(v, \lambda, \mu) = \tag{25}$$
$$= \int_\Omega (-\sum_{i=1}^n \frac{\partial a_i(Du)}{\partial x_i} - f)(v - u)\, dx + \int_\Omega \lambda(w_1(x) - v(x))\, dx + \int_\Omega \mu(v(x) - w_2(x))\, dx,$$

thanks to Theorem 7, there exists a saddle point $(\lambda^*, \mu^*) \in C$, namely,

$$\mathcal{L}(u, \lambda, \mu) \leq \mathcal{L}(u, \lambda^*, \mu^*) \leq \mathcal{L}(v, \lambda^*, \mu^*) \quad \forall v \in L^2(\Omega), \; \forall (\lambda, \mu) \in C, \tag{26}$$

and

$$\int_\Omega \lambda^*(w_1(x) - u(x))\, dx = 0, \quad \int_\Omega \mu^*(u(x) - w_2(x))\, dx = 0, \tag{27}$$

that is,

$$\lambda^*(w_1(x) - u(x)) = 0, \quad \mu^*(u(x) - w_2(x)) = 0, \quad \text{a.e. in } \Omega. \tag{28}$$

Using variational arguments (see [12]), it follows

$$-\sum_{i=1}^n \frac{\partial a_i(Du)}{\partial x_i} - f - \lambda^* + \mu^* = 0 \quad \text{a.e. in } \Omega. \tag{29}$$

Now, we consider the coincidence set $I = \{x \in \Omega : u(x) = w_1(x) \text{ or } u(x) = w_2(x)\}$ and the non-coincidence set $N = \{x \in \Omega : w_1(x) < u(x) < w_2(x)\}$.

From [26], Theorem 5.1, we have that $|Dw_1(x)| = |Dw_2(x)| = \sqrt{g(x)}$ a.e. in Ω, then

$$|Du| = \sqrt{g(x)} \text{ in } I. \tag{30}$$

Moreover, from (28) and (29) it follows that $\lambda^* = \mu^* = 0$ a.e. in N and

$$-\sum_{i=1}^n \frac{\partial a_i(Du)}{\partial x_i} = f \quad \text{a.e. in } N. \tag{31}$$

Thanks to the regularity of u, stated in Theorem 8, and since f is a constant function, we follow the same steps used in [35], Lemma III.10. We differentiate (31) with respect to x_k, multiply it by $\frac{\partial u}{\partial x_k}$ and sum it with respect to k. Then, it follows that

$$\sum_{i,j,k=1}^{n} \frac{\partial}{\partial x_k}\left(\frac{\partial a_i(Du)}{\partial p_j}\right) \frac{\partial^2 u}{\partial x_j \partial x_i} \frac{\partial u}{\partial x_k} + \sum_{i,j,k=1}^{n} \frac{\partial a_i(Du)}{\partial p_j} \frac{\partial^3 u}{\partial x_j \partial x_i \partial x_k} \frac{\partial u}{\partial x_k} = 0. \tag{32}$$

It follows that

$$\frac{1}{2}\frac{\partial}{\partial x_i}\left[\sum_{j=1}^{n} \frac{\partial a_i(Du)}{\partial p_j} \frac{\partial}{\partial x_j}\left(|Du|^2 - g(x)\right)\right] = \sum_{i,j,k=1}^{n} \frac{\partial}{\partial x_i}\left(\frac{\partial a_i(Du)}{\partial p_j}\right) \frac{\partial u}{\partial x_k} \frac{\partial^2 u}{\partial x_k \partial x_j}$$
$$+ \sum_{i,j,k=1}^{n} \frac{\partial a_i(Du)}{\partial p_j} \frac{\partial^2 u}{\partial x_k \partial x_j} \frac{\partial^2 u}{\partial x_k \partial x_i} + \sum_{i,j,k=1}^{n} \frac{\partial a_i(Du)}{\partial p_j} \frac{\partial u}{\partial x_k} \frac{\partial^3 u}{\partial x_j \partial x_i \partial x_k} \tag{33}$$
$$- \frac{1}{2}\sum_{i,j=1}^{n} \frac{\partial}{\partial x_i}\left(\frac{\partial a_i(Du)}{\partial p_j} \frac{\partial g(x)}{\partial x_j}\right).$$

From assumptions (6) and (7), we have

$$\frac{1}{2}\frac{\partial}{\partial x_i}\left[\sum_{j=1}^{n} \frac{\partial a_i(Du)}{\partial p_j} \frac{\partial}{\partial x_j}\left(|Du|^2 - g(x)\right)\right]$$
$$\geq \sum_{i,j,k=1}^{n} \left[\frac{\partial}{\partial x_i}\left(\frac{\partial a_i(Du)}{\partial p_j}\right) \frac{\partial^2 u}{\partial x_k \partial x_j} - \frac{\partial}{\partial x_k}\left(\frac{\partial a_i(Du)}{\partial p_j}\right) \frac{\partial^2 u}{\partial x_j \partial x_i}\right] \frac{\partial u}{\partial x_k} \tag{34}$$
$$= \sum_{i,j,k=1}^{n} \left[\sum_{l=1}^{n} \frac{\partial^2 a_i(Du)}{\partial p_j \partial p_l} \frac{\partial^2 u}{\partial x_l \partial x_i} \frac{\partial^2 u}{\partial x_k \partial x_j} - \sum_{l=1}^{n} \frac{\partial^2 a_i(Du)}{\partial p_j \partial p_l} \frac{\partial^2 u}{\partial x_k \partial x_l} \frac{\partial^2 u}{\partial x_j \partial x_i}\right] \frac{\partial u}{\partial x_k} = 0.$$

Finally, since the coefficients are bounded, N is an open set, applying the maximum principle to the operator

$$-\mathcal{A}(\varphi) = -\frac{1}{2}\sum_{i,j=1}^{n} \frac{\partial}{\partial x_i}\left(\frac{\partial a_i}{\partial p_j} \frac{\partial \varphi}{\partial x_j}\right),$$

acting on $|Du|^2 - g(x)$ on N, we have

$$|Du(x)| < \sqrt{g(x)} \quad \text{a.e.} \in N. \tag{35}$$

From (30) and (35) it follows that, if $u \in K$ is a solution to (3), then

$$|Du(x)| \leq \sqrt{g(x)} \quad \text{a.e.} \in \Omega. \tag{36}$$

Taking into account the uniqueness of the solution, we may conclude that the solution to (3) is also the solution to (2) and Theorem 1 is proved.

Finally, the following interesting coincidence of sets follows from (30) and (35)

$$E = \{x \in \Omega : |Du| < \sqrt{g(x)}\} = N.$$

5. Lagrange Multipliers

In this section we provide the proofs of the existence of Lagrange multipliers.

A first result, the existence of L^2 Lagrange multipliers, holds under the assumption $f \equiv \text{constant} > 0$ and a strongly monotone operator. It follows from (28) and (29) as in the proof of Theorem 1.

The second result holds assuming that $f \in L^p(\Omega)$, $p > 1$, and the operator a is strictly monotone. In this case the Lagrange multipliers exist in the dual of L^∞.

Indeed, we set

$$X = S = W_0^{1,\infty}(\Omega); \quad C = \{v \in L^\infty(\Omega) \,:\, v(x) \geq 0 \text{ a.e. in } \Omega\}.$$

In this case C has a nonempty interior, then we may apply the classical strong duality theory (see [33]).

We may rewrite problem (2) as

$$\text{Find } u \in K_1 = \left\{ v \in H_0^{1,\infty}(\Omega) : \sum_{i=1}^{n}\left(\frac{\partial v}{\partial x_i}\right)^2 \leq g(x), \text{ a.e. on } \Omega \right\} \text{ such that:}$$

$$\int_\Omega \left\{ \sum_{i=1}^{n} a_i(Du)(D_iv - D_iu) - f(v-u) \right\} dx \geq 0, \quad \forall v \in K_1. \tag{37}$$

Following the same steps as in [19], we may prove that C is closed and the generalized Slater condition is verified. Moreover, since F and G are convex, then the composite mapping (F,G) is convex-like, namely all the assumptions of Theorems 6.7 and 6.11 in [33] are fulfilled.

Then, it follows that there exists $\mu^* \in C^*$ solution to the dual problem

$$\max_{\mu \in C^*} \inf_{v \in S}[F(v) + \langle \mu, G(v) \rangle], \tag{38}$$

with

$$F(v) = \int_\Omega \left\{ \sum_{i=1}^{n} a_i(Du)(D_iv - D_iu) - f(v-u) \right\} dx \tag{39}$$

and

$$G(v) = |Dv|^2 - g(x).$$

Moreover, (u, μ^*) is a saddle point of the Lagrange functional

$$\mathcal{L}(v,\mu) = F(v) + \langle \mu, G(v) \rangle, \, \forall v \in H_0^{1,\infty}(\Omega), \forall \mu \in C^*,$$

that is

$$\mathcal{L}(u,\mu) \leq \mathcal{L}(u,\mu^*) \leq \mathcal{L}(v,\mu^*), \, \forall v \in H_0^{1,\infty}(\Omega), \forall \mu \in C^*. \tag{40}$$

Using variational arguments as in [19], we obtain that $\mu^* \in (L^\infty(\Omega))^*$ satisfies conditions (10).

6. Discussions

The paper adds to the already existing literature on nonconstant gradient constrained problem further results related to the relationship with double obstacle problem and the existence of Lagrange multipliers.

In particular, in the paper we focused on the nonconstant gradient constraint $|Du| \leq g(x)$ associated with a nonlinear monotone operator $a(Du)$.

The existence of Lagrange multipliers as Lebesgue functions is guaranteed in the case $f \equiv constant > 0$ and strong monotonicity assumption on the operator, whereas the Lagrange multipliers exist as Radon measure in the case $f \in L^p$, $p > 1$, and strict monotonicity assumption is required.

In the future, several studies could be carried out in several directions in this framework. For example it will be interesting to consider a regular, nonconstant, free term f, or studying the problem associated with different nonlinear operators. Moreover, the properties of the Lagrange multiplier may be investigated. Finally, one could analyze the natural parabolic counterpart.

Funding: This research received no external funding.

Data Availability Statement: No new data were created or analyzed in this study.

Acknowledgments: This research was partly supported by GNAMPA of Italian INdAM (National Institute of High Mathematics).

Conflicts of Interest: The author declares no conflict of interest.

References

1. Von Mises, R. Three remarks on the theory of the ideal plastic body. In *Reissner Anniversary Volume*; Edwards: Ann Arbor, MI, USA, 1949.
2. Caffarelli, L.A.; Friedman, A. The free boundary for elastic-plastic torsion problems. *Trans. Am. Math. Soc.* **1979**, *252*, 65–97. [CrossRef]
3. Lanchon, H. Solution du probleme de torsion élastoplastic d'une bare cylindrique de section quelconque. *C. R. Acad. Sci. Paris Ser. A* **1969**, *114*, 791–794.
4. Ting, T.W. Elastic-plastic torsion of a square bar. *Trans. Am. Math. Soc.* **1966**, *113*, 369–401. [CrossRef]
5. Brezis, H. Moltiplicateur de Lagrange en Torsion Elasto-Plastique. *Arch. Rational Mech. Anal.* **1972**, *49*, 32–40. [CrossRef]
6. Glowinski, R.; Lions, J.L.; Tremolieres, R. *Numerical Analysis of Variational Inequalities*; Elsevier: Amsterdam, The Netherlands, 1981.
7. Brezis, H.; Sibony, M. Equivalence de Deux Inequation Variationnelles et Application. *Arch. Rational Mech. Anal.* **1971**, *41*, 254–265. [CrossRef]
8. Chiadó-Piat, V.; Percivale, D. Generalized Lagrange multipliers in elastoplastic torsion. *Differ. Equ.* **1994**, *114*, 570–579. [CrossRef]
9. Daniele, P.; Giuffrè, S.; Maugeri, A.; Raciti, F. Duality theory and applications to unilateral problems. *J. Optim. Theory Appl.* **2014**, *162*, 718–734. [CrossRef]
10. Giuffrè, S.; Maugeri, A. New results on infinite dimensional duality in elastic-plastic torsion. *Filomat* **2012**, *26*, 1029–1036. [CrossRef]
11. Giuffrè, S.; Maugeri, A. A Measure-type Lagrange Multiplier for the Elastic-Plastic Torsion. *Nonlinear Anal.* **2014**, *102*, 23–29. [CrossRef]
12. Giuffrè, S.; Maugeri, A.; Puglisi, D. Lagrange multipliers in elastic-plastic torsion problem for nonlinear monotone operators. *Differ. Equ.* **2015**, *259*, 817–837.
13. Figalli, A.; Shahgholian, H. An overview of unconstrained free boundary problems. *Philos. Trans. R. Soc.* **2015**, *373*, 20140281. [CrossRef] [PubMed]
14. Evans, L. A second order elliptic equation with gradient constraint. *Commun. Partial Differ. Equ.* **1979**, *4*, 555–572. [CrossRef]
15. Cimatti, G. The plane stress problem of Ghizetti in elastoplasticity. *Appl. Math. Optim.* **1976**, *3*, 15–26. [CrossRef]
16. Ishii, H.; Koike, S. Boundary regularity and uniqueness for an elliptic equation with gradient constraint. *Commun. Partial Differ. Equ.* **1983**, *8*, 317–346.
17. Jensen, R. Regularity for elastoplastic type variational inequalities. *Indiana Univ. Math. J.* **1983**, *32*, 407–423. [CrossRef]
18. Wiegner, M. The $C^{1,1}$-character of solutions of second order elliptic equations with gradient constraint. *Commun. Partial Differ. Equ.* **1981**, *6*, 361–371. [CrossRef]
19. Giuffrè, S. Lagrange multipliers and non-constant gradient constrained problem. *Differ. Equ.* **2020**, *269*, 542–562. [CrossRef]
20. Santos, L. Variational problems with non-constant gradient constraints. *Port. Math.* **2002**, *59*, 205–248.
21. Santos, L. Lagrange multipliers and transport densities. *J. Math. Pures Appl.* **2017**, *108*, 592–611.
22. Treu, G.; Vornicescu, M. On the equivalence of two variational problems. *Calc. Var.* **2000**, *11*, 307–319. [CrossRef]
23. Giuffrè, S.; Marcianò, A. Lagrange Multipliers and Nonlinear Variational Inequalities with Gradient Constraints. *Philos. Trans. R. Soc. A* **2022**, *380*, 20210355. [CrossRef] [PubMed]
24. Stampacchia, G. Variational equalities. In Proceedings of the Nato Advanced Study Institute. Theory and Applications of Monotone Operators, Venice, Italy, 17–30 June 1968; pp. 101–192.
25. Hartman, P.; Stampacchia, G. On some nonlinear elliptic differential functional equations. *Acta Math.* **1966**, *115*, 271–310. [CrossRef]
26. Lions, P.L. *Generalized Solutions for Hamilton-Jacobi Equations*; Pitman Advanced Publishing Program: London, UK, 1982.
27. Ceng, L.C.; Wen, C.F.; Liou, Y.C.; Yao, J.C. A General Class of Differential Hemivariational Inequalities Systems in Reflexive Banach Spaces. *Mathematics* **2021**, *9*, 3173. [CrossRef]
28. Baranovskii, E.S. Steady flows of an Oldroyd fluid with threshold slip. *Commun. Pure Appl. Anal.* **2019**, *18*, 735–750.
29. Baranovskii, E.S. On Flows of Bingham-Type Fluids with Threshold Slippage. *Adv. Math. Phys.* **2017**, *2017*, 7548328. [CrossRef]
30. Zhao, J.; He, J.; Migórski, S.; Dudek, S. An inverse problem for Bingham type fluids. *J. Comput. Appl. Math.* **2022**, *404*, 113906. [CrossRef]
31. Pascale, L.D.; Evans, L.C.; Pratelli, A. Integral estimates for transport densities. *Bull. Lond. Math. Soc.* **2004**, *36*, 383–395. [CrossRef]
32. Igbida, N. Equivalent formulations for Monge-Kantorovich equation. *Nonlinear Anal.* **2009**, *71*, 3805–3813. [CrossRef]
33. Jahn, J. *Introduction to the Theory of Nonlinear Optimization*; Springer: Berlin/Heidelberg, Germany, 1996.

34. Rodriguez, J.F. *Obstacle Problems in Mathematical Physics*; Elsevier: Amsterdam, The Netherlands, 1987.
35. Brezis, H.; Stampacchia, G. Sur la régularité de la solution d'inéquations elliptiques. *Bull. Soc. Math. Fr.* **1968**, *96*, 53–180. [CrossRef]
36. Donato, M.B. The infinite dimensional Lagrange multiplier rule for convex optimization problems. *J. Funct. Anal.* **2011**, *261*, 2083–2093. [CrossRef]

Disclaimer/Publisher's Note: The statements, opinions and data contained in all publications are solely those of the individual author(s) and contributor(s) and not of MDPI and/or the editor(s). MDPI and/or the editor(s) disclaim responsibility for any injury to people or property resulting from any ideas, methods, instructions or products referred to in the content.

Article

New Class of K-G-Type Symmetric Second Order Vector Optimization Problem

Chetan Swarup [1], Ramesh Kumar [2], Ramu Dubey [2,*] and Dowlath Fathima [3]

- [1] Department of Basic Science, College of Science and Theoretical Studies, Saudi Electronic University, Riyadh-Male Campus, Riyadh 13316, Saudi Arabia; c.swarup@seu.edu.sa
- [2] Department of Mathematics, J.C. Bose University of Science and Technology, YMCA, Faridabad 121 006, India; rameshgoswami2619@gmail.com
- [3] Basic Sciences Department, College of Science and Theoretical Studies, Saudi Electronic University, Jeddah 23442, Saudi Arabia; d.fathima@seu.edu.sa
- * Correspondence: rdubeyjiya@gmail.com

Abstract: In this paper, we present meanings of K-G_f-bonvexity/K-G_f-pseudobonvexity and their generalization between the above-notice functions. We also construct various concrete non-trivial examples for existing these types of functions. We formulate K-G_f-Wolfe type multiobjective second-order symmetric duality model with cone objective as well as cone constraints and duality theorems have been established under these aforesaid conditions. Further, we have validates the weak duality theorem under those assumptions. Our results are more generalized than previous known results in the literature.

Keywords: K-G_f-pseudobonvexity; second-order; K-G_f-Wolfe type; efficient solution; multiobjective programming; arbitrary cones; strong duality; generalized assumptions

MSC: 90C26; 90C30; 90C32; 90C46

Citation: Swarup, C.; Kumar, R.; Dubey, R.; Fathima, D.I. New Class of K-G-Type Symmetric Second Order Vector Optimization Problem. *Axioms* **2023**, *12*, 571. https://doi.org/10.3390/axioms12060571

Academic Editor: Mircea Merca, Siamak Pedrammehr and Mohammad Reza Chalak Qazani

Received: 24 April 2023
Revised: 1 June 2023
Accepted: 2 June 2023
Published: 8 June 2023

Copyright: © 2023 by the authors. Licensee MDPI, Basel, Switzerland. This article is an open access article distributed under the terms and conditions of the Creative Commons Attribution (CC BY) license (https://creativecommons.org/licenses/by/4.0/).

1. Introduction

The field of optimization theory has progressed far beyond anyone's expectations. Due to its wide variety of uses, it has made its way into all disciplines of science and engineering. When approximations are utilized, one of the most important practical applications of duality is that it provides bounds on the value of the objective functions because there are more factors involved, second-order duality has a greater computational benefit than first-order duality. For intriguing applications and breakthroughs in multiobjective optimization, we refer to [1], and the references cited therein. Dorn [2] presented the primary symmetric duality definition for quadratic programming in 1965. Dantzig et al. [3] and Mond [4] proposed a pair of symmetric dual Duality plays a vital role in investigating nonlinear programming problem solutions. Several writers have proposed several duality models, such as Wolfe dual [5] and Mond-Weir dual [6]. Nanda and Das [7] introduced four different forms of duality models for the nonlinear programming problem with cone constraints. The work of Bazaraa and Goode [8] and Hanson and Mond [9] inspired these findings.

Mangasian [10] established the duality theorem in the context of a second-order dual problem in nonlinear programming, where none of the constraints imposed convexity restrictions on all functions. Mond [11] introduced second-order symmetric dual models and established second-order symmetric duality theorems under second-order convexity conditions for the first time. In mathematical programming, Hasnson [12] defined the second-order invexity of a differentiable function and studied it. In 1999, Mishra [13] proposed a pair of second-order vector symmetric dual multiobjective models for arbitrary cones based on the Wolfe and Mond-Weir types. In addition 2006, ref. [14] a couple of Mond–Weir type second-order symmetric duality multiobjective calculations for cone second-order pseudoinvex and emphatically cone second-order pseudoinvex algorithm were presented. A couple of Mond–Weir type second-order symmetric dual multiobjective projects over discretion cones is created under pseudoinvexity/$K\tilde{\ }F$-convexity assumptions by Gulati [15], which is as:

Primal(MP):

$$K\text{-minimize} \quad \psi(\iota, \kappa)$$

subject to

$$-\left(\nabla_\kappa(\lambda^T\psi)(\iota,\kappa) + \nabla_{\kappa\kappa}(w^T\phi)(\iota,\kappa)p\right) \in C_2^*,$$

$$\kappa^T\left(\nabla_\kappa(\lambda^T\psi)(\iota,\kappa) + \nabla_{\kappa\kappa}(w^T\phi)(\iota,\kappa)p\right) \geqq 0,$$

$$\lambda \in intK^*, \quad \iota \in C_1$$

Dual(MD):

$$K\text{-maximize} \quad \psi(\mu, \nu)$$

subject to

$$\left(\nabla_\iota(\lambda^T\psi)(\mu,\nu) + \nabla_u(w^T\phi)(\mu,\nu)p\right) \in C_1^*,$$

$$\mu^T\left(\nabla_\iota(\lambda^T\psi)(\mu,\nu) + \nabla_u(w^T\phi)(\mu,\nu)r\right) \leqq 0,$$

$$\lambda \in intK^*, \quad \iota \in C_2,$$

where,

(i) $R_1 \subseteq \mathbb{R}^n, R_2 \subseteq \mathbb{R}^m$ are open sets,
(ii) $\psi, \phi : R_1 \times R_2 \to \mathbb{R}^k$ is a twice differentiable function of ι and κ, is a differentiable function of ι and κ,
(iii) $\lambda \in \mathbb{R}^k, w \in \mathbb{R}^q, p \in \mathbb{R}^m$ and $r \in \mathbb{R}^n$,
(iv) for i=1,2, $C_i \subset S_i$ is a closed convex cone with non-empty interior and C_i^* is its positive polar cone.

Aside from them, a number of other researchers are working in this field. For additional information, see [16–20].

In this paper be start by defining in section 2, K-G_f-bonvexity as well as pseduobonvexity and construct non-trivial numerical examples for clear understanding the concept introduced by authors. We identify several examples lying exclusively K-G_f-bonvex and not in the class of K-invex function with respect to same η already exist in the literature. We illustrate an example which is K-G_f-pseudobonvex but not K-G_f-bonvex with respect to same η. In the next section, we formulate a new pair of multiobjective symmetric second order K-G_f-primal-dual models over arbitrary cone and drive duality results under K-G_f-bonvex as well as K-G_f-pseudobonvex assumptions. We, also construct a non-trivial example for validate the weak duality theorem presented in the paper. we also introduced geometry figure for clear understanding the concept through figure.

2. Preliminaries and Definitions

In this paper, we used $\mathbb{R}^n$ for n-dimensional Euclidean space and $\mathbb{R}^n_+$ for semi-positive orthant. Also, here C_1 and C_2 used for closed convex cone $\mathbb{R}^n$ and $\mathbb{R}^m$ respectively, with non-void interiors. For a real-valued twice differentiable function $g(\varphi, \vartheta)$ described on an open set in $\mathbb{R}^n \times \mathbb{R}^m$, indicate by $\nabla_\varphi g(\bar{\varphi}, \bar{\vartheta})$ the gradient vector of g with respect to a at $(\bar{\varphi}, \bar{\vartheta})$, $\nabla_{\varphi\varphi} g(\bar{\varphi}, \bar{\vartheta})$ the Hessian matrix with respect to φ an at $(\bar{\varphi}, \bar{\vartheta})$. Throughout the paper $\tilde{N} = \{1, 2, ..., k\}$, $\tilde{O} = \{1, 2, ..., m\}$.

A differentiable function $f : X \times Y \to R^k$, $\eta_1 : X \times Y \to R^k$, $\eta_2 : X \times Y \to R^k$,

$G_f = (G_{f_1}, G_{f_2}, ..., G_{f_k}) : R \to R^k$, $G_{f_i} : I_{f_i}(X) \to R$ is range f_i for $i = \tilde{N}$. Also, K is used for pointed convex cone with non-void interiors in $\mathbb{R}^k$, for $\vartheta, z \in \mathbb{R}^k$ and we specify cone orders with respect to K as follows:

$$\vartheta \leqq z \iff z - \vartheta \in K; \quad \vartheta \leq z \iff z - \vartheta \in K \setminus \{0\}; \quad \vartheta < z \iff z - \vartheta \in intK.$$

Let $f : X \to \mathbb{R}^k$ be a differentiable function defined on open set $\phi \neq X \subseteq \mathbb{R}^n$ and $I_{f_i}(X), i \in \tilde{N}$ be the range of f_i.

Consider the following multiobjective programming problem with cone objective as well as constraints as :

(MP) $\quad$ K-min $f(\varphi)$
$\quad\quad\quad$ subject to

$$\varphi \in X^0 = \left\{ \varphi \in S : g(\varphi) \in Q \right\}.$$

where $S \subseteq \mathbb{R}^n, f : S \to \mathbb{R}^k, g : S \to \mathbb{R}^m$. Q is a closed convex cone with a non-empty interior in $\mathbb{R}^m$.

Definition 1 ([21]). *$\bar{\varphi} \in X^0$ is a weak efficient solution of (MP), $\nexists \ \varphi \in X$ such that*

$$f(\bar{\varphi}) - f(\varphi) \in intK.$$

Definition 2 ([21]). *$\bar{\varphi} \in X^0$ is an efficient solution of (MP), $\nexists \ \varphi \in X$ such that*

$$f(\bar{\varphi}) - f(\varphi) \in K \setminus \{0\}.$$

Now, we consider the following multiobjective programming with cone objective and cone constraints as:

(GMP) $\quad$ $K-$min $G_f(f(z))$

$$\text{subject to } z \in Z^0 = \left\{ z \in S : -G_g(g(z)) \in Q \right\}.$$

Definition 3 ([21]). *$\bar{z} \in Z^0$ is a weak efficient solution of (GMP), $\nexists \ z \in Z^0$ s.t.*

$$G_f(f(\bar{z})) - G_f(f(z)) \in intK.$$

Definition 4 ([21]). *$\bar{z} \in Z^0$ is a efficient solution of (GMP), $\nexists \ z \in Z^0$ s.t. $G_f(f(\bar{z})) - G_f(f(z)) \in K \setminus \{0\}$.*

Definition 5 ([21]). *The positive polar cone C_i^* of C_i (i=1,2) is defined as $C_i^* = \left\{ z : \varphi^T z \geqq 0, \forall \varphi \in C_1 \right\}$.*

Suppose that $S_1 \subseteq \mathbb{R}^n$ and $S_2 \subseteq \mathbb{R}^m$ are open sets such that

$$C_1 \times C_2 \subset S_1 \times S_2.$$

A differentiable function $f : X \to R^k$ and G_f such that every component G_{f_i} is strictly increasing on the range of I_{f_i}.

Definition 6. *If $\exists \, G_f$ and η such that $\forall \, \varphi \in X$ and $p_i \in R^n$, we have*

$$\left\{ G_{f_1}(f_1(\varphi)) - G_{f_1}(f_1(\delta)) + \frac{1}{2}p_1^T \left[G''_{f_1}(f_1(\delta))\nabla_\varphi f_1(\delta)(\nabla_\varphi f_1(\delta))^T + G'_{f_1}(f_1(\delta))\nabla_{\varphi\varphi} f_1(\delta) \right] p_1 - \eta^T(\varphi,\delta) \left[G'_{f_1}(f_1(\delta))\nabla_\varphi f_1(\delta) \right. \right.$$
$$\left. + \left\{ G''_{f_1}(f_1(\delta))\nabla_\varphi f_1(\delta)(\nabla_\varphi f_1(\delta))^T + G'_{f_1}(f_1(\delta))\nabla_{\varphi\varphi} f_1(\delta) \right\} p_1 \right], \ldots, G_{f_k}(f_k(\varphi)) - G_{f_k}(f_k(\delta)) + \frac{1}{2}p_k^T \left[G''_{f_k}(f_k(\delta))\nabla_\varphi f_k(\delta)(\nabla_\varphi f_k(\delta))^T \right.$$
$$\left. \left. + G'_{f_k}(f_k(\delta))\nabla_{\varphi\varphi} f_k(\delta) \right] p_k - \eta^T(\varphi,\delta) \left[G'_{f_k}(f_k(\delta))\nabla_\varphi f_k(\delta) + \left\{ G''_{f_k}(f_k(\delta))\nabla_\varphi f_k(\delta)(\nabla_\varphi f_k(\delta))^T + G'_{f_k}(f_k(\delta))\nabla_{\varphi\varphi} f_k(\delta) \right\} p_k \right] \right\} \in K,$$

then f is K-G_f-bonvex at $\delta \in X$ with respect to η.

Definition 7. *If $\exists \, G_f$ and η such that $\forall \, \varphi \in X$ and $p_i \in R^m$, we have*

$$\left\{ G_{f_1}(f_1(\varphi)) - G_{f_1}(f_1(\delta)) + \frac{1}{2}p_1^T \left[G''_{f_1}(f_1(\delta))\nabla_\varphi f_1(\delta)(\nabla_\varphi f_1(\delta))^T + G'_{f_1}(f_1(\delta))\nabla_{\varphi\varphi} f_1(\delta) \right] p_1 - \eta^T(\varphi,\delta) \left[G'_{f_1}(f_1(\delta))\nabla_\varphi f_1(\delta) \right. \right.$$
$$\left. + \left\{ G''_{f_1}(f_1(\delta))\nabla_\varphi f_1(\delta)(\nabla_\varphi f_1(\delta))^T + G'_{f_1}(f_1(\delta))\nabla_{\varphi\varphi} f_1(\delta) \right\} p_1 \right], \ldots, G_{f_k}(f_k(\varphi)) - G_{f_k}(f_k(\delta)) + \frac{1}{2}p_k^T \left[G''_{f_k}(f_k(\delta))\nabla_\varphi f_k(\delta)(\nabla_\varphi f_k(\delta))^T \right.$$
$$\left. \left. + G'_{f_k}(f_k(\delta))\nabla_{\varphi\varphi} f_k(\delta) \right] p_k - \eta^T(\varphi,\delta) \left[G'_{f_k}(f_k(\delta))\nabla_\varphi f_k(\delta) + \left\{ G''_{f_k}(f_k(\delta))\nabla_\varphi f_k(\delta)(\nabla_\varphi f_k(\delta))^T + G'_{f_k}(f_k(\delta))\nabla_{\varphi\varphi} f_k(\delta) \right\} p_k \right] \right\} \in -K,$$

then f is K-G_f-boncave at $\delta \in X$ with respect to η.

Generalized the above definitions on two variable, as follows,

Definition 8. *If $\exists$ and G_f and η_1 such that $\forall \, \varphi \in X$ and $q_i \in R^n$, we have*

$$\left\{ G_{f_1}(f_1(\varphi,\ell)) - G_{f_1}(f_1(\delta,\ell)) + \frac{1}{2}q_1^T \left[G''_{f_1}(f_1(\delta,\ell))\nabla_\varphi f_1(\delta,\ell)(\nabla_\varphi f_1(\delta,\ell))^T + G'_{f_1}(f_1(\delta,\ell))\nabla_{\varphi\varphi} f_1(\delta,\ell) \right] q_1 - \eta_1^T(\varphi,\delta) \left[G'_{f_1}(f_1(\delta,\ell)) \right. \right.$$
$$\nabla_\varphi f_1(\delta,\ell) + \{ G''_{f_1}(f_1(\delta,\ell))\nabla_\varphi f_1(\delta,\ell)(\nabla_\varphi f_1(\delta,\ell))^T + G'_{f_1}(f_1(\delta,\ell))\nabla_{\varphi\varphi} f_1(\delta,\ell) \} q_1 \right], \ldots, G_{f_k}(f_k(\varphi,\ell)) - G_{f_k}(f_k(\delta,\ell))$$
$$+ \frac{1}{2}q_k^T \left[G''_{f_k}(f_k(\delta,\ell))\nabla_\varphi f_k(\delta,\ell)(\nabla_\varphi f_k(\delta,\ell))^T + G'_{f_k}(f_k(\delta,\ell))\nabla_{\varphi\varphi} f_k(\delta,\ell) \right] q_k$$
$$\left. - \eta_1^T(\varphi,\delta) \left[G'_{f_k}(f_k(\delta))\nabla_\varphi f_k(\delta,\ell) + \left\{ G''_{f_k}(f_k(\delta,\ell))\nabla_\varphi f_k(\delta,\ell)(\nabla_\varphi f_k(\delta,\ell))^T + G'_{f_k}(f_k(\delta,\ell))\nabla_{\varphi\varphi} f_k(\delta,\ell) \right\} q_k \right] \right\} \in K,$$

then, f is K-G_f-bonvex in the first variable at $\delta \in X$ for fixed $\ell \in Y$ with η_1,

and

If $\exists \, G_f \, \eta_2$ such that $\forall \, \vartheta \in Y$ and $p_i \in R^m$, we have

$$\left\{ G_{f_1}(f_1(\delta,\vartheta)) - G_{f_1}(f_1(\delta,\ell)) + \frac{1}{2}p_1^T \left[G''_{f_1}(f_1(\delta,\ell))\nabla_\vartheta f_1(\delta,\ell)(\nabla_\vartheta f_1(\delta,\ell))^T + G'_{f_1}f_1(\delta,\ell)\nabla_{\vartheta\vartheta} f_1(\delta,\ell) \right] p_1 - \eta_2^T(\ell,\vartheta) \left[G'_{f_1}(f_1(\delta,\ell)) \right. \right.$$
$$\nabla_\vartheta f_1(\delta,\ell) + \{ G''_{f_1}(f_1(\delta,\ell))\nabla_\vartheta f_1(\delta,\ell)(\nabla_\vartheta f_1(\delta,\ell))^T + G'_{f_1}(f_1(\delta,\ell))\nabla_{\vartheta\vartheta} f_1(\delta,\ell) \} p_1 \right], \ldots, G_{f_k}(f_k(\delta,\vartheta)) - G_{f_k}(f_k(\delta,\ell))$$
$$+ \frac{1}{2}p_k^T \left[G''_{f_k}(f_k(\delta,\ell))\nabla_\vartheta f_k(\delta,\ell)(\nabla_\vartheta f_k(\delta,\ell))^T + G'_{f_k}(f_k(\delta,\ell))\nabla_{\vartheta\vartheta} f_k(\delta,\ell) \right] p_k$$
$$\left. - \eta_2^T(\ell,\vartheta) \left[G'_{f_k}(f_k(\delta,\ell))\nabla_\vartheta f_k(\delta,\ell) + \left\{ G''_{f_k}(f_k(\delta,\ell))\nabla_\vartheta f_k(\delta,\ell)(\nabla_\vartheta f_k(\delta,\ell))^T + G'_{f_k}(f_k(\delta,\ell))\nabla_{\vartheta\vartheta} f_k(\delta,\ell) \right\} p_k \right] \right\} \in K,$$

then, f is K-G_f-bonvex in the second variable at $\ell \in Y$ for fixed $\delta \in X$ with η_2.

Definition 9. *If* $\exists G_f$ *and* η_1 *such that* $\forall \varphi \in X$ *and* $q_i \in R^n$, *we have*

$$\left\{ G_{f_1}(f_1(\varphi,\ell)) - G_{f_1}(f_1(\delta,\ell)) + \frac{1}{2}q_1^T\left[G''_{f_1}(f_1(\delta,\ell))\nabla_\varphi f_1(\delta,\ell)(\nabla_\varphi f_1(\delta,\ell))^T + G'_{f_1}(f_1(\delta,\ell))\nabla_{\varphi\varphi}f_1(\delta,\ell)\right]q_1 - \eta_1^T(\varphi,\delta)\left[G'_{f_1}(f_1(\delta,\ell))\right.\right.$$
$$\nabla_\varphi f_1(\delta,\ell) + \{G''_{f_1}(f_1(\delta,\ell))\nabla_\varphi f_1(\delta,\ell)(\nabla_\varphi f_1(\delta,\ell))^T + G'_{f_1}(f_1(\delta,\ell))\nabla_{\varphi\varphi}f_1(\delta,\ell)\}q_1\bigg],...,G_{f_k}(f_k(\varphi,\ell)) - G_{f_k}(f_k(\delta,\ell))$$
$$+ \frac{1}{2}q_k^T\left[G''_{f_k}(f_k(\delta,\ell))\nabla_\varphi f_k(\delta,\ell)(\nabla_\varphi f_k(\delta,\ell))^T + G'_{f_k}(f_k(\delta,\ell))\nabla_{\varphi\varphi}f_k(\delta,\ell)\right]q_k$$
$$- \eta_1^T(\varphi,\delta)\left[G'_{f_k}(f_k(\delta))\nabla_\varphi f_k(\delta,\ell) + \{G''_{f_k}(f_k(\delta,\ell))\nabla_\varphi f_k(\delta,\ell)(\nabla_\varphi f_k(\delta,\ell))^T + G'_{f_k}(f_k(\delta,\ell))\nabla_{\varphi\varphi}f_k(\delta,\ell)\}q_k\right]\right\} \in -K,$$

then, f is K-G_f-boncave in the first variable at $\delta \in X$ for fixed $\ell \in Y$ with respect to η_1, and

If $\exists G_f$ *and* η_2 *such that* $\forall \vartheta \in Y$ *and* $p_i \in R^m$, *we have*

$$\left\{ G_{f_1}(f_1(\delta,\vartheta)) - G_{f_1}(f_1(\delta,\ell)) + \frac{1}{2}p_1^T\left[G''_{f_1}(f_1(\delta,\ell))\nabla_\vartheta f_1(\delta,\ell)(\nabla_\vartheta f_1(\delta,\ell))^T + G'_{f_1}(f_1(\delta,\ell))\nabla_{\vartheta\vartheta}f_1(\delta,\ell)\right]p_1 - \eta_2^T(\ell,\vartheta)\left[G'_{f_1}(f_1(\delta,\ell))\right.\right.$$
$$\nabla_\vartheta f_1(\delta,\ell) + \{G''_{f_1}(f_1(\delta,\ell))\nabla_\vartheta f_1(\delta,\ell)(\nabla_\vartheta f_1(\delta,\ell))^T + G'_{f_1}(f_1(\delta,\ell))\nabla_{\vartheta\vartheta}f_1(\delta,\ell)\}p_1\bigg],...,G_{f_k}(f_k(\delta,\vartheta)) - G_{f_k}(f_k(\delta,\ell))$$
$$+ \frac{1}{2}p_k^T\left[G''_{f_k}(f_k(\delta,\ell))\nabla_\vartheta f_k(\delta,\ell)(\nabla_\vartheta f_k(\delta,\ell))^T\right.$$
$$- \eta_2^T(\ell,\vartheta)[G'_{f_k}(f_k(\delta,\ell))\nabla_\vartheta f_k(\delta,\ell) + \{G''_{f_k}(f_k(\delta,\ell))\nabla_\vartheta f_k(\delta,\ell)(\nabla_\vartheta f_k(\delta,\ell))^T + G'_{f_k}(f_k(\delta,\ell))\nabla_{\vartheta\vartheta}f_k(\delta,\ell)\}p_k\big|\right\} \in -K,$$

then function f is K-G_f-boncave in the second variable at $\ell \in Y$ for fixed $\delta \in X$ with respect to η_2.

Example 1. *Let* $X = [1,2] \subseteq \mathbb{R}, n = m = 1$ *and* $k = 2$. *Consider* $f : X \to \mathbb{R}^2$ *be defined by*

$$f(\varphi) = \left(f_1(\varphi), f_2(\varphi)\right),$$

where,

$$f_1(\varphi) = \varphi \sin\left(\frac{1}{\varphi}\right), \quad f_2(\varphi) = \cos\varphi.$$

Next, $G_f : (G_{f_1}, G_{f_2}) : \mathbb{R} \to \mathbb{R}^2$ *defined by*

$$G_{f_1} = t^2, \quad G_{f_2} = t^4.$$

Let $K = \left\{(\varphi,\vartheta); \varphi \geqq 0 \text{ and } \vartheta \geqq 0\right\}$ *and* $\eta : X \times X \to \mathbb{R}$ *be given by*

$$\eta(\varphi,\delta) = (1-\delta^2).$$

Now, we have to claim that f is $K - G_f$-bonvex, for this, we have driven that the following expression as

$$\left\{ G_{f_1}(f_1(\varphi)) - G_{f_1}(f_1(\delta)) + \frac{1}{2}p_1^T\left[G''_{f_1}(f_1(\delta))\nabla_\varphi f_1(\delta)(\nabla_\varphi f_1(\delta))^T + G'_{f_1}(f_1(\delta))\nabla_{\varphi\varphi}f_1(\delta)\right]p_1 - \eta^T(\varphi,\delta)\left[G'_{f_1}(f_1(\delta))\nabla_\varphi f_1(\delta)\right.\right.$$
$$+\{G''_{f_1}(f_1(\delta))\nabla_\varphi f_1(\delta)(\nabla_\varphi f_1(\delta))^T + G'_{f_1}(f_1(\delta))\nabla_{\varphi\varphi}f_1(\delta)\}p_1\bigg], G_{f_2}(f_2(\varphi)) - G_{f_2}(f_2(\delta)) + \frac{1}{2}p_2^T\left[G''_{f_2}(f_2(\delta))\nabla_\varphi f_2(\delta)(\nabla_\varphi f_2(\delta))^T\right.$$
$$+ G'_{f_2}(f_2(\delta))\nabla_{\varphi\varphi}f_2(\delta)\big]p_2 - \eta^T(\varphi,\delta)[G'_{f_2}(f_2(\delta))\nabla_\varphi f_2(\delta) + \{G''_{f_2}(f_2(\delta))\nabla_\varphi f_2(\delta)(\nabla_\varphi f_2(\delta))^T + G'_{f_2}(f_2(\delta))\nabla_{\varphi\varphi}f_2(\delta)\}p_2]\right\} \in K.$$

Let

$$\Pi = \left\{ G_{f_1}(f_1(\varphi)) - G_{f_1}(f_1(\delta)) + \frac{1}{2}p_1^T \left[G''_{f_1}(f_1(\delta))\nabla_\varphi f_1(\delta)(\nabla_\varphi f_1(\delta))^T + G'_{f_1}(f_1(\delta))\nabla_{\varphi\varphi} f_1(\delta) \right] p_1 - \eta^T(\varphi,\delta) \left[G'_{f_1}(f_1(\delta))\nabla_\varphi f_1(\delta) \right. \right.$$
$$+ \left\{ G''_{f_1}(f_1(\delta))\nabla_\varphi f_1(\delta)(\nabla_\varphi f_1(\delta))^T + G'_{f_1}(f_1(\delta))\nabla_{\varphi\varphi} f_1(\delta) \right\} p_1 \right], G_{f_2}(f_2(\varphi)) - G_{f_2}(f_2(\delta)) + \frac{1}{2}p_2^T \left[G''_{f_2}(f_2(\delta))\nabla_\varphi f_2(\delta)(\nabla_\varphi f_2(\delta))^T \right.$$
$$+ \left. G'_{f_2}(f_2(\delta))\nabla_{\varphi\varphi} f_2(\delta) \right] p_2 - \eta^T(\varphi,\delta) \left[G'_{f_2}(f_2(\delta))\nabla_\varphi f_2(\delta) + \left\{ G''_{f_2}(f_2(\delta))\nabla_\varphi f_2(\delta)(\nabla_\varphi f_2(\delta))^T + G'_{f_2}(f_2(\delta))\nabla_{\varphi\varphi} f_2(\delta) \right\} p_2 \right] \right\}.$$

Substituting the values of $f_1, f_2, G_{f_1}, G_{f_2}$ and η, we obtain

$$\Pi = \left\{ \varphi^2 sin^2 \frac{1}{\varphi^2} - \delta^2 sin^2 \frac{1}{\delta^2} + \frac{1}{2}p^2 \left[2\left(sin\frac{1}{\delta} - \frac{1}{\delta}cos\frac{1}{\delta}\right)^2 + 2\delta sin\frac{1}{\delta}\left(-\frac{1}{\delta^3}sin\frac{1}{\delta}\right) \right] - (1-\delta^2)\left[2\delta sin\frac{1}{\delta}\left(sin\frac{1}{\delta} - \frac{1}{\delta}cos\frac{1}{\delta}\right) \right. \right.$$
$$+ \left. p\left[2\left(sin\frac{1}{\delta} - \frac{1}{\delta}cos\frac{1}{\delta}\right)^2 + 2\delta sin\frac{1}{\delta}\left(-\frac{1}{\delta^3}sin\frac{1}{\delta}\right) \right] \right], cos^4\varphi - cos^4\delta + \frac{1}{2}p^2[12cos^2\delta(-sin\delta)^2$$
$$+ 4cos^3\delta(-cos\delta)] - (1-\delta^2)[4cos^3\delta(-sin\delta) + p(12cos^2\delta(-sin\delta)^2 + 4cos^3\delta(-cos\delta))] \right\}.$$

Now, we consider

$$\Psi = \varphi^2 sin^2 \frac{1}{\varphi^2} - \delta^2 sin^2 \frac{1}{\delta^2} + \frac{1}{2}p^2 \left[2\left(sin\frac{1}{\delta} - \frac{1}{\delta}cos\frac{1}{\delta}\right)^2 + 2\delta sin\frac{1}{\delta}\left(-\frac{1}{\delta^3}sin\frac{1}{\delta}\right) \right]$$
$$- (1-\delta^2)\left[2\delta sin\frac{1}{\delta}\left(sin\frac{1}{\delta} - \frac{1}{\delta}cos\frac{1}{\delta}\right) + p\left[2\left(sin\frac{1}{\delta} - \frac{1}{\delta}cos\frac{1}{\delta}\right)^2 + 2\delta sin\frac{1}{\delta}\left(-\frac{1}{\delta^3}sin\frac{1}{\delta}\right) \right] \right].$$

Let us apply the following ansatz:

$$\Psi = \Psi_1 + \Psi_2 \ (say),$$

consider

$$\Phi = \left\{ cos^4\varphi - cos^4\delta + \frac{1}{2}p^2 \left[12cos^2\delta(-sin\delta)^2 + 4cos^3\delta(-cos\delta) \right] \right.$$
$$- (1-\delta^2)\left[4cos^3\delta(-sin\delta) + p\left(12cos^2\delta(-sin\delta)^2 + 4cos^3\delta(-cos\delta)\right) \right] \right\} \in K.$$

The above expression breaks in Φ_1 and Φ_2 (say) as follows:

$$\Phi = \Phi_1 + \Phi_2,$$

where

$$\Psi_1 = \varphi^2 sin^2 \frac{1}{\varphi^2} - \delta^2 sin^2 \frac{1}{\delta^2} - (1-\delta^2)\left[2\delta sin\frac{1}{\delta}\left(sin\frac{1}{\delta} - \frac{1}{\delta}cos\frac{1}{\delta}\right) \right].$$

It is easily verified from Figure 1, we have

$$\Psi_1 \geqq 0, \ \forall \ \varphi, \delta \in X.$$

$$\Psi_2 = \frac{1}{2}p^2 \left[2\left(sin\frac{1}{\delta} - \frac{1}{\delta}cos\frac{1}{\delta}\right)^2 + 2\delta sin\frac{1}{\delta}\left(-\frac{1}{\delta^3}sin\frac{1}{\delta}\right) \right] + p\left[2\left(sin\frac{1}{\delta} - \frac{1}{\delta}cos\frac{1}{\delta}\right)^2 + 2\delta sin\frac{1}{\delta}\left(-\frac{1}{\delta^3}sin\frac{1}{\delta}\right) \right].$$

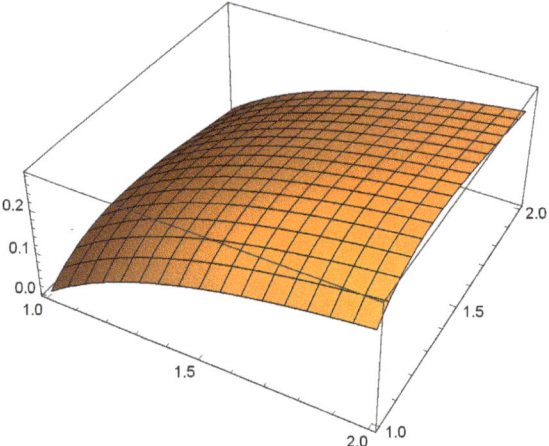

Figure 1. $\Psi_1 = \left\{ \varphi^2 \sin^2 \frac{1}{\varphi^2} - \delta^2 \sin^2 \frac{1}{\delta^2} - (1-\delta^2)\left[2\delta \sin\frac{1}{\delta}\left(\sin\frac{1}{\delta} - \frac{1}{\delta}\cos\frac{1}{\delta}\right)\right]\right\}$.

It is clear from Figure 2, we obtain

$$\Psi_2 \geqq 0, \ \forall \, \delta \in X \text{ and } p \in \left[-\frac{1}{10^{10}}, -1\right].$$

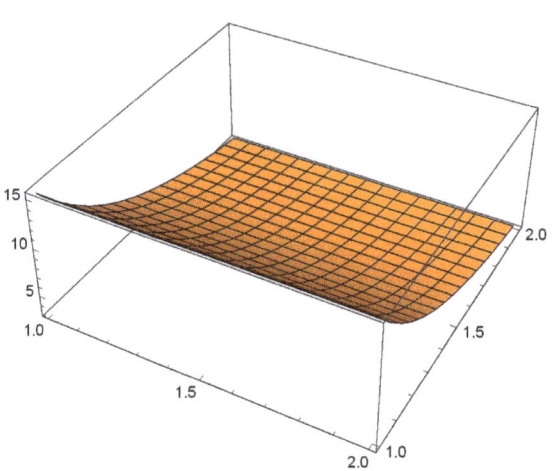

Figure 2. $\Psi_2 = \frac{1}{2}p^2\left[2\left(\sin\frac{1}{\delta} - \frac{1}{\delta}\cos\frac{1}{\delta}\right)^2 + 2\delta\sin\frac{1}{\delta}\left(-\frac{1}{\delta^3}\sin\frac{1}{\delta}\right)\right] + p\left[2\left(\sin\frac{1}{\delta} - \frac{1}{\delta}\cos\frac{1}{\delta}\right)^2 + 2\delta\sin\frac{1}{\delta}\left(-\frac{1}{\delta^3}\sin\frac{1}{\delta}\right)\right]$.

Now,

$$\Phi_1 = \cos^4\varphi - \cos^4\delta + -(1-\delta^2)\left[4\cos^3\delta(-\sin\delta)\right],$$

as can be seen from Figure 3.

$$\Phi_1 \geqq 0 \ \forall \, \varphi, \delta \in X,$$

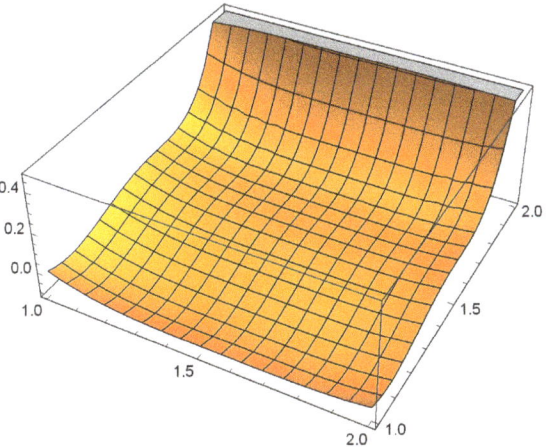

Figure 3. $\Phi_1 = \left\{ \cos^4\varphi - \cos^4\delta + -(1-\delta^2)4\cos^3\delta(-\sin\delta) \right\}$.

and

$$\Phi_2 = \frac{1}{2}p^2\left[12\cos^2\delta(-\sin\delta)^2 + 4\cos^3\delta(-\cos\delta) + p\left(12\cos^2\delta(-\sin\delta)^2 + 4\cos^3\delta(-\cos\delta)\right)\right].$$

As can be seen from Figure 4. $\Phi_2 \geqq 0$, $\forall \delta \in X$ and $p_1, p_2 \in [-\frac{1}{10^{10}}, -1]$. (From Figure 4).

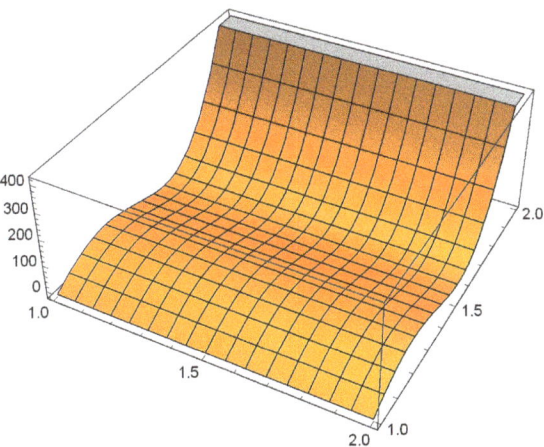

Figure 4. $\Phi_2 = \frac{1}{2}p^2\left[12\cos^2\delta(-\sin\delta)^2 + 4\cos^3\delta(-\cos\delta) + p\left(12\cos^2\delta(-\sin\delta)^2 + 4\cos^3\delta(-\cos\delta)\right)\right]$.

Hence, $\Psi \geqq 0$ and $\Phi \geqq 0$. This gives $\psi + \phi \geqq 0$. Thus, we can find that $(\Psi, \Phi) \in K$.

Hence, f is K-G_f-bonvex function at (Ψ, Φ) w.r.t. η.

We will show that f is not invex. For this it is either

$$f_1(\varphi) - f_1(\delta) - \eta^T(\varphi, \delta)\nabla_\varphi f_1(\delta) \ngeq 0$$

or

$$f_2(\varphi) - f_2(\delta) - \eta^T(\varphi, \delta)\nabla_\varphi f_2(\delta) \ngeq 0.$$

Since $f_1(\varphi) - f_1(\delta) - \eta^T(\varphi, \delta) \nabla_\varphi f_1(\delta) = \varphi \sin\frac{1}{\varphi} - \delta \sin\frac{1}{\delta} - (1 - \delta^2)\sin\frac{1}{\delta} - \frac{1}{\delta}\cos\frac{1}{\delta} \not\geq 0$, is not $\forall \varphi, \delta \in X$ as can be seen from Figure 5. Also, $f_2(\varphi) - f_1(\delta) - \eta^T(\varphi, \delta) \nabla_\varphi f_2(\delta) = \cos\varphi - \cos\delta + (1 - \delta^2)\sin\delta \not\geq 0$, is not $\forall \varphi, \delta \in X$ as can be seen from Figure 6.

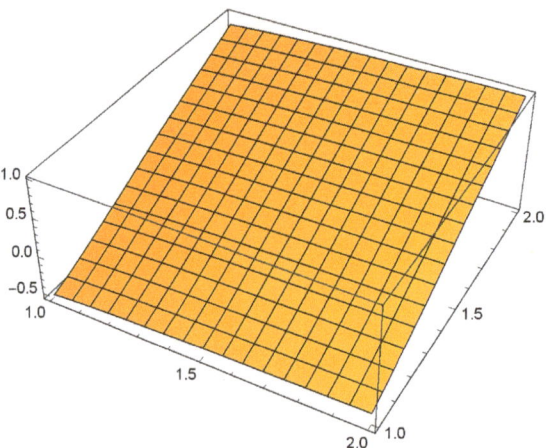

Figure 5. $\varphi \sin\frac{1}{\varphi} - \delta \sin\frac{1}{\delta} - (1 - \delta^2)\sin\frac{1}{\delta} - \frac{1}{\delta}\cos\frac{1}{\delta}$.

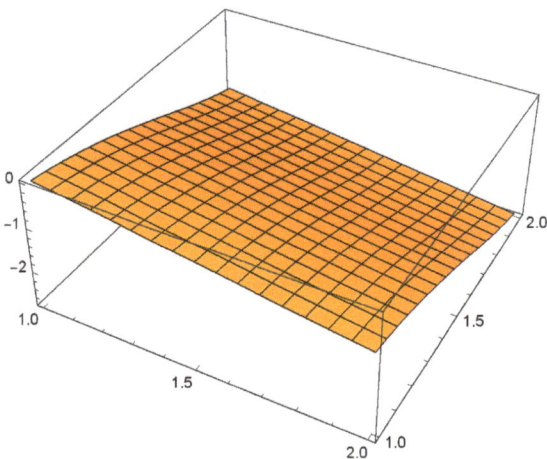

Figure 6. $\cos\varphi - \cos\delta + (1 - \delta^2)\sin\delta$.

Therefore, from the above example, it shows that f is K-G_f-bonvex, but it is not invex with respect to same η.

Definition 10. *If* $\exists\ G_f$ *and* η *such that* $\forall\ \varphi \in X$ *and* $q_i \in R^n$, *we have*

$$\eta^T(\varphi, \delta) \Big\{ G'_{f_1}(f_1(\delta)) \nabla_\varphi f_1(\delta) + q_1 \Big\{ G''_{f_1}(f_1(\delta))(\nabla_\varphi f_1(\delta))^T + G'_{f_1}(f_1(\delta)) \nabla_{\varphi\varphi} f_1(\delta) \Big\}, ..., G'_{f_k}(f_k(\delta)) \nabla_\varphi f_k(\delta) + q_k \Big\{ G''_{f_k}(f_k(\delta))(\nabla_\varphi f_k(\delta))^T + G'_{f_k}(f_k(\delta)) \nabla_{\varphi\varphi} f_k(\delta) \Big\} \Big\} \in K \Rightarrow \Big[G_{f_1}(f_1(\varphi)) - G_{f_1}(f_1(\delta)) + \frac{1}{2} q_1^T \Big\{ G''_{f_1}(f_1(\delta)) \nabla_\varphi f_1(\delta)(\nabla_\varphi f_1(\delta))^T + G'_{f_1}(f_1(\delta)) \nabla_{\varphi\varphi} f_1(\delta) \Big\} q_1, ..., G_{f_k}(f_k(\varphi)) - G_{f_k}(f_k(\delta)) + \frac{1}{2} q_k^T \Big\{ G''_{f_k}(f_k(\delta)) \nabla_\varphi f_k(\delta)(\nabla_\varphi f_k(\delta))^T + G'_{f_k}(f_k(\delta)) \nabla_{\varphi\varphi} f_k(\delta) \Big\} q_k \Big] \in K,$$

then, f *is* G_f*-pseudobonvex at* $\delta \in X$ *with* η.

Definition 11. *If $\exists\, G_f$ and η such that $\forall\, \varphi \in X$ and $q_1 \in R^n$, we have*

$$\eta^T(\varphi,\delta)\Big\{G'_{f_1}(f_1(\delta))\nabla_\varphi f_1(\delta) + q_1\Big\{G''_{f_1}(f_1(\delta))(\nabla_\varphi f_1(\delta))^T + G'_{f_1}(f_1(\delta))\nabla_{\varphi\varphi}f_1(\delta)\Big\},\ldots,G'_{f_k}(f_k(\delta))\nabla_\varphi f_k(\delta) + q_k\Big\{G''_{f_k}(f_k(\delta))(\nabla_\varphi f_k(\delta))^T$$
$$+ G'_{f_k}(f_k(\delta))\nabla_{\varphi\varphi}f_k(\delta)\Big\}\Big\} \in -K \Rightarrow \Big[G_{f_1}(f_1(\varphi)) - G_{f_1}(f_1(\delta)) + \tfrac{1}{2}q_1^T\Big\{G''_{f_1}(f_1(\delta))\nabla_\varphi f_1(\delta)(\nabla_\varphi f_1(\delta))^T + G'_{f_1}(f_1(\delta))\nabla_{\varphi\varphi}f_1(\delta)\Big\}q_1$$
$$,\ldots,G_{f_k}(f_k(\varphi)) - G_{f_k}(f_k(\delta)) + \tfrac{1}{2}q_k^T\Big\{G''_{f_k}(f_k(\delta))\nabla_\varphi f_k(\delta)(\nabla_\varphi f_k(\delta))^T + G'_{f_k}(f_k(\delta))\nabla_{\varphi\varphi}f_k(\delta)\Big\}q_k\Big] \in -K,$$

then f is G_f-pseudoboncave at $\delta \in X$ with respect to η.

We generalized the above definition as follows:

Definition 12. *If $\exists\, G_f$ and η_1 such that $\forall\, \varphi \in X$ and $q_i \in R^n$, we have*

$$\eta_1^T(\varphi,\delta)\Big\{G'_{f_1}(f_1(\delta,\ell))\nabla_\varphi f_1(\delta,\ell) + q_1\Big\{G''_{f_1}(f_1(\delta,\ell))(\nabla_\varphi f_1(\delta,\ell))^T + G'_{f_1}(f_1(\delta,\ell))\nabla_{\varphi\varphi}f_1(\delta,\ell)\Big\},\ldots,G'_{f_k}(f_k(\delta,\ell))\nabla_\varphi f_k(\delta,\ell)$$
$$+ q_k\Big\{G''_{f_k}(f_k(\delta,\ell))(\nabla_\varphi f_k(\delta,\ell))^T + G'_{f_k}(f_k(\delta,\ell))\nabla_{\varphi\varphi}f_k(\delta,\ell)\Big\}\Big\} \in K$$
$$\Rightarrow \Big[G_{f_1}(f_1(\varphi,\ell)) - G_{f_1}(f_1(\delta,\ell)) + \tfrac{1}{2}q_1^T\Big\{G''_{f_1}(f_1(\delta,\ell))\nabla_\varphi f_1(\delta,\ell)(\nabla_\varphi f_1(\delta,\ell))^T + G'_{f_1}(f_1(\delta,\ell))\nabla_{\varphi\varphi}f_1(\delta,\ell)\Big\}q_1,\ldots,G_{f_k}(f_k(\varphi,\ell))$$
$$- G_{f_k}(f_k(\delta,\ell)) + \tfrac{1}{2}q_k^T\Big\{G''_{f_k}(f_k(\delta,\ell))\nabla_\varphi f_k(\delta,\ell)(\nabla_\varphi f_k(\delta,\ell))^T + G'_{f_k}(f_k(\delta,\ell))\nabla_{\varphi\varphi}f_k(\delta,\ell)\Big\}q_k\Big] \in K,$$

then f is K-G_f-bonvex in the first variable at $\delta \in X$ for fixed $\ell \in Y$ with η_1,

and

if $\exists\, G_f$ and η_2 such that $\forall\, \vartheta \in Y$ and $p_i \in R^m$, we have

$$\eta_2^T(\delta,\vartheta)\Big\{G'_{f_1}(f_1(\delta,\vartheta))\nabla_\vartheta f_1(\delta,\ell) + \Big\{G''_{f_1}(f_1(\delta,\ell))(\nabla_\vartheta f_1(\delta,\ell))^T + G'_{f_1}(f_1(\delta,\ell))\nabla_{\vartheta\vartheta}f_1(\delta,\ell)\Big\}p_1,\ldots,G'_{f_k}(f_k(\delta,\ell))\nabla_\vartheta f_k(\delta,\ell)$$
$$+ p_k\Big\{G''_{f_k}(f_k(\delta,\ell))(\nabla_\vartheta f_k(\delta,\ell))^T + G'_{f_k}(f_k(\delta,\ell))\nabla_{\vartheta\vartheta}f_k(\delta,\ell)\Big\}\Big\} \in K$$
$$\Rightarrow \Big[G_{f_1}(f_1(\delta,\vartheta)) - G_{f_1}(f_1(\delta,\ell)) + \tfrac{1}{2}p_1^T\Big\{G''_{f_1}(f_1(\delta,\ell))\nabla_\vartheta f_1(\delta,\ell)(\nabla_\vartheta f_1(\delta,\ell))^T + G'_{f_1}(f_1(\delta,\ell))\nabla_{\vartheta\vartheta}f_1(\delta,\ell)\Big\}p_1,\ldots,G_{f_k}(f_k(\delta,\vartheta))$$
$$- G_{f_k}(f_k(\delta,\ell)) + \tfrac{1}{2}p_k^T\Big\{G''_{f_k}(f_k(\delta,\ell))\nabla_\vartheta f_k(\delta,\ell)(\nabla_\vartheta f_k(\delta,\ell))^T + G'_{f_k}(f_k(\delta,\ell))\nabla_{\vartheta\vartheta}f_k(\delta,\ell)\Big\}p_k\Big] \in K,$$

then f is K-G_f-bonvex in the second variable at $\ell \in Y$ for fixed $\delta \in X$ with η_2.

Definition 13. *If $\exists\, G_f$ and η_1 such that $\forall\, \varphi \in X$ and $q_i \in R^n$, we have*

$$\eta_1^T(\varphi,\delta)\Big\{G'_{f_1}(f_1(\delta,\ell))\nabla_\varphi f_1(\delta,\ell) + q_1\Big\{G''_{f_1}(f_1(\delta,\ell))(\nabla_\varphi f_1(\delta,\ell))^T + G'_{f_1}(f_1(\delta,\ell))\nabla_{\varphi\varphi}f_1(\delta,\ell)\Big\},\ldots,G'_{f_k}(f_k(\delta,\ell))\nabla_\varphi f_k(\delta,\ell)$$
$$+ q_k\Big\{G''_{f_k}(f_k(\delta,\ell))(\nabla_\varphi f_k(\delta,\ell))^T + G'_{f_k}(f_k(\delta,\ell))\nabla_{\varphi\varphi}f_k(\delta,\ell)\Big\}\Big\} \in -K$$
$$\Rightarrow \Big[G_{f_1}(f_1(\varphi,\ell)) - G_{f_1}(f_1(\delta,\ell)) + \tfrac{1}{2}q_1^T\Big\{G''_{f_1}(f_1(\delta,\ell))\nabla_\varphi f_1(\delta,\ell)(\nabla_\varphi f_1(\delta,\ell))^T + G'_{f_1}(f_1(\delta,\ell))\nabla_{\varphi\varphi}f_1(\delta,\ell)\Big\}q_1,\ldots,G_{f_k}(f_k(\varphi,\ell))$$
$$- G_{f_k}(f_k(\delta,\ell)) + \tfrac{1}{2}q_k^T\Big\{G''_{f_k}(f_k(\delta,\ell))\nabla_\varphi f_k(\delta,\ell)(\nabla_\varphi f_k(\delta,\ell))^T + G'_{f_k}(f_k(\delta,\ell))\nabla_{\varphi\varphi}f_k(\delta,\ell)\Big\}q_k\Big] \in -K,$$

then f is K-G_f-bonvex in the first variable at $\delta \in X$ for fixed $\ell \in Y$ with η_1,

and

If $\exists\, G_f$ and η_2 such that $\forall\, \vartheta \in Y$ and $p_i \in R^m$, we have

$$\eta_2^T(\delta,\vartheta)\Big\{G'_{f_1}(f_1(\delta,\vartheta))\nabla_\vartheta f_1(\delta,\ell) + \Big\{G''_{f_1}(f_1(\delta,\ell))(\nabla_\vartheta f_1(\delta,\ell))^T + G'_{f_1}(f_1(\delta,\ell))\nabla_{\vartheta\vartheta}f_1(\delta,\ell)\Big\}p_1,\ldots,G'_{f_k}(f_k(\delta,\ell))\nabla_\vartheta f_k(\delta,\ell)$$
$$+ p_k\Big\{G''_{f_k}(f_k(\delta,\ell))(\nabla_\vartheta f_k(\delta,\ell))^T + G'_{f_k}(f_k(\delta,\ell))\nabla_{\vartheta\vartheta}f_k(\delta,\ell)\Big\}\Big\} \in -K$$
$$\Rightarrow \Big[G_{f_1}(f_1(\delta,\vartheta)) - G_{f_1}(f_1(\delta,\ell)) + \tfrac{1}{2}p_1^T\Big\{G''_{f_1}(f_1(\delta,\ell))\nabla_\vartheta f_1(\delta,\ell)(\nabla_\vartheta f_1(\delta,\ell))^T + G'_{f_1}(f_1(\delta,\ell))\nabla_{\vartheta\vartheta}f_1(\delta,\ell)\Big\}p_1,\ldots,G_{f_k}(f_k(\delta,\vartheta))$$
$$- G_{f_k}(f_k(\delta,\ell)) + \tfrac{1}{2}p_k^T\Big\{G''_{f_k}(f_k(\delta,\ell))\nabla_\vartheta f_k(\delta,\ell)(\nabla_\vartheta f_k(\delta,\ell))^T + G'_{f_k}(f_k(\delta,\ell))\nabla_{\vartheta\vartheta}f_k(\delta,\ell)\Big\}p_k\Big] \in -K.$$

then f is K-G_f-boncave in the second variable at $\ell \in Y$ for fixed $\delta \in X$ with respect to η_2.

Remark 1. If $G_f(t) = t$, then above definition reduces in $K - \eta$-pseudo bonvex w.r.t. η,

$$\eta^T(\varphi,\delta)\left[\nabla_\varphi f_1(\delta) + \nabla_{\varphi\varphi}f_1(\delta)q_1, \ldots, \nabla_\varphi f_k(\delta) + \nabla_{\varphi\varphi}f_k(\delta)q_k\right] \in K$$

$$\Rightarrow \left[f_1(\varphi) - f_1(\delta) + \frac{1}{2}q_1^T\nabla_{\varphi\varphi}f_1(\delta)q_1, \ldots, f_k(\varphi) - f_k(\delta) + \frac{1}{2}q^T\nabla_{\varphi\varphi}f_k(\delta)q_k\right] \in K.$$

Example 2. Let $X = [-10, 10]$ and $K = \{(\varphi, \vartheta) : \varphi \geqq 0, \varphi \leqq \vartheta\}$. Consider the function $f : X \to \mathbb{R}^2$ defined by

$$f(\varphi) = (f_1(\varphi), f_2(\varphi)),$$

where

$$f_1(\varphi) = \sin\varphi, \quad f_2(\varphi) = e^\varphi$$

Define $G_f = (G_{f_1}, G_{f_2}) : R^2 \to R$ given by

$$G_{f_1} = t^2, G_{f_2} = t^3, \eta = \varphi^2 - \delta^2, \text{ and } q_1 = q_2 \in [2, \infty].$$

We have to claim that function f is K-G_f-pseudobonvex at point δ, i.e.,

$$\eta^T(\varphi,\delta)\left\{G'_{f_1}(f_1(\delta))\nabla_\varphi f_1(\delta) + q_1\left\{G''_{f_1}(f_1(\delta))(\nabla_\varphi f_1(\delta))^T + G'_{f_1}(f_1(\delta))\nabla_{\varphi\varphi}f_1(\delta)\right\}, G'_{f_2}(f_2(\delta))\nabla_\varphi f_2(\delta) + q_2\left\{G''_{f_2}(f_2(\delta))(\nabla_\varphi f_2(\delta))^T + G'_{f_2}(f_2(\delta))\nabla_{\varphi\varphi}f_2(\delta)\right\}\right\} \in K \Rightarrow \left\{G_{f_1}(f_1(\varphi)) - G_{f_1}(f_1(\delta)) + \frac{1}{2}q_1^T\left\{G''_{f_1}(f_1(\delta))\nabla_\varphi f_1(\delta)(\nabla_\varphi f_1(\delta))^T + G'_{f_1}(f_1(\delta))\nabla_{\varphi\varphi}f_1(\delta)\right\}q_1, G_{f_2}(f_2(\varphi)) - G_{f_2}(f_2(\delta)) + \frac{1}{2}q_2^T\left\{G''_{f_2}(f_2(\delta))\nabla_\varphi f_2(\delta)(\nabla_\varphi f_2(\delta))^T + G'_{f_2}(f_2(\delta))\nabla_{\varphi\varphi}f_2(\delta)\right\}q_2\right\} \in K.$$

Consider

$$\tau = \eta^T(\varphi,\delta)\left\{G'_{f_1}(f_1(\delta))\nabla_\varphi f_1(\delta) + q_1\left\{G''_{f_1}(f_1(\delta))(\nabla_\varphi f_1(\delta))^T + G'_{f_1}(f_1(\delta))\nabla_{\varphi\varphi}f_1(\delta)\right\}, G'_{f_2}(f_2(\delta))\nabla_\varphi f_2(\delta) + q_2\left\{G''_{f_2}(f_2(\delta))(\nabla_\varphi f_2(\delta))^T + G'_{f_2}(f_2(\delta))\nabla_{\varphi\varphi}f_2(\delta)\right\}\right\}.$$

Putting the values of $f_1, f_2, G_{f_1}, G_{f_2}$ and η, we have

$$\tau = (\varphi^2 - \delta^2)\left(\sin 2\delta + 2q_1(\cos\delta - \sin^2\delta), \ 3e^{3\delta} + 9e^{2\delta}q_2\right).$$

At the point $\delta = 0$, the value of above expression becomes

$$\tau = \left\{2\varphi^2 q_1, \ 3\varphi^2(1 + 3q_2)\right\}, \quad \forall \, q_1 = q_2 \in [2, \infty)$$

Obviously,

$$\tau = \left\{2\varphi^2 q_1, \ 3\varphi^2(1 + 3q_2)\right\} \in K.$$

Next, consider

$$\Psi = \left\{G_{f_1}(f_1(\varphi)) - G_{f_1}(f_1(\delta)) + \frac{1}{2}q_1^T\{G''_{f_1}(f_1(\delta))\nabla_\varphi f_1(\delta)(\nabla_\varphi f_1(\delta))^T + G'_{f_1}(f_1(\delta))\nabla_{\varphi\varphi}f_1(\delta)\}q_1, \ G_{f_2}(f_2(\varphi)) - G_{f_2}(f_2(\delta)) + \frac{1}{2}q_2^T\{G''_{f_2}(f_2(\delta))\nabla_\varphi f_2(\delta)(\nabla_\varphi f_2(\delta))^T + G'_{f_2}(f_2(\delta))\nabla_{\varphi\varphi}f_2(\delta)\}q_2\right\}.$$

Putting the values of f_1, f_2, G_{f_1}, G_{f_2} and η, we have

$$\Psi = \left\{\sin^2\varphi - \sin^2\delta + \frac{1}{2}q_1^2(2\cos^2\delta - 2\sin^2\delta), \ e^{3\varphi} - e^{3\delta} + \frac{9}{2}q_2^2 e^{3\delta}\right\}.$$

The value of above expression at the point $\delta = 0$, we get

$$\Psi = \left\{\sin^2\varphi + q_1^2, \ e^{3\varphi} + \frac{9}{2}q_2^2 - 1\right\} \in K.$$

From the Figure 7. We can easily observe that the value of φ-coordinate always less than ϑ-coordinate in K, so $\varphi \in K$.

Hence, f is K-G_f-pseudobonvex at the point $\delta = 0$ with respect to η.

Next,

$$\left\{ G_{f_1}(f_1(\varphi)) - G_{f_1}(f_1(\delta)) + \frac{1}{2}p_1^T \left[G''_{f_1}(f_1(\delta)) \nabla_\varphi f_1(\delta) (\nabla_\varphi f_1(\delta))^T + G'_{f_1}(f_1(\delta)) \nabla_{\varphi\varphi} f_1(\delta) \right] p_1 - \eta^T(\varphi, \delta) \left[G'_{f_1}(f_1(\delta)) \nabla_\varphi f_1(\delta) \right. \right.$$
$$\left. + \{ G''_{f_1}(f_1(\delta)) \nabla_\varphi f_1(\delta) (\nabla_\varphi f_1(\delta))^T + G'_{f_1}(f_1(\delta)) \nabla_{\varphi\varphi} f_1(\delta) \} p_1 \right],$$
$$G_{f_2}(f_2(\varphi)) - G_{f_2}(f_2(\delta)) + \frac{1}{2}p_2^T \left[G''_{f_2}(f_2(\delta)) \nabla_\varphi f_2(\delta) (\nabla_\varphi f_2(\delta))^T \right.$$
$$\left. \left. + G'_{f_2} f_2(\delta) \nabla_{\varphi\varphi} f_2(\delta) \right] p_2 - \eta^T(\varphi, \delta) \left[G'_{f_2} f_2(\delta) \nabla_\varphi f_2(\delta) + \{ G''_{f_2}(f_2(\delta)) \nabla_\varphi f_2(\delta) (\nabla_\varphi f_2(\delta))^T + G'_{f_2} f_2(\delta) \nabla_{\varphi\varphi} f_2(\delta) \} p_2 \right] \right\} \notin K.$$

Let

$$\Psi = \left\{ G_{f_1}(f_1(\varphi)) - G_{f_1}(f_1(\delta)) + \frac{1}{2}p_1^T \left[G''_{f_1}(f_1(\delta)) \nabla_\varphi f_1(\delta) (\nabla_\varphi f_1(\delta))^T + G'_{f_1}(f_1(\delta)) \nabla_{\varphi\varphi} f_1(\delta) \right] p_1 - \eta^T(\varphi, \delta) \left[G'_{f_1}(f_1(\delta)) \nabla_\varphi f_1(\delta) \right. \right.$$
$$\left. + \{ G''_{f_1}(f_1(\delta)) \nabla_\varphi f_1(\delta) (\nabla_\varphi f_1(\delta))^T + G'_{f_1}(f_1(\delta)) \nabla_{\varphi\varphi} f_1(\delta) \} p_1 \right], G_{f_2}(f_2(\varphi)) - G_{f_2}(f_2(\delta)) + \frac{1}{2}p_2^T \left[G''_{f_2}(f_2(\delta)) \nabla_\varphi f_2(\delta) (\nabla_\varphi f_2(\delta))^T \right.$$
$$\left. \left. + G'_{f_2} f_2(\delta) \nabla_{\varphi\varphi} f_2(\delta) \right] p_2 - \eta^T(\varphi, \delta) \left[G'_{f_2} f_2(\delta) \nabla_\varphi f_2(\delta) + \{ G''_{f_2}(f_2(\delta)) \nabla_\varphi f_2(\delta) (\nabla_\varphi f_2(\delta))^T + G'_{f_2} f_2(\delta) \nabla_{\varphi\varphi} f_2(\delta) \} p_2 \right] \right\}.$$

Substituting the values of $f_1, f_2, G_{f_1}, G_{f_2}$ and η, we obtain

$$\Psi = \left\{ \sin^2 \varphi - \sin^2 \delta + p_1^2(\cos^2 \delta - \sin^2 \delta) - (\varphi^2 - \delta^2)(\sin 2\delta + 2p_1(\cos \delta - \sin^2 \delta)), \; e^{3\varphi} - e^{3\delta} + \frac{9}{2}p_2^2 e^{3\delta} - (\varphi^2 - \delta^2)(3e^{3\delta} + 9e^{2\delta} p_2) \right\}.$$

At the point $\delta = 0$, it follows that

$$\Psi = \left\{ \sin^2 \varphi + p_1^2 - 2p_1 \varphi^2, \; e^{3\varphi} + \frac{9}{2}p_2^2 - 1 - \varphi^2(3 + 9p_2) \right\}, \quad p_1 = p_2 \in [2, \infty).$$

Take particular point $\varphi = -\frac{\pi}{2}$ and $p_1 = p_2 = 2 \in [2, \infty)$, we obtain,

$$\Psi = (-4.86, \; -34.80) \notin K.$$

Hence, f is K-G_f-pseudobonvex, but it is not K-G_f-bonvex at $\delta = 0$ with respect to η.

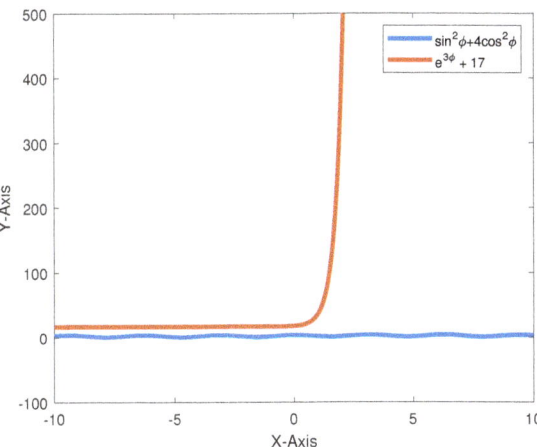

Figure 7. $\left(\sin^2 \varphi + 4\cos^2 \varphi, e^{3\varphi} + 17 \right)$.

In the following example, we showed that the function f is K-G_f-pseudobonvex, but it is not K-G_f-bonvex function with same η.

Example 3. Let $X = [0, \frac{\pi}{2}]$ and $K = \{(\varphi, \vartheta) : \varphi \geqq 0, \vartheta \geqq \varphi\}$. Consider $G_f = (G_{f_1}, G_{f_2}) : R^2 \to R$ and $f : X \to \mathbb{R}^2$ given by

$$f(\varphi) = (f_1(\varphi), f_2(\varphi)),$$

where

$$f_1(\varphi) = \sin\varphi, \quad f_2(\varphi) = \varphi,$$

$$G_{f_1} = t, \; G_{f_2} = t^2.$$

Define $\eta : X \times X \to R^n$ given by

$$\eta(\varphi, \delta) = \varphi - \delta \text{ and } q_1, q_2 \in [1, \infty].$$

Solution: In this example, we will try to derive that f is K-G_f-pseudobonvex i.e.,

$\eta^T(\varphi,\delta)\{G'_{f_1}(f_1(\delta))\nabla_\varphi f_1(\delta) + q_1\{G''_{f_1}(f_1(\delta))(\nabla_\varphi f_1(\delta))^T + G'_{f_1}(f_1(\delta))\nabla_{\varphi\varphi} f_1(\delta)\}, G'_{f_2}(f_2(\delta))\nabla_\varphi f_2(\delta) + q_2\{G''_{f_2}(f_2(\delta))(\nabla_\varphi f_2(\delta))^T + G'_{f_2}(f_2(\delta))\nabla_{\varphi\varphi} f_2(\delta)\}\} \in K \Rightarrow \{G_{f_1}(f_1(\varphi)) - G_{f_1}(f_1(\delta)) + \frac{1}{2}q_1^T\{G''_{f_1}(f_1(\delta))\nabla_\varphi f_1(\delta)(\nabla_\varphi f_1(\delta))^T + G'_{f_1}(f_1(\delta))\nabla_{\varphi\varphi} f_1(\delta)\}q_1, G_{f_2}(f_2(\varphi)) - G_{f_2}(f_2(\delta)) + \frac{1}{2}q_2^T\{G''_{f_2}(f_2(\delta))\nabla_\varphi f_2(\delta)(\nabla_\varphi f_2(\delta))^T + G'_{f_2}(f_2(\delta))\nabla_{\varphi\varphi} f_2(\delta)\}q_2\} \in K.$

Consider

$\Pi_1 = \eta^T(\varphi,\delta)\{G'_{f_1}(f_1(\delta))\nabla_\varphi f_1(\delta) + q_1\{G''_{f_1}(f_1(\delta))(\nabla_\varphi f_1(\delta))^T + G'_{f_1}(f_1(\delta))\nabla_{\varphi\varphi} f_1(\delta)\}, G'_{f_2}(f_2(\delta))\nabla_\varphi f_2(\delta) + q_2\{G''_{f_2}(f_2(\delta))(\nabla_\varphi f_2(\delta))^T + G'_{f_2}(f_2(\delta))\nabla_{\varphi\varphi} f_2(\delta)\}\}.$

Putting the values of $f_1, f_2, G_{f_1}, G_{f_2}$ and η, we have

$$\Pi_1 = \{(\varphi - \delta)\cos\delta, \; (\varphi - \delta)(2\delta + 2q_2)\}.$$

The value of above expression at the point $\delta = 0$, we get

$$\Pi_1 = \{\varphi, 2\delta q_2\} \in K.$$

Next, let

$\Pi_2 = \{G_{f_1}(f_1(\varphi)) - G_{f_1}(f_1(\delta)) + \frac{1}{2}q_1^T\{G''_{f_1}(f_1(\delta))\nabla_\varphi f_1(\delta)(\nabla_\varphi f_1(\delta))^T + G'_{f_1}(f_1(\delta))\nabla_{\varphi\varphi} f_1(\delta)\}q_1, \; G_{f_2}(f_2(\varphi)) - G_{f_2}(f_2(\delta)) + \frac{1}{2}q_2^T\{G''_{f_2}(f_2(\delta))\nabla_\varphi f_2(\delta)(\nabla_\varphi f_2(\delta))^T + G'_{f_2}(f_2(\delta))\nabla_{\varphi\varphi} f_2(\delta)\}q_2\}.$

Putting the values of $f_1, f_2, G_{f_1}, G_{f_2}$ and η, we have

$$\Pi_2 = \left\{\sin\varphi - \sin\delta + \frac{1}{2}q_1^2(-\sin\delta), \varphi - \delta + q_2^2\right\}.$$

After simplifying and the value at $\delta = 0$, it follows that

$$\Pi_2 = \left\{\sin\varphi, \varphi + q_2^2\right\} \in K.$$

Hence, f is K-G_f-pseudobonvex at the point $\delta = 0$ with respect to η.

Next,

$$\left\{ G_{f_1}(f_1(\varphi)) - G_{f_1}(f_1(\delta)) + \frac{1}{2}p_1^T \left[G_{f_1}''(f_1(\delta))\nabla_\varphi f_1(\delta)(\nabla_\varphi f_1(\delta))^T + G_{f_1}'(f_1(\delta))\nabla_{\varphi\varphi}f_1(\delta) \right] p_1 - \eta^T(\varphi,\delta) \left[G_{f_1}'(f_1(\delta))\nabla_\varphi f_1(\delta) \right. \right.$$
$$\left. + \{ G_{f_1}''(f_1(\delta))\nabla_\varphi f_1(\delta)(\nabla_\varphi f_1(\delta))^T + G_{f_1}'(f_1(\delta))\nabla_{\varphi\varphi}f_1(\delta)\}p_1 \right],$$
$$G_{f_2}(f_2(\varphi)) - G_{f_2}(f_2(\delta)) + \frac{1}{2}p_2^T \left[G_{f_2}''(f_2(\delta))\nabla_\varphi f_2(\delta)(\nabla_\varphi f_2(\delta))^T \right.$$
$$\left. \left. + G_{f_2}'f_2(\delta)\nabla_{\varphi\varphi}f_2(\delta) \right]p_2 - \eta^T(\varphi,\delta) \left[G_{f_2}'f_2(\delta)\nabla_\varphi f_2(\delta) + \{G_{f_2}''(f_2(\delta))\nabla_\varphi f_2(\delta)(\nabla_\varphi f_2(\delta))^T + G_{f_2}'f_2(\delta)\nabla_{\varphi\varphi}f_2(\delta)\}p_2 \right] \right\} \notin K.$$

Let

$$\Psi = \left\{ G_{f_1}(f_1(\varphi)) - G_{f_1}(f_1(\delta)) + \frac{1}{2}p_1^T \left[G_{f_1}''(f_1(\delta))\nabla_\varphi f_1(\delta)(\nabla_\varphi f_1(\delta))^T + G_{f_1}'(f_1(\delta))\nabla_{\varphi\varphi}f_1(\delta) \right] p_1 - \eta^T(\varphi,\delta) \left[G_{f_1}'(f_1(\delta))\nabla_\varphi f_1(\delta) \right. \right.$$
$$\left. + \{G_{f_1}''(f_1(\delta))\nabla_\varphi f_1(\delta)(\nabla_\varphi f_1(\delta))^T + G_{f_1}'(f_1(\delta))\nabla_{\varphi\varphi}f_1(\delta)\}p_1 \right\}, G_{f_2}(f_2(\varphi)) - G_{f_2}(f_2(\delta)) + \frac{1}{2}p_2^T \left[G_{f_2}''(f_2(\delta))\nabla_\varphi f_2(\delta)(\nabla_\varphi f_2(\delta))^T \right.$$
$$\left. \left. + G_{f_2}'f_2(\delta)\nabla_{\varphi\varphi}f_2(\delta) \right]p_2 - \eta^T(\varphi,\delta) \left[G_{f_2}'f_2(\delta)\nabla_\varphi f_2(\delta) + \{G_{f_2}''(f_2(\delta))\nabla_\varphi f_2(\delta)(\nabla_\varphi f_2(\delta))^T + G_{f_2}'f_2(\delta)\nabla_{\varphi\varphi}f_2(\delta)\}p_2 \right] \right\}.$$

Substituting the values of $f_1, f_2, G_{f_1}, G_{f_2}$ and η, we obtain

$$\Psi = \left\{ \sin\varphi - \sin\delta + \frac{1}{2}p_1^2(-\sin\delta) - (\varphi - \delta)p_1\cos\delta, \ \varphi^2 + p_2^2 - 2(\varphi - \delta)p_2 \right\}.$$

At the point $\delta = 0$, it follows that

$$\Psi = \left\{ \sin\varphi - p_1\varphi, (\varphi - p_2)^2 \right\} \notin K.$$

Hence, f is K-G_f-pseudobonvex, but it is not K-G_f-bonvex at $\delta = 0$ with respect to η.

3. K-G_f-Wolfe Type Second-Order Symmetric Primal-Dual Pair with Cones

The study of second-order duality is more significant due to computational advantage over first order duality as it provides tighter bounds for the objective functions, when approximation is used.

The motivated by [21–27] several researches in this area, we formulated a new type K-G_f-Wolfe type primal dual pair, with cone objectives as well as cone constraint as follows:

Primal Problem (GWPP):

$$K\text{-min } L(\varphi, \vartheta, \lambda, p) = \left\{ L_1(\varphi, \vartheta, \lambda, p), L_2(\varphi, \vartheta, \lambda, p), L_3(\varphi, \vartheta, \lambda, p), ..., L_k(\varphi, \vartheta, \lambda, p) \right\},$$

where

$$L_i(\varphi, \vartheta, \lambda, p) = G_{f_i}(f_i(\varphi, \vartheta)) - \vartheta^T \sum_{i=1}^{k} \lambda_i \left[G_{f_i}'(f_i(\varphi, \vartheta))\nabla_\vartheta f_i(\varphi, \vartheta) + \{ G_{f_i}''(f_i(\varphi, \vartheta))\nabla_\vartheta f_i(\varphi, \vartheta)(\nabla_\vartheta f_i(\varphi, \vartheta))^T \right.$$
$$\left. + G_{f_i}'(f_i(\varphi, \vartheta))\nabla_{\varphi,\vartheta} f_i(\varphi, \vartheta) \} p_i \right] - \frac{1}{2} \sum_{i=1}^{k} \lambda_i p_i \left\{ G_{f_i}''(f_i(\varphi, \vartheta))\nabla_\vartheta f_i(\varphi, \vartheta)(\nabla_\vartheta f_i(\varphi, \vartheta))^T + G_{f_i}'(f_i(\varphi, \vartheta))\nabla_{\vartheta\vartheta} f_i(\varphi, \vartheta) \right\} p_i,$$

subject to

$$-\sum_{i=1}^{k} \lambda_i \left[G_{f_i}'(f_i(\varphi, \vartheta))\nabla_\vartheta f_i(\varphi, \vartheta) + \left\{ G_{f_i}''(f_i(\varphi, \vartheta))\nabla_\vartheta f_i(\varphi, \vartheta)(\nabla_\vartheta f_i(\varphi, \vartheta))^T + G_{f_i}'(f_i(\varphi, \vartheta))\nabla_{\vartheta\vartheta} f_i(\varphi, \vartheta) \right\} p_i \right] \in C_2^*, \quad (1)$$

$$\lambda^T e_k = 1, \ \lambda \in \text{int}K^*, \ \varphi \in C_1. \quad (2)$$

Dual Problem (GWDP):

$$K\text{-max } M(\delta, \ell, \lambda, q) = \left\{ M_1(\delta, \ell, q), M_2(\delta, \ell, \lambda, q), M_3(\delta, \ell, \lambda, q), ..., M_k(\delta, \ell, \lambda, q) \right\},$$

where

$$M_i(\delta, \ell, \lambda, q) = G_{f_i}(f_i(\delta, \ell)) - \delta^T \sum_{i=1}^{k} \lambda_i \Big[G'_{f_i}(f_i(\delta, \ell)) \nabla_\varphi f_i(\delta, \ell) + \Big\{ G''_{f_i}(f_i(\delta, \ell)) \nabla_\varphi f_i(\delta, \ell)(\nabla_\varphi f_i(\delta, \ell))^T$$
$$+ G'_{f_i}(f_i(\delta, \ell)) \nabla_{\varphi\varphi} f_i(\delta, \ell) \Big\} q_i \Big] - \tfrac{1}{2} \sum_{i=1}^{k} \lambda_i q_i \Big[G''_{f_i}(f_i(\delta, \ell)) \nabla_\varphi f_i(\delta, \ell)(\nabla_\varphi f_i(\delta, \ell))^T + G'_{f_i}(f_i(\delta, \ell)) \nabla_{\varphi\varphi} f_i(\delta, \ell) \Big] q_i,$$

subject to

$$\sum_{i=1}^{k} \lambda_i \Big[G'_{f_i}(f_i(\delta, \ell)) \nabla_\varphi f_i(\delta, \ell) + \Big\{ G''_{f_i}(f_i(\delta, \ell)) \nabla_\varphi f_i(\delta, \ell)(\nabla_\varphi f_i(\delta, \ell))^T + G'_{f_i}(f_i(\delta, \ell)) \nabla_{\varphi\varphi} f_i(\delta, \ell) \Big\} q_i \Big] \in C_1^*, \tag{3}$$

$$\lambda^T e_k = 1, \ \lambda \in \mathrm{int} K^*, \ \delta \in C_2, \tag{4}$$

where, for $i \in \tilde{Q}$,

- $f_i : R_1 \times R_2 \to R$, is a differential function of φ and ϑ, $e_k = (1, 1, ..., 1)^T \in R^k$,
- q_i and p_i are vectors in R^n and R^m, respectively and $\lambda \in R^k$.

Let V^* and W^* be the sets of feasible solutions of (GWPP) and (GWDP) respectively.

Theorem 1 (Weak duality). *Let $(\varphi, \vartheta, \lambda, p) \in V^*$ and $(\delta, \ell, \lambda, q) \in W^*$. Let, for $i \in \tilde{N}$*

(i) $\Big\{ f_1(., \ell), f_2(., \ell), ..., f_k(., \ell) \Big\}$ *be K-G_{f_i}-bonvex at δ w.r.t. η_1,*

(ii) $\Big\{ f_1(\varphi, .), f_2(\varphi, .), ..., f_k(\varphi, .) \Big\}$ *be K-G_{f_i}-boncave in ϑ w.r.t. η_2,*

(iii) $\eta_1(\varphi, \delta) + \delta \in C_1, \forall \ (\varphi, \delta) \in C_1 \times C_2,$

(iv) $\eta_2(\ell, \vartheta) + \vartheta \in C_2, \forall \ (\ell, \vartheta) \in C_1 \times C_2,$

Then, $L(\varphi, \vartheta, \lambda, p) - M(\delta, \ell, \lambda, q) \notin -K \setminus \{0\}$.

Proof. If possible, then suppose

$$L(\varphi, \vartheta, \lambda, p) - M(\delta, \ell, \lambda, q) \in -K \setminus \{0\},$$

or

$$\Big\{ G_{f_i}(f_1(\varphi, \vartheta)) - \vartheta^T \sum_{i=1}^{k} \lambda_i \Big(G'_{f_i}(f_i(\varphi, \vartheta)) \nabla_\vartheta f_i(\varphi, \vartheta) + \Big\{ G''_{f_i}(f_i(\varphi, \vartheta)) (\nabla_\vartheta f_i(\varphi, \vartheta))(\nabla_\vartheta f_i(\varphi, \vartheta))^T + G'_{f_i}(f_i(\varphi, \vartheta)) \nabla_{\vartheta\vartheta} f_i(\varphi, \vartheta) \Big\} p_i \Big)$$
$$- \tfrac{1}{2} \sum_{i=1}^{k} \lambda_i p_i^T \Big\{ G''_{f_i}(f_i(\varphi, \vartheta))(\nabla_\vartheta f_i(\varphi, \vartheta))(\nabla_\vartheta f_i(\varphi, \vartheta))^T + G'_{f_i}(f_i(\varphi, \vartheta)) \nabla_{\vartheta\vartheta} f_i(\varphi, \vartheta) \Big\} p_i, ..., G_{f_k}(f_k(\varphi, \vartheta))$$
$$- \vartheta^T \sum_{i=1}^{k} \lambda_i \Big(G'_{f_i}(f_i(\varphi, \vartheta)) \nabla_\vartheta f_i(\varphi, \vartheta) + \Big\{ G''_{f_i}(f_i(\varphi, \vartheta))(\nabla_\vartheta f_i(\varphi, \vartheta))(\nabla_\vartheta f_i(\varphi, \vartheta))^T + G'_{f_i}(f_i(\varphi, \vartheta)) \nabla_{\vartheta\vartheta} f_i(\varphi, \vartheta) \Big\} p_i \Big)$$
$$- \tfrac{1}{2} \sum_{i=1}^{k} \lambda_i p_i^T \Big\{ G''_{f_i}(f_i(\varphi, \vartheta))(\nabla_\vartheta f_i(\varphi, \vartheta))(\nabla_\vartheta f_i(\varphi, \vartheta))^T + G'_{f_i}(f_i(\varphi, \vartheta)) \nabla_{\vartheta\vartheta} f_i(\varphi, \vartheta) \Big\} p_i - G_{f_i}(f_1(\delta, \ell)) - \delta^T \sum_{i=1}^{k} \lambda_i \Big(G'_{f_i}(f_i(\delta, \ell))$$
$$\nabla_\varphi f_i(\delta, \ell) + \Big\{ G''_{f_i}(f_i(\delta, \ell))(\nabla_\varphi f_i(\delta, \ell))(\nabla_\varphi f_i(\delta, \ell))^T + G'_{f_i}(f_i(\delta, \ell)) \nabla_{\varphi\varphi} f_i(\delta, \ell) \Big\} q_i \Big) - \tfrac{1}{2} \sum_{i=1}^{k} \lambda_i q_i^T \Big\{ G''_{f_i}(f_i(\delta, \ell))(\nabla_\varphi f_i(\delta, \ell))(\nabla_\varphi f_i(\delta, \ell))^T$$
$$+ G'_{f_i}(f(\delta, \ell)) \nabla_{\varphi\varphi} f_i(\delta, \ell) \Big\} q_i, ..., G_{f_k}(f_k(\delta, \ell)) - \delta^T \sum_{i=1}^{k} \lambda_i \Big(G'_{f_i}(f_i(\delta, \ell)) \nabla_\varphi f_i(\delta, \ell) + \Big\{ G''_{f_i}(f_i(\delta, \ell))(\nabla_\varphi f_i(\delta, \ell))(\nabla_\varphi f_i(\delta, \ell))^T$$
$$+ G'_{f_i}(f_i(\delta, \ell)) \nabla_{\varphi\varphi} f_i(\delta, \ell) \Big\} q_i \Big) - \tfrac{1}{2} \sum_{i=1}^{k} \lambda_i q_i^T \Big\{ G''_{f_i}(f_i(\delta, \ell))(\nabla_\varphi f_i(\delta, \ell))(\nabla_\varphi f_i(\delta, \ell))^T + G'_{f_i}(f(\delta, \ell)) \nabla_{\varphi\varphi} f_i(\delta, \ell) \Big\} q_i \Big\} \in -K \setminus \{0\}.$$

Since $\lambda \in \mathrm{int} K^*$, we get

$$\sum_{i=1}^{k} \lambda_i \Big\{ G_{f_i}(f_i(\varphi, \vartheta)) - \vartheta^T \sum_{i=1}^{k} \lambda_i \Big[G'_{f_i}(f_i(\varphi, \vartheta)) \nabla_\vartheta f_i(\varphi, \vartheta) + \Big\{ G''_{f_i}(f_i(\varphi, \vartheta)) \nabla_\vartheta f_i(\varphi, \vartheta)(\nabla_\vartheta f_i(\varphi, \vartheta))^T$$
$$+ G'_{f_i}(f_i(\varphi, \vartheta)) \nabla_{\vartheta\vartheta} f_i(\varphi, \vartheta) \Big\} p_i \Big] - \delta^T \sum_{i=1}^{k} \lambda_i \Big[G'_{f_i}(f_i(\delta, \ell)) \nabla_\varphi f_i(\delta, \ell) + \Big\{ G''_{f_i}(f_i(\delta, \ell)) \nabla_\varphi f_i(\delta, \ell)$$
$$(\nabla_\varphi f_i(\delta, \ell))^T \Big\} \Big] - \tfrac{1}{2} \sum_{i=1}^{k} \lambda_i p_i^T \Big\{ G''_{f_i}(f_i(\varphi, \vartheta)) \nabla_\vartheta f_i(\varphi, \vartheta)(\nabla_\vartheta f_i(\varphi, \vartheta))^T + G'_{f_i}(f_i(\varphi, \vartheta)) \nabla_{\vartheta\vartheta} f_i(\varphi, \vartheta) \Big\} - \Big\{ G_{f_i}(f_i(\delta, \ell))$$
$$+ G'_{f_i}(f_i(\delta, \ell)) \nabla_{\varphi\varphi} f_i(\delta, \ell) \Big\} - \tfrac{1}{2} \sum_{i=1}^{k} \lambda_i q_i^T \Big\{ G''_{f_i}(f_i(\delta, \ell))(\nabla_\varphi f_i(\delta, \ell))(\nabla_\varphi f_i(\delta, \ell))^T + G'_{f_i}(f_i(\delta, \ell)) \nabla_{\varphi\varphi} f_i(\varphi, \vartheta) \Big\} q_i \Big\} < 0. \tag{5}$$

By hypothesis (i) and using $\lambda \in \mathrm{int} K^*$, we get

$$\sum_{i=1}^{k} \lambda_i \left\{ G_{f_i}(f_i(\varphi,\ell)) - G_{f_i}(f_i(\delta,\ell)) + \frac{1}{2} q_i^T \left\{ G''_{f_i}(f_i(\delta,\ell))(\nabla_\varphi f_i(\delta,\ell))\nabla_\varphi f_i(\delta,\ell)^T + G'_{f_i}(f_i(\delta,\ell))\nabla_{\varphi\varphi} f_i(\delta,\ell) \right\} q_i \right\}$$
$$- \eta_1^T(\varphi,\delta) \left[G'_{f_i}(f_i(\delta,\ell))\nabla_\varphi f_i(\delta,\ell) + \left\{ G''_{f_i}(f_i(\delta,\ell))(\nabla_\varphi f_i(\delta,\ell))\nabla_\varphi f_i(\delta,\ell)^T + G'_{f_i}(f_i(\delta,\ell))\nabla_{\varphi\varphi} f_i(\delta,\ell) \right\} q_i \right] \right\} \geqq 0,$$

Using feasibility of dual problem (GWDP) & using dual constraints with assumption (iii), it yields

$$\left(\eta_1(\varphi,\delta) + \delta \right)^T \sum_{i=1}^{k} \lambda_i \left[G'_{f_i}(f_i(\delta,\ell))\nabla_\varphi f_i(\delta,\ell) + \left\{ G''_{f_i}(f_i(\delta,\ell))(\nabla_\varphi f_i(\delta,\ell))(\nabla_\varphi f_i(\delta,\ell))^T + G'_{f_i}(f_i(\delta,\ell))\nabla_\varphi f_i(\delta,\ell) \right\} q_i \right] \geqq 0,$$

it implies that

$$\sum_{i=1}^{k} \lambda_i \left[G_{f_i}(f_i(\varphi,\ell)) - G_{f_i}(f_i(\delta,\ell)) + \frac{1}{2} q_i^T \left\{ G''_{f_i}(f_i(\delta,\ell))(\nabla_\varphi f_i(\delta,\ell))(\nabla_\varphi f_i(\delta,\ell))^T + G'_{f_i}(f_i(\delta,\ell))\nabla_{\varphi\varphi} f_i(\delta,\ell) \right\} q_i \right]$$
$$\geqq -\delta^T \sum_{i=1}^{k} \lambda_i \left[G'_{f_i}(f_i(\delta,\ell))\nabla_\varphi(f_i(\delta,\ell)) + \left\{ G''_{f_i}(f_i(\delta,\ell))(\nabla_\varphi f_i(\delta,\ell))(\nabla_\varphi f_i(\delta,\ell))^T + G'_{f_i}(f_i(\delta,\ell))\nabla_{\varphi\varphi} f_i(\delta,\ell) \right\} q_i \right]. \quad (6)$$

Similarly, using hypotheses (ii), (iv), feasible conditions of primal problem (GWPP), dual constraint and $\lambda \in intK^*$, we get

$$\sum_{i=1}^{k} \lambda_i \left[G_{f_i}(f_i(\varphi,\vartheta)) - G_{f_i}(f_i(\varphi,\ell)) + \frac{1}{2} p_i^T \left\{ G''_{f_i}(f_i(\delta,\ell))(\nabla_\vartheta f_i(\delta,\ell))(\nabla_\vartheta f_i(\delta,\ell))^T + G'_{f_i}(f_i(\delta,\ell))\nabla_{\varphi\varphi} f_i(\delta,\ell) \right\} p_i \right]$$
$$\geqq \vartheta^T \sum_{i=1}^{k} \lambda_i \left[G'_{f_i}(f_i(\delta,\ell))\nabla_\vartheta(f_i(\delta,\ell)) + \left\{ G''_{f_i}(f_i(\delta,\ell))(\nabla_\varphi f_i(\delta,\ell))(\nabla_\varphi f_i(\delta,\ell))^T + G'_{f_i}(f_i(\delta,\ell))\nabla_{\varphi\varphi} f_i(\delta,\ell) \right\} p_i \right]. \quad (7)$$

Now, from inequalities (6), (7) and using the fact that $\lambda^T e_k = 1$, we find that

$$\sum_{i=1}^{k} \lambda_i \left[G_{f_i}(f_i(\varphi,\vartheta)) - \vartheta^T \sum_{i=1}^{k} \lambda_i \left[G'_{f_i}(f_i(\varphi,\vartheta))\nabla_\vartheta(f_i(\varphi,\vartheta)) + \left\{ G''_{f_i}(f_i(\varphi,\vartheta))(\nabla_\vartheta f_i(\delta,\ell))(\nabla_\vartheta f_i(\delta,\ell))^T + G'_{f_i}(f_i(\varphi,\vartheta))\nabla_{\vartheta\vartheta} f_i(\varphi,\vartheta) \right\} p_i \right]$$
$$- \frac{1}{2} \sum_{i=1}^{k} \lambda_i p_i^T \left\{ G''_{f_i}(f_i(\varphi,\vartheta))(\nabla_\vartheta f_i(\varphi,\vartheta))(\nabla_\vartheta f_i(\varphi,\vartheta))^T + G'_{f_i}(f_i(\varphi,\vartheta))\nabla_{\vartheta\vartheta} f_i(\varphi,\vartheta) \right\} - G_{f_i}(f_i(\delta,\ell))$$
$$- \delta^T \sum_{i=1}^{k} \lambda_i \left[G'_{f_i}(f_i(\delta,\ell))\nabla_\varphi(f_i(\delta,\ell)) + \left\{ G''_{f_i}(f_i(\delta,\ell))(\nabla_\varphi f_i(\delta,\ell))(\nabla_\varphi f_i(\delta,\ell))^T + G'_{f_i}(f_i(\delta,\ell))\nabla_{\varphi\varphi} f_i(\delta,\ell) \right\} \right]$$
$$- \frac{1}{2} \delta^T \sum_{i=1}^{k} \lambda_i q_i^T \left\{ G''_{f_i}(f_i(\delta,\ell))(\nabla_\varphi f_i(\delta,\ell))(\nabla_\varphi f_i(\delta,\ell))^T + G'_{f_i}(f_i(\delta,\ell))(\nabla_\varphi f_i(\delta,\ell)) q_i \right\} \right] \geqq 0,$$

we arrive at contradiction. □

Through following example, we validate the Weak duality theorem as:

Example 4. Let $n=m=1$, $k=2$, $X = [1,2]$, $p \in [2^2, 2^{10}]$, $q \in [10^{-19}, 10^{19}]$, $K = \left\{ (\varphi, \vartheta); \varphi \geqq 0, \varphi \geqq \vartheta \right\}$ and

$$- K = \left\{ (\varphi, \vartheta); \varphi \leq 0, \varphi \leq \vartheta \right\}, R_1 = R_2 = R_+. \text{ Let } f_i : R_1 \times R_2 \to R \text{ and } G_{f_i} \text{ for } i = 1, 2. \text{ be defined as}$$

$$f_1(\varphi, \vartheta) = \varphi + \cos\vartheta, \ f_2(\varphi, \vartheta) = \sin\vartheta, \ G_{f_1}(t) = t^2, \ G_{f_2}(t) = t.$$

Further, let

$$\eta_1(\varphi, \delta) = \varphi\delta, \ \eta_2(\ell, \vartheta) = \ell - \vartheta.$$

Assume that $C_1 = C_2 = C_1^* = C_2^* = R_+$.

(GWPP) K-minimize $L(\varphi, \vartheta, \lambda, p) = \{L_1(\varphi, \vartheta, \lambda, p),\ L_2(\varphi, \vartheta, \lambda, p)\}$

Subject to constraints

$$\lambda_1 \left[2(\varphi + \cos\vartheta)(-\sin\vartheta) + \{2\sin^2\vartheta + 2(\varphi + \cos\vartheta)(-\cos\vartheta)\} p_1 \right] + \lambda_2 \left[\cos\vartheta - p_2 \sin\vartheta \right] \leqq 0, \tag{8}$$

$$\lambda_1 + \lambda_2 = 1, \lambda_i \in \text{int} K^*, \varphi \in C_1, i = 1, 2. \tag{9}$$

(GWDP) K-maximize $M(\delta, \ell, \lambda, q) = \{M_1(\delta, \ell, \lambda, q),\ M_2(\delta, \ell, \lambda, q)\}$

Subject to constraints

$$\lambda_1 \left[2(\varphi + \cos\vartheta) + 2q_1 \right] \geqq 0, \tag{10}$$

$$\lambda_1 + \lambda_2 = 1,\ \lambda_i \in \text{int} K^*,\ \varphi \in C_2,\ i = 1, 2. \tag{11}$$

(A1). $\{f_1(.,\ell), f_2(.,\ell)\}$ is K-G_f-bonvex at $\delta = 0$ w.r.t. η_1, $\forall\ \varphi \in S_1$, i.e.,

$$\Big\{ G_{f_1}(f_1(\varphi,\ell)) - G_{f_1}(f_1(\delta,\ell)) + \frac{1}{2} p_1^T \left[G''_{f_1}(f_1(\delta,\ell)) \nabla_\varphi f_1(\delta,\ell)(\nabla_\varphi f_1(\delta,\ell))^T + G'_{f_1}(f_1(\delta,\ell)) \nabla_{\varphi\varphi} f_1(\delta,\ell) \right] p_1$$
$$-\eta^T(\varphi,\delta)\left[G'_{f_1}(f_1(\delta,\ell)) \nabla_\varphi f_1(\delta,\ell) + \{G''_{f_1}(f_1(\delta,\ell)) \nabla_\varphi f_1(\delta,\ell)(\nabla_\varphi f_1(\delta,\ell))^T + G'_{f_1}(f_1(\delta,\ell)) \nabla_{\varphi\varphi} f_1(\delta,\ell)\} p_1 \right],$$
$$G_{f_2}(f_2(\varphi,\ell)) - G_{f_2}(f_2(\delta,\ell)) + \frac{1}{2} p_2^T \left[G''_{f_2}(f_2(\delta,\ell)) \nabla_\varphi f_2(\delta,\ell)(\nabla_\varphi f_2(\delta,\ell))^T + G'_{f_2}(f_2(\delta,\ell)) \nabla_{\varphi\varphi} f_2(\delta,\ell) \right] p_2$$
$$-\eta^T(\varphi,\delta)\left[G'_{f_2}(f_2(\delta,\ell)) \nabla_\varphi f_2(\delta,\ell) + \{G''_{f_2}(f_2(\delta,\ell)) \nabla_\varphi f_2(\delta,\ell)(\nabla_\varphi f_2(\delta,\ell))^T + G'_{f_2}(f_2(\delta,\ell)) \nabla_{\varphi\varphi} f_2(\delta,\ell)\} p_2 \right] \Big\} \in K. \tag{12}$$

Consider

$$\Psi = \Big\{ G_{f_1}(f_1(\varphi,\ell)) - G_{f_1}(f_1(\delta,\ell)) + \frac{1}{2} p_1^T \left[G''_{f_1}(f_1(\delta,\ell)) \nabla_\varphi f_1(\delta,\ell)(\nabla_\varphi f_1(\delta,\ell))^T + G'_{f_1}(f_1(\delta,\ell)) \nabla_{\varphi\varphi} f_1(\delta,\ell) \right] p_1$$
$$-\eta^T(\varphi,\delta)\left[G'_{f_1}(f_1(\delta,\ell)) \nabla_\varphi f_1(\delta,\ell) + \{G''_{f_1}(f_1(\delta,\ell)) \nabla_\varphi f_1(\delta,\ell)(\nabla_\varphi f_1(\delta,\ell))^T + G'_{f_1}(f_1(\delta,\ell)) \nabla_{\varphi\varphi} f_1(\delta,\ell)\} p_1 \right],$$
$$G_{f_2}(f_2(\varphi,\ell)) - G_{f_2}(f_2(\delta,\ell)) + \frac{1}{2} p_2^T \left[G''_{f_2}(f_2(\delta,\ell)) \nabla_\varphi f_2(\delta,\ell)(\nabla_\varphi f_2(\delta,\ell))^T + G'_{f_2}(f_2(\delta,\ell)) \nabla_{\varphi\varphi} f_2(\delta,\ell) \right] p_2$$
$$-\eta^T(\varphi,\delta)\left[G'_{f_2}(f_2(\delta,\ell)) \nabla_\varphi f_2(\delta,\ell) + \{G''_{f_2}(f_2(\delta,\ell)) \nabla_\varphi f_2(\delta,\ell)(\nabla_\varphi f_2(\delta,\ell))^T + G'_{f_2}(f_2(\delta,\ell)) \nabla_{\varphi\varphi} f_2(\delta,\ell)\} p_2 \right] \Big\}. \tag{13}$$

Putting the values of $f_1, f_2, G_{f_1}, G_{f_2}$ and η_1 at the point $\delta = 0$, and simplifying, we get

$$\Psi = \left(\varphi^2 + 2\varphi \cos\ell + p^2,\ 0 \right).$$

It is clear that

$$\Psi = \left(\varphi^2 + 2\varphi \cos\ell + p^2,\ 0 \right) \in K.$$

(A2). $\{f_1(\varphi,.), f_2(\varphi,.)\}$ is K-G_f-boncave at $\vartheta = 0$ w.r.t. η_2, $\ell \in S_2$,

$$\Big\{ G_{f_1}(f_1(\varphi,\ell)) - G_{f_1}(f_1(\varphi,\vartheta)) + \frac{1}{2} p_1^T \left[G''_{f_1}(f_1(\varphi,\vartheta)) \nabla_\vartheta f_1(\varphi,\vartheta)(\nabla_\vartheta f_1(\varphi,\vartheta))^T + G'_{f_1}(f_1(\varphi,\vartheta)) \nabla_{\vartheta\vartheta} f_1(\varphi,\vartheta) \right] p_1$$
$$-\eta^T(\ell,\vartheta)\left[G'_{f_1}(f_1(\varphi,\vartheta)) \nabla_\vartheta f_1(\varphi,\vartheta) + \{G''_{f_1}(f_1(\varphi,\vartheta)) \nabla_\vartheta f_1(\varphi,\vartheta)(\nabla_\vartheta f_1(\varphi,\vartheta))^T + G'_{f_1}(f_1(\varphi,\vartheta)) \nabla_{\vartheta\vartheta} f_1(\varphi,\vartheta)\} p_1 \right],$$
$$G_{f_2}(f_2(\varphi,\ell)) - G_{f_2}(f_2(\varphi,\vartheta)) + \frac{1}{2} p_2^T \left[G''_{f_2}(f_2(\varphi,\vartheta)) \nabla_\vartheta f_2(\varphi,\vartheta)(\nabla_\vartheta f_2(\varphi,\vartheta))^T + G'_{f_2}(f_2(\varphi,\vartheta)) \nabla_{\vartheta\vartheta} f_2(\varphi,\vartheta) \right] p_2$$

$$-\eta^T(\ell,\vartheta)\left[G'_{f_2}(f_2(\varphi,\vartheta))\nabla_\vartheta f_2(\varphi,\vartheta) + \left\{G''_{f_2}(f_2(\varphi,\vartheta))\nabla_\vartheta f_2(\varphi,\vartheta)(\nabla_\vartheta f_2(\varphi,\vartheta))^T + G'_{f_2}(f_2(\varphi,\vartheta))\nabla_{\vartheta\vartheta} f_2(\varphi,\vartheta)\right\}p_2\right]\right] \in -K. \quad (14)$$

Let $\Psi_1 = \Big\{ G_{f_1}(f_1(\varphi,\ell)) - G_{f_1}(f_1(\varphi,\vartheta)) + \frac{1}{2}p_1^T\Big[G''_{f_1}(f_1(\varphi,\vartheta))\nabla_\vartheta f_1(\varphi,\vartheta)(\nabla_\vartheta f_1(\varphi,\vartheta))^T + G'_{f_1}(f_1(\varphi,\vartheta))\nabla_{\vartheta\vartheta} f_1(\varphi,\vartheta)\Big]p_1$
$-\eta^T(\ell,\vartheta)\Big[G'_{f_1}(f_1(\varphi,\vartheta))\nabla_\vartheta f_1(\varphi,\vartheta) + \big\{G''_{f_1}(f_1(\varphi,\vartheta))\nabla_\vartheta f_1(\varphi,\vartheta)(\nabla_\vartheta f_1(\varphi,\vartheta))^T + G'_{f_1}(f_1(\varphi,\vartheta))\nabla_{\vartheta\vartheta} f_1(\varphi,\vartheta)\big\}p_1\Big],$
$G_{f_2}(f_2(\varphi,\ell)) - G_{f_2}(f_2(\varphi,\vartheta)) + \frac{1}{2}p_2^T\Big[G''_{f_2}(f_2(\varphi,\vartheta))\nabla_\vartheta f_2(\varphi,\vartheta)(\nabla_\vartheta f_2(\varphi,\vartheta))^T + G'_{f_2}(f_2(\varphi,\vartheta))\nabla_{\vartheta\vartheta} f_2(\varphi,\vartheta)\Big]p_2$
$-\eta^T(\ell,\vartheta)\Big[G'_{f_2}(f_2(\varphi,\vartheta))\nabla_\vartheta f_2(\varphi,\vartheta) + \big\{G''_{f_2}(f_2(\varphi,\vartheta))\nabla_\vartheta f_2(\varphi,\vartheta)(\nabla_\vartheta f_2(\varphi,\vartheta))^T + G'_{f_2}(f_2(\varphi,\vartheta))\nabla_{\vartheta\vartheta} f_2(\varphi,\vartheta)\big\}p_2\Big]\Big\}. \quad (15)$

Putting the values of $f_1, f_2, G_{f_1}, G_{f_2}$ and η_2 at $\vartheta = 0$, we obtain

$$\Psi_1 = \Big((\varphi+\cos\ell)^2 - (\varphi+1)^2 - p_1^2(\varphi+1) + 2\ell(\varphi+1),\ \sin\ell - \ell\Big).$$

$$\Psi_1 = \Big((\varphi+\cos\ell)^2 - (\varphi+1)^2 - p_1^2(\varphi+1) + 2\ell(\varphi+1),\ \sin\ell - \ell\Big) \in -K.$$

(A3). $\eta_1(\varphi,\delta) + \delta \in C_1,\ \forall\ \varphi \in C_1.$

(A4). $\eta_2(\ell,\vartheta) + \vartheta \in C_2,\ \forall\ \ell \in C_2.$

Validation: To validate Weak duality theorem it is enough to claim that any point $(\varphi, 0, \lambda_1, \lambda_2, p)$ such that $\varphi \geqq 0, \lambda_1 + \lambda_2 = 1$ are feasible to $(GWPP)$. Also, the points $(0, \ell, \lambda_1, \lambda_2, q)$ such that $\ell \geqq 0, \lambda_1 + \lambda_2 = 1$ are feasible to $(GWDP)$. Now, at these feasible points,

$$L = (L_1, L_2) = \Big((\varphi+1)^2 + \lambda_1 p_1^2(\varphi+1),\ \lambda_1 p_1^2(\varphi+1)\Big),$$

and

$$M = (M_1, M_2) = \Big(\cos^2\ell - \lambda_1 q_1^2,\ \sin\ell - \lambda_1 q_1^2\Big).$$

Now, calculate the value at above feasible points, we have

$$L(\varphi,\vartheta,\lambda,p) - M(\delta,\ell,\lambda,q) = \Big((\varphi+1)^2 + \lambda_1 p_1^2(\varphi+1) - \cos^2\ell + \lambda_1 q_1^2,\ \lambda_1 p_1^2(\varphi+1) - \sin\ell + \lambda_1 q_1^2\Big) \notin K\setminus\{0\}. \quad (16)$$

In particular, the points $\left(\varphi,\vartheta,\lambda_1,\lambda_2,p\right) = \left(1,0,\frac{1}{2},\frac{1}{2},4\right)$ and $\left(\delta,\ell,\lambda_1,\lambda_2,q\right) = \left(0,\frac{22}{14},\frac{1}{2},\frac{1}{2},2\right)$ are feasible solutions for $(GWPP)$ and $(GWDP)$, respectively. Also

$$L(\varphi,\vartheta,\lambda,p) - M(\delta,\ell,\lambda,q) = (22,17) \notin -K\setminus\{0\}. \quad (17)$$

Hence, this validate the results.

Remark 2. *Every pseudoconvex function is convex function. On the same pattern we can proof that K-G_f-pseudobonvex is K-G_f-bonvex with respect to same η. So, above proof of Weak duality 3.2 follows on same pattern as Theorem 1.*

Theorem 2 (Weak duality). *Let $(\varphi,\vartheta,\lambda,p) \in V^*$ and $(\delta,\ell,\lambda,q) \in W^*$. Let, For $i \in \tilde{N}$*

(i) $\{f_1(.,\ell), f_2(.,\ell), ..., f_k(.,\ell)\}$ *be K-G_f-pseudobonvex at ℓ w.r.t. η_1,*

(ii) $\{f_1(\varphi,.), f_2(\varphi,.), ..., f_k(\varphi,.)\}$ *be K-G_f-pseudoboncave at ϑ, w.r.t. η_2,*

(iii) $\eta_1(\varphi,\delta) + \delta \in C_1, \forall\ (\varphi,\delta) \in C_1 \times C_2,$

(iv) $\eta_2(\ell, \vartheta) + \vartheta \in C_2, \forall (\ell, \vartheta) \in C_1 \times C_2$,

Then, $L(\varphi, \vartheta, \lambda, p) - M(\delta, \ell, \lambda, q) \notin -K \setminus \{0\}$.

Proof. Proof follows on same lines as Weak Duality Theorem 1. □

Example 5. *For* $n = m = 1$, $k = 2$, $X = [2,3]$, $p \in [0,1]$, $q \in [2, 2^{10}]$, $K = \{(\varphi, \vartheta); \varphi \leqq 0, \vartheta \geqq 0, |\varphi| \geqq \vartheta\}$,

$$R_1 = R_2 = R_+. \text{ Let } f_i : R_1 \times R_2 \to R \text{ be given as}$$

$$f_1(\varphi, \vartheta) = \varphi + \vartheta^2, \ f_2(\varphi, \vartheta) = 1 - \vartheta, \ G_{f_1}(t) = t^2, \ G_{f_2}(t) = t.$$

Further, Let

$$\eta_1(\varphi, \delta) = \varphi\delta, \ \eta_2(\ell, \vartheta) = \ell - \vartheta.$$

Assume that $C_1 = C_2 = C_1^* = C_2^* = R_+$.

(GWPP) K-minimize $L(\varphi, \vartheta, \lambda, p) = \{L_1(\varphi, \vartheta, \lambda, p), \ L_2(\varphi, \vartheta, \lambda, p)\}$

Subject to constraints

$$\lambda_1 \left[4\vartheta(\varphi + \vartheta^2) + p_1\{8\vartheta^2 + 4(\varphi + \vartheta^2)\} \right] - \lambda_2 \leqq 0, \tag{18}$$

$$\lambda_1 + \lambda_2 = 1, \ \lambda_i \in \text{int} K^*, \ \varphi \in C_1, \ i = 1, 2. \tag{19}$$

(GWDP) K-maximize $M(\delta, \ell, \lambda, q) = \{M_1(\delta, \ell, \lambda, q), \ M_2(\delta, \ell, \lambda, q)\}$

Subject to constraints

$$\lambda_1 \left[2(\delta + \ell^2 + q) \right] \geqq 0, \tag{20}$$

$$\lambda_1 + \lambda_2 = 1, \ \lambda_i \in \text{int} K^*, \ \delta \in C_2, \ i = 1, 2. \tag{21}$$

(A1). $\{f_1(., \ell), \ f_2(., \ell)\}$ is K-G_f-pseudobonvex at δ with respect to η_1, $\varphi \in R_1$, so that

$$\eta_1^T(\varphi, \delta) \Big\{ G'_{f_1}(f_1(\delta, \ell)) \nabla_\varphi f_1(\delta, \ell) + p \Big\{ G''_{f_1}(f_1(\delta, \ell)) (\nabla_\varphi f_1(\delta, \ell))^T + G'_{f_1}(f_1(\delta, \ell)) \nabla_{\varphi\varphi} f_1(\delta, \ell) \Big\},$$

$$G'_{f_2}(f_2(\delta, \ell)) \nabla_\varphi f_2(\delta, \ell) + p \Big\{ G''_{f_2}(f_2(\delta, \ell)) (\nabla_\varphi f_2(\delta, \ell))^T + G'_{f_2}(f_2(\delta, \ell)) \nabla_{\varphi\varphi} f_2(\delta, \ell) \Big\} \Big\} \in K. \tag{22}$$

Let

$$\Pi_1 = \eta_1^T(\varphi, \delta) \Big\{ G'_{f_1}(f_1(\delta, \ell)) \nabla_\varphi f_1(\delta, \ell) + p \Big\{ G''_{f_1}(f_1(\delta, \ell)) (\nabla_\varphi f_1(\delta, \ell))^T + G'_{f_1}(f_1(\delta, \ell)) \nabla_{\varphi\varphi} f_1(\delta, \ell) \Big\},$$

$$G'_{f_2}(f_2(\delta, \ell)) \nabla_\varphi f_2(\delta, \ell) + p \Big\{ G''_{f_2}(f_2(\delta, \ell)) (\nabla_\varphi f_2(\delta, \ell))^T + G'_{f_2}(f_2(\delta, \ell)) \nabla_{\varphi\varphi} f_2(\delta, \ell) \Big\} \Big\}. \tag{23}$$

Next, let

$$\Pi_2 = \Big[G_{f_1}(f_1(\varphi, \ell)) - G_{f_1}(f_1(\delta, \ell)) + \frac{1}{2} p^T \Big\{ G''_{f_1}(f_1(\delta, \ell)) \nabla_\varphi f_1(\delta, \ell) (\nabla_\varphi f_1(\delta, \ell))^T + G'_{f_1}(f_1(\delta, \ell)) \nabla_{\varphi\varphi} f_1(\delta, \ell) \Big\} p,$$

$$G_{f_2}(f_2(\varphi, \ell)) - G_{f_2}(f_2(\delta, \ell)) + \frac{1}{2} p^T \Big\{ G''_{f_2}(f_2(\delta, \ell)) \nabla_\varphi f_2(\delta, \ell) (\nabla_\varphi f_2(\delta, \ell))^T + G'_{f_2}(f_2(\delta, \ell)) \nabla_{\varphi\varphi} f_2(\delta, \ell) \Big\} p \Big]. \tag{24}$$

After simplification, substituting the value of f_1, f_2, G_{f_1}, G_{f_2} and η_1 at $\delta = 0$, we get

$$\Pi_1 = (0, 0) \in K \Rightarrow \Pi_2 = (\varphi^2 - 2\varphi\ell^2 + p^2, 0) \in K.$$

(A2). $\{f_1(\varphi, .), f_2(\varphi, .)\}$ is K-G_f-pseudoboncave at ϑ with respect to η_2 for fixed φ for all $\ell \in S_2$, i.e.,

$$\eta_2^T(\varphi, \delta)\{G'_{f_1}(f_1(\varphi, \vartheta))\nabla_\vartheta f_1(\varphi, \vartheta) + q\{G''_{f_1}(f_1(\varphi, \vartheta))(\nabla_\vartheta f_1(\varphi, \vartheta))^T + G'_{f_1}(f_1(\varphi, \vartheta))\nabla_{\vartheta\vartheta} f_1(\varphi, \vartheta)\}, G'_{f_2}(f_2(\varphi, \vartheta))\nabla_\vartheta f_2(\varphi, \vartheta)$$
$$+ q\{G''_{f_2}(f_2(\varphi, \vartheta))(\nabla_\vartheta f_2(\varphi, \vartheta))^T + G'_{f_2}(f_2(\varphi, \vartheta))\nabla_{\vartheta\vartheta} f_2(\varphi, \vartheta)\}\} \in K$$
$$\Rightarrow \left[G_{f_1}(f_1(\varphi, \ell)) - G_{f_1}(f_1(\varphi, \vartheta)) + \frac{1}{2}q^T\{G''_{f_1}(f_1(\varphi, \vartheta))\nabla_\vartheta f_1(\varphi, \vartheta)(\nabla_\vartheta f_1(\varphi, \vartheta))^T + G'_{f_1}(f_1(\varphi, \vartheta))\nabla_{\vartheta\vartheta} f_1(\varphi, \vartheta)\}q,\right.$$

$$G_{f_2}(f_2(\varphi, \ell)) - G_{f_2}(f_2(\varphi, \vartheta)) + \frac{1}{2}q^T\{G''_{f_2}(f_2(\varphi, \vartheta))\nabla_\vartheta f_2(\varphi, \vartheta)(\nabla_\vartheta f_2(\varphi, \vartheta))^T + G'_{f_2}(f_2(\varphi, \vartheta))\nabla_{\vartheta\vartheta} f_2(\varphi, \vartheta)\}q\right] \in -K. \tag{25}$$

Let $\Pi_3 = \eta_2^T(\varphi, \delta)\{G'_{f_1}(f_1(\varphi, \vartheta))\nabla_\vartheta f_1(\varphi, \vartheta) + q\{G''_{f_1}(f_1(\varphi, \vartheta))(\nabla_\vartheta f_1(\varphi, \vartheta))^T + G'_{f_1}(f_1(\varphi, \vartheta))\nabla_{\vartheta\vartheta} f_1(\varphi, \vartheta)\},$

$$G'_{f_2}(f_2(\varphi, \vartheta))\nabla_\vartheta f_2(\varphi, \vartheta) + q\{G''_{f_2}(f_2(\varphi, \vartheta))(\nabla_\vartheta f_2(\varphi, \vartheta))^T + G'_{f_2}(f_2(\varphi, \vartheta))\nabla_{\vartheta\vartheta} f_2(\varphi, \vartheta)\}\}, \tag{26}$$

and

$$\Pi_4 = \left[G_{f_1}(f_1(\varphi, \ell)) - G_{f_1}(f_1(\varphi, \vartheta)) + \frac{1}{2}q^T\{G''_{f_1}(f_1(\varphi, \vartheta))\nabla_\vartheta f_1(\varphi, \vartheta)(\nabla_\vartheta f_1(\varphi, \vartheta))^T + G'_{f_1}(f_1(\varphi, \vartheta))\nabla_{\vartheta\vartheta} f_1(\varphi, \vartheta)\}q,\right.$$

$$\left.G_{f_2}(f_2(\varphi, \ell)) - G_{f_2}(f_2(\varphi, \vartheta)) + \frac{1}{2}q^T\{G''_{f_2}(f_2(\varphi, \vartheta))\nabla_\vartheta f_2(\varphi, \vartheta)(\nabla_\vartheta f_2(\varphi, \vartheta))^T + G'_{f_2}(f_2(\varphi, \vartheta))\nabla_{\vartheta\vartheta} f_2(\varphi, \vartheta)\}q\right]. \tag{27}$$

Substituting the value of f_1, f_2, G_{f_1}, G_{f_2} and η_2 at the point $\delta = 0$ and simplify, we get

$$\Pi_3 = \left(4vq\varphi, -1\right) \in -K \Rightarrow \Pi_4 = \left(\ell^4 + 2\varphi\ell^2, -\ell\right) \in -K.$$

(A3). $\eta_1(\varphi, \delta) + \delta \in C_1, \forall \varphi \in C_1$.

(A4). $\eta_2(\ell, \vartheta) + \vartheta \in C_2, \forall \ell \in C_2$.

Validation: To prove our result its enough to prove that any point $\left(\varphi, 0, \lambda_1, \lambda_2, p\right)$ such that $\varphi \geqq 0$, $\lambda_1 + \lambda_2 = 1$ are feasible to $(GWPP)$. Also, the points $\left(0, \ell, \lambda_1, \lambda_2, q\right)$ such that $\ell \geqq 0$, $\lambda_1 + \lambda_2 = 1$ are feasible to $(GWDP)$. Now, at these feasible points,

$$L = \left(L_1, L_2\right) = \left(\varphi^2 - 2\varphi\lambda_1 p^2, 1 - 2\varphi\lambda_1 p^2\right)$$

and

$$M = \left(M_1, M_2\right) = \left(\ell^4 - \lambda_1 q^2, 1 - \ell - \lambda_1 q^2\right).$$

Now at above feasible condition

$$L - M = \left(\varphi^2 - 2\varphi\lambda_1 p^2 - \ell^4 + \lambda_1 q^2, \ell - 2\varphi\lambda_1 p^2 + \lambda_1 q^2\right) \notin K\setminus\{0\}. \tag{28}$$

In particular, the points $\left(\varphi, \vartheta, \lambda_1, \lambda_2, p\right) = \left(2, 0, \frac{1}{2}, \frac{1}{2}, 1\right)$ and $\left(\delta, \ell, \lambda_1, \lambda_2, q\right) = \left(0, 2, \frac{1}{2}, \frac{1}{2}, 2\right)$ are

feasible for $(GWPP)$ and $(GWDP)$ respectively,
Now, calculate
$$L(\varphi, \vartheta, \lambda, p) - M(\delta, \ell, \lambda, q) = (-12, 2) \notin K \setminus \{0\}. \quad (29)$$

Hence, this validate the Weak duality Theorem 2.

Theorem 3 (Strong duality). *Let $(\bar{\varphi}, \bar{\vartheta}, \bar{\lambda}, \bar{p}_1 = \bar{p}_2 = \bar{p}_3 = ... = \bar{p}_k)$ is an efficient solution of $(GWPP)$; fix $\lambda = \bar{\lambda}$ in $(GWDP)$ such that*

(i) *for all* $i \in \tilde{N}$, $\left[G''_{f_i}(f_i(\bar{\varphi}, \bar{\vartheta})) \nabla_\vartheta f_i(\bar{\varphi}, \bar{\vartheta}) (\nabla_\vartheta f_i(\bar{\varphi}, \bar{\vartheta}))^T + G'_{f_i}(f_i(\bar{\varphi}, \bar{\vartheta})) \nabla_{\vartheta\vartheta} f_i(\bar{\varphi}, \bar{\vartheta}) \right]$ *is nonsingular,*

(ii) *the vector* $\sum_{i=1}^{k} \bar{\lambda}_i \nabla_\vartheta \left[\bar{p}_i \{ G''_{f_i}(f_i(\bar{\varphi}, \bar{\vartheta})) \nabla_\vartheta f_i(\bar{\varphi}, \bar{\vartheta}) (\nabla_\vartheta f_i(\bar{\varphi}, \bar{\vartheta}))^T + G'_{f_i}(f_i(\bar{\varphi}, \bar{\vartheta})) \nabla_{\vartheta\vartheta} f_i(\bar{\varphi}, \bar{\vartheta}) \} \bar{p}_i \right]$

$\notin span \left\{ G'_{f_1}(f_1(\bar{\varphi}, \bar{\vartheta})) \nabla_\vartheta f_1(\bar{\varphi}, \bar{\vartheta}), G'_{f_2}(f_2(\bar{\varphi}, \bar{\vartheta})) \nabla_\vartheta f_2(\bar{\varphi}, \bar{\vartheta}), ..., G'_{f_i}(f_i(\bar{\varphi}, \bar{\vartheta})) \nabla_\vartheta f_i(\bar{\varphi}, \bar{\vartheta}) \right\}$,

(iii) *the set of vectors* $\left\{ G'_{f_1}(f_1(\bar{\varphi}, \bar{\vartheta})) \nabla_\vartheta f_1(\bar{\varphi}, \bar{\vartheta}), G'_{f_2}(f_2(\bar{\varphi}, \bar{\vartheta})) \nabla_\vartheta f_2(\bar{\varphi}, \bar{\vartheta}), ..., G'_{f_k}(f_k(\bar{\varphi}, \bar{\vartheta})) \nabla_\vartheta f_k(\bar{\varphi}, \bar{\vartheta}) \right\}$ *are linearly independent,*

(iv) $\sum_{i=1}^{k} \bar{\lambda}_i \nabla_\vartheta \left[\bar{p}_i \{ G''_{f_i}(f_i(\bar{\varphi}, \bar{\vartheta})) \nabla_\vartheta f_i(\bar{\varphi}, \bar{\vartheta}) (\nabla_\vartheta f_i(\bar{\varphi}, \bar{\vartheta}))^T + G'_{f_i}(f_i(\bar{\varphi}, \bar{\vartheta})) \nabla_{\vartheta\vartheta} f_i(\bar{\varphi}, \bar{\vartheta}) \} \bar{p}_i \right] = 0 \Rightarrow \bar{p}_i = 0, \, \forall \, i$, *and*

(v) *K is closed convex pointed cone with $R^k_+ \subseteq K$.*

Then, $(\bar{\varphi}, \bar{\vartheta}, \bar{\lambda}, \bar{q}_1 = \bar{q}_2 = \bar{q}_3 = ... = \bar{q}_k = 0) \in W^*$ and $L(\bar{\varphi}, \bar{\vartheta}, \bar{p}) = M(\bar{\varphi}, \bar{\vartheta}, \bar{q})$. Also, if the hypotheses of Theorem 1 or Theorem 2 are satisfied for all feasible solutions for $(GWPP)$ and $(GWDP)$, then $(\bar{\varphi}, \bar{\vartheta}, \bar{\lambda}, \bar{p})$ and $(\bar{\varphi}, \bar{\vartheta}, \bar{\lambda}, \bar{q})$ is an efficient solution for $(GWPP)$ and $(GWDP)$, respectively.

Proof. Since $(\bar{\varphi}, \bar{\vartheta}, \bar{\lambda}, \bar{p}_1, \bar{p}_2, \bar{p}_3, ..., \bar{p}_k)$, is an efficient solution of $(GWPP)$, there exist $\alpha \in K^*$, $\beta \in C_2$ and $\bar{\eta} \in R$ such that the following Fritz-John optimality condition stated by [28] are satisfied at $(\bar{\varphi}, \bar{\vartheta}, \bar{\lambda}, \bar{p}_1, \bar{p}_2, \bar{p}_3, ..., \bar{p}_k)$:

$$(\varphi - \bar{\varphi})^T \left[\sum_{i=1}^{k} \alpha_i \left[G'_{f_i}(f_i(\bar{\varphi}, \bar{\vartheta})) \nabla_\varphi f_i(\bar{\varphi}, \bar{\vartheta}) \right] + \sum_{i=1}^{k} \bar{\lambda}_i \left[G''_{f_i}(f_i(\bar{\varphi}, \bar{\vartheta})) \nabla_\vartheta f_i(\bar{\varphi}, \bar{\vartheta}) \nabla_\varphi f_i(\bar{\varphi}, \bar{\vartheta}) + G'_{f_i}(f_i(\bar{\varphi}, \bar{\vartheta})) \nabla_{\varphi\vartheta} f_i(\bar{\varphi}, \bar{\vartheta}) \right] \left[\beta - (\bar{\alpha}^T e_k) \bar{\vartheta} \right]$$
$$+ \sum_{i=1}^{k} \bar{\lambda}_i \nabla_\varphi \left[(G''_{f_i}(f_i(\bar{\varphi}, \bar{\vartheta})) \nabla_\vartheta f_i(\bar{\varphi}, \bar{\vartheta}) (\nabla_\vartheta f_i(\bar{\varphi}, \bar{\vartheta}))^T + G'_{f_i}(f_i(\bar{\varphi}, \bar{\vartheta})) \nabla_{\vartheta\vartheta} f_i(\bar{\varphi}, \bar{\vartheta})) \bar{p}_i \right] \left(\beta - (\bar{\alpha}^T e_k) \left(\bar{\vartheta} + \frac{1}{2} \bar{p}_i \right) \right) \right] \geqq 0, \, \forall \, \varphi \in C_1, \quad (30)$$

$$(\vartheta - \bar{\vartheta})^T \left\{ \sum_{i=1}^{k} \alpha_i \left[G'_{f_i}(f_i(\bar{\varphi}, \bar{\vartheta})) \nabla_\vartheta f_i(\bar{\varphi}, \bar{\vartheta}) \right] + \sum_{i=1}^{k} \bar{\lambda}_i \left[G''_{f_i}(f_i(\bar{\varphi}, \bar{\vartheta})) \nabla_\vartheta f_i(\bar{\varphi}, \bar{\vartheta}) (\nabla_\vartheta f_i(\bar{\varphi}, \bar{\vartheta}))^T + G'_{f_i}(f_i(\bar{\varphi}, \bar{\vartheta})) \nabla_{\vartheta\vartheta} f_i(\bar{\varphi}, \bar{\vartheta}) \right] \right.$$
$$\left(\bar{\beta} - (\bar{\alpha}^T e_k) \bar{\vartheta} \right) + \sum_{i=1}^{k} \bar{\lambda}_i \nabla_\vartheta \left[(G''_{f_i}(f_i(\bar{\varphi}, \bar{\vartheta})) \nabla_\vartheta f_i(\bar{\varphi}, \bar{\vartheta}) (\nabla_\vartheta f_i(\bar{\varphi}, \bar{\vartheta}))^T + G'_{f_i}(f_i(\bar{\varphi}, \bar{\vartheta})) \nabla_{\vartheta\vartheta} f_i(\bar{\varphi}, \bar{\vartheta})) \bar{p}_i \right]$$
$$\left[\bar{\beta} - (\bar{\alpha}^T e_k) \left(\bar{\vartheta} + \frac{1}{2} \bar{p}_i \right) \right] - \sum_{i=1}^{k} \bar{\lambda}_i \left[G'_{f_i}(f_i(\bar{\varphi}, \bar{\vartheta})) \nabla_\vartheta f_i(\bar{\varphi}, \bar{\vartheta}) \right.$$
$$\left. \left. + (G''_{f_i}(f_i(\bar{\varphi}, \bar{\vartheta})) \nabla_\vartheta f_i(\bar{\varphi}, \bar{\vartheta}) (\nabla_\vartheta f_i(\bar{\varphi}, \bar{\vartheta}))^T + G'_{f_i}(f_i(\bar{\varphi}, \bar{\vartheta})) \nabla_{\vartheta\vartheta} f_i(\bar{\varphi}, \bar{\vartheta})) \bar{p}_i \right] (\bar{\alpha}^T e_k) \right\} \geqq 0, \, \forall \, \vartheta \in R^m, \quad (31)$$

$$G'_{f_i}(f_i(\bar{\varphi}, \bar{\vartheta})) \nabla_\vartheta f_i(\bar{\varphi}, \bar{\vartheta}) \left(\bar{\beta} - (\bar{\alpha}^T e_k) \bar{\vartheta} \right) + \bar{\eta} e_k + \left\{ \left\{ \beta - (\bar{\alpha}^T e_k) \left(\bar{\vartheta} + \frac{1}{2} \bar{p}_1 \right) \right\}^T \left(G''_{f_i}(f_i(\bar{\varphi}, \bar{\vartheta})) \nabla_\vartheta f_i(\bar{\varphi}, \bar{\vartheta}) (\nabla_\vartheta f_i(\bar{\varphi}, \bar{\vartheta}))^T \right. \right.$$
$$\left. + G'_{f_i}(f_i(\bar{\varphi}, \bar{\vartheta})) \nabla_{\vartheta\vartheta} f_i(\bar{\varphi}, \bar{\vartheta}) \right) \bar{p}_1, \left\{ \left\{ \beta - (\bar{\alpha}^T e_k) \left(\bar{\vartheta} + \frac{1}{2} \bar{p}_2 \right) \right\}^T \left(G''_{f_i}(f_i(\bar{\varphi}, \bar{\vartheta})) \nabla_\vartheta f_i(\bar{\varphi}, \bar{\vartheta}) (\nabla_\vartheta f_i(\bar{\varphi}, \bar{\vartheta}))^T \right. \right.$$
$$\left\{ \left\{ \beta - (\bar{\alpha}^T e_k) \left(\bar{\vartheta} + \frac{1}{2} \bar{p}_3 \right) \right\}^T \left(G''_{f_i}(f_i(\bar{\varphi}, \bar{\vartheta})) \nabla_\vartheta f_i(\bar{\varphi}, \bar{\vartheta}) (\nabla_\vartheta f_i(\bar{\varphi}, \bar{\vartheta}))^T + G'_{f_i}(f_i(\bar{\varphi}, \bar{\vartheta})) \nabla_{\vartheta\vartheta} f_i(\bar{\varphi}, \bar{\vartheta}) \right) \bar{p}_3, ..., \right.$$
$$\left\{ \left\{ \beta - (\bar{\alpha}^T e_k) \left(\bar{\vartheta} + \frac{1}{2} \bar{p}_3 \right) \right\}^T \left(G''_{f_i}(f_i(\bar{\varphi}, \bar{\vartheta})) \nabla_\vartheta f_i(\bar{\varphi}, \bar{\vartheta}) (\nabla_\vartheta f_i(\bar{\varphi}, \bar{\vartheta}))^T + G'_{f_i}(f_i(\bar{\varphi}, \bar{\vartheta})) \nabla_{\vartheta\vartheta} f_i(\bar{\varphi}, \bar{\vartheta}) \right) \bar{p}_k \right\} = 0, \quad (32)$$

$$\left[G''_{f_i}(f_i(\bar{\varphi},\bar{\vartheta}))\nabla_\vartheta f_i(\bar{\varphi},\bar{\vartheta})(\nabla_\vartheta f_i(\bar{\varphi},\bar{\vartheta}))^T + G'_{f_i}(f_i(\bar{\varphi},\bar{\vartheta}))\nabla_{\vartheta\vartheta} f_i(\bar{\varphi},\bar{\vartheta})\right]\left((\bar{\beta}-(\bar{\alpha}^T e_k)(\bar{p}_i+\bar{\vartheta}))\bar{\lambda}_i\right) = 0, \ i \in \tilde{N}, \quad (33)$$

$$\bar{\beta}^T \sum_{i=1}^{k} \bar{\lambda}_i \left[G'_{f_i}(f_i(\bar{\varphi},\bar{\vartheta}))\nabla_\vartheta f_i(\bar{\varphi},\bar{\vartheta}) + \left\{G''_{f_i}(f_i(\bar{\varphi},\bar{\vartheta}))\nabla_\varphi f_i(\bar{\varphi},\bar{\vartheta})(\nabla_\vartheta f_i(\bar{\varphi},\bar{\vartheta}))^T + G'_{f_i}(f_i(\bar{\varphi},\bar{\vartheta}))\nabla_{\vartheta\vartheta} f_i(\bar{\varphi},\bar{\vartheta})\right\}\bar{p}_i\right] = 0, \quad (34)$$

$$\bar{\eta}^T\left[\bar{\lambda}^T e_k - 1\right] = 0, \quad (35)$$

$$\left(\bar{\alpha},\bar{\beta},\bar{\eta}\right) \geqq 0, \ \left(\bar{\alpha},\bar{\beta},\bar{\eta}\right) \neq 0. \quad (36)$$

Inequalities (31) and (32) can be rewritten in the following expressions:

$$\sum_{i=1}^{k} \alpha_i \left[G'_{f_i}(f_i(\bar{\varphi},\bar{\vartheta}))\nabla_\vartheta f_i(\bar{\varphi},\bar{\vartheta})\right] + \sum_{i=1}^{k} \bar{\lambda}_i \left[G''_{f_i}(f_i(\bar{\varphi},\bar{\vartheta}))\nabla_\vartheta f_i(\bar{\varphi},\bar{\vartheta})(\nabla_\vartheta f_i(\bar{\varphi},\bar{\vartheta}))^T + G'_{f_i}(f_i(\bar{\varphi},\bar{\vartheta}))\nabla_{\vartheta\vartheta} f_i(\bar{\varphi},\bar{\vartheta})\right]$$

$$\left(\bar{\beta} - (\bar{\alpha}^T e_k)\bar{\vartheta}\right) + \sum_{i=1}^{k} \bar{\lambda}_i \nabla_\vartheta \left[(G''_{f_i}(f_i(\bar{\varphi},\bar{\vartheta}))\nabla_\vartheta f_i(\bar{\varphi},\bar{\vartheta})(\nabla_\vartheta f_i(\bar{\varphi},\bar{\vartheta}))^T + G'_{f_i}(f_i(\bar{\varphi},\bar{\vartheta}))\nabla_{\vartheta\vartheta} f_i(\bar{\varphi},\bar{\vartheta}))\bar{p}_i\right]$$

$$\left[\bar{\beta} - (\bar{\alpha}^T e_k)\left(\bar{\vartheta} + \frac{1}{2}\bar{p}_i\right)\right] - \sum_{i=1}^{k} \bar{\lambda}_i \Big[G'_{f_i}(f_i(\bar{\varphi},\bar{\vartheta}))\nabla_\vartheta f_i(\bar{\varphi},\bar{\vartheta})$$

$$+ \left(G''_{f_i}(f_i(\bar{\varphi},\bar{\vartheta}))\nabla_\vartheta f_i(\bar{\varphi},\bar{\vartheta})(\nabla_\vartheta f_i(\bar{\varphi},\bar{\vartheta}))^T + G'_{f_i}(f_i(\bar{\varphi},\bar{\vartheta}))\nabla_{\vartheta\vartheta} f_i(\bar{\varphi},\bar{\vartheta})\right)\bar{p}_i\Big](\bar{\alpha}^T e_k) = 0. \quad (37)$$

$$G'_{f_i}(f_i(\bar{\varphi},\bar{\vartheta}))\nabla_\vartheta f_i(\bar{\varphi},\bar{\vartheta})\left(\bar{\beta} - (\bar{\alpha}^T e_k)\bar{\vartheta}\right) + \left\{\left\{\beta - (\bar{\alpha}^T e_k)\left(\bar{\vartheta} + \frac{1}{2}\bar{p}_i\right)\right\}^T\right.$$

$$\left.\left(G''_{f_i}(f_i(\bar{\varphi},\bar{\vartheta}))\nabla_\vartheta f_i(\bar{\varphi},\bar{\vartheta})(\nabla_\vartheta f_i(\bar{\varphi},\bar{\vartheta}))^T + G'_{f_i}(f_i(\bar{\varphi},\bar{\vartheta}))\nabla_{\vartheta\vartheta} f_i(\bar{\varphi},\bar{\vartheta})\right)\bar{p}_i\right\} + \bar{\eta} = 0, \ i \in \tilde{N}. \quad (38)$$

Now, from hypothesis (iv), it is given that $R_+^k \subseteq K \Rightarrow \text{int } K^* \subseteq \text{int } R_+^k$.

Obviously, $\bar{\lambda} > 0$ because $\bar{\lambda} \in \text{int } K^*$.

By hypothesis (i), (33) gives

$$\beta = (\bar{\alpha}^T e_k)(\bar{p}_i + \bar{\vartheta}), \ i \in \tilde{N}. \quad (39)$$

Suppose $\bar{\alpha} = 0$, then (39) yields $\bar{\beta} = 0$. Further, from (38) gives $\bar{\eta} = 0$. Now, we reach at contradiction (36). Hence, $\bar{\alpha} \neq 0$. Further, $\bar{\alpha} \in K^* \subseteq R_+^k$ implies

$$\bar{\alpha}^T e_k > 0. \quad (40)$$

Now, we have to claim that $\bar{p}_i = 0, \ i \in \tilde{N}$. Using (39) and (40) in (38), we get

$$\sum_{i=1}^{k} \bar{\lambda}_i \left[\nabla_\vartheta \left\{\frac{1}{2}\bar{p}_i(G''_{f_i}(f_i(\bar{\varphi},\bar{\vartheta}))\nabla_\vartheta f_i(\bar{\varphi},\bar{\vartheta})(\nabla_\vartheta f_i(\bar{\varphi},\bar{\vartheta}))^T + G'_{f_i}(f_i(\bar{\varphi},\bar{\vartheta}))\nabla_{\vartheta\vartheta} f_i(\bar{\varphi},\bar{\vartheta}))\bar{p}_i\right\}\right]$$

$$= -\frac{1}{\mu}\sum_{i=1}^{k}\left(\alpha_i - \mu\bar{\lambda}_i\right)[G'_{f_i}(f_i(\bar{\varphi},\bar{\vartheta}))\nabla_\vartheta f_i(\bar{\varphi},\bar{\vartheta})], \quad (41)$$

By hypothesis (ii), we get

$$\sum_{i=1}^{k} \bar{\lambda}_i \left[\nabla_\vartheta \left\{\bar{p}_i(G''_{f_i}(f_i(\bar{\varphi},\bar{\vartheta}))\nabla_\vartheta f_i(\bar{\varphi},\bar{\vartheta})(\nabla_\vartheta f_i(\bar{\varphi},\bar{\vartheta}))^T + G'_{f_i}(f_i(\bar{\varphi},\bar{\vartheta}))\nabla_{\vartheta\vartheta} f_i(\bar{\varphi},\bar{\vartheta}))\bar{p}_i\right\}\right] = 0. \quad (42)$$

Again, from hypothesis (iv), we have

$$\bar{p}_i = 0, \ \forall \ i \in \tilde{N}. \tag{43}$$

From (39) implies

$$\bar{\beta} = (\bar{\alpha}^T e_k) \bar{\vartheta}. \tag{44}$$

Using (42) and (43) in (37), we obtain

$$\sum_{i=1}^{k} \left(\alpha_i - (\bar{\alpha}^T e_k) \bar{\lambda}_i \right) \left[G'_{f_i}(f_i(\bar{\varphi}, \bar{\vartheta})) \nabla_\vartheta f_i(\bar{\varphi}, \bar{\vartheta}) \right] = 0. \tag{45}$$

From hypothesis (iii), it yields

$$\alpha_i = (\bar{\alpha}^T e_k) \bar{\lambda}_i, \ i \in \tilde{N}. \tag{46}$$

Using (43) and (44) in (30), we get

$$(\varphi \quad \bar{\varphi})^T \sum_{i=1}^{k} \alpha_i \left[G'_{f_i}(f_i(\bar{\varphi}, \bar{\vartheta})) \nabla_\varphi f_i(\bar{\varphi}, \bar{\vartheta}) \right] \geqq 0.$$

Using (40), (43), (44) and (46) in (30), we find that

$$(\varphi - \bar{\varphi})^T \sum_{i=1}^{k} \bar{\lambda}_i \left[G'_{f_i}(f_i(\bar{\varphi}, \bar{\vartheta})) \nabla_\varphi f_i(\bar{\varphi}, \bar{\vartheta}) \right] \geqq 0, \ \forall \ \varphi \in C_1. \tag{47}$$

Let $\varphi \in C_1$. Then, $\varphi + \bar{\varphi} \in C_1$ and inequality (47) gives that

$$\bar{\varphi}^T \sum_{i=1}^{k} \bar{\lambda}_i \left[G'_{f_i}(f_i(\bar{\varphi}, \bar{\vartheta})) \nabla_\varphi f_i(\bar{\varphi}, \bar{\vartheta}) \right] \geqq 0, \ \forall \ \varphi \in C_1. \tag{48}$$

Therefore,

$$\sum_{i=1}^{k} \bar{\lambda}_i \left[G'_{f_i}(f_i(\bar{\varphi}, \bar{\vartheta})) \nabla_\varphi f_i(\bar{\varphi}, \bar{\vartheta}) \right] \in C_1^*. \tag{49}$$

Also, from (44), we obtain

$$\bar{\vartheta} = \frac{\bar{\beta}}{\bar{\alpha}^T e_k} \in C_2. \tag{50}$$

Therefore, $(\bar{\varphi}, \bar{\vartheta}, \bar{\lambda}, \bar{q}_1 = \bar{q}_2 = \bar{q}_3 = ... = \bar{q}_k = 0)$ satisfies the constraint of (GWDP) and is therefore a feasible solution for the dual problem (GWDP).

Now, letting $\varphi = 0$ and $\varphi = 2\bar{\varphi}$ in (47), we obtain

$$\bar{\varphi}^T \sum_{i=1}^{k} \bar{\lambda}_i \left[G'_{f_i}(f_i(\bar{\varphi}, \bar{\vartheta})) \nabla_\varphi f_i(\bar{\varphi}, \bar{\vartheta}) \right] = 0. \tag{51}$$

Further, from (34), (40), (43) and (44), we get

$$\bar{\vartheta}^T \sum_{i=1}^{k} \bar{\lambda}_i \left[G'_{f_i}(f_i(\bar{\varphi}, \bar{\vartheta})) \nabla_\vartheta f_i(\bar{\varphi}, \bar{\vartheta}) \right] = 0. \tag{52}$$

Therefore, using (43), (51) and (52), we obtain

$$\begin{aligned}
&\bigg(G_{f_1}(f_1(\bar{\varphi}, \bar{\vartheta})) - \bar{\vartheta}^T \sum_{i=1}^{k} \bar{\lambda}_i \Big[G'_{f_i}(f_i(\bar{\varphi}, \bar{\vartheta})) \nabla_\vartheta f_i(\bar{\varphi}, \bar{\vartheta}) + \big\{ G''_{f_i}(f_i(\bar{\varphi}, \bar{\vartheta})) \nabla_\vartheta f_i(\bar{\varphi}, \bar{\vartheta})(\nabla_\vartheta f_i(\bar{\varphi}, \bar{\vartheta}))^T + G'_{f_i}(f_i(\bar{\varphi}, \bar{\vartheta})) \nabla_{\vartheta\vartheta} f_i(\bar{\varphi}, \bar{\vartheta}) \big\} \bar{p}_i \Big] \\
&- \frac{1}{2} \sum_{i=1}^{k} \lambda_i \bar{p}_i \Big\{ G''_{f_i}(f_i(\bar{\varphi}, \bar{\vartheta})) \nabla_\vartheta f_i(\bar{\varphi}, \bar{\vartheta})(\nabla_\vartheta f_i(\bar{\varphi}, \bar{\vartheta}))^T + G'_{f_i}(f_i(\bar{\varphi}, \bar{\vartheta})) \nabla_{\vartheta\vartheta} f_i(\bar{\varphi}, \bar{\vartheta}) \Big\} \bar{p}_i \Big], \ldots, G_{f_k}(f_k(\bar{\varphi}, \bar{\vartheta})) - \bar{\vartheta}^T \sum_{i=1}^{k} \bar{\lambda}_i \Big[G'_{f_i}(f_i(\bar{\varphi}, \bar{\vartheta})) \\
&\nabla_\vartheta f_i(\bar{\varphi}, \bar{\vartheta}) + \big\{ G''_{f_i}(f_i(\bar{\varphi}, \bar{\vartheta})) \nabla_\vartheta f_i(\bar{\varphi}, \bar{\vartheta})(\nabla_\vartheta f_i(\bar{\varphi}, \bar{\vartheta}))^T + G'_{f_i}(f_i(\bar{\varphi}, \bar{\vartheta})) \nabla_{\vartheta\vartheta} f_i(\bar{\varphi}, \bar{\vartheta}) \big\} \bar{p}_i \Big] - \frac{1}{2} \sum_{i=1}^{k} \lambda_i \bar{p}_i \Big\{ G''_{f_i}(f_i(\bar{\varphi}, \bar{\vartheta})) \nabla_\vartheta f_i(\bar{\varphi}, \bar{\vartheta})(\nabla_\vartheta f_i(\bar{\varphi}, \bar{\vartheta}))^T \\
&\quad + G'_{f_i}(f_i(\bar{\varphi}, \bar{\vartheta})) \nabla_{\vartheta\vartheta} f_i(\bar{\varphi}, \bar{\vartheta}) \big\} \bar{p}_i \Big] \bigg) \\
&= \bigg(G_{f_1}(f_1(\bar{\varphi}, \bar{\vartheta})) - \bar{\varphi}^T \sum_{i=1}^{k} \bar{\lambda}_i \Big[G'_{f_i}(f_i(\bar{\varphi}, \bar{\vartheta})) \nabla_\varphi f_i(\bar{\varphi}, \bar{\vartheta}) + \big\{ G''_{f_i}(f_i(\bar{\varphi}, \bar{\vartheta})) \nabla_\varphi f_i(\bar{\varphi}, \bar{\vartheta})(\nabla_\varphi f_i(\bar{\varphi}, \bar{\vartheta}))^T + G'_{f_i}(f_i(\bar{\varphi}, \bar{\vartheta})) \nabla_{\varphi\varphi} f_i(\bar{\varphi}, \bar{\vartheta}) \big\} \bar{q}_i \Big] \\
&- \frac{1}{2} \sum_{i=1}^{k} \lambda_i \bar{q}_i \Big\{ G''_{f_i}(f_i(\bar{\varphi}, \bar{\vartheta})) \nabla_\varphi f_i(\bar{\varphi}, \bar{\vartheta})(\nabla_\varphi f_i(\bar{\varphi}, \bar{\vartheta}))^T + G'_{f_i}(f_i(\bar{\varphi}, \bar{\vartheta})) \nabla_{\varphi\varphi} f_i(\bar{\varphi}, \bar{\vartheta}) \Big\} \bar{q}_i \Big], \ldots, G_{f_k}(f_k(\bar{\varphi}, \bar{\vartheta})) - \bar{\varphi}^T \sum_{i=1}^{k} \bar{\lambda}_i \Big[G'_{f_i}(f_i(\bar{\varphi}, \bar{\vartheta})) \\
&\nabla_\varphi f_i(\bar{\varphi}, \bar{\vartheta}) + \big\{ G''_{f_i}(f_i(\bar{\varphi}, \bar{\vartheta})) \nabla_\varphi f_i(\bar{\varphi}, \bar{\vartheta})(\nabla_\varphi f_i(\bar{\varphi}, \bar{\vartheta}))^T + G'_{f_i}(f_i(\bar{\varphi}, \bar{\vartheta})) \nabla_{\varphi\varphi} f_i(\bar{\varphi}, \bar{\vartheta}) \big\} \bar{q}_i \Big] - \frac{1}{2} \sum_{i=1}^{k} \lambda_i \bar{q}_i \Big\{ G''_{f_i}(f_i(\bar{\varphi}, \bar{\vartheta})) \nabla_\varphi f_i(\bar{\varphi}, \bar{\vartheta})(\nabla_\varphi f_i(\bar{\varphi}, \bar{\vartheta}))^T \\
&\quad + G'_{f_i}(f_i(\bar{\varphi}, \bar{\vartheta})) \nabla_{\varphi\varphi} f_i(\bar{\varphi}, \bar{\vartheta}) \big\} \bar{q}_i \Big] \bigg).
\end{aligned}$$

This shows that the objective values are equal.

Finally, we have to claim that $(\bar{\varphi}, \bar{\vartheta}, \bar{\lambda}, \bar{q}_1 = \bar{q}_2 = \bar{q}_3 = \ldots = \bar{q}_k = 0)$ is an efficient solution of $(GWDP)$.

If possible, then suppose that $(\bar{\varphi}, \bar{\vartheta}, \bar{\lambda}, \bar{q}_1 = \bar{q}_2 = \bar{q}_3 = \ldots = \bar{q}_k = 0)$ is not an efficient solution of $(GWDP)$, then there exist $(\bar{\delta}, \bar{\ell}, \bar{\lambda}, \bar{q}_1 = \bar{q}_2 = \bar{q}_3 = \ldots = \bar{q}_k = 0)$ is efficient solution of $(GWDP)$ such that

$$\begin{aligned}
&\bigg(G_{f_1}(f_1(\bar{\varphi}, \bar{\vartheta})) - \bar{\varphi}^T \sum_{i=1}^{k} \bar{\lambda}_i \Big[G'_{f_i}(f_i(\bar{\varphi}, \bar{\vartheta})) \nabla_\varphi f_i(\bar{\varphi}, \bar{\vartheta}) + \big\{ G''_{f_i}(f_i(\bar{\varphi}, \bar{\vartheta})) \nabla_\varphi f_i(\bar{\varphi}, \bar{\vartheta})(\nabla_\varphi f_i(\bar{\varphi}, \bar{\vartheta}))^T + G'_{f_i}(f_i(\bar{\varphi}, \bar{\vartheta})) \nabla_{\varphi\varphi} f_i(\bar{\varphi}, \bar{\vartheta}) \big\} \bar{q}_i \Big] \\
&- \frac{1}{2} \sum_{i=1}^{k} \lambda_i \bar{q}_i \Big\{ G''_{f_i}(f_i(\bar{\varphi}, \bar{\vartheta})) \nabla_\varphi f_i(\bar{\varphi}, \bar{\vartheta})(\nabla_\varphi f_i(\bar{\varphi}, \bar{\vartheta}))^T + G'_{f_i}(f_i(\bar{\varphi}, \bar{\vartheta})) \nabla_{\varphi\varphi} f_i(\bar{\varphi}, \bar{\vartheta}) \Big\} \bar{q}_i \Big], \ldots, G_{f_k}(f_k(\bar{\varphi}, \bar{\vartheta})) - \bar{\varphi}^T \sum_{i=1}^{k} \bar{\lambda}_i \Big[G'_{f_i}(f_i(\bar{\varphi}, \bar{\vartheta})) \\
&\nabla_\varphi f_i(\bar{\varphi}, \bar{\vartheta}) + \big\{ G''_{f_i}(f_i(\bar{\varphi}, \bar{\vartheta})) \nabla_\varphi f_i(\bar{\varphi}, \bar{\vartheta})(\nabla_\varphi f_i(\bar{\varphi}, \bar{\vartheta}))^T + G'_{f_i}(f_i(\bar{\varphi}, \bar{\vartheta})) \nabla_{\varphi\varphi} f_i(\bar{\varphi}, \bar{\vartheta}) \big\} \bar{q}_i \Big] - \frac{1}{2} \sum_{i=1}^{k} \lambda_i \bar{q}_i \Big\{ G''_{f_i}(f_i(\bar{\varphi}, \bar{\vartheta})) \nabla_\varphi f_i(\bar{\varphi}, \bar{\vartheta})(\nabla_\varphi f_i(\bar{\varphi}, \bar{\vartheta}))^T \\
&\quad + G'_{f_i}(f_i(\bar{\varphi}, \bar{\vartheta})) \nabla_{\varphi\varphi} f_i(\bar{\varphi}, \bar{\vartheta}) \big\} \bar{q}_i \Big] - G_{f_1}(f_1(\bar{\delta}, \bar{\ell})) - \bar{\delta}^T \sum_{i=1}^{k} \bar{\lambda}_i \Big[G'_{f_i}(f_i(\bar{\delta}, \bar{\ell})) \nabla_\varphi f_i(\bar{\delta}, \bar{\ell}) + \big\{ G''_{f_i}(f_i(\bar{\delta}, \bar{\ell})) \nabla_\varphi f_i(\bar{\delta}, \bar{\ell})(\nabla_\varphi f_i(\bar{\delta}, \bar{\ell}))^T \\
&+ G'_{f_i}(f_i(\bar{\delta}, \bar{\ell})) \nabla_{\varphi\varphi} f_i(\bar{\delta}, \bar{\ell}) \big\} \bar{q}_i \Big] \\
&- \frac{1}{2} \sum_{i=1}^{k} \lambda_i \bar{q}_i \Big\{ G''_{f_i}(f_i(\bar{\delta}, \bar{\ell})) \nabla_\varphi f_i(\bar{\delta}, \bar{\ell})(\nabla_\varphi f_i(\bar{\delta}, \bar{\ell}))^T + G'_{f_i}(f_i(\bar{\delta}, \bar{\ell})) \nabla_{\varphi\varphi} f_i(\bar{\delta}, \bar{\ell}) \Big\} \bar{q}_i \Big], \ldots, G_{f_k}(f_k(\bar{\delta}, \bar{\ell})) - \bar{\delta}^T \sum_{i=1}^{k} \bar{\lambda}_i \Big[G'_{f_i}(f_i(\bar{\delta}, \bar{\ell})) \\
&\nabla_\varphi f_i(\bar{\delta}, \bar{\ell}) + \big\{ G''_{f_i}(f_i(\bar{\delta}, \bar{\ell})) \nabla_\varphi f_i(\bar{\delta}, \bar{\ell})(\nabla_\varphi f_i(\bar{\delta}, \bar{\ell}))^T + G'_{f_i}(f_i(\bar{\delta}, \bar{\ell})) \nabla_{\varphi\varphi} f_i(\bar{\delta}, \bar{\ell}) \big\} \bar{q}_i \Big] - \frac{1}{2} \sum_{i=1}^{k} \lambda_i \bar{q}_i \Big\{ G''_{f_i}(f_i(\bar{\delta}, \bar{\ell})) \nabla_\varphi f_i(\bar{\delta}, \bar{\ell})(\nabla_\varphi f_i(\bar{\delta}, \bar{\ell}))^T \\
&\quad + G'_{f_i}(f_i(\bar{\delta}, \bar{\ell})) \nabla_{\varphi\varphi} f_i(\bar{\delta}, \bar{\ell}) \big\} \bar{q}_i \Big] \bigg) \in -K \setminus \{0\}.
\end{aligned}$$

As

$$\bar{\varphi}^T \sum_{i=1}^{k} \bar{\lambda}_i G'_{f_i}(f_i(\bar{\varphi}, \bar{\vartheta})) \nabla_\varphi f_i(\bar{\varphi}, \bar{\vartheta}) = \bar{\vartheta}^T \sum_{i=1}^{k} \bar{\lambda}_i G'_{f_i}(f_i(\bar{\varphi}, \bar{\vartheta})) \nabla_\vartheta f_i(\bar{\varphi}, \bar{\vartheta}) \text{ and } \bar{p}_i = 0, \ i \in \hat{N},$$

$$\left(G_{f_1}(f_1(\bar{\varphi}, \bar{\vartheta})) - \bar{\vartheta}^T \sum_{i=1}^{k} \bar{\lambda}_i \left[G'_{f_i}(f_i(\bar{\varphi}, \bar{\vartheta})) \nabla_\vartheta f_i(\bar{\varphi}, \bar{\vartheta}) + \left\{ G''_{f_i}(f_i(\bar{\varphi}, \bar{\vartheta})) \nabla_\varphi f_i(\bar{\varphi}, \bar{\vartheta}) (\nabla_\varphi f_i(\bar{\varphi}, \bar{\vartheta}))^T + G'_{f_i}(f_i(\bar{\varphi}, \bar{\vartheta})) \nabla_{\varphi\varphi} f_i(\bar{\varphi}, \bar{\vartheta}) \right\} \bar{q}_i \right] \right.$$

$$- \frac{1}{2} \sum_{i=1}^{k} \lambda_i \bar{q}_i \left\{ G''_{f_i}(f_i(\bar{\varphi}, \bar{\vartheta})) \nabla_\varphi f_i(\bar{\varphi}, \bar{\vartheta}) (\nabla_\varphi f_i(\bar{\varphi}, \bar{\vartheta}))^T + G'_{f_i}(f_i(\bar{\varphi}, \bar{\vartheta})) \nabla_{\varphi\varphi} f_i(\bar{\varphi}, \bar{\vartheta}) \right\} \bar{q}_i \right], \ldots, G_{f_k}(f_k(\bar{\varphi}, \bar{\vartheta})) - \bar{\varphi}^T \sum_{i=1}^{k} \bar{\lambda}_i \left[G'_{f_i}(f_i(\bar{\varphi}, \bar{\vartheta})) \right.$$

$$\nabla_\varphi f_i(\bar{\varphi}, \bar{\vartheta}) + \left\{ G''_{f_i}(f_i(\bar{\varphi}, \bar{\vartheta})) \nabla_\varphi f_i(\bar{\varphi}, \bar{\vartheta}) (\nabla_\varphi f_i(\bar{\varphi}, \bar{\vartheta}))^T + G'_{f_i}(f_i(\bar{\varphi}, \bar{\vartheta})) \nabla_{\varphi\varphi} f_i(\bar{\varphi}, \bar{\vartheta}) \right\} \bar{q}_i \right] - \frac{1}{2} \sum_{i=1}^{k} \lambda_i \bar{q}_i \left\{ G''_{f_i}(f_i(\bar{\varphi}, \bar{\vartheta})) \nabla_\varphi f_i(\bar{\varphi}, \bar{\vartheta}) (\nabla_\varphi f_i(\bar{\varphi}, \bar{\vartheta}))^T \right.$$

$$+ G'_{f_i}(f_i(\bar{\varphi}, \bar{\vartheta})) \nabla_{\varphi\varphi} f_i(\bar{\varphi}, \bar{\vartheta}) \right\} \bar{q}_i \right] - G_{f_1}(f_1(\bar{\delta}, \bar{\ell})) - \bar{\delta}^T \sum_{i=1}^{k} \bar{\lambda}_i \left[G'_{f_i}(f_i(\bar{\varphi}, \bar{\vartheta})) \nabla_\varphi f_i(\bar{\delta}, \bar{\ell}) + \right.$$

$$\left\{ G''_{f_i}(f_i(\bar{\delta}, \bar{\ell})) \nabla_\varphi f_i(\bar{\delta}, \bar{\ell}) (\nabla_\varphi f_i(\bar{\delta}, \bar{\ell}))^T + G'_{f_i}(f_i(\bar{\delta}, \bar{\ell})) \nabla_{\varphi\varphi} f_i(\bar{\delta}, \bar{\ell}) \right\} \bar{q}_i \right]$$

$$- \frac{1}{2} \sum_{i=1}^{k} \lambda_i \bar{q}_i \left\{ G''_{f_i}(f_i(\bar{\delta}, \bar{\ell})) \nabla_\varphi f_i(\bar{\delta}, \bar{\ell}) (\nabla_\varphi f_i(\bar{\delta}, \bar{\ell}))^T + G'_{f_i}(f_i(\bar{\delta}, \bar{\ell})) \nabla_{\varphi\varphi} f_i(\bar{\delta}, \bar{\ell}) \right\} \bar{q}_i \right], \ldots, G_{f_k}(f_k(\bar{\delta}, \bar{\ell})) - \bar{\delta}^T \sum_{i=1}^{k} \bar{\lambda}_i \left[G'_{f_i}(f_i(\bar{\delta}, \bar{\ell})) \right.$$

$$\nabla_\varphi f_i(\bar{\delta}, \bar{\ell}) + \left\{ G''_{f_i}(f_i(\bar{\delta}, \bar{\ell})) \nabla_\varphi f_i(\bar{\delta}, \bar{\ell}) (\nabla_\varphi f_i(\bar{\delta}, \bar{\ell}))^T + G'_{f_i}(f_i(\bar{\delta}, \bar{\ell})) \nabla_{\varphi\varphi} f_i(\bar{\delta}, \bar{\ell}) \right\} \bar{q}_i \right] - \frac{1}{2} \sum_{i=1}^{k} \lambda_i \bar{q}_i \left\{ G''_{f_i}(f_i(\bar{\delta}, \bar{\ell})) \nabla_\varphi f_i(\bar{\delta}, \bar{\ell}) (\nabla_\varphi f_i(\bar{\delta}, \bar{\ell}))^T \right.$$

$$\left. + G'_{f_i}(f_i(\bar{\delta}, \bar{\ell})) \nabla_{\varphi\varphi} f_i(\bar{\delta}, \bar{\ell}) \right\} \bar{q}_i \right] \right) \in -K \setminus \{0\},$$

which contradicts the Weak duality Theorem 1 or Theorem 2. Hence, completes the proof. □

Theorem 4 (Converse duality). *Let* $(\bar{\delta}, \bar{\ell}, \bar{\lambda}, \bar{q})$ *is an efficient solution of* $(GWDP)$*; fix* $\lambda = \bar{\lambda}$ *in* $(GWPP)$ *such that*

(i) *for all* $i \in \{1, 2, \ldots, k\}$, $\left[G''_{f_i}(f_i(\bar{\delta}, \bar{\ell})) \nabla_\varphi f_i(\bar{\delta}, \bar{\ell}) (\nabla_\varphi f_i(\bar{\delta}, \bar{\ell}))^T + G'_{f_i}(f_i(\bar{\delta}, \bar{\ell})) \nabla_{\varphi\varphi} f_i(\bar{\delta}, \bar{\ell}) \right]$ *is non singular,*

(ii) $\sum_{i=1}^{k} \bar{\lambda}_i \nabla_\varphi \left[\bar{q}_i \left\{ G''_{f_i}(f_i(\bar{\delta}, \bar{\ell})) \nabla_\varphi f_i(\bar{\delta}, \bar{\ell}) (\nabla_\varphi f_i(\bar{\delta}, \bar{\ell}))^T + G'_{f_i}(f_i(\bar{\delta}, \bar{\ell})) \nabla_{\varphi\varphi} f_i(\bar{\delta}, \bar{\ell}) \right\} \bar{q}_i \right]$

$\notin \text{span} \left\{ G'_{f_1}(f_1(\bar{\delta}, \bar{\ell})) \nabla_\varphi f_1(\bar{\delta}, \bar{\ell}), G'_{f_2}(f_2(\bar{\delta}, \bar{\ell})) \nabla_\varphi f_2(\bar{\delta}, \bar{\ell}), \ldots, G'_{f_i}(f_i(\bar{\delta}, \bar{\ell})) \nabla_\varphi f_i(\bar{\delta}, \bar{\ell}) \right\}.$

(iii) *the set of vectors* $\left\{ G'_{f_1}(f_1(\bar{\delta}, \bar{\ell})) \nabla_\varphi f_1(\bar{\delta}, \bar{\ell}), G'_{f_2}(f_2(\bar{\delta}, \bar{\ell})) \nabla_\varphi f_2(\bar{\delta}, \bar{\ell}), \ldots, G'_{f_k}(f_k(\bar{\delta}, \bar{\ell})) \nabla_\varphi f_k(\bar{\delta}, \bar{\ell}) \right\}$ *are linearly independent,*

(iv) $\sum_{i=1}^{k} \bar{\lambda}_i \nabla_\vartheta \left[\bar{q}_i \left\{ G''_{f_i}(f_i(\bar{\delta}, \bar{\ell})) \nabla_\varphi f_i(\bar{\delta}, \bar{\ell}) (\nabla_\varphi f_i(\bar{\delta}, \bar{\ell}))^T + G'_{f_i}(f_i(\bar{\delta}, \bar{\ell})) \nabla_{\varphi\varphi} f_i(\bar{\delta}, \bar{\ell}) \right\} \bar{q}_i \right] = 0 \Rightarrow \bar{q}_i = 0, \ \forall \ i,$

(v) K *is closed convex pointed cone with* $R^k_+ \subseteq K$.

Then, $(\bar{\delta}, \bar{\ell}, \bar{\lambda}, \bar{p} = 0)$ *is a feasible solution for* $(GWPP)$ *and the objective values of* $(GWDP)$ *and* $(GWPP)$ *are equal. Furthermore, if the hypotheses of Theorem 1 or Theorem 2 are satisfied for all feasible solutions of* $(GWDP)$ *and* $(GWPP)$*, then* $(\bar{\delta}, \bar{\ell}, \bar{\lambda}, \bar{p} = 0)$ *is an optimal solution of* $(GWPP)$. *Also, if the hypotheses of Theorem 1 or Theorem 2 are satisfied for all feasible solutions for* $(GWDP)$ *and* $(GWPP)$*, then* $(\bar{\delta}, \bar{\ell}, \bar{\lambda}, \bar{q})$ *and* $(\bar{\delta}, \bar{\ell}, \bar{\lambda}, \bar{p})$ *is an efficient solution for* $(GWDP)$ *and* $(GWPP)$*, respectively.*

Proof. It follows on the lines of Theorem 3. □

4. Conclusions

In this paper, we have presented a novel generalized group of definitions and illustrated various non-trivial numerical examples for existing such type of functions. Numerical examples have also been illustrated to justify the weak duality theorem. Furthermore, we have studied a new class of K-G_f-Wolfe type primal-dual model with cone objective as well as constraint and proved duality theorem under K-G_f-bonvexity and K-G_f-pseudobonvexity. This work can further be extended to higher order symmetric fractional programming problem and variational control problem over cones. This will be feature task for the researchers.

Author Contributions: All authors contributed equally. All authors have read and agreed to the published version of the manuscript.

Funding: This research received no external funding.

Data Availability Statement: Not applicable.

Conflicts of Interest: The authors declare no conflict of interest.

References

1. Chinchuluun, A.; Pardalos, P.M. A survey of recent developments in multiobjective optimization. *Ann. Oper. Res.* **2007**, *154*, 29–50. [CrossRef]
2. Dorn, W.S. A symmetric dual theorem for quadratic programming. *J. Oper. Res. Soc. Jpn.* **1960**, *2*, 93–97.
3. Dantzig, G.B.; Eisenberg, E.; Cottle, R.W. Symmetric dual non-linear programs. *Pac. J. Math.* **1965**, *15*, 809–812. [CrossRef]
4. Mond, B. A symmetric dual theorem for non-linear programs. *Q. J. Appl. Math.* **1965**, *23*, 265–269. [CrossRef]
5. Mangasarian, O.L. *Nonlinear Programming*; McGraw-Hill: New York, NY, USA, 1969.
6. Mond, B.; Weir, T. Generalized concavity and duality, *Gen. Concavity Optim. Econ.* **1981**, 263–279.
7. Nanda, S.; Das, L.N. Pseudo-invexity and duality in nonlinear programming. *Eur. J. Oper. Res.* **1996**, *88*, 572–577. [CrossRef]
8. Bazaraa, M.S.; Goode, J.J.; On symmetric duality in nonlinear programming. *Oper. Res.* **1973**, *21*, 1–9. [CrossRef]
9. Hanson, M.A.; Mond, B. Further generalization of convexity in mathematical programming. *J. Inf. Optim. Sci.* **1982**, *3*, 25–32. [CrossRef]
10. Mangasarian, O.L. Second and higher order duality in non-linear programming. *J. Math. Anal. Appl.* **1975**, *51*, 607–620. [CrossRef]
11. Mond, B. Second order duality for non-linear programs. *Opsearch* **1974**, *11*, 90–99.
12. Hanson, M.A. Second order invexity and duality in mathematical programming. *Opsearch* **1993**, *30*, 313–320.
13. Mishra, S.K. Multiobjective second order symmetric duality with cone constraints. *Eur. J. Oper. Res.* **2000**, *126*, 675–682. [CrossRef]
14. Mishra, S.K.; Lai, K.K. Second order symmetric duality in multiobjective programming involving generalized cone-invex functions. *Eur. J. Oper. Res.* **2007**, *178*, 20–26. [CrossRef]
15. Gulati, T.R. Mond-Weir type second-order symmetric duality in multiobjective programming over cones. *Appl. Math. Lett.* **2010**, *23*, 466–471. [CrossRef]
16. Dhingra, V.; Kailey, N. Optimality and duality for second-order interval-valued variational problems. *J. Appl. Math. Comput.* **2021**, *68*, 3147–3162. [CrossRef]
17. Dar, B.A.; Jayswal, A.; Singh, D. Optimality, duality and saddle point analysis for interval-valued nondifferentiable multiobjective fractional programming problems. *Optimization* **2021**, *70*, 1275–1305. [CrossRef]
18. García-Alonso, C.R.; Pérez-Naranjo, L.M.; Fernández-Caballero, J.C. Multiobjective evolutionary algorithms to identify highly autocorrelated areas: The case of spatial distribution in financially compromised farms. *Ann. Oper. Res.* **2014**, *219*, 187–202. [CrossRef]
19. Yang, X.M.; Yang, X.Q.; Teo, K.L.; Hou, S.H. Second order symmetric duality in non-differentiable multiobjective programming with F-convexity. *Eur. J. Oper. Res.* **2005**, *164*, 406–416. [CrossRef]
20. Yang, X.M.; Yang, X.Q.; Teo, K.L.; Hou, S.H. Multiobjective second-order symmetric duality with F-convexity. *Eur. J. Oper. Res.* **2005**, *165*, 585–591. [CrossRef]
21. Jayswal, A.; Prasad, A.K. Second order symmetric duality in nondifferentiable multiobjective fractional programming with cone convex functions. *J. Appl. Math. Comput.* **2014**, *45*, 15–33. [CrossRef]
22. Chuong, T.D. Second-order cone programming relaxations for a class of multiobjective convex polynomial problems. *Ann. Oper. Res.* **2020**, *311*, 1017–1033. [CrossRef]
23. Dubey, R.; Mishra, L.N.; Ali, R. Special class of second order nondifferentiable duality problems with (G, α)-pseudobonvexity assumptions. *Mathematics* **2019**, *7*, 763. [CrossRef]
24. Dubey, R.; Mishra, V.N.; Tomar, P. Duality relations for second-order programming problem under (G, α)-bonvexity. *Asian-Eur. J. Math.* **2020**, *13*, 2050044. [CrossRef]
25. Dubey, R.; Mishra, V.N.; Karateke, S. A class of second order nondifferentiable symmetric duality relations under generalized assumptions. *J. Math. Comput. Sci.* **2020**, *21*, 120–126. [CrossRef]
26. Jayswal, A.; Jha, S. Second order symmetric duality in fractional variational problems over cone constraints, *Yugosl. J. Oper. Res.* **2018**, *28*, 39–57.

27. Kapoor, M. Vector optimization over cones involving support functions using generalized (ϕ,ρ)-convexity. *Opsearch* **2017**, *54*, 351–364. [CrossRef]
28. Kaur, A.; Sharma, M.K. Higher order symmetric duality for multiobjective fractional programming problems over cones. *Yugosl. J. Oper. Res.* **2021**, *32*, 29–44. [CrossRef]

Disclaimer/Publisher's Note: The statements, opinions and data contained in all publications are solely those of the individual author(s) and contributor(s) and not of MDPI and/or the editor(s). MDPI and/or the editor(s) disclaim responsibility for any injury to people or property resulting from any ideas, methods, instructions or products referred to in the content.

Article

Predicting Sit-to-Stand Body Adaptation Using a Simple Model

Sarra Gismelseed *, Amur Al-Yahmedi, Riadh Zaier, Hassen Ouakad and Issam Bahadur

Department of Mechanical & Industrial Engineering, College of Engineering, Sultan Qaboos University, Muscat 123, Oman; amery@squ.edu.om (A.A.-Y.); zaier@squ.edu.om (R.Z.); houakad@squ.edu.om (H.O.); bahdoor@squ.edu.om (I.B.)
* Correspondence: sarraabbasher@gmail.com

Abstract: Mathematical models that simulate human motion are used widely due to their potential in predicting basic characteristics of human motion. These models have been involved in investigating various aspects of gait and human-related tasks, especially walking and running. This study uses a simple model to study the impact of different factors on sit-to-stand motion through the formulation of an optimization problem that aims at minimizing joint torques. The simulated results validated experimental results reported in the literature and showed the ability of the model to predict the changes in kinetic and kinematic parameters as adaptation to any change in the speed of motion, reduction in the joint strength, and change in the seat height. The model discovered that changing one of these determinants would affect joint angular displacement, joint torques, joint angular velocities, center of mass position, and ground reaction force.

Keywords: sit-to-stand; discrete mechanics; optimization; sit-to-stand determinates

MSC: 37N99

Citation: Gismelseed, S.; Al-Yahmedi, A.; Zaier, R.; Ouakad, H.; Bahadur, I. Predicting Sit-to-Stand Body Adaptation Using a Simple Model. *Axioms* **2023**, *12*, 559. https://doi.org/10.3390/axioms12060559

Academic Editors: Siamak Pedrammehr and Mohammad Reza Chalak Qazani

Received: 14 April 2023
Revised: 25 May 2023
Accepted: 31 May 2023
Published: 5 June 2023

Copyright: © 2023 by the authors. Licensee MDPI, Basel, Switzerland. This article is an open access article distributed under the terms and conditions of the Creative Commons Attribution (CC BY) license (https:// creativecommons.org/licenses/by/ 4.0/).

1. Introduction

Mathematical models that simulate human motion and capture the basic pattern of human motor characteristics in the absence of empirical data (or what is known as predictive simulation [1]), were used to study many human kinetic characteristics, such as targeting a specific kinetic speed while reducing the metabolic cost associated with this movement [1,2]. By applying dynamic optimization processes while considering physical and physiological constraints [3,4], researchers were able to derive whole body dynamics, aiding in the production of movements that closely resemble human motion by controlling relevant parameters. Most of the predictive simulation studies were done to study human gait characteristics since it is the main feature of human beings [3,5,6]; however, Sit-to-Stand (STS) motion is also one of the main daily activities, which is also considered as a distinctive feature of human beings.

STS motion has been attracting scientists and physical therapists to experimentally study and analyze the aspects of how humans perform this task that is mainly defined by the process of going to a standing position from a sitting position [7,8]. This motion has a direct effect on humans' quality of life, and the significance of this motion will not be appreciated until it becomes physically or cognitively challenging, which can be temporary due to injury or permanent due to aging or illness. All the previous reasons may cause difficulties in completing this motion successfully, especially in an elderly population. Studies showed that at the age of 55 years and above, 45% of women and 30% of men suffer from moderate to serious inabilities in rising from sitting [9]. Inability to properly perform the STS motion may be associated with decreased mobility and balance, with an increased risk of falling, as well. Several factors influencing the performance of STS motion are considered as determinants, as they can either facilitate successful completion of the task or make it more challenging [10,11]. The determinants of STS motion have been categorized into different groups according to the source of the determinates, which are strategy-related determinants such as speed, foot position, trunk rotation, etc. [8,11]; subject-related determinants such as age, muscle force, and disease [7,12,13]; and chair-related determinants [14,15] such as seat height, armrests, and backrest [16,17]. The impact of these determinants on body behavior and movement performance differs according to the type of determinants, and it has been studied in order to investigate how the body adapts to the changes of these determinants.

The predictive simulation has been involved in studying the STS motion [6,18] to have a better understanding of how we usually move and when this movement occurs [18]. A good understanding of the normal way of movement during STS will help as well in applying this knowledge to some cases of predictive simulation that involve studying losing mobility or some difficulties in performing this task. The complexity of biomechanical models used to study STS motion varies from simple to complicated based on the number of segments and muscles included in these models, in addition to the number of planes used in the modeling [9,19]. Most of the models were modeled as 2D models in the sagittal plane [20] since most of the joints' movement occur in this plane; however, few were modeled as 3D models. These models were involved in studying various aspects of STS motion and the effect of different parameters on this motion, including the effect of chair height, the effect of initial foot position, the effect of muscle strength, etc. Garner proposed a biomechanical model modeled in the sagittal plane that has three rigid segments (i.e., thigh, leg, and HAT (Head, Arms, and Torso) and eight muscles [19]. Garner used dynamic optimization to explain the execution of this motion by minimizing a cost function split into two parts; the first part is aimed at minimizing muscle stress until the time the biped leaves the chair, and the second part is aimed at minimizing peak forces developed by the muscles from the time the biped leaves the chair until the time required to accomplish this task [19]. This cost function produced simulation results that were very similar to the experimental results. The model of Garner is further enhanced by Daigle by adding a foot segment and increasing the number of muscles to 18 [20], and the model was used to understand the difficulties related to muscle strength and its effect on accomplishing this task by using an optimization formulation that minimizes the motion time with different muscle strength varied from 50% to 200% [20]. The model was able to define which muscles have a great contribution and power activation in the sit-to-stand task [20]. On other hand, Domire used a sagittal plane model that consists of three links connected with three joints and actuated by eight muscles to study the effect of seat height on STS motion [21]. Domire predicted the effect of seat height using the same objective function described by Garner and simulated the movement during STS from different seat heights, adjusted by rotating the thigh segment at four different angles: 80°, 90°, 98°, and 100° [21]. The study concluded that as the seat height decreased, the movement of STS became more difficult, and it was impossible at the lowest seat height corresponding to the 100° thigh angle.

In this study, a simple 2D model is used to predict the effect of changing three STS determinants (speed, joint strength, and seat height) on lower limb and upper body kinetic and kinematic parameters by applying dynamic optimization to minimize the joint torques. First, the derivation of the proposed model and the formulation of the optimization problem are shown in the following section. Then, the simulation results are shown in the third section of this study with the validation of some simulation results with experimental results from the literature. In the fourth section, results from this study are discussed and compared to reported results and conclusions from experimental studies. Finally, we summarize our work with the main conclusions in the last section.

2. Materials and Methods

Accurately predicting STS motion requires a biomechanics model that accurately represents the human body, as well as an understanding of how to identify the specific movements involved in STS motion. The model proposed in this study is modeled in the sagittal plane since the movement of humans' joints are mostly obvious when it is seen from the sagittal plane compared to the other planes [22]. This will allow for simplifying the human body to a three-links model, as shown in Figure 1, through assuming that the two legs are symmetrical and can be modeled as one leg with two segments, tibia and femur, in addition to the torso segment. A male subject of height 1.70 m and mass 70 kg is considered for approximating the model physical parameters. The physical parameters shown in Table 1 were calculated using anthropometric percentages compiled by different investigators (the detailed calculations are given in Appendix A) [23–25].

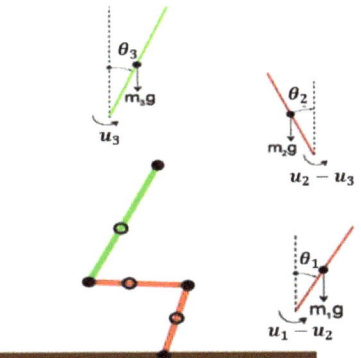

Figure 1. Three-links model, u_i is the torque applied at each joint, and each link is assigned with a number: 1 = stance tibia, 2 = stance femur, 3 = trunk.

Table 1. Physical parameters.

Link	Body Segment	Length of Segment (m) l_i	Distance from Center of Mass to Next Joint (m) d_i	Mass of Segment (kg) m_i	Moment of Inertia of Segment (kg·m^2) I_i
1	tibia	0.390	0.182	6.650	0.088
2	femur	0.420	0.170	14.70	0.163
3	torso	0.690	0.372	46.60	2.068

The problem is formulated as an optimization problem in the goal is to minimize a given cost function while satisfying constraints imposed by the task. Due to the high degree of nonlinearity of the problem, the use of the direct (single) shooting method to solve the resulting optimization problem may likely cause the algorithm to fail to find a solution. One can either use collocation methods or use direct discretization of the Lagrange-d'Alembert Principle for the system. We chose to use direct discretization of the Lagrange-d'Alembert Principle (discrete mechanics) [26,27]. Discrete mechanics requires that the Lagrange equation of the system be derived first. The Lagrange equation of the model is given by:

$$\begin{aligned}\mathcal{L} = &\tfrac{1}{2}\big(m_1(l_1-d_1)^2 + m_2 l_1^2 + m_3 l_1^2\big)\dot{\theta}_1^2 + \tfrac{1}{2}\big(m_2(l_2-d_2)^2 + m_3 l_2^2\big)\dot{\theta}_2^2 + \tfrac{1}{2}m_3 d_3^2 \dot{\theta}_3^2 \\ &-(m_2 l_1(l_2-d_2) + m_3 l_1 l_2)\dot{\theta}_1\dot{\theta}_2 \cos(\theta_1+\theta_2) + m_3 l_1 d_3 \dot{\theta}_1\dot{\theta}_3 \cos(\theta_1-\theta_3) \\ &- m_3 l_2 d_3 \dot{\theta}_2 \dot{\theta}_3 \cos(\theta_2+\theta_3) - g(m_1(l_1-d_1) + m_2 l_1 + m_3 l_1)\cos\theta_1 \\ &- g(m_2(l_2-d_2) + m_3 l_2)\cos\theta_2 - m_3 g d_3 \cos\theta_3\end{aligned} \qquad(1)$$

the discrete Lagrange equation is derived from the continuous Lagrange equation, using the mid-point rule as follows (for the detailed derivations, check Appendix A):

$$\mathcal{L}(q,\dot{q}) \rightarrow h\mathcal{L}_d\big(\frac{q_{k+1}+q_k}{2}, \frac{q_{k+1}-q_k}{h}\big) \qquad(2)$$

The system dynamics is then:

$$D_1\mathcal{L}_d(\theta_{1k}, \theta_{1k+1}, \theta_{2k}, \theta_{2k+1}, \theta_{3k}, \theta_{3k+1}) + f_d^-(\theta_{1k}, \theta_{1k+1}, \theta_{2k}, \theta_{2k+1}, \theta_{3k}, \theta_{3k+1})$$
$$+D_2\mathcal{L}_d(\theta_{1k-1}, \theta_{1k}, \theta_{2k-1}, \theta_{2k}, \theta_{3k-1}, \theta_{3k}) \quad (3)$$
$$+f_d^+(\theta_{1k-1}, \theta_{1k}, \theta_{2k-1}, \theta_{2k}, \theta_{3k-1}, \theta_{3k}) = 0$$

where $D_1\mathcal{L}_d(\theta_{1k}, \theta_{1k+1}, \theta_{2k}, \theta_{2k+1}, \theta_{3k}, \theta_{3k+1})$ is the first derivative of the discrete Lagrange with respect to current coordinates (i.e., θ_{1k}, θ_{2k}, and θ_{3k}), and is the first derivative of the discrete Lagrange with respect to future coordinates (i.e., $\theta_{1k+1}, \theta_{2k+1}$, and θ_{3k+1}).

$$D_1\mathcal{L}_d = \begin{bmatrix} \frac{\partial \mathcal{L}_d}{\partial \theta_{1k}}(\theta_{1k}, \theta_{1k+1}, \theta_{2k}, \theta_{2k+1}, \theta_{3k}, \theta_{3k+1}) \\ \frac{\partial \mathcal{L}_d}{\partial \theta_{2k}}(\theta_{1k}, \theta_{1k+1}, \theta_{2k}, \theta_{2k+1}, \theta_{3k}, \theta_{3k+1}) \\ \frac{\partial \mathcal{L}_d}{\partial \theta_{3k}}(\theta_{1k}, \theta_{1k+1}, \theta_{2k}, \theta_{2k+1}, \theta_{3k}, \theta_{3k+1}) \end{bmatrix} \quad (4)$$

$$D_2\mathcal{L}_d = \begin{bmatrix} \frac{\partial \mathcal{L}_d}{\partial \theta_{1k+1}}(\theta_{1k}, \theta_{1k+1}, \theta_{2k}, \theta_{2k+1}, \theta_{3k}, \theta_{3k+1}) \\ \frac{\partial \mathcal{L}_d}{\partial \theta_{2k+1}}(\theta_{1k}, \theta_{1k+1}, \theta_{2k}, \theta_{2k+1}, \theta_{3k}, \theta_{3k+1}) \\ \frac{\partial \mathcal{L}_d}{\partial \theta_{3k+1}}(\theta_{1k}, \theta_{1k+1}, \theta_{2k}, \theta_{2k+1}, \theta_{3k}, \theta_{3k+1}) \end{bmatrix} \quad (5)$$

Both discrete torques, i.e., left and right forces, are defined as follows.

$$u_d^- = u_d^+ = \begin{bmatrix} u_{1k} - u_{2k} \\ u_{2k} - u_{3k} \\ u_{3k} \end{bmatrix} \quad (6)$$

To raise the body from the sitting position to the standing position, it is necessary to provide an appropriate amount of torque at the joints. Therefore, an optimization problem is formulated to mimic the Sit-to-Stand function with the aim of minimizing the effort required to complete this motion, which is represented as the total torque-squared applied by each joint [28]. The torques are equally minimized ($\alpha_1 = \alpha_2 = \alpha_3 = 1$) to study the effect of speed and seat height on the motion; however, α_2 (coefficient of the knee torque) is increased to study the effect of knee strength while keeping $\alpha_1 = \alpha_3 = 1$, assuming that the model is mimicking sitting on a desk chair in which the femur is making a 90° angle with the vertical axis, whereas the tibias and torso are allowed to have unfixed initial states but within reasonable bounded range. Conversely, the standing position requires all joints to make around 0° with the vertical as defined in our model. Then, the optimization problem can be simplified as follows:

$$\min J = \sum_{k=1}^{N}\sum_{i=1}^{3}\alpha_i u_i^2(N) = \sum_{k=1}^{N} \alpha_1 u_1^2(N) + \alpha_2 u_2^2(N) + \alpha_3 u_3^2(N) \quad (7)$$

with both decision variables θ_i and u_i subjected to the following constraints:

- System dynamics

$$D_1\mathcal{L}_d(\theta_{1k}, \theta_{1k+1}, \theta_{2k}, \theta_{2k+1}, \theta_{3k}, \theta_{3k+1}) + f_d^-(\theta_{1k}, \theta_{1k+1}, \theta_{2k}, \theta_{2k+1}, \theta_{3k}, \theta_{3k+1})$$
$$+D_2\mathcal{L}_d(\theta_{1k-1}, \theta_{1k}, \theta_{2k-1}, \theta_{2k}, \theta_{3k-1}, \theta_{3k})$$
$$+f_d^+(\theta_{1k-1}, \theta_{1k}, \theta_{2k-1}, \theta_{2k}, \theta_{3k-1}, \theta_{3k}) = 0$$

- Boundary constraints

$$\theta_3(1) = 0°, \theta_2(1) = 90°$$

$$\theta_1(N+1) = 0°, \theta_2(N+1) = 0°, \theta_3(N+1) = 0°$$

- Path constraints

$$\theta_{i\ min} \leq \theta_i \leq \theta_{i\ max}$$

$$u_{i\ min} \leq u_i \leq u_{i\ max}$$

The optimization problem was solved using the MATLAB® and SNOPT® (Sparse Nonlinear OPTimizer) toolbox, and the simulation was run with different initial conditions for each case in this study.

3. Results

The results of the optimization provided a unique solution for each case that describes the optimal STS movement for the given conditions. The normal pattern of STS can be explained using the ground force and the velocity of Center of Mass (COM) by dividing the STS motion into phases, starting from the model at sitting position and ending when the velocity of center of mass approaches zero [29]. The first phase starts at the sitting position and initiates the movement by bending the torso forward, and it ends by raising both thighs, as seen in Figure 2. Bending the torso forward helps to get torso flexion, which shifts COM forward. This phase transfers momentum to the next phase, and it occurs quickly. Therefore, it requires the generation of an efficient flexion momentum to be able to transfer a lot of it to the lower extremities in the next phase. Before standing up, the tibia segment is placed backward behind the knee, which results in ankle dorsiflexion. The results showed that the profile of GRF directed forward under the feet and the velocity of COM have a bell shape with a peak just before seat off, as seen in Figures 3 and 4 respectively [29]. The GRF for the model and the experimental results [30] have the same pattern; however, for the case of the experimental results, the GRF starts from zero due to the presence of the chair that holds the weight of the person. For the model, the GRF as a percentage of body weight starts from one because we assume that the model is at the sitting position on foot (no chair). Moreover, we noticed that the model obtained the same profile of COM velocity reported in the literature [29].

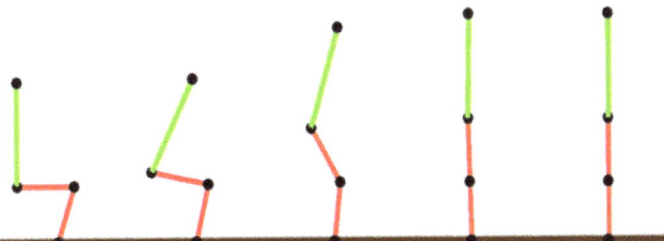

Figure 2. The normal pattern of STS can be explained using the ground force reaction and the velocity of center of mass by dividing the movement into phases starting from the model sitting and ending when the velocity of center of mass approaches zero.

Then, the model is considered to be in the second phase once it is no longer in the sitting position. The hip will continue to flex, and the model uses the flexion momentum transferred from the previous phase, which was generated from torso flexion and distributed to all segments, but more to the lower segments. For human beings, the flexion momentum produced in the first phase is for the upper body, since the thighs are still on the seat. Whenever the thighs are taken off the seat, this flexion momentum can be transferred to the total body and into the legs, as well. Meanwhile, we will have continued flexion of the hips and continued ankle dorsiflexion in this phase. One of the most important characteristics of this phase is that it has the largest amount of ground reaction force among all four phases of STS. This is because during this phase, all the body weight is on the feet. Looking at the pattern of Ground Reaction Force (GRF), we see that there is a basic need to produce ground force greater than body weight in order to accelerate the body in the upward direction [30].

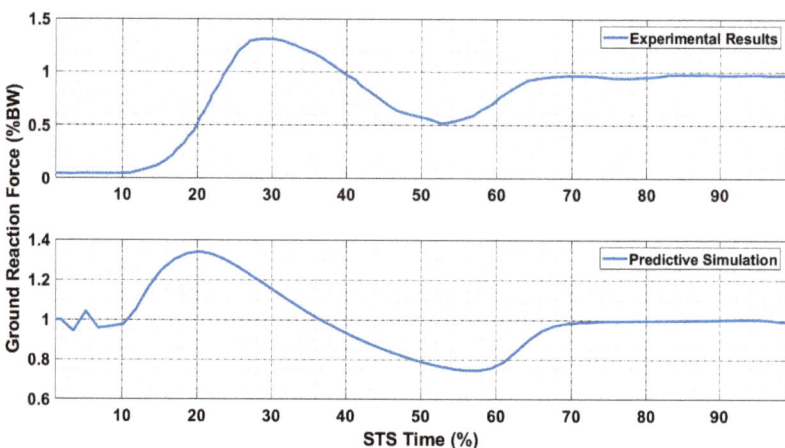

Figure 3. The profile of GRF directed forward under the feet from simulation and experimental results [30].

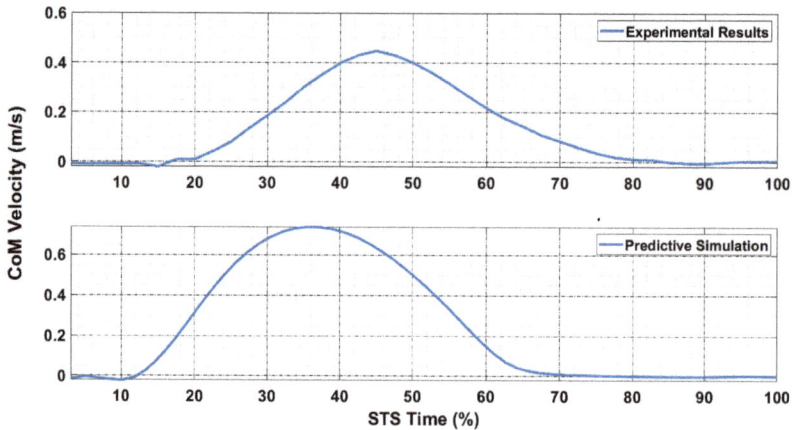

Figure 4. The velocity of COM of the model and the experimental results [29].

The third phase starts at maximum ankle dorsiflexion and ends at hip extension. It includes a sequence of lower limb extensions, knee extension, hip extension, and ankle extension. When a person stands up to a standing position from the point of maximum ankle dorsiflexion, the foot does not change position, but the tibia will move backward on the ankle. Therefore, the angle between tibia and the foot will be around 60° in this phase, whereas in the standing position it will be around 90°. In the previous phase, muscles are activated to flex the knee, whereas in this phase, the muscles are activated to extend the knee.

The GRF will start to decrease from its maximum value, indicating that the thigh is leaving the seat [30]. Again, the ground reaction force will start to increase once the body is in the upward standing position [31]. This phase is terminated once the hip reaches its maximum extension. The last phase is mainly about stabilizing the body and preventing it from falling down, since the body is already in a standing position. In this phase, the velocity of COM will approach zero, indicating the termination of STS movement.

3.1. STS Speed

The effect of STS speed on joints' kinetic and kinematics was investigated using the three-links model by changing the time required to stand up from sitting position. In order to stand up from the sitting position, the model flexes the torso forward with the presence of the hip flexion. The results show that as the speed increases (time to stand up is reduced), the torso remains flexed for a longer time interval as a percentage of total STS duration, as seen in Figure 5. Additionally, at very short time of STS, the model stands up with a flexed torso. This means that the duration of the stabilization phase reduces as the speed increases. In addition to the increment in the flexion duration of the torso, the torso angular velocity tends to increase as the speed increases, as shown in Figure 6.

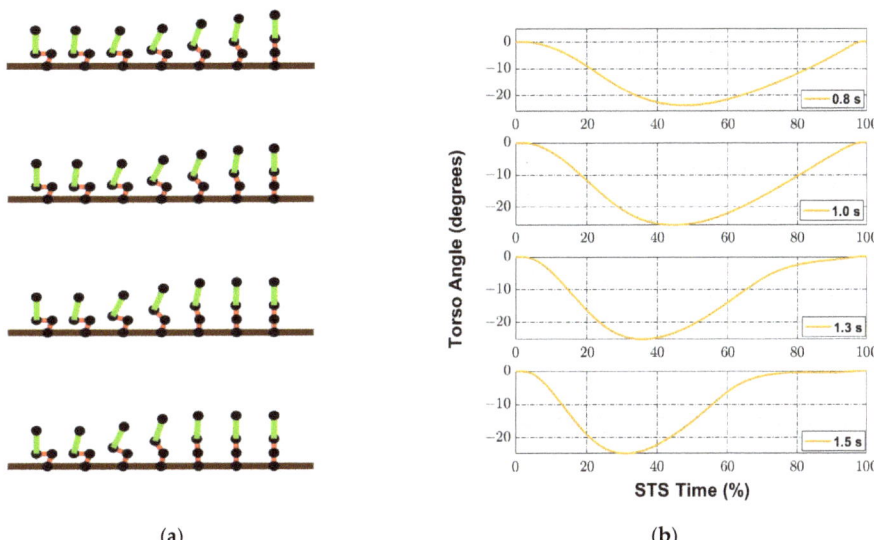

Figure 5. (a) The model performing the sit-to-stand task within different timeframes; (b) Torso angle during standing from sitting position within different timeframes.

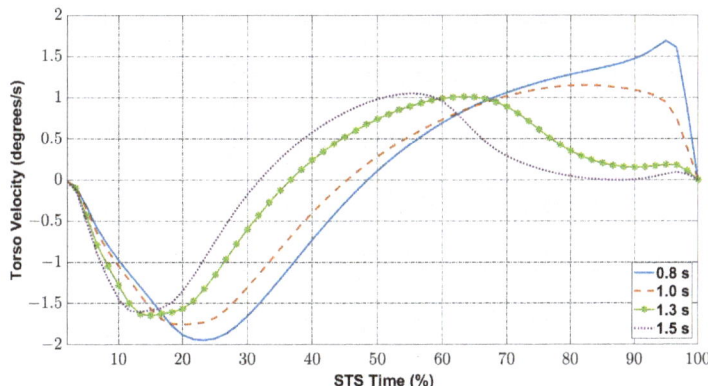

Figure 6. Torso angular velocity at different STS speeds.

An initial flexion angular velocity (negative) is observed at the hip joint as the torso is leaning forwards, followed by a positive angular velocity indicating the extension of the hip joint, which is continuous until the standing position is attained, as is clear from Figure 7. On the other hand, the velocity of the knee joint shows a smooth increase and decrease in the negative direction (extension velocity), demonstrating the control of the movement towards the full extension position, as shown in Figure 7. The peak of the angular velocity increases as the speed of rising increases, indicating the presence of exaggerated knee joint loading and causing an increment in the knee joint torque, as portrayed in Figure 8.

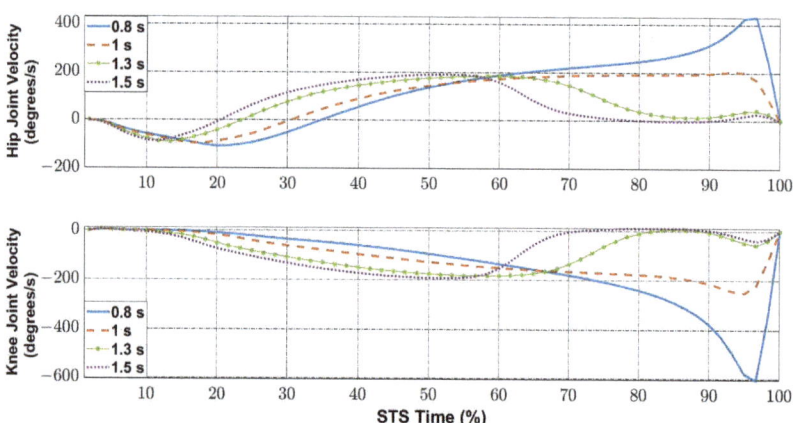

Figure 7. Hip joint velocity and knee joint velocity at different STS speeds.

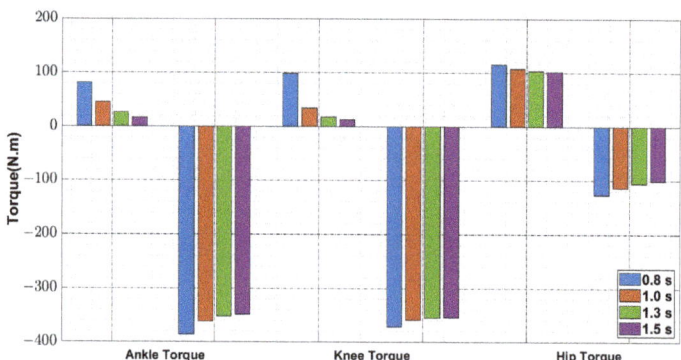

Figure 8. Ankle, knee, and hip torques at different STS speeds.

A sufficient torque needs to be generated at the joints to overcome the challenges that will need to be faced to accomplish this task successfully, including moving the body's center of mass forward and raising it vertically to the standing position.

The results have shown that the increment in the speed of STS increases the ankle dorsiflexion, knee extension, and hip flexion joint torques, and among the models' joints, the results of the optimization demonstrated that the knee is the most affected joint by increasing speed, as displayed in Figure 8.

3.2. Reduction in Joint Strength

To investigate the effect of reduced knee strength on STS motion, the model is used to optimize the STS motion with minimum joint torques and especially the knee joint torque. This can be accomplished by reformulating the cost function in Equation (7) to have a larger coefficient for the knee joint torque. The optimizer was run with different coefficients for the knee joint torque (α_2 = 1, 3, 5, and 7). The results of the optimization showed that as the coefficient of knee joint torque increases, the model tends to flex the knee and the torso as well while standing up and start to extend them at the moment just before the standing position, which is as shown in Figure 9.

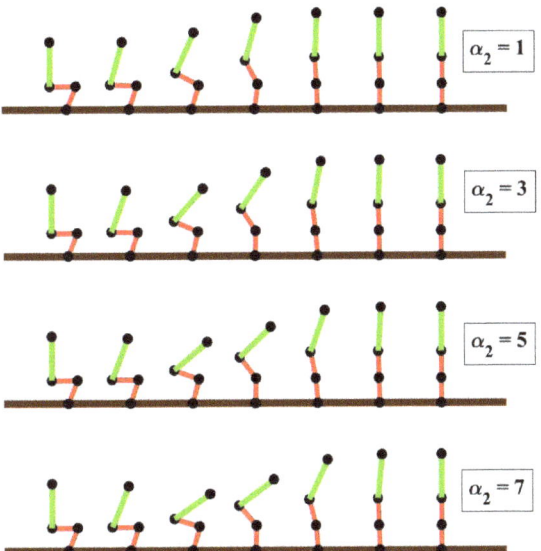

Figure 9. The model standing up with reduced knee joint strength corresponds to different coefficients of knee joint torque (α_2 = 1, α_2 = 3, α_2 = 5, and α_2 = 7).

Increasing the coefficient of knee joint torque to indicate the difficulties in rising due to the knee joint seems to increase the angular velocity of hip flexion and angular velocity of knee extension as seen in Figure 10. Moreover, an increment in the hip joint torque was observed in Figure 11 when increasing the coefficient of knee joint torque, indicating that the model depends on the hip joint to accommodate for the losing of some knee joint strength.

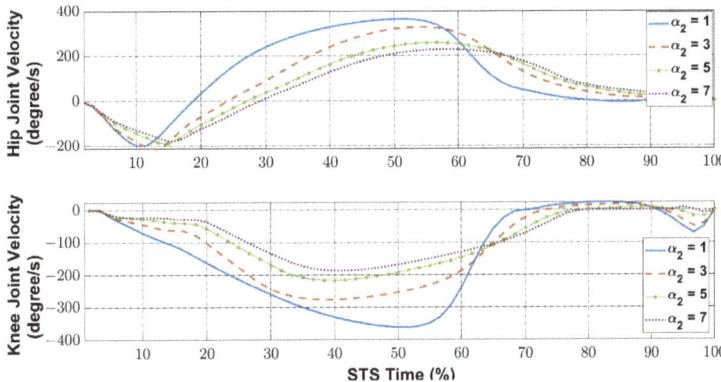

Figure 10. The angular velocity of the model with reduced knee joint strength corresponds to different coefficients of knee joint torque (α_2 = 1, α_2 = 3, α_2 = 5, and α_2 = 7).

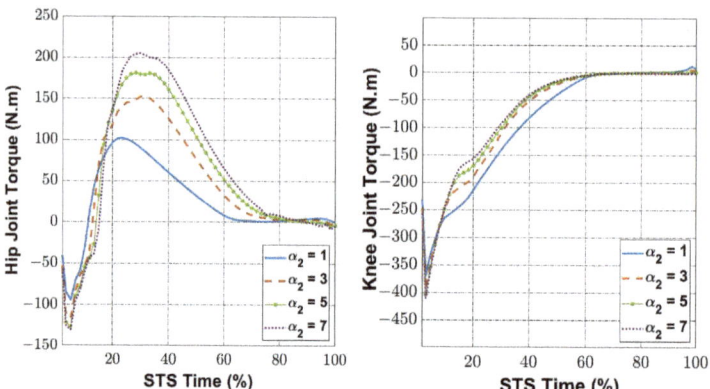

Figure 11. The Hip and knee joint torques of the model with reduced knee joint strength correspond to different coefficients of knee joint torque ($\alpha_2 = 1$, $\alpha_2 = 3$, $\alpha_2 = 5$, and $\alpha_2 = 7$).

Furthermore, the effect of reduced knee strength was studied at two speeds, fast and slow, corresponding to STS duration of 1.5 s and 0.8 s, respectively. The results of different STS speeds showed a similar pattern of joint motion, as shown in Figure 12. The model first flexed the hip while still at the sitting position with the knee initially flexed at 90°, and then performed a series of extension movements by extending the hip and knee (after a short delay) joints while plantar flexing the ankle during the remaining time of the standing. Immoderate hip flexion is resisted by the contraction of muscles, which at the same time motivates the knee flexion just prior standing up. Knee flexion is also controlled by the contraction of muscles to avoid excessive knee flexion. Figure 12 shows that the joint angle profiles for the case of larger knee torque coefficients were identical to the normal case at a slow speed; however, the range of joint motion with reduced knee strength was slightly decreased at a fast speed. On the other hand, for the same case (normal knee strength or reduced knee strength), increasing the speed resulted in increased joint range of motion.

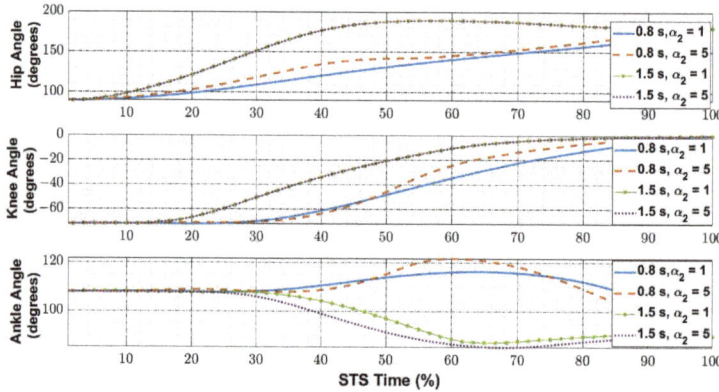

Figure 12. Hip angle, Knee angle, and Ankle angle at different STS speeds with normal and reduced knee joint strength ($\alpha_2 = 1$ and $\alpha_2 = 5$, respectively).

With normal knee strength, and as a consequence of a more upright torso during standing up, as stated in the previous section, the body's center of mass exhibited a more posterior location (behind the foot) in the cases of a fast speed that corresponds to a standing duration of 0.8 s and 1.0 s. However, with reduced knee strength, the increment in the speed increases the horizontal position of the center of mass, as seen in Figure 13. On the other hand, with normal knee strength and reduced knee strength, the vertical position of the body's center of mass starts to increase earlier for the cases of slow motion, indicating that the torso is remaining flexed while standing up for the cases of fast motion. However, the impact of speed on the vertical position of center of mass is clearer for the case of reduced knee strength than normal knee strength.

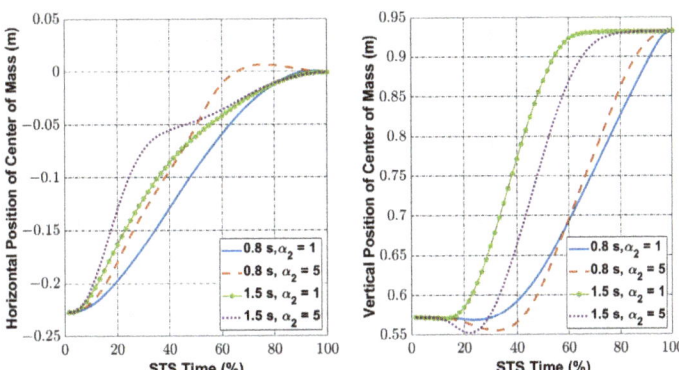

Figure 13. Horizontal and vertical positions of the center of mass at different STS speeds with normal and reduced knee joint strength ($\alpha_2 = 1$ and $\alpha_2 = 5$, respectively).

Figure 14 shows that the increment and decrement in the angular velocity of the hip and knee joints tends to be rough at a fast STS motion for $\alpha_2 = 5$ with a significant increment in the peak value of knee angular velocity compared to the hip angular velocity.

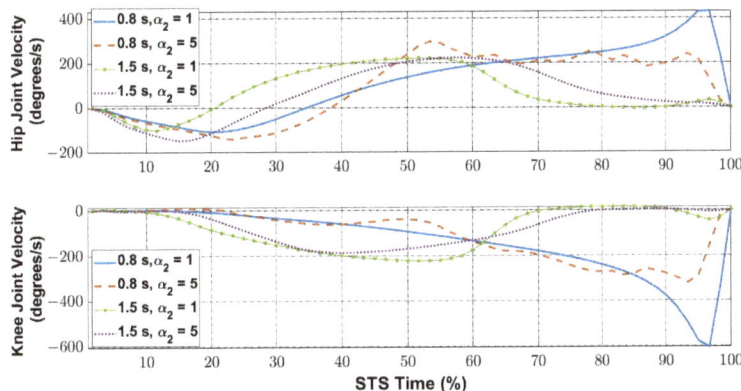

Figure 14. Hip joint velocity and knee joint velocity at different STS speeds with normal and reduced knee joint strength ($\alpha_2 = 1$ and $\alpha_2 = 5$, respectively).

3.3. Seat Height

The results of the optimization of four seat heights (30 cm, 33 cm, 37 cm, and 44 cm) showed almost a similar time taken by the model to stand from the sitting position, although the time required to attain the full standing position was longer for the lowest seat height. Moreover, the torso angle showed noticeable differences in the forward movement by showing an increment in the maximum torso angle, as seen in Figure 15, as the seat height decreases with larger angular displacements of the joints due to the larger space needing to be covered.

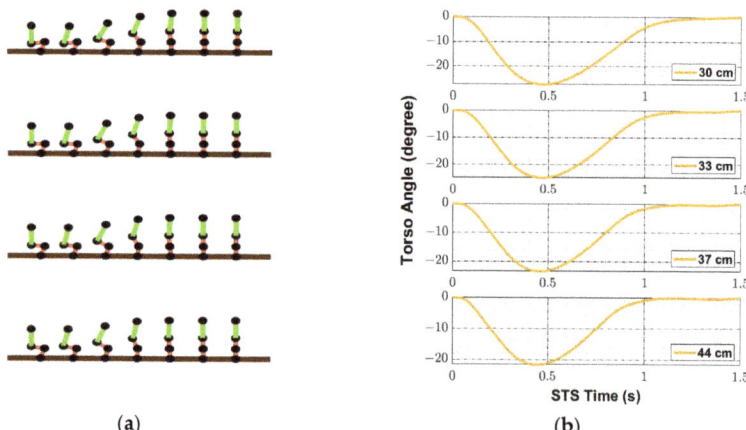

Figure 15. (**a**) Model standing up from different seat heights; (**b**) Torso angle of the model standing up from four seat heights (30 cm, 33 cm, 37 cm, and 44 cm).

The results apparently showed that as the seat height decreases, the hip and knee extension velocity increases, as seen in Figure 16, resulting in more foot repositioning, which led to an increase in the ground reaction force, as shown in Figure 17.

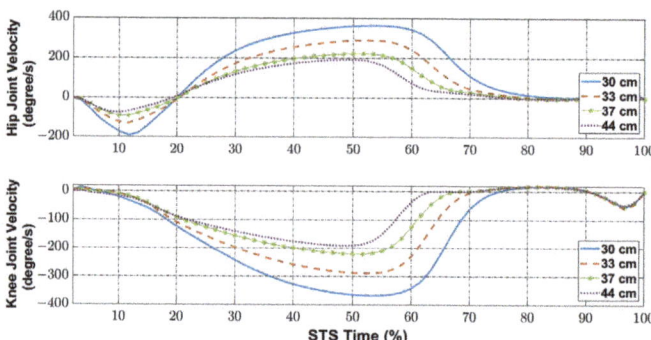

Figure 16. Hip and knee joint velocities of the model standing up from four seat heights (30 cm, 33 cm, 37 cm, and 44 cm).

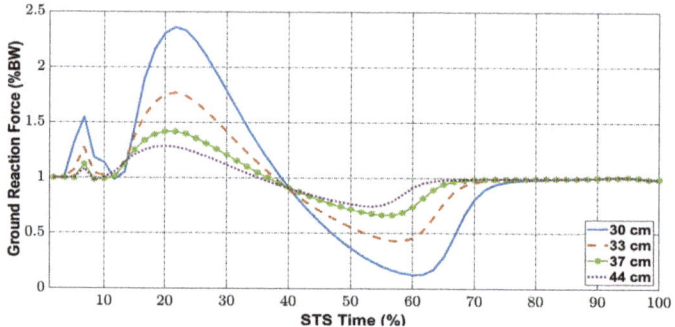

Figure 17. Ground Reaction Force of the model (as a percentage of body weight) standing up from four seat heights (30 cm, 33 cm, 37 cm, and 44 cm).

We have found that lowering the seat height increases the hip torque before and after the seat off, as well; however, reducing the height decreases the knee torque before seat off while increases it after seat off, as clear from Figure 18.

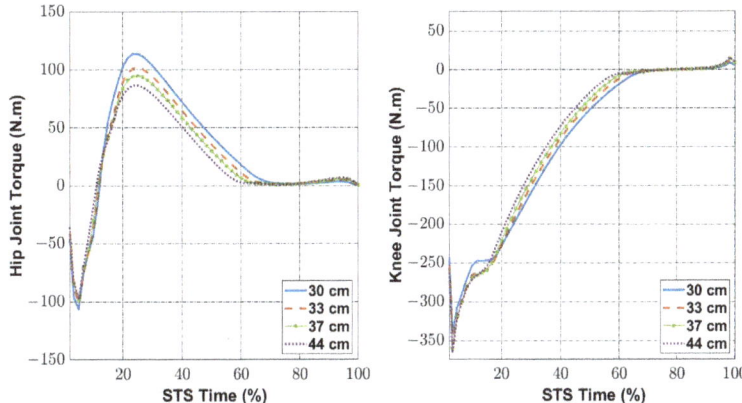

Figure 18. Hip joint and knee joint torque of the model standing up from four seat heights (30 cm, 33 cm, 37 cm, and 44 cm).

4. Discussion

We have found that increasing STS speed resulted in a shorter duration of STS phases, which agrees with reported experimental studies in the literature [32,33] and a more upright position of the torso at lift-off. Furthermore, in order to speed up the motion of STS by reducing the duration of phases, the joint torque was significantly affected, which agrees with reported experimental studies in the literature [7,13,34,35]. It is also found that increasing the speed of STS motion increased the hip flexion torque, knee extension torque, and ankle dorsiflexion torque for the model with both normal knee strength and reduced knee strength, and this validates the results of other experimental studies on healthy people and people with weakened knees [7,13,34,35]. However, between the model joints, the knee joint was the most affected joint, and it was clear from the significant increment in the knee extension moment and knee extension velocity [8,35]. This impact may be due to the load of body weight on the knee at the moment of standing up, since the model was standing with a flexed torso.

Therefore, due to the great increment in the knee joint torque, more attention was paid to the knee joint by increasing the coefficient of knee joint torque in the cost function to represent individuals with weakened or impaired knee joints, such as patients with some knee osteoarthritis or elderly people, and investigated the effect of this on STS motion. Furthermore, it was observed that as the strength of the knee joint was reduced (increasing the coefficient of knee joint torque), the angular velocities of hip and knee joints slightly increased; however, the increment in the hip joint torque was very significant. This indicated that the hip joint was trying to compensate for the reduction in the available knee joint torque. To avoid the load on the knee joint, a person can stand up slowly, especially when there are abnormalities in the knee joint; however, fast STS motion is required not only as a daily life activity, but also to do some clinical settings and tests like fast STS tests, in which patients are asked to stand up as quickly as possible. Regarding the kinetic parameters of lower limb joints and how they are affected by speed, the results of fast STS motion for the model with normal and reduced knee strength was characterized by increased knee and hip peak velocities, similar results being reported in experimental studies in the literature [7,8] and they tended to be unsmooth at fast speed as we increased the coefficient of knee joint torque. We have found that as the speed of motion was increased, the horizontal position of center of mass also increased, which can be related to the upright position of the torso while standing up, and the results of this simulation are in agreement with reported experimental studies reported in the literature [35,36]. However, the pattern of lower limb joints, including the hip, was similar when performing STS motion at fast and slow speeds for both normal knee strength and reduced knee strength [36].

Conversely, we have investigated the effects of seat height on the kinetic and kinematic parameters of the model during STS motion, as it has been considered as the most influential factor related to the chair properties [16,37,38]. The results indicated that reducing the seat height increases the angular velocity of the hip and knee joints required to stand up, which was a consequence of the increment in the torso angular velocity required to move the torso further forward from a lower seat height before seat off [16,37,38]. The higher angular velocity resulted in a higher torque at the hip joint, which transferred to the lower limb joints after leaving the seat. It is also noticed that the model exhibited an increment in the torso movement which was demonstrated by Weiner et al. as a result of increasing the demand to move the center of mass closer to the knees and reduce the required effort [39]. The higher torque at the hip joint was used by the model to assist in the remaining phases of STS, which was also due to the high forward velocity of the torso at seat off [39]. The increment in the joints' angular displacement exhibited by the model as the seat height is decreased is also confirmed by other studies [11,40], and the reason behind that was demonstrated by Yamada and Demura as reported in [17] that standing up from a lower seat height is more difficult due to the increment in the distance that must be covered by the person in order to stand up. The increase in the distance covered will also lead to an increment in the muscle activity of the lower limbs, which is represented by the increment of the model's joint torques in this study [11]. It has been known that the increment in the torso's forward movement increases the chance of falling down due to the huge torso mass compared to lower limbs; therefore, more feet repositioning was observed by the model when lowering the seat height as a stabilizing strategy [37,38], which resulted in an increment in the peak of the ground reaction force.

5. Conclusions

In this study, we have used a mathematical model to investigate its ability to predict STS body adaptations by formulating an optimization problem that minimizes joints' torques. The model was able to predict basic features of STS motion by following the constraints of the optimization problem. We have found that STS motion may be influenced by different factors such as motion speed, reduced joint strength, and seat height. We have first investigated the effect of motion speed by changing the total time required to stand up from the sitting position while equally optimizing the joint torques. Then, we reduced the knee joint strength, since it was the most affected joint, by increasing the coefficient of joint torque in the cost function for the purpose of optimizing it more than the other joints torques. Finally, we studied the effect of seat height on the STS motion by changing the femur link to get different seat heights, and again equally optimized the joints torque.

The results of this study for the three cases agreed with published experimental results, indicating that the model was able to predict the STS body adaptation. Increasing STS motion speed, reducing knee strength, and reducing seat height was found to increase joints torque and joints angular velocity, whereas reducing the knee strength was found to decrease the range of joints motion. On the other hand, we have found that reducing knee strength and reducing seat height led to increased torso flexion, while increasing STS motion speed led to standing up with an upright torso position. Moreover, the model expressed higher ground reaction force as the height of the seat was reduced and more posterior center of mass position as the knee strength was reduced.

Since STS motion is used for clinical investigation as well as daily activity as human beings, it is very important to pay attention to the factors that may impact this motion. Therefore, the model involved in this study can help in understanding these factors and determining the ability of the person to complete this motion and the challenges that may be faced.

Author Contributions: Conceptualization, S.G., A.A.-Y. and R.Z.; methodology, S.G.; software, S.G.; validation, S.G.; formal analysis, S.G., A.A.-Y. and R.Z.; investigation, S.G., A.A.-Y. and R.Z.; resources, S.G.; data curation, S.G.; writing—original draft preparation, S.G.; writing—review and editing, S.G., A.A.-Y., R.Z., H.O. and I.B.; visualization, S.G., A.A.-Y. and R.Z.; supervision, A.A.-Y. and R.Z.; project administration, A.A.-Y. All authors have read and agreed to the published version of the manuscript.

Funding: This research was funded by the former Research Council, grant number RC/ENG/MIED/15/2.

Data Availability Statement: Not applicable.

Acknowledgments: The authors would like to thank Sultan Qaboos University (SQU) and the former Research Council for supporting this research.

Conflicts of Interest: The authors declare no conflict of interest.

Appendix A

The model under study consists of three segments: the torso, the femur, and the tibia. This model is simplified as we study human motion in the sagittal plane in which we can assume that the two legs move in an asymmetric manner, so we can include one leg only. The system dynamics are derived using direct discretization of the Lagrange-d'Alembert Principle (discrete mechanics). First, we define the positions of center of mass of each link in the x and y coordinates:

$$x_{c1} = -(l_1 - d_1)sin\theta_1 \tag{A1}$$

$$y_{c1} = (l_1 - d_1)cos\theta_1 \tag{A2}$$

$$x_{c2} = -l_1 sin\theta_1 - (l_2 - d_2)sin\theta_2 \tag{A3}$$

$$y_{c2} = l_1 cos\theta_1 + (l_2 - d_2)cos\theta_2 \tag{A4}$$

$$x_{c3} = -l_1 sin\theta_1 - l_2 sin\theta_2 - (l_3 - d_3)sin\theta_3 \tag{A5}$$

$$y_{c3} = l_1 cos\theta_1 + l_2 cos\theta_2 + (l_3 - d_3)cos\theta_3 \tag{A6}$$

The velocities of center of mass of each link in the x and y coordinates are:

$$\dot{x}_{c1} = -(l_1 - d_1)\dot{\theta}_1 cos\theta_1 \tag{A7}$$

$$\dot{y}_{c1} = -(l_1 - d_1)\dot{\theta}_1 sin\theta_1 \tag{A8}$$

$$\dot{x}_{c2} = -l_1 \dot{\theta}_1 cos\theta_1 - (l_2 - d_2)\dot{\theta}_2 cos\theta_2 \tag{A9}$$

$$\dot{y}_{c2} = -l_1 \dot{\theta}_1 sin\theta_1 - (l_2 - d_2)\dot{\theta}_2 sin\theta_2 \tag{A10}$$

$$\dot{x}_{c3} = -l_1 \dot{\theta}_1 cos\theta_1 - l_2 \dot{\theta}_2 cos\theta_2 - d_3 \dot{\theta}_3 cos\theta_3 \tag{A11}$$

$$\dot{y}_{c3} = -l_1 \dot{\theta}_1 sin\theta_1 - l_2 \dot{\theta}_2 sin\theta_2 - d_3 \dot{\theta}_3 sin\theta_3 \tag{A12}$$

The kinetic energy of each link:

$$KE_1 = \frac{1}{2}m_1 v_{c1}^2 = \frac{1}{2}m_1(l_1 - d_1)^2 \dot{\theta}_1^2 + \frac{1}{2}I_1 \dot{\theta}_1^2 \tag{A13}$$

$$KE_2 = \frac{1}{2}m_2 v_{c2}^2 = \frac{1}{2}m_2 l_1^2 \dot{\theta}_1^2 + \frac{1}{2}m_2(l_2 - d_2)^2 \dot{\theta}_2^2 + \frac{1}{2}I_2 \dot{\theta}_2^2 + m_2 l_1(l_2 - d_2)\dot{\theta}_1 \dot{\theta}_2 cos(\theta_1 - \theta_2) \tag{A14}$$

$$KE_3 = \tfrac{1}{2}m_3 v_{c3}^2 = \tfrac{1}{2}m_3 l_1^2 \dot{\theta}_1^2 + \tfrac{1}{2}m_3 l_2^2 \dot{\theta}_2^2 + \tfrac{1}{2}m_3 (l_3 - d_3)^2 \dot{\theta}_3^2 + \tfrac{1}{2}I_3 \dot{\theta}_3^2$$
$$+ m_3 l_1 l_2 \dot{\theta}_1 \dot{\theta}_2 \cos(\theta_1 - \theta_2) + m_3 l_1 (l_3 - d_3) \dot{\theta}_1 \dot{\theta}_3 \cos(\theta_1 - \theta_3) \quad \text{(A15)}$$
$$+ m_3 l_2 (l_3 - d_3) \dot{\theta}_2 \dot{\theta}_3 \cos(\theta_2 - \theta_3)$$

The potential energy of each link:

$$PE_1 = m_1 g y_1 = m_1 g (l_1 - d_1) \cos\theta_1 \quad \text{(A16)}$$

$$PE_2 = m_2 g y_2 = m_2 g l_1 \cos\theta_1 + m_2 g (l_2 - d_2) \cos\theta_2 \quad \text{(A17)}$$

$$PE_3 = m_3 g y_3 = m_3 g l_1 \cos\theta_1 + m_3 g l_2 \cos\theta_2 + m_3 g (l_3 - d_3) \cos\theta_3 \quad \text{(A18)}$$

Now we derive the Lagrange equation of the model:

$$\mathcal{L} = \text{total kinetic energy} - \text{total potential energy} = KE - PE \quad \text{(A19)}$$

$$\mathcal{L} = \tfrac{1}{2}\left(m_1(l_1 - d_1)^2 + m_2 l_1^2 + m_3 l_1^2\right)\dot{\theta}_1^2 + \tfrac{1}{2}\left(m_2(l_2 - d_2)^2 + m_3 l_2^2\right)\dot{\theta}_2^2 + \tfrac{1}{2}m_3 d_3^2 \dot{\theta}_3^2$$
$$- (m_2 l_1 (l_2 - d_2) + m_3 l_1 l_2)\dot{\theta}_1 \dot{\theta}_2 \cos(\theta_1 + \theta_2)$$
$$+ m_3 l_1 d_3 \dot{\theta}_1 \dot{\theta}_3 \cos(\theta_1 - \theta_3) - m_3 l_2 d_3 \dot{\theta}_2 \dot{\theta}_3 \cos(\theta_2 + \theta_3) \quad \text{(A20)}$$
$$- g(m_1(l_1 - d_1) + m_2 l_1 + m_3 l_1)\cos\theta_1$$
$$- g(m_2(l_2 - d_2) + m_3 l_2)\cos\theta_2 - m_3 g d_3 \cos\theta_3$$

Now we convert the continuous Lagrange equation into a discrete Lagrange equation using the mid-point rule as follows:

$$\mathcal{L}(q, \dot{q}) \rightarrow h\mathcal{L}_d\left(\frac{q_{k+1} + q_k}{2}, \frac{q_{k+1} - q_k}{h}\right) \quad \text{(A21)}$$

$$L_d = \tfrac{1}{2h}a_1 \Delta\theta_{1k}^2 + \tfrac{1}{2h}a_2 \Delta\theta_{2k}^2 + \tfrac{1}{2h}a_3 \Delta\theta_{3k}^2 + \tfrac{1}{h}b_1 \Delta\theta_{1k}\Delta\theta_{2k}\cos\left(\tfrac{\Sigma\theta_{1k}}{2} - \tfrac{\Sigma\theta_{2k}}{2}\right)$$
$$+ \tfrac{1}{h}b_2 \Delta\theta_{1k}\Delta\theta_{3k}\cos\left(\tfrac{\Sigma\theta_{1k}}{2} - \tfrac{\Sigma\theta_{3k}}{2}\right)$$
$$+ \tfrac{1}{h}b_3 \Delta\theta_{2k}\Delta\theta_{3k}\cos\left(\tfrac{\Sigma\theta_{2k}}{2} - \tfrac{\Sigma\theta_{3k}}{2}\right) - ghc_1 \cos\left(\tfrac{\Sigma\theta_{1k}}{2}\right) \quad \text{(A22)}$$
$$- ghc_2 \cos\left(\tfrac{\Sigma\theta_{2k}}{2}\right) - ghc_3 \cos\left(\tfrac{\Sigma\theta_{3k}}{2}\right)$$

where:

$$a_1 = I_1 + m_1(l_1 - d_1)^2 + m_2 l_1^2 + m_3 l_1^2 \quad \text{(A23)}$$

$$a_2 = I_2 + m_2(l_2 - d_2)^2 + m_3 l_2^2 \quad \text{(A24)}$$

$$a_3 = I_3 + m_3(l_3 - d_3)^2 \quad \text{(A25)}$$

$$b_1 = m_2 l_1 (l_2 - d_2) + m_3 l_1 l_2 \quad \text{(A26)}$$

$$b_2 = m_3 l_1 (l_3 - d_3) \quad \text{(A27)}$$

$$b_3 = m_3 l_2 (l_3 - d_3) \quad \text{(A28)}$$

$$c_1 = m_1(l_1 - d_1) + m_2 l_1 + m_3 l_1 \quad \text{(A29)}$$

$$c_2 = m_2(l_2 - d_2) + m_3 l_2 \tag{A30}$$

Now find $D_1 L_d(\theta_{1k}, \theta_{1k+1}, \theta_{2k}, \theta_{2k+1}, \theta_{3k}, \theta_{3k+1})$ and $D_2 L_d(\theta_{1k}, \theta_{1k+1}, \theta_{2k}, \theta_{2k+1}, \theta_{3k}, \theta_{3k+1})$.

$D_1 L_d(\theta_{1k}, \theta_{1k+1}, \theta_{2k}, \theta_{2k+1}, \theta_{3k}, \theta_{3k+1})$: The first derivative of the discrete Lagrange with respect to the current coordinates (i.e., θ_{1k}, θ_{2k}, and θ_{3k})

$$\begin{aligned} D_1 \mathcal{L}_d = \frac{\partial \mathcal{L}_d}{\partial \theta_{1k}} \quad & (\theta_{1k}, \theta_{1k+1}, \theta_{2k}, \theta_{2k+1}, \theta_{3k}, \theta_{3k+1}) \\ = & -\tfrac{1}{h} a_1 \Delta\theta_{1k} - \tfrac{1}{h} b_1 \Delta\theta_{2k} \cos\left(\tfrac{\Sigma\theta_{1k}}{2} - \tfrac{\Sigma\theta_{2k}}{2}\right) \\ & -\tfrac{1}{2h} b_1 \Delta\theta_{1k} \Delta\theta_{2k} \sin\left(\tfrac{\Sigma\theta_{1k}}{2} - \tfrac{\Sigma\theta_{2k}}{2}\right) - \tfrac{1}{h} b_2 \Delta\theta_{3k} \cos\left(\tfrac{\Sigma\theta_{1k}}{2} - \tfrac{\Sigma\theta_{3k}}{2}\right) \\ & -\tfrac{1}{2h} b_2 \Delta\theta_{1k} \Delta\theta_{3k} \sin\left(\tfrac{\Sigma\theta_{1k}}{2} - \tfrac{\Sigma\theta_{3k}}{2}\right) + \tfrac{ghc_1}{2} \sin\left(\tfrac{\Sigma\theta_{1k}}{2}\right) \end{aligned} \tag{A31}$$

$$\begin{aligned} D_1 \mathcal{L}_d = \frac{\partial \mathcal{L}_d}{\partial \theta_{2k}} \quad & (\theta_{1k}, \theta_{1k+1}, \theta_{2k}, \theta_{2k+1}, \theta_{3k}, \theta_{3k+1}) \\ = & -\tfrac{1}{h} a_2 \Delta\theta_{2k} - \tfrac{1}{h} b_1 \Delta\theta_{1k} \cos\left(\tfrac{\Sigma\theta_{1k}}{2} - \tfrac{\Sigma\theta_{2k}}{2}\right) \\ & +\tfrac{1}{2h} b_1 \Delta\theta_{1k} \Delta\theta_{2k} \sin\left(\tfrac{\Sigma\theta_{1k}}{2} - \tfrac{\Sigma\theta_{2k}}{2}\right) - \tfrac{1}{h} b_3 \Delta\theta_{3k} \cos\left(\tfrac{\Sigma\theta_{2k}}{2} - \tfrac{\Sigma\theta_{3k}}{2}\right) \\ & -\tfrac{1}{2h} b_3 \Delta\theta_{2k} \Delta\theta_{3k} \sin\left(\tfrac{\Sigma\theta_{2k}}{2} - \tfrac{\Sigma\theta_{3k}}{2}\right) \tfrac{ghc_2}{2} \sin\left(\tfrac{\Sigma\theta_{2k}}{2}\right) \end{aligned} \tag{A32}$$

$$\begin{aligned} D_1 \mathcal{L}_d = \frac{\partial \mathcal{L}_d}{\partial \theta_{3k}} \quad & (\theta_{1k}, \theta_{1k+1}, \theta_{2k}, \theta_{2k+1}, \theta_{3k}, \theta_{3k+1}) \\ = & -\tfrac{1}{h} a_3 \Delta\theta_{3k} - \tfrac{1}{h} b_2 \Delta\theta_{1k} \cos\left(\tfrac{\Sigma\theta_{1k}}{2} - \tfrac{\Sigma\theta_{3k}}{2}\right) \\ & +\tfrac{1}{2h} b_2 \Delta\theta_{1k} \Delta\theta_{3k} \sin\left(\tfrac{\Sigma\theta_{1k}}{2} - \tfrac{\Sigma\theta_{3k}}{2}\right) - \tfrac{1}{h} b_3 \Delta\theta_{2k} \cos\left(\tfrac{\Sigma\theta_{2k}}{2} - \tfrac{\Sigma\theta_{3k}}{2}\right) \\ & +\tfrac{1}{2h} b_3 \Delta\theta_{2k} \Delta\theta_{3k} \sin\left(\tfrac{\Sigma\theta_{2k}}{2} - \tfrac{\Sigma\theta_{3k}}{2}\right) + \tfrac{ghc_3}{2} \sin\left(\tfrac{\Sigma\theta_{3k}}{2}\right) \end{aligned} \tag{A33}$$

$D_2 L_d(\theta_{1k}, \theta_{1k+1}, \theta_{2k}, \theta_{2k+1}, \theta_{3k}, \theta_{3k+1})$: The first derivative of the discrete Lagrange with respect to the current coordinates (i.e., $\theta_{1k+1}, \theta_{2k+1}$, and θ_{3k+1})

$$\begin{aligned} D_2 \mathcal{L}_d = \frac{\partial \mathcal{L}_d}{\partial \theta_{1k+1}} \quad & (\theta_{1k}, \theta_{1k+1}, \theta_{2k}, \theta_{2k+1}, \theta_{3k}, \theta_{3k+1}) \\ = & \tfrac{1}{h} a_1 \Delta\theta_{1k} + \tfrac{1}{h} b_1 \Delta\theta_{2k} \cos\left(\tfrac{\Sigma\theta_{1k}}{2} - \tfrac{\Sigma\theta_{2k}}{2}\right) \\ & -\tfrac{1}{2h} b_1 \Delta\theta_{1k} \Delta\theta_{2k} \sin\left(\tfrac{\Sigma\theta_{1k}}{2} - \tfrac{\Sigma\theta_{2k}}{2}\right) + \tfrac{1}{h} b_2 \Delta\theta_{3k} \cos\left(\tfrac{\Sigma\theta_{1k}}{2} - \tfrac{\Sigma\theta_{3k}}{2}\right) \\ & -\tfrac{1}{2h} b_2 \Delta\theta_{1k} \Delta\theta_{3k} \sin\left(\tfrac{\Sigma\theta_{1k}}{2} - \tfrac{\Sigma\theta_{3k}}{2}\right) + ghc_1 \sin\left(\tfrac{\Sigma\theta_{1k}}{2}\right) \end{aligned} \tag{A34}$$

$$\begin{aligned} D_2 \mathcal{L}_d = \frac{\partial \mathcal{L}_d}{\partial \theta_{2k+1}} \quad & (\theta_{1k}, \theta_{1k+1}, \theta_{2k}, \theta_{2k+1}, \theta_{3k}, \theta_{3k+1}) \\ = & \tfrac{1}{h} a_2 \Delta\theta_{2k} + \tfrac{1}{h} b_1 \Delta\theta_{1k} \cos\left(\tfrac{\Sigma\theta_{1k}}{2} - \tfrac{\Sigma\theta_{2k}}{2}\right) \\ & +\tfrac{1}{2h} b_1 \Delta\theta_{1k} \Delta\theta_{2k} \sin\left(\tfrac{\Sigma\theta_{1k}}{2} - \tfrac{\Sigma\theta_{2k}}{2}\right) + \tfrac{1}{h} b_3 \Delta\theta_{3k} \cos\left(\tfrac{\Sigma\theta_{2k}}{2} - \tfrac{\Sigma\theta_{3k}}{2}\right) \\ & -\tfrac{1}{2h} b_3 \Delta\theta_{2k} \Delta\theta_{3k} \sin\left(\tfrac{\Sigma\theta_{2k}}{2} - \tfrac{\Sigma\theta_{3k}}{2}\right) + ghc_2 \sin\left(\tfrac{\Sigma\theta_{2k}}{2}\right) \end{aligned} \tag{A35}$$

$$\begin{aligned} D_2 \mathcal{L}_d = \frac{\partial \mathcal{L}_d}{\partial \theta_{3k+1}} \quad & (\theta_{1k}, \theta_{1k+1}, \theta_{2k}, \theta_{2k+1}, \theta_{3k}, \theta_{3k+1}) \\ = & \tfrac{1}{h} a_3 \Delta\theta_{3k} + \tfrac{1}{h} b_2 \Delta\theta_{1k} \cos\left(\tfrac{\Sigma\theta_{1k}}{2} - \tfrac{\Sigma\theta_{3k}}{2}\right) \\ & +\tfrac{1}{2h} b_2 \Delta\theta_{1k} \Delta\theta_{3k} \sin\left(\tfrac{\Sigma\theta_{2k}}{2} - \tfrac{\Sigma\theta_{3k}}{2}\right) + \tfrac{1}{h} b_3 \Delta\theta_{2k} \cos\left(\tfrac{\Sigma\theta_{1k}}{2} - \tfrac{\Sigma\theta_{3k}}{2}\right) \\ & +\tfrac{1}{2h} b_3 \Delta\theta_{2k} \Delta\theta_{3k} \sin\left(\tfrac{\Sigma\theta_{2k}}{2} - \tfrac{\Sigma\theta_{3k}}{2}\right) + ghc_3 \sin\left(\tfrac{\Sigma\theta_{3k}}{2}\right) \end{aligned} \tag{A36}$$

After several investigations, we came out with the proper and most commonly used set of anthropometric information. Table A1 provides the weight of each segment as a percentage of the total body weight, the length of each segment as a percentage of total body height [25,26], the location of Center of Mass (COM) of each segment, measured as percentage of segment length [26], the segments' radius of gyration in the frontal plane (perpendicular to the sagittal plane) as a percentage of segment length [24], and it will be used to calculate the Moment of Inertia (MOI) for each segment. Based on this information, the required anthropometric data of the model is calculated for a male with 70 kg mass and 1.70 m height.

Table A1. Anthropometric percentages of different body segments required for the model.

Body Segment	Segment Mass as a PERCENTAGE of Body Mass	Segment Length as a Percentage of Total Body Height	Distance of Segment COM from Proximal End as a Percentage of Segment Length	Radius of Gyration of Body Segments in Frontal Plane as a Percentage of Segment Length
Head and Neck	8.2	10.75	56.7	31.5
Trunk	46.84	30.00	56.2	38.3
Upper arm	3.25	17.20	43.6	31.0
Forearm	1.8	15.70	43.0	28.4
Hand	0.65	5.75	46.8	23.3
Thigh	10.5	23.20	43.3	26.7
Calf	4.75	24.70	43.4	27.5

The moment of inertia for each segment is calculated using the anthropometric data associated with each segment. For instance, evaluation of MOI of the head and neck will be as follows:

- Mass of the head and neck segment is considered to be 8.2% of total body mass according to the data provided in Table A1, and hence, $m_{HN} = 5.78$ kg.
- According to Table A1, the length of the head and neck segment is 10.75% of the body height and is found to be $L_{HN} = 0.18$ m.
- Radius of gyration of the head and neck in the frontal axis is 31.5%, and hence, $k_{HN} = 0.058$ m.
- Now, the MOI of the head and neck can be determined using the following equation:

$$I_{HN} = m_{HN} k_{HN}^2 = 5.78 \times 0.058^2 = 0.0192 \text{ kg·m}^2 \quad (A37)$$

Using the same technique, the MOI of torso, hand segments, and leg segments are calculated, and the values are given in Table A2 with the other anthropometric measurements of each segment. The mass and moment of inertia of the head, the arms, and the torso (HAT) segment is simply found by summing up the individual mass of these segments; however, the center of mass is found using the parallel axis theorem [41]:

$$m_{HAT} d_{HAT} = m_{HN} d_{HN} + m_T d_T + 2 * m_{UA} d_{UA} + 2 * m_{FA} d_{FA} + 2 * m_H d_H \quad (A38)$$

The distance of the COM of the head and neck from the top of the head is d_{HN} and is calculated directly from Table A1. The distance of the COM of the torso from the top of the head is d_T, and it is equivalent to the total length of the head and neck segment and the distance from the neck to the COM of the torso. The same procedure is followed to calculate the distance from the top of the head to the COM of each segment of the arm.

$$\begin{aligned}(5.78 + 32.8 + 2 \times 2.275 &+ 2 \times 1.309 + 2 \times 0.455) d_{HAT} \\ &= 5.78 \times 0.078 + 32.8 \times 0.4034 + 2 \times 2.275 \times 0.3075 + 2 \times 1.309 \times 0.585 \\ &+ 2 \times 0.455 \times 0.84\end{aligned} \quad (A39)$$

$$d_{HAT} = \frac{17.379}{46.66} = 0.3725 \text{ m} \tag{A40}$$

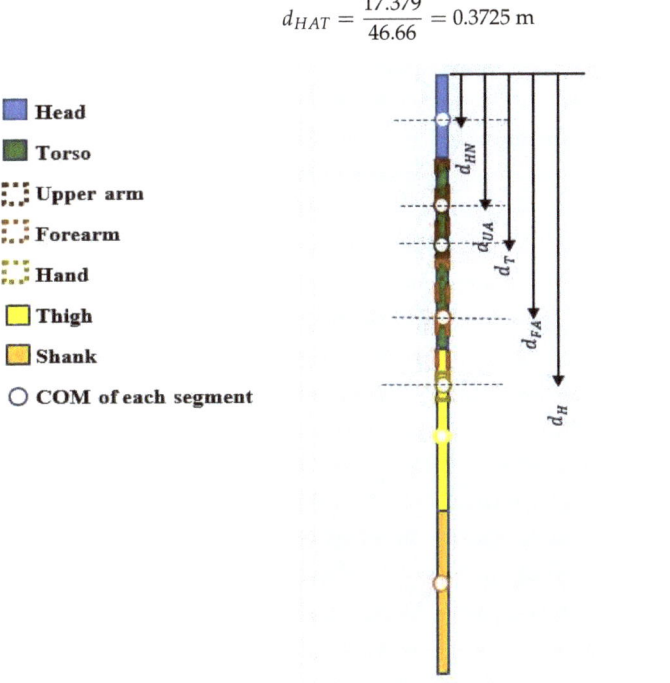

Figure A1. COM of body segments in the sagittal plane.

The MOI of upper body segments around the axis of rotation, which is the y-axis, can be approximated using the principle Parallel Axes Theorem. For applying the theorem, we need to determine the offset (r) for each segment, which is the shortest distance between the axis of rotation and the other axis passing through the COG of that segment. For example, the offset distance between the axis of rotation and the axis of the head and neck segment is defined as r_{HN}, and it can be found as the distance between the COG of the head and neck segment to the joint of the shoulder and the distance from the joint of the shoulder to the COG of the HAT segment.

$$r_{HN} = d_{HAT} - d_{HN} = 0.3725 - 0.078 = 0.2945 \text{ m} \tag{A41}$$

The MOI of the head and neck about the axis of rotation is found as shown below.

$$I_{HN}' = I_{HN} + m_{HN} r_{HN}^2 = 0.0192 + \left(5.78 \times 0.2945^2\right) = 0.5205 \text{ kg·m}^2 \tag{A42}$$

Using the same procedure, we found the offset distances and the moments of inertia about the axis of rotation for the other segments:

For the torso:

$$r_T = d_T - d_{HAT} = 0.4034 - 0.3725 = 0.0309 \text{ m} \tag{A43}$$

$$I_T' = I_T + m_T r_T^2 = 1.251 + \left(32.8 \times 0.0309^2\right) = 1.2823 \text{ kg·m}^2 \tag{A44}$$

For the upper arms:

$$r_{UA} = d_{HAT} - d_{UA} = 0.3725 - 0.3075 = 0.065 \text{ m} \tag{A45}$$

$$I_{UA}' = I_{UA} + m_{UA}r_{UA}^2 = 0.0187 + \left(2.275 \times 0.065^2\right) = 0.0283 \text{ kg·m}^2 \tag{A46}$$

For the forearms:

$$r_{FA} = d_{FA} - d_{HAT} = 0.585 - 0.3075 = 0.2775 \text{ m} \tag{A47}$$

$$I_{FA}' = I_{FA} + m_{FA}r_{FA}^2 = 0.00752 + \left(1.309 \times 0.2775^2\right) = 0.1083 \text{ kg·m}^2 \tag{A48}$$

For the hands:

$$r_H = d_H - d_{HAT} = 0.84 - 0.3075 = 0.5325 \text{ m} \tag{A49}$$

$$I_H' = I_H + m_H r_H^2 = 0.000236 + \left(0.455 \times 0.5325^2\right) = 0.1292 \text{ kg·m}^2 \tag{A50}$$

Then, the total MOI of the HAT segment about the axis of rotation is found by summing up the MOI of the individual segments about the same axis of rotation:

$$\begin{aligned} I_{HAT}' &= I_{HN}' + I_T' + I_{UA}' + I_{FA}' + I_H' \\ &= 0.5205 + 1.2823 + 0.0283 + 0.1083 + 0.1292 = 2.0686 \text{ kg·m}^2 \end{aligned} \tag{A51}$$

The table below shows the physical parameters for a male with 70 kg and 1.70 m required to build the model. Since the model does not include the head and the arms, the head and the three segments of the arms will be considered as one segment with the torso, represented as HAT (Head, Arms, and Torso).

Table A2. Model physical parameters based on a male with 70 kg mass and 1.70 m height.

Body Segment	Segment Mass (KG)	Segment Length (m)	Distance of Segment COM from Proximal (m)	Moment of Inertia
Head & Neck	0.18	5.782	0.10361925	0.019160814
Trunk	0.51	32.788	0.28662	1.250987086
Upper arm	0.29	2.275	0.1274864	0.018692162
Forearm	0.27	1.309	0.1155677	0.007520963
Hand	0.10	0.455	0.045747	0.000236024
Thigh	0.39	7.35	0.1707752	0.081504892
Calf	0.42	3.325	0.1822366	0.044335212
HAT	0.69	46.648	0.214937	2.0686

References

1. Dorn, T.W.; Wang, J.M.; Hicks, J.L.; Delp, S.L. Predictive simulation generates human adaptations during loaded and inclined walking. *PLoS ONE* **2015**, *10*, e0121407. [CrossRef] [PubMed]
2. Abdel-Malek, K.; Arora, J. *Human Motion Simulation: Predictive Dynamics*; Academic Press: Cambridge, MA, USA, 2013.
3. Geyer, H. Simple Models of Legged Locomotion Based on Compliant Limb Behavior = Grundmodelle Pedaler Lokomotion Basierend auf Nachgiebigem Beinverhalten. Ph.D. Thesis, Friedrich-Schiller-Universitat, Jena, Germany, 2005.
4. Seipel, J.; Kvalheim, M.; Revzen, S.; Sharbafi, M.A.; Seyfarth, A. *Conceptual Models of Legged Locomotion, in Bioinspired Legged Locomotion*; Elsevier: Amsterdam, The Netherlands, 2017; pp. 55–131.
5. Khan, A.T.; Li, S.; Zhou, X. Trajectory optimization of 5-link biped robot using beetle antennae search. *IEEE Trans. Circuits Syst. II Express Briefs* **2021**, *68*, 3276–3280. [CrossRef]
6. Xiang, Y.; Chung, H.-J.; Kim, J.H.; Bhatt, R.; Rahmatalla, S.; Yang, J.; Marler, T.; Arora, J.S.; Abdel-Malek, K. Predictive dynamics: An optimization-based novel approach for human motion simulation. *Struct. Multidiscip. Optim.* **2010**, *41*, 465–479. [CrossRef]
7. Gross, M.; Stevenson, P.; Charette, S.; Pyka, G.; Marcus, R. Effect of muscle strength and movement speed on the biomechanics of rising from a chair in healthy elderly and young women. *Gait Posture* **1998**, *8*, 175–185. [CrossRef] [PubMed]

8. Mak, M.K.; Hui-Chan, C.W. The speed of sit-to-stand can be modulated in Parkinson's disease. *Clin. Neurophysiol.* **2005**, *116*, 780–789. [CrossRef] [PubMed]
9. Odding, E. *Locomotor Disability in the Elderly: An Epidemiological Study of Its Occurrence and Determinants in a General Population of 55 Years and Over: The Rotterdam Study*; Erasmus University Rotterdam: Rotterdam, The Netherlands, 1994.
10. Janssen, W. *The Sit-to-Stand Movement Recovery after Stroke and Objective Assessment*; Optima Grafische Communicatie: Rotterdam, The Netherlands, 2008.
11. Janssen, W.G.; Bussmann, H.B.; Stam, H.J. Determinants of the sit-to-stand movement: A review. *Phys. Ther.* **2002**, *82*, 866–879. [CrossRef]
12. Anan, M.; Shinkoda, K.; Suzuki, K.; Yagi, M.; Ibara, T.; Kito, N. Do patients with knee osteoarthritis perform sit-to-stand motion efficiently? *Gait Posture* **2015**, *41*, 488–492. [CrossRef]
13. Rogers, M.W.; Chan, C.W. Motor planning is impaired in Parkinson's disease. *Brain Res.* **1988**, *438*, 271–276. [CrossRef]
14. Honda, K.; Sekiguchi, Y.; Sasaki, A.; Shimazaki, S.; Suzuki, R.; Suzuki, T.; Kanetaka, H.; Izumi, S.-I. Effects of seat height on whole-body movement and lower limb muscle power during sit-to-stand movements in young and older individuals. *J. Biomech.* **2021**, *129*, 110813. [CrossRef]
15. Hurley, S.T.; Rutherford, D.J.; Hubley-Kozey, C. The effect of age and seat height on sit-to-stand transfer biomechanics and muscle activation. *Phys. Occup. Ther. Geriatr.* **2016**, *34*, 169–185. [CrossRef]
16. Su, F.C.; Lai, K.; Hong, W. Rising from chair after total knee arthroplasty. *Clin. Biomech.* **1998**, *13*, 176–181. [CrossRef] [PubMed]
17. Yamada, T.; Demura, S.-I. Influence of the relative difference in chair seat height according to different lower thigh length on floor reaction force and lower-limb strength during sit-to-stand movement. *J. Physiol. Anthropol. Appl. Hum. Sci.* **2004**, *23*, 197–203. [CrossRef]
18. Yamasaki, H.R.; Kambara, H.; Koike, Y. Dynamic optimization of the sit-to-stand movement. *J. Appl. Biomech.* **2011**, *27*, 306–313. [CrossRef]
19. Garner, B. A Dynamic Musculoskeletal Computer Model for Rising from a Squatting or Sitting Position. Master's Thesis, The University of Texas at Austin, Austin, TX, USA, 1992.
20. Daigle, K.E. The Effect of Muscle Strength on the Coordination of Rising from a Chair in Minimum Time: Predictions of an Optimal Control Model. Master's Thesis, The University of Texas at Austin, Austin, TX, USA, 1994.
21. Domire, Z.J. A Biomechanical Analysis of Maximum Vertical Jumps and Sit to Stand. Ph.D. Thesis, The Pennsylvania State University, University Park, PA, USA, 2004.
22. Dodig, M. Models and modelling of dynamic moments of inertia of human body. *Int. J. Sport. Sci.* **2016**, *6*, 247–256.
23. Erdmann, W.S. Geometry and inertia of the human body-review of research. *Acta Bioeng. Biomech.* **1999**, *1*, 23–35.
24. Hall, S.J. *Basic Biomechanics, 8e*; McGraw-Hill: New York, NY, USA, 2019.
25. Williams, R. *Engineering Biomechanics of Human Motion*; Supplement Notes; Mechanical/Biomedical Engineering, Ohio University: Athens, OH, USA, 2014; p. 5670.
26. Ober-Blobaum, S.; Junge, O.; Marsden, J.E. Discrete mechanics and optimal control: An analysis. *ESAIM Control. Optim. Calc. Var.* **2011**, *17*, 322–352. [CrossRef]
27. Schultz, J.; Johnson, E.; Murphey, T.D. Trajectory optimization in discrete mechanics. In *Differential-Geometric Methods in Computational Multibody System Dynamics*; Springer International Publishing: Cham, Switzerland, 2015.
28. Inoue, Y.; Takahashi, M. Time-constrained Optimization of Sit-to-stand Movements in Contact with the Environment. *IFAC-PapersOnLine* **2022**, *55*, 358–363. [CrossRef]
29. Hirschfeld, H.; Thorsteinsdottir, M.; Olsson, E. Coordinated ground forces exerted by buttocks and feet are adequately programmed for weight transfer during sit-to-stand. *J. Neurophysiol.* **1999**, *82*, 3021–3029. [CrossRef]
30. Yamada, T.; Demura, S. The relationship of force output characteristics during a sit-to-stand movement with lower limb muscle mass and knee joint extension in the elderly. *Arch. Gerontol. Geriatr.* **2010**, *50*, e46–e50. [CrossRef]
31. Headon, R.; Curwen, R. Recognizing movements from the ground reaction force. In Proceedings of the 2001 Workshop on Perceptive User Interfaces, Orlando, FL, USA, 15–16 November 2001.
32. A Hanke, T.; Pai, Y.-C.; Rogers, M.W. Reliability of measurements of body center-of-mass momentum during sit-to-stand in healthy adults. *Phys. Ther.* **1995**, *75*, 105–113. [CrossRef]
33. Linden, D.W.V.; Brunt, D.; McCulloch, M.U. Variant and invariant characteristics of the sit-to-stand task in healthy elderly adults. *Arch. Phys. Med. Rehabil.* **1994**, *75*, 653–660. [CrossRef] [PubMed]
34. Bieryla, K.A.; Anderson, D.E.; Madigan, M.L. Estimations of relative effort during sit-to-stand increase when accounting for variations in maximum voluntary torque with joint angle and angular velocity. *J. Electromyogr. Kinesiol.* **2009**, *19*, 139–144. [CrossRef] [PubMed]
35. Wang, J.; Severin, A.C.; Siddicky, S.F.; Barnes, C.L.; Mannen, E.M. Effect of movement speed on lower and upper body biomechanics during sit-to-stand-to-sit transfers: Self-selected speed vs. fast imposed speed. *Hum. Mov. Sci.* **2021**, *77*, 102797. [CrossRef]
36. Lord, S.R.; Murray, S.M.; Chapman, K.; Munro, B.; Tiedemann, A. Sit-to-stand performance depends on sensation, speed, balance, and psychological status in addition to strength in older people. *J. Gerontol. Ser. A Biol. Sci. Med. Sci.* **2002**, *57*, M539–M543. [CrossRef] [PubMed]
37. Hughes, M.A.; Weiner, D.K.; Schenkman, M.L.; Long, R.M.; Studenski, S.A. Chair rise strategies in the elderly. *Clin. Biomech.* **1994**, *9*, 187–192. [CrossRef]
38. Schenkman, M.; Riley, P.; Pieper, C. Sit to stand from progressively lower seat heights—Alterations in angular velocity. *Clin. Biomech.* **1996**, *11*, 153–158. [CrossRef]

39. Weiner, D.K.; Long, R.; Hughes, M.A.; Chandler, J.; Studenski, S. When older adults face the chair-rise challenge: A study of chair height availability and height-modified chair-rise performance in the elderly. *J. Am. Geriatr. Soc.* **1993**, *41*, 6–10. [CrossRef]
40. Munro, B.J.; Steele, J.R.; Bashford, G.M.; Ryan, M.; Britten, N. A kinematic and kinetic analysis of the sit-to-stand transfer using an ejector chair: Implications for elderly rheumatoid arthritic patients. *J. Biomech.* **1997**, *31*, 263–271. [CrossRef]
41. Dempster, W.T. *Space Requirements of the Seated Operator, Geometrical, Kinematic, and Mechanical Aspects of the Body with Special Reference to the Limbs*; Michigan State Univ East Lansing: East Lansing, MI, USA, 1955.

Disclaimer/Publisher's Note: The statements, opinions and data contained in all publications are solely those of the individual author(s) and contributor(s) and not of MDPI and/or the editor(s). MDPI and/or the editor(s) disclaim responsibility for any injury to people or property resulting from any ideas, methods, instructions or products referred to in the content.

Article

Efficient Method to Solve the Monge–Kantarovich Problem Using Wavelet Analysis

Juan Rafael Acosta-Portilla [1], Carlos González-Flores [2], Raquiel Rufino López-Martínez [3] and Armando Sánchez-Nungaray [3,*]

[1] Instituto de Investigaciones y Estudios Superiores Económicos y Sociales, Universidad Veracruzana, Veracruz 94294, Mexico; juaacosta@uv.mx
[2] Escuela Superior de Ingeniería Mecánica y Eléctrica Zacatenco, Instituto Politécnico Nacional, Mexico City 07738, Mexico; cfgonzalez@esimez.mx
[3] Facultad de Matemáticas, Universidad Veracruzana, Veracruz 94294, Mexico; ralopez@uv.mx
* Correspondence: armsanchez@uv.mx

Abstract: In this paper, we present and justify a methodology to solve the Monge–Kantorovich mass transfer problem through Haar multiresolution analysis and wavelet transform with the advantage of requiring a reduced number of operations to carry out. The methodology has the following steps. We apply wavelet analysis on a discretization of the cost function level j and obtain four components comprising one corresponding to a low-pass filter plus three from a high-pass filter. We obtain the solution corresponding to the low-pass component in level $j-1$ denoted by μ^*_{j-1}, and using the information of the high-pass filter components, we get a solution in level j denoted by $\hat{\mu}_j$. Finally, we make a local refinement of $\hat{\mu}_j$ and obtain the final solution μ^σ_j.

Keywords: mass transfer problem; wavelets; multiresolution analysis

MSC: 42C40; 49Q20; 65T60

1. Introduction

In recent years, schemes to approximate infinite linear programs have become very important in theory. The authors of [1] showed that under suitable assumptions, the program's optimum value can be approximated by the values of finite-dimensional linear programs and that every accumulation point of a sequence of optimal solutions for the approximating programs is an optimal solution for the original problem. In particular, in [2] the authors studied the Monge–Kantorovich mass transfer (MT) problem on metric spaces. They considered conditions under the MT problem as solvable and, furthermore, that an optimal solution can be obtained as the weak limit of a sequence of optimal solutions to suitably approximate MT problems.

Moreover, in [3], the authors presented a numerical approximation for the value of the mass transfer (MT) problem on compact metric spaces. A sequence of transportation problems was built, and it proved that the value of the MT problem is a limit of the optimal values of these problems. Moreover, they gave an error bound for the numerical approximation. A generalization of this scheme of approximation was presented in [4,5]. They proposed an approximation scheme for the Monge–Kantorovich (MK) mass transfer problem on compact spaces that consisted of reducing to solve a sequence of finite transport problems. The method presented in that work uses a metaheuristic algorithm inspired by a scatter search in order to reduce the dimensionality of each transport problem. Finally, they provided some examples of that method.

On the other hand, the authors of [6] provided orthonormal bases for $L^2(\mathbb{R}^n)$ that have properties that are similar to those enjoyed by the classical Haar basis for $L^2(\mathbb{R})$. For example, each basis consists of appropriate dilates and translates of a finite collection of "piecewise constant" functions. The construction is based on the notion of multiresolution analysis and reveals an interesting connection between the theory of compactly supported wavelet bases and the theory of self-similar tilings. Recent applications of the wavelet filter methodology have been used in various problems arising in communication systems and detection of thermal defects (see, for example, [7,8], respectively).

In [9], the authors gave a scheme to approximate the MK problem based on the symmetries of the underlying spaces. They took a Haar-type MRA constructed according to the geometry of the spaces. Thus, they applied the Haar-type MRA based on symmetries to the MK problem and obtained a sequence-of-transport problem that approximates the original MK problem for each MRA space. Note that in the case of Haar's classical wavelet, this methodology coincides with the methods presented in [2,3].

It is important to note that various scientific problems are modeled through the Monge–Kantorovich approach; therefore, providing new efficient methodologies to find approximations of such problems turns out to be very useful. Within the applications of problems whose solutions are the Monge–Kantorovich problem are found: the use of the transport problem for the analysis of elastic image registration (see, for example, [10–12]). Other optimization problems related to this topic and differential equation tools can be found in recent works such as [13,14].

The main goal of this paper is to present a scheme of approximation of the MK problem based on wavelet analysis in which we use wavelet filters to split the original problem. That is, we apply the filter to the discrete cost function in level j, which results in a cost function of level $j-1$ and three components of wavelet analysis. Using the information of the cost function given by the low-pass filter, which belongs to level $j-1$, we construct μ_{j-1}^* a solution of the MK problem for that level $j-1$, and using the additional information, the other three components of wavelet analysis are extended to $\hat{\mu}_j$, which is a solution to level j, where the projection of $\hat{\mu}_j$ to level $j-1$ is μ_{j-1}^*. Finally, we make a local analysis of the solution $\hat{\mu}_j$ to obtain an improved solution based on the type of points of that solution (we have two type of points that are defined in the base in the connectedness of the solution).

This work has three non-introductory sections. In the first of them we present the Haar multiresolution analysis (MRA) in one and two dimensions. Next, we relate this to the absolutely continuous measures over a compact in $\mathbb{R}^2$. We finish with the definition of the Monge–Kantorovich mass transfer problem and its relation to the MRA.

In the second section, we define a proximity criterion for the components of the support of the simple solutions of the MK problem and study in detail the problem of, given a solution μ_{j-1}^* at level $j-1$ of resolution for the MK problem, construct a feasible solution $\hat{\mu}_j$ for the MK problem at level of resolution j such that it is a refinement of the solution with lees resolution.

On the other hand, in the third section we present a methodological proposal to solve the MK^j problem such that it can be summarized in a simple algorithm of six steps:

Step 1. We consider a discretization of the cost function for the level j, denoted by c_j.

Step 2. We apply the wavelet transform to c_j; we obtain the low-pass component c_{j-1} and three high-pass components, denoted by Ψ_1, Ψ_2 and Ψ_3, respectively.

Step 3. Using c_{j-1} and the methodology of [3,4,9], we obtain a solution μ_{j-1}^* for MK^{j-1} associated with this cost function.

Step 4. We classify the points of the support of the solution μ_{j-1}^* by proximity criteria as points of Type I or Type II.

Step 5. Using the solution μ_{j-1}^*, the information of the high-pass components and Lemma 1, we obtain a feasible solution for the level j, which is denoted by $\hat{\mu}_j$. This feasible solution has the property that its projection to the level $j-1$ is equal to μ_{j-1}^*; moreover, the support of $\hat{\mu}_j$ is contained in the support of μ_{j-1}^*.

Step 6. The classification of the points of μ_{j-1}^* induce classification of the points in $\hat{\mu}_j$ by contention in the support. Over the points of Type I of the solution $\hat{\mu}_j$, we do not move those points. For the points of Type II, we apply a permutation to the solution over the two points that better improves the solution, and we repeat the process with the rest of the points.

Finally, we present a series of examples that use the proposed methodology based on wavelet analysis and compare their results with those obtained applying the methodology of [3,4,9].

2. Preliminaries

2.1. One-Dimensional MRA

The results of this and the following subsection are well known, and for a detailed exposition, we recommend consulting [15–17]. We begin by defining a general multiresolution analysis and developing the particular case of the Haar multiresolution analysis on $\mathbb{R}$. Given $a > 0$ and $b \in \mathbb{R}$, the dilatation operator D_a and the translation operator T_b are defined by

$$(D_a f)(x) = a^{1/2} f(ax) \quad \text{and} \quad (T_b f)(x) = f(x - b) \tag{1}$$

for every $f \in L^2(\mathbb{R})$, where the latter denotes the usual Hilbert space of square integrable real functions defined on $\mathbb{R}$. A multiresolution analysis (MRA) on $\mathbb{R}$ is a sequence of subspaces $(V_j)_{j \in \mathbb{Z}}$ of $L^2(\mathbb{R})$ such that it satisfies the following properties:

(1) $V_j \subset V_{j+1}$ for every $j \in \mathbb{Z}$.
(2) $L^2(\mathbb{R}) = \overline{\text{span}} \bigcup_{j \in \mathbb{Z}} V_j$.
(3) $\bigcap_{j \in \mathbb{Z}} V_j = \{0\}$.
(4) $V_j = D_{2^j} V_0$.
(5) There exists a function $\varphi \in L^2$, called the scaling function, such that the collection $\{T_j \varphi\}_{j \in \mathbb{Z}}$ is an orthonormal system of translates and

$$V_0 = \overline{\text{span}}\{T_j \varphi\}_{i \in \mathbb{Z}}. \tag{2}$$

We denote as χ_A the characteristic function of the set A. Then, the Haar scaling function is defined by

$$\varphi(x) = \chi_{[0,1)}(x). \tag{3}$$

For each pair $j, k \in \mathbb{Z}$, we call

$$I_{j,k} = [2^{-j}k, 2^{-j}(k+1)). \tag{4}$$

Hence, we define the function

$$\begin{aligned}
\varphi_{j,k}(x) &= (T_k D_{2^j} \varphi)(x) \\
&= 2^{j/2} \varphi(2^j x - k) \\
&= 2^{j/2} \chi_{I_{j,k}}(x).
\end{aligned} \tag{5}$$

The collection $\{\varphi_{j,k}\}_{j,k \in \mathbb{Z}}$ is called the system of Haar scaling functions. For $j_0 \in \mathbb{Z}$, the collection $\{\varphi_{j_0,k}\}_{k \in \mathbb{Z}}$ is referred to as the system of scale j_0 Haar scaling functions. The Haar function is defined by

$$\psi(x) = \chi_{[0,1/2)}(x) - \chi_{[1/2,1)}(x). \tag{6}$$

For each pair $j, k \in \mathbb{Z}$, we define the function

$$\begin{aligned}
\psi_{j,k}(x) &= (T_k D_{2^j} \psi)(x) \\
&= 2^{j/2} \psi(2^j x - k) \\
&= 2^{j/2} (\chi_{I_{j+1,2k}} - \chi_{I_{j+1,2k+1}})(x).
\end{aligned} \tag{7}$$

The collection $\{\psi_{j,k}\}_{j,k\in\mathbb{Z}}$ is referred to as the Haar system on $\mathbb{R}$. For $j_0 \in \mathbb{Z}$, the collection $\{\psi_{j_0,k}\}_{k\in\mathbb{Z}}$ is referred to as the system of scale j_0 Haar functions. It is well known that with respect to the usual inner product $\langle\cdot,\cdot\rangle$ in $L^2(\mathbb{R})$, the Haar system on $\mathbb{R}$ is an orthonormal system. Moreover, for each $j_0 \in \mathbb{Z}$, the collection of scale j_0 Haar scaling functions is an orthonormal system. Thus, for each $j \in \mathbb{Z}$, the approximation operator P_j on $L^2(\mathbb{R})$ is defined by

$$(P_j f)(x) = \sum_k \langle f, \varphi_{j,k}\rangle \varphi_{j,k}(x), \text{ for all } f \in L^2(\mathbb{R}), \tag{8}$$

and the approximation space V_j by

$$V_j = \overline{\mathrm{span}}\{\varphi_{j,k}\}_{k\in\mathbb{Z}}. \tag{9}$$

The collection $\{V_j\}_{j\in\mathbb{Z}}$ is called Haar multiresolution analysis. Similarly, we have that for each $j_0 \in \mathbb{Z}$, the detail operator Q_j on $L^2(\mathbb{R})$ is defined by

$$(Q_j f)(x) = (P_{j+1} f)(x) - (P_j f)(x), \text{ for all } f \in L^2(\mathbb{R}), \tag{10}$$

and the wavelet space W_j by

$$W_j = \overline{\mathrm{span}}\{\psi_{j,k}\}_{k\in\mathbb{Z}}. \tag{11}$$

Note that $V_{j+1} = V_j \oplus W_j$ for all $j \in \mathbb{Z}$. Hence, the collection

$$\{\varphi_{j_0,k}, \psi_{j,k} : j \geq j_0, k \in \mathbb{Z}\} \tag{12}$$

is a complete orthonormal system on $\mathbb{R}$; this system is called the scale j_0 Haar system on $\mathbb{R}$. As a consequence, the Haar system $\{\psi_{j,k}\}_{j,k\in\mathbb{Z}}$ is a complete orthonormal system on $\mathbb{R}$.

2.2. Two-Dimensional MRA

To obtain the Haar MRA on $\mathbb{R}^2$, we consider the Haar MRA on $\mathbb{R}$ defined in the previous subsection with scaling and Haar functions φ and ψ, and from them, through a tensor product approach we can construct a two-dimensional scaling and Haar function. First, we define the four possible products:

$$\begin{aligned}\Phi(x,y) &= \varphi(x)\varphi(y), & \Psi^{(1)}(x,y) &= \varphi(x)\psi(y) \\ \Psi^{(2)}(x,y) &= \psi(x)\varphi(y), & \Psi^{(3)}(x,y) &= \psi(x)\psi(y),\end{aligned} \tag{13}$$

which are the scaling function associated with the unitary square and three Haar functions, respectively. Hence, for each $j, k_1, k_2 \in \mathbb{Z}$, we define naturally the scaling and Haar function systems:

$$\begin{aligned}\Phi_{j,k_1,k_2}(x,y) &= \varphi_{j,k_1}(x)\varphi(y)_{j,k_2}, & \Psi^{(1)}_{j,k_1,k_2}(x,y) &= \varphi(x)_{j,k_1}\psi(y)_{j,k_2} \\ \Psi^{(2)}_{j,k_1,k_2}(x,y) &= \psi(x)_{j,k_1}\varphi(y)_{j,k_2}, & \Psi^{(3)}_{j,k_1,k_2}(x,y) &= \psi_{j,k_1}(x)\psi(y)_{j,k_2}.\end{aligned} \tag{14}$$

Then for $j_0 \in \mathbb{Z}$, as in the one-dimensional case, we have that the collection

$$\{\Phi_{j_0,k_1,k_2} : k_1, k_2 \in \mathbb{Z}\} \cup \{\Psi^{(i)}_{j,k_1,k_2} : 1 \leq i \leq 3, j \geq j_0\} \tag{15}$$

is an orthonormal basis on $L^2(\mathbb{R}^2)$. Thus, the collection

$$\{\Psi^{(i)}_{j,k_1,k_2} : 1 \leq i \leq 3, j, k_1, k_2 \in \mathbb{Z}\} \tag{16}$$

is an orthonormal basis on $L^2(\mathbb{R}^2)$. Then for $j \in \mathbb{Z}$ and $f \in L^2(\mathbb{R}^2)$, the approximation operator is defined by

$$(\mathbf{P}_j f)(x,y) = \sum_{k_1} \sum_{k_2} \langle f, \Phi_{j,k_1,k_2} \rangle \Phi_{j,k_1,k_2}(x,y), \tag{17}$$

and for $i = 1, 2, 3$, the detail operators are

$$(\mathbf{Q}_j^{(i)} f)(x,y) = \sum_{k_1} \sum_{k_2} \langle f, \Psi_{j,k_1,k_2}^{(i)} \rangle \Psi_{j,k_1,k_2}^{(i)}(x,y). \tag{18}$$

Hence, the projection can be written as

$$(\mathbf{P}_{j+1} f)(x,y) = (\mathbf{P}_j f)(x,y) + (\mathbf{Q}_j^{(1)} f)(x,y) + (\mathbf{Q}_j^{(2)} f)(x,y) + (\mathbf{Q}_j^{(3)} f)(x,y). \tag{19}$$

We will describe the approximation $\mathbf{P}_j$ and detail operators $\mathbf{Q}_j^{(i)}$ from the geometric point of view. First of all, we fix some $j, k_1, k_2 \in \mathbb{Z}$ and define the square

$$\begin{aligned} S(j,k_1,k_2) &= I_{j,k_1} \times I_{j,k_2} \\ &= [2^{-j} k_1, 2^{-j}(k_1+1)) \times [2^{-j} k_2, 2^{-j}(k_2+1)). \end{aligned} \tag{20}$$

Then, we have that Φ_{j,k_1,k_2} is the characteristic function of $S(j,k_1,k_2)$, in symbols

$$\Phi_{j,k_1,k_2}(x,y) = \chi_S(x,y) \tag{21}$$

where $S = S(j,k_1,k_2)$. Therefore for $f \in L^2(\mathbb{R}^2)$, the operator $\mathbf{P}_j f$ acts as a discretization of f that is constant over the disjointed $S(j,k_1,k_2)$ squares. On the other hand, we can split $S(j,k_1,k_2)$ as follows (see Figure 1):

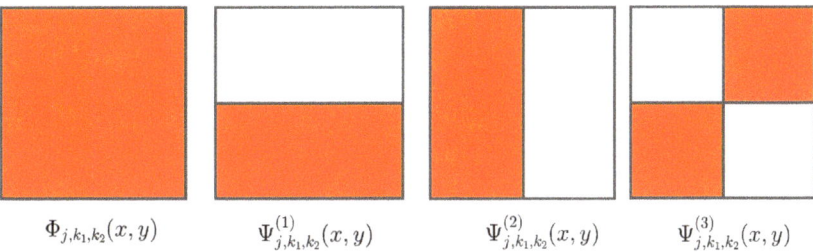

Figure 1. Functions Φ_{j,k_1,k_2}, $\Psi_{j,k_1,k_2}^{(1)}$, $\Psi_{j,k_1,k_2}^{(2)}$ and $\Psi_{j,k_1,k_2}^{(3)}$.

(i) Into two rectangles with half the height and the same width as $S(j,k_1,k_2)$, namely, the sets

$$\begin{aligned} A_1(j,k_1,k_2) &= [2^{-j} k_1, 2^{-j}(k_1+1)) \times [2^{-j-1} 2k_2, 2^{-j-1}(2k_2+1)) \text{ and} \\ A_2(j,k_1,k_2) &= [2^{-j} k_1, 2^{-j}(k_1+1)) \times [2^{-j-1} 2k_2 + 1, 2^{-j-1}(2k_2+2)). \end{aligned} \tag{22}$$

(ii) Into two rectangles with the same height and half the width as $S(j,k_1,k_2)$, namely,

$$\begin{aligned} B_1(j,k_1,k_2) &= [2^{-j-1} 2k_1, 2^{-j-1}(2k_1+1)) \times [2^{-j} k_2, 2^{-j}(k_2+1)) \text{ and} \\ B_2(j,k_1,k_2) &= [2^{-j-1} 2k_1 + 1, 2^{-j-1}(2k_1+2)) \times [2^{-j} k_2, 2^{-j}(k_2+1)). \end{aligned} \tag{23}$$

(iii) Into four squares with half the side lengths of $S(j,k_1,k_2)$, namely,

$$C_1(j,k_1,k_2) = [2^{-j-1}2k_1, 2^{-j-1}(2k_1+1)) \times [2^{-j-1}2k_2, 2^{-j-1}(2k_2+1)),$$
$$C_2(j,k_1,k_2) = [2^{-j-1}2k_1+1, 2^{-j-1}(2k_1+2)) \times [2^{-j-1}2k_2, 2^{-j-1}(2k_2+1)),$$
$$C_3(j,k_1,k_2) = [2^{-j-1}2k_1, 2^{-j-1}(2k_1+1)) \times [2^{-j-1}2k_2+1, 2^{-j-1}(2k_2+2)) \text{ and}$$
$$C_4(j,k_1,k_2) = [2^{-j-1}2k_1+1, 2^{-j-1}(2k_1+2)) \times [2^{-j-1}2k_2+1, 2^{-j-1}(2k_2+2)).$$
(24)

Hence, for $i = 1, 2, 3$, the function $\Psi_{j,k_1,k_2}^{(i)}$ is defined by

$$\Psi_{j,k_1,k_2}^{(1)}(x,y) = \chi_{A_1}(x,y) - \chi_{A_2}(x,y) \text{ with } A_l = A_l(j,k_1,k_2) \text{ for } l = 1, 2.$$
$$\Psi_{j,k_1,k_2}^{(2)}(x,y) = \chi_{B_1}(x,y) - \chi_{B_2}(x,y) \text{ with } B_l = B_l(j,k_1,k_2) \text{ for } l = 1, 2.$$
(25)
$$\Psi_{j,k_1,k_2}^{(3)}(x,y) = \chi_{C_1 \cup C_4}(x,y) - \chi_{C_2 \cup C_3}(x,y) \text{ with } C_l = C_l(j,k_1,k_2) \text{ for } l = 1, 2, 3, 4.$$

(see Figure 1). Thus, the image of $f \in L^2(\mathbb{R}^2)$ under the detail operator $\mathbf{Q}_j^{(i)}$ is a function $\mathbf{Q}_j^{(i)} f$ formed by pieces that oscillate symmetrically on each square $S(j,k_1,k_2)$.

Now we have the elements to define an MRA on $\mathbb{R}^2$; to do this, we will use the notation introduced for the one-dimensional MRA on $\mathbb{R}$ defined in the previous subsection. For each $j \in \mathbb{Z}$, we define

$$\mathbf{V}_j = V_j \otimes V_j.$$
(26)

Then the collection $\{\mathbf{V}_j\}_{j \in \mathbb{Z}}$ is the Haar multiresolution analysis on $\mathbb{R}^2$, where the dilatation and translation operators are defined by

$$\mathbf{D}_{2^j} = D_{2^j} \otimes D_{2^j} \text{ and } \mathbf{T}_{m,n} = T_m \otimes T_n,$$
(27)

respectively. Note that we have the following relation:

$$\mathbf{V}_{j+1} = \mathbf{V}_j \oplus \mathbf{W}_j^{(1)} \oplus \mathbf{W}_j^{(2)} \oplus \mathbf{W}_j^{(3)},$$
(28)

where $\mathbf{W}_j^{(1)} = V_j \otimes W_j$, $\mathbf{W}_j^{(2)} = W_j \otimes V_j$ and $\mathbf{W}_j^{(3)} = W_j \otimes W_j$. For more detail with respect to the Haar MRA, see [15].

2.3. Measures and MRA

In this subsection, we will use the two previous ones and the [9] approach to relate measures over $\mathbb{R}^2$ with the Haar MRA on $\mathbb{R}^2$. The results and definitions presented in this and the following subsection can be found in the classical references [18,19]. We consider a compact subset X of $\mathbb{R}^2$ and a measure μ such that it is absolutely continuous with respect to the Lebesgue measure λ. We call

$$f_\mu = \frac{d\mu}{d\lambda}$$
(29)

the Radon–Nikodym derivative of μ with respect to λ. By construction, it necessary holds that $f_\mu \in L^1(X)$. We additionally suppose that $f_\mu \in L^2(X)$. Then, as a consequence of the Haar MRA on $\mathbb{R}^2$, we have that

$$\|\mathbf{P}_j f_\mu - f_\mu\|_2 \to 0 \text{ as } j \to \infty.$$
(30)

Moreover, the compactness of X ensures that

$$\|\mathbf{P}_j f_\mu - f_\mu\|_1 \le \lambda(X)^{1/2} \|\mathbf{P}_j f_\mu - f_\mu\|_2.$$
(31)

The above allow us to define μ_j, the approximation of the measure μ to the level $j \in \mathbb{Z}$ of the Haar MRA on $\mathbb{R}^2$, as the measure induced by the projection of the Radon–Nikodym to the level j. That is, μ_j is defined by the relation

$$d\mu_j = \mathbf{P}_j f_\mu \, d\lambda. \tag{32}$$

We denote the expectation of a function $g \in L(\mathbb{R}^2)$ with respect to λ as

$$\mathbb{E}[g] = \int_{\mathbb{R}^2} g \, d\lambda. \tag{33}$$

Then Theorem 4 and Corollary 5 in [9] ensure that for each $g \in L^2(\mathbb{R}^2)$ and $j \in \mathbb{Z}$, it is fulfilled that

$$\mathbb{E}[\mathbf{P}_j g] = \mathbb{E}[g]. \tag{34}$$

Thus, μ_j is absolutely continuous with respect to the Lebesgue measure. If, additionally, we suppose that μ is a measure with support on X, then (μ_j) converges to μ in the L^1 and L^2 sense. That is, by the Riesz Theorem, we can associate each of these measures μ_j to an integrable function $\hat{\mu}_j \in \mathbf{P}_j L^2(\mathbb{R}^2)$ such that for each Lebesgue measurable set $A \subset \mathbb{R}^2$,

$$\begin{aligned}\mu_j(A) &= \int_A \hat{\mu}_j \, d\lambda \\ &= \int \hat{\mu}_j \chi_A \, d\lambda \\ &= \mathbb{E}[\hat{\mu}_j \chi_A],\end{aligned} \tag{35}$$

and we apply the respective convergence mode. Further, the compact support of measures ensures that the sequence (μ_j) converges weakly to the measure μ, proof of which can be found in [9] Theorem 7.

2.4. M-K Problem and MRA

In this subsection, we study the Monge–Kantorovich problem from the point of view of the Haar MRA on $\mathbb{R}^2$ (for a detailed exposition, we recommend consulting [9]). Let X and Y be two compact subsets of $\mathbb{R}^2$. We denote by $M^+(X \times Y)$ the family of finite measures on $X \times Y$. Given $\mu \in M^+(X \times Y)$, we denote its marginal measures on X and Y as

$$\Pi_1 \mu(E_1) = \mu(E_1 \times Y) \tag{36}$$

and

$$\Pi_2 \mu(E_2) = \mu(X \times E_2) \tag{37}$$

for each μ-measurable set $E_1 \subset X$ and $E_2 \subset Y$. Let c be a real function defined on $X \times Y$, and η^1, η^2 are two measures defined on X and Y, respectively. The Monge–Kantorovich mass transfer problem is given as follows:

$$\begin{aligned}\text{MK: minimize} \quad & \langle \mu, c \rangle := \int c \, d\mu \\ \text{subject to:} \quad & \Pi_1 \mu = \eta^1, \quad \Pi_2 \mu = \eta^2, \quad \mu \in M^+(X \times Y).\end{aligned} \tag{38}$$

A measure $\mu \in M^+(X \times Y)$ is said to be a feasible solution for the MK problem if it satisfies (38) and $\langle \mu, c \rangle$ is finite. We said that the MK problem is solvable if there is a feasible solution μ^* that attains the optimal value for it. So μ^* is called an optimal solution for (38). If, additionally, we assume that μ, η^1 and η^2 are absolutely continuous with respect to the Lebesgue measures on $\mathbb{R}^2$ and $\mathbb{R}$, then in a natural way, we can discretize the MK problem through the Haar MRA on $\mathbb{R}^2$ as follows. For $j \in \mathbb{Z}$, we define the MK problem of level j by:

$$\begin{aligned}
\text{MK}_j\text{: minimize} \quad & \langle \mu_j, c \rangle := \int c \, d\mu_j \\
\text{subject to:} \quad & \Pi_1 \mu_j = \eta_j^1, \quad \Pi_2 \mu_j = \eta_j^2, \quad \mu \in M^+(X \times Y).
\end{aligned} \quad (39)$$

where μ_j, η_j^1 and η_j^2 are the projections to level j of the measures μ, η^1 and η^2, respectively, to the Haar MRA.

3. Technical Results

In this section, we present a series of results that ensure the good behavior of the methodological proposal of the next section. In order to do this, we start by assuming an MK problem with cost function $c = c(x, y)$, base sets $X = Y = [0, 1]$ and measure restrictions $\eta^1 = \eta^2 = \lambda|_{[0,1]}$. In other words, we consider the problem of moving a uniform distribution to a uniform one with the minimum movement cost. Since in applications we work with discretized problems, then as a result of applying the MRA on $\mathbb{R}^2$, we have that our objective is to solve:

$$\begin{aligned}
\text{MK}_j\text{: minimize} \quad & \sum_{i,k} \mu_{i,k}^j c_{i,k}^j \\
\text{subject to:} \quad & \sum_i \mu_{i,k}^j = \frac{1}{2^j}, \text{ for each } k = 1, \ldots, 2^j. \\
& \sum_k \mu_{i,k}^j = \frac{1}{2^j}, \text{ for each } i = 1, \ldots, 2^j. \\
& \sum_{i,k} \mu_{i,k}^j = 1. \\
& \mu_{i,k}^j \geq 0, \text{ for each } i, k = 1, \ldots, 2^j.
\end{aligned} \quad (40)$$

where $\mu_{i,k}^j$ is the portion of the initial value $\frac{1}{2^j}$ in the position $I_{j,i}$ of the x-axis allocated to the position $I_{j,k}$ of the y-axis. We call j-discrete unit square the grid formed by the squares $S(j, k_1, k_2)$ (see (20)), dividing the set $[0, 1] \times [0, 1]$ in $2^j \times 2^j$ blocks, in a such way that each one is identified with the point (k_1, k_2). We suppose that there is a simple solution μ for (40). That is, μ is a feasible solution such that, given $i_0, k_0 \in \{1, \ldots, 2^j\}$ with $\mu_{i_0,k_0} \neq 0$, it necessarily holds that $\mu_{i_0,k} = 0$ for each $k \neq k_0$ and $\mu_{i,k_0} = 0$ for each $i \neq i_0$. Geometrically, if the measure μ is plotted as a discrete heat map in the j-discrete unit square, then no color element in the plot has another color element in its same row and column, as can be seen in Figure 2.

Definition 1. *We define a proximity criteria in the j-discrete unit square as follows: (i, k) is a neighbor of (l, m) if*

$$|i - l| = 1 \text{ or } |k - m| = 1. \quad (41)$$

In Figure 2, we plot the support of the hypothetical simple solution μ. Hence, the neighbors of the position in the middle of the cross are those that touch the yellow stripes. Then in this example, the middle point has four neighbors.

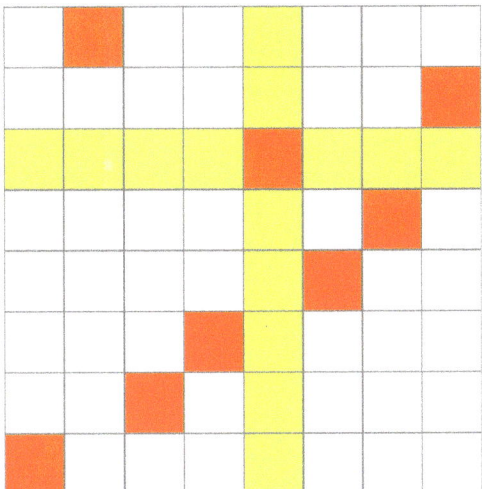

Figure 2. Support of μ and the proximity criteria.

With this in mind, we can classify the points in support(μ) as follows.

Definition 2. *We say that $(k_1, k_2) \in$ support(μ) is a border point if k_1 or k_2 equals 0 or 1; otherwise, we call it an interior point. It is clear that a border point has at least one neighbor and at most three, whereas an interior point has at least two neighbors and at most four. Hence, we can partition* support(μ) *into two sets as follows.*

The set of the points of Type I is given by

$$T_1 = \{(i,k) \in \text{support}(\mu) \mid (i,k) \text{ has minimun neighbors}\}, \tag{42}$$

and the set of the points of Type II is given by

$$T_2 = \text{support}(\mu) \setminus T_1. \tag{43}$$

Intuitively, the set T_1 is composed of well-controlled points, whereas the set T_2 has the points that admit permutations between them, since, as we will see in the next section, in the proposed algorithm they will be permuted. See Figures 3 and 4. Naturally, since μ is a feasible solution for (40), then given elements $(k_1, k_2), (m_1, m_2) \in$ support(μ) and for $i = 1, 2$ permutations σ_i over $\{k_i, m_i\}$, the measure μ^σ defined by

$$\mu^\sigma(a,b) = \mu(\sigma_1(a), \sigma_2(b)) \tag{44}$$

is a feasible solution.

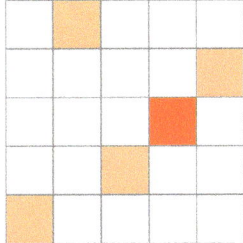

Figure 3. Classification of the points in support(μ): Type I points.

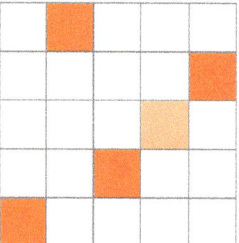

Figure 4. Classification of the points in support(μ): Type II points.

Refining Projections

In this subsection, we study the problem of improving an optimal solution μ_{j-1}^* for (40) on level $j-1 \in \mathbb{Z}$ to a feasible solution $\hat{\mu}_j$ for the next level j. Let μ_{j-1}^* be an optimal solution for level $j-1$. Then we are looking for $\hat{\mu}_j$ such that:

$$\begin{aligned}&(1)\quad \hat{\mu}_j \text{ is a feasible solution.}\\&(2)\quad \mathbf{P}_{j-1}\hat{\mu}_j = \mu_{j-1}^*.\end{aligned} \qquad (45)$$

As described in the previous section, the measure $\hat{\mu}_j \in L^2(\mathbb{R}^2)$ can be decomposed in

$$\hat{\mu}_j = \mu_{j-1}^* + \nu_1 + \nu_2 + \nu_3 \qquad (46)$$

where

$$\begin{aligned}\nu_i(x,y) &= (\mathbf{Q}_j^{(i)}\hat{\mu}_j)(x,y)\\&= \sum_{k_1}\sum_{k_2}\langle \hat{\mu}_j, \Psi_{j,k_1,k_2}^{(i)}\rangle \Psi_{j,k_1,k_2}^{(i)}(x,y).\end{aligned} \qquad (47)$$

From the geometric point of view, the projections ν_i are formed from differences of characteristic functions, as we mentioned in Section 2.2. So we have the following result:

Lemma 1. *Let $j \in \mathbb{Z}$ and μ_{j-1}^* be an optimal solution for (40) at level $j-1$. Then for each positive measure $\hat{\mu}_j \in \mathbf{P}_j L^2(\mathbb{R}^2)$ such that $\mathbf{P}_{j-1}\hat{\mu}_j = \mu_{j-1}^*$ and $\hat{\mu}_j = \mu_{j-1}^* + \nu_1 + \nu_2 + \nu_3$, it necessarily holds that*

$$\mu_{j-1}^*(A) = 0 \text{ implies } \nu_i(A) = 0 \qquad (48)$$

for each Lebesgue measurable set $A \subset \mathbb{R}^2$ and each $i = 1,2,3$. Therefore, the support of $\hat{\mu}_j$ is contained in the support of μ_{j-1}^*.

Proof. We only make the proof for the case $i = 1$, since the other two are very similar. To simplify the notation, we use the symbols μ_- and ν_- as measures or functions in the respective subspace of $L^2(\mathbb{R}^2)$. Since when setting a level $j \in \mathbb{Z}$ all the measures in question are constant in pairs of rectangles dividing $S(j, k_1, k_2)$, as we prove in Section 2.2, then it is enough to prove that (65) is valid on this rectangles. Let

$$\begin{aligned}A_1 &= A_1(j,k_1',k_2')\\&= [2^{-j}k_1', 2^{-j}(k_1'+1)) \times [2^{-j-1}2k_2', 2^{-j-1}(2k_2'+1)).\end{aligned} \qquad (49)$$

and

$$\begin{aligned}A_2 &= A_2(j,k_1',k_2')\\&= [2^{-j}k_1', 2^{-j}(k_1'+1)) \times [2^{-j-1}2k_2'+1, 2^{-j-1}(2k_2'+2)),\end{aligned} \qquad (50)$$

as in (22). Then for $l = 1, 2$, we have that

$$\hat{\mu}_j(A_l) = \mu^*_{j-1}(A_l) + \sum_{i=1}^{3} \nu_i(A_l)$$
$$= \mathbb{E}[\mu^*_{j-1}\chi_{A_l}] + \sum_{i=1}^{3} \mathbb{E}[\nu_i\chi_{A_l}]. \tag{51}$$

Now we will calculate each one of the expectations separately. By (17), (18) and (25), we have that

$$\mu^*_{j-1}(x,y) = \sum_{k_1} \sum_{k_2} \langle \mu^*_{j-1}, \Phi_{j,k_1,k_2} \rangle \Phi_{j,k_1,k_2}(x,y) \tag{52}$$

and

$$\nu_1(x,y) = \sum_{k_1} \sum_{k_2} \langle \nu_1, \Psi^{(1)}_{j,k_1,k_2} \rangle \Psi^{(1)}_{j,k_1,k_2}(x,y)$$
$$= \sum_{k_1} \sum_{k_2} \langle \nu_1, \Psi^{(1)}_{j,k_1,k_2} \rangle [\chi_{A_1(j,k_1,k_2)}(x,y) - \chi_{A_2(j,k_1,k_2)}(x,y)]. \tag{53}$$

Then for $l = 1$ and by (15), (16) and (22), we have that

$$\mathbb{E}[\mu^*_{j-1}\chi_{A_1}] = \mathbb{E}[\chi_{A_1} \sum_{k_1} \sum_{k_2} \langle \mu^*_{j-1}, \Phi_{j,k_1,k_2} \rangle \Phi_{j,k_1,k_2}]$$
$$= \langle \mu^*_{j-1}, \Phi_{j,k'_1,k'_2} \rangle \mathbb{E}[\chi_{A_1} \Phi_{j,k'_1,k'_2}]]$$
$$= d\mathbb{E}[\chi_{A_1}]$$
$$= d\frac{1}{2^{2j+1}} \tag{54}$$

where $d = \langle \mu^*_{j-1}, \Phi_{j,k'_1,k'_2} \rangle$ and

$$\mathbb{E}[\nu_1\chi_{A_1}] = \mathbb{E}[\chi_{A_1} \sum_{k_1} \sum_{k_2} \langle \nu_1, \Psi^{(1)}_{j,k_1,k_2} \rangle (\chi_{A_1(j,k_1,k_2)} - \chi_{A_2(j,k_1,k_2)})]$$
$$= \langle \nu_1, \Psi^{(1)}_{j,k'_1,k'_2} \rangle \mathbb{E}\chi_{A_1}$$
$$= c\mathbb{E}[\chi_{A_1}]$$
$$= c\frac{1}{2^{2j+1}} \tag{55}$$

where $c = \langle \nu_1, \Psi^{(1)}_{j,k'_1,k'_2} \rangle$. Similarly, but using (23) and (24), we can prove that

$$\mathbb{E}[\nu_2\chi_{A_1}] = 0 \tag{56}$$

and

$$\mathbb{E}[\nu_3\chi_{A_1}] = 0. \tag{57}$$

Then

$$\hat{\mu}_j(A_1) = d\frac{1}{2^{2j+1}} + c\frac{1}{2^{2j+1}}$$
$$= \mu^*_{j-1}(A_1) + \nu(A_1) \tag{58}$$

Now, we will make an analogous argument for the case $l = 2$. Hence,

$$\mathbb{E}[\mu_{j-1}^* \chi_{A_2}] = \mathbb{E}[\chi_{A_2} \sum_{k_1} \sum_{k_2} \langle \mu_{j-1}^*, \Phi_{j,k_1,k_2}\rangle \Phi_{j,k_1,k_2}]$$
$$= \langle \mu_{j-1}^*, \Phi_{j,k_1,k_2}\rangle \mathbb{E}[\chi_{A_2}\Phi_{j,k_1',k_2'}]] \qquad (59)$$
$$= d\mathbb{E}[\chi_{A_2}]$$
$$= d\frac{1}{2^{2j+1}}$$

and

$$\mathbb{E}[\nu_1 \chi_{A_2}] = \mathbb{E}[\chi_{A_2} \sum_{k_1} \sum_{k_2} \langle \nu_1, \Psi_{j,k_1,k_2}^{(1)}\rangle (\chi_{A_1(j,k_1,k_2)} - \chi_{A_2(j,k_1,k_2)})]$$
$$= -\langle \nu_1, \Psi_{j,k_1',k_2'}^{(1)}\rangle \mathbb{E}\chi_{A_2} \qquad (60)$$
$$= -c\mathbb{E}[\chi_{A_2}]$$
$$= -c\frac{1}{2^{2j+1}}.$$

Thus,

$$\hat{\mu}_j(A_2) = d\frac{1}{2^{2j+1}} - c\frac{1}{2^{2j+1}}$$
$$= \mu_{j-1}^*(A_2) + \nu(A_2) \qquad (61)$$

and by (54), (55), (59) and (60), we have that

$$\mu_{j-1}^*(A_1) = \mu_{j-1}^*(A_2) \qquad (62)$$

and

$$\nu_1(A_1) = -\nu_1(A_2). \qquad (63)$$

Therefore, it follows from (58), (61), (62), (63) and the fact that $\hat{\mu}_j$ is a positive measure, that

$$|\nu_1(A_1)| = |\nu_1(A_2)|$$
$$\leq |\mu_{j-1}^*(A_1)| \qquad (64)$$
$$= |\mu_{j-1}^*(A_2)|$$

From which we conclude that $\mu_{j-1}^*(A) = 0$ implies $\nu_1(A) = 0$. Similarly, it can be shown that $\mu_{j-1}^*(A) = 0$ implies $\nu_i(A) = 0$ for $i = 2, 3$; for this, analogous proofs are carried out, with the difference being that for $i = 2$, the sets to be considered are B_1 and B_2 as in (23), whereas $C_1 \cup C_4$ and $C_2 \cup C_3$ as in (24) are the respective sets when $i = 3$. □

We have proved that if it is intended to go back to the preimage of the projection of the approximation operator $\mathbf{P}$ from a level $j - 1$ to a level j, the support of the level $j - 1$ delimits that of the j level. Now, we will prove that for every measure $\hat{\mu}_j$ that satisfies (45) and (46), it necessarily holds that $\nu_1 = \nu_2 = 0$.

Lemma 2. *Let $j \in \mathbb{Z}$ and μ_{j-1}^* be an optimal simple solution for (40) at level $j - 1$. Then for each feasible solution $\hat{\mu}_j \in \mathbf{P}_j L^2(\mathbb{R}^2)$ to (40) at level j such that $\mathbf{P}_{j-1}\hat{\mu}_j = \mu_{j-1}^*$ and $\hat{\mu}_j = \mu_{j-1}^* + \nu_1 + \nu_2 + \nu_3$. It necessarily holds that*

$$\nu_1 = \nu_2 = 0. \qquad (65)$$

Proof. In order to perform this proof, we use the restrictions of the MK problem (40), which in turn, are related to the marginal measures. Therefore, we will only complete the proof for one of the projections, since the other is analogous. From the linearity of the Radon–Nikodym derivative, it follows that

$$\begin{aligned} \eta_j^1 &= \Pi_1 \hat{\mu}_j \\ &= \Pi(\mu_{j-1}^* + \nu_1 + \nu_2 + \nu_3) \\ &= \Pi \mu_{j-1}^* + \Pi \nu_1 + \Pi \nu_2 + \Pi \nu_3. \end{aligned} \quad (66)$$

Let $k' \in \mathbb{Z}$ and $I_{j+1,2k'} = [2^{-j-1}2k', 2^{-j-1}(2k'+1))$. Thus, by (39) and (66), we have that

$$\begin{aligned} \Pi_1 \hat{\mu}_j(I_{j+1,2k'}) &= \eta_j^1(I_{j+1,2k'}) \\ &= \Pi_1 \mu_{j-1}^*(I_{j+1,2k'}) \\ &= \alpha. \end{aligned} \quad (67)$$

That is, we are evaluating feasible solutions on rectangles whose height is half the size of the squares with which they are discretized at the j level of the Haar MRA. Now, we will develop in detail (66) evaluated on $I_{j,k'}$. Since μ_{j-1}^* is a simple solution, we call $l' \in \mathbb{Z}$ the only number such that $\mu_{j-1}^+(S(j,k',l')) > 0$, where $S(j,k_1,k_2)$ is defined as in (20). With the aim of simplifying the notation, we define $\mathcal{I} = I_{j+1,2k'} \times \mathbb{R}$. By (16) and (25), we have that

$$\begin{aligned} \Pi_1 \nu_1(I_{j+1,2k'}) &= \nu_i(\mathcal{I}) \\ &= \mathbb{E}[\chi_{\mathcal{I}} \nu_1] \\ &= \mathbb{E}[\chi_{\mathcal{I}} \sum_{k_1} \sum_{k_2} \langle \nu_1, \Psi_{j,k_1,k_2}^{(1)} \rangle (\chi_{A_1(j,k_1,k_2)} - \chi_{A_2(j,k_1,k_2)})] \\ &= \mathbb{E}[\chi_{\mathcal{I}} \sum_{k_2} \langle \nu_1, \Psi_{j,k',k_2}^{(1)} \rangle (\chi_{A_1(j,k',k_2)} - \chi_{A_2(j,k',k_2)})] \\ &= \mathbb{E}[\chi_{\mathcal{I}} \langle \nu_1, \Psi_{j,k',l'}^{(1)} \rangle (\chi_{A_1(j,k',l')} - \chi_{A_2(j,k',l')})] \end{aligned} \quad (68)$$

By the way $\mathcal{I}$ was defined, necessarily in the last equality it must be fulfilled that one of the terms in the expectation is equal to 0. Hence, it is fulfilled that

$$\begin{aligned} \Pi_1 \nu_1(I_{j+1,2k'}) &= \langle \nu_1, \Psi_{j,k',l'}^{(1)} \rangle \mathbb{E}[\chi_{\mathcal{I}}] \\ &= \frac{1}{2^{2j+1}} \langle \nu_1, \Psi_{j,k',l'}^{(1)} \rangle. \end{aligned} \quad (69)$$

By a similar argument, it can be proved that

$$\Pi \nu_2(I_{j+1,2k'}) = 0 \quad (70)$$

and

$$\Pi \nu_2(I_{j+1,2k'}) = 0. \quad (71)$$

Then from (66) to (71), it follows that

$$\alpha = \alpha + \frac{1}{2^{2j+1}} \langle \nu_1, \Psi_{j,k',l'}^{(1)} \rangle + 0 + 0. \quad (72)$$

Hence,

$$\langle \nu_1, \Psi_{j,k',l'}^{(1)} \rangle = 0. \quad (73)$$

Therefore, $\nu_1 = 0$. In a similar way, we can prove that $\nu_2 = 0$. □

Suppose we have a simple optimal solution μ^*_{j-1} for the MK problem discretized through the Haar MRA at level $j-1 \in \mathbb{Z}$ and that we are interested in refining that solution to the next level j. By Lemmas 1 and 2, any $\hat{\mu}_j$ that satisfies (45) has its support contained in the support of μ^*_{j-1} and has components $\nu_1 = \nu_2 = 0$. Then the problem of constructing a feasible solution $\hat{\mu}_j$ such that it refines μ^*_{j-1} is reduced to construct

$$\hat{\mu}_j(x,y) = \mu^*_{j-1}(x,y) + \nu_3(x,y)$$
$$= \mu^*_{j-1}(x,y) + \sum_{k_1}\sum_{k_2} \langle \hat{\mu}_j, \Psi^{(i)}_{j,k_1,k_2}\rangle \Psi^{(i)}_{j,k_1,k_2}(x,y), \quad (74)$$

which is equivalent to chosing for each $k_1, k_2 \in \mathbb{Z}$ a value $\nu^3_{k_1,k_2}$ such that

$$\hat{\mu}^j_{k_1,k_2} = \mu^{*,j-1}_{k_1,k_2} + \nu^3_{k_1,k_2}. \quad (75)$$

By Lemma 1 for each $k_1, k_2 \in \mathbb{Z}$, it is fulfilled that

$$|\nu^3_{k_1,k_2}| \leq \mu^{*,j-1}_{k_1,k_2}. \quad (76)$$

Therefore, the choice of $\nu^3_{k_1,k_2}$ is restricted to a compact collection, and since $\hat{\mu}_j$ is a solution of the linear program (40), then

$$|\nu^3_{k_1,k_2}| = \mu^{*,j-1}_{k_1,k_2}. \quad (77)$$

Thus, the sign of $\nu^3_{k_1,k_2}$ must be such that it minimizes $\nu^3_{k_1,k_2} c^j_{k_1,k_2}$. That is,

$$\nu^3_{k_1,k_2} c^j_{k_1,k_2} \leq 0 \quad (78)$$

4. Methodological Proposal

In this section, we show through examples a process that builds solutions to the MK problem with a reduced number of operations. First, we consider the MK problem with cost function $c : [0,1] \times [0,1] \to \mathbb{R}$ defined by

$$c(x,y) = 4x^2y - xy^2 \quad (79)$$

and homogeneous restrictions ν_1, ν_2 over $[0,1]$. So that the algorithm can be graphically appreciated, we take a small level of discretization, namely $j = 6$. Thus, in the Haar MRA over $\mathbb{R}^2$ at level $j = 6$, the cost function has the form shown in Figure 5, which can be stored in a vector of size $2^{2j} = 2^{2(6)} = 2^{12}$.

Now, we apply the filtering process to the cost function at level $j = 6$, which results in four functions

$$c_6(x,y) = c_5(x,y) + \Psi^{(1)}(x,y) + \Psi^{(2)}(x,y) + \Psi^{(3)}(x,y); \quad (80)$$

see Figures 6–9.

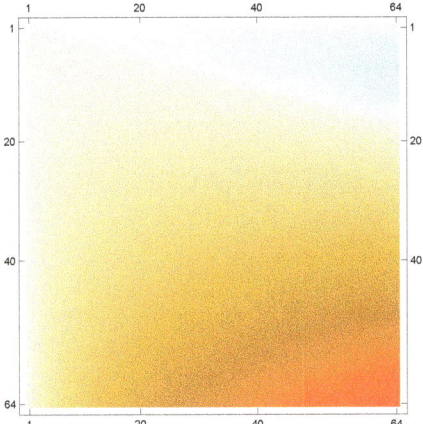

Figure 5. Step 1. Discretization of the cost function to the level j, which is denoted by c_j. In particular, the cost function is $c(x,y) = 4x^2y - xy^2$ for lever $j = 6$.

Step 2. Filtering the original discrete function using the high-pass filter, which yield three discrete functions denoted by Ψ_1, Ψ_2 and Ψ_3, that functions correspond to Figures 7, 8 and 9, respectively, each describing local changes in the original discrete function. It is then low-pass filtered to produce the approximate discrete function c_5, which is given by Figure 6.

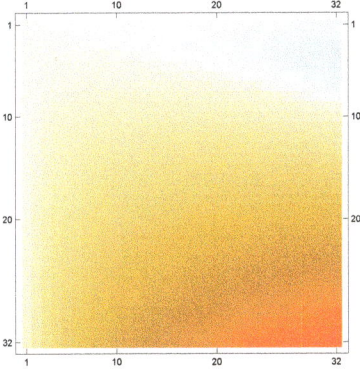

Figure 6. $c_5(x,y)$.

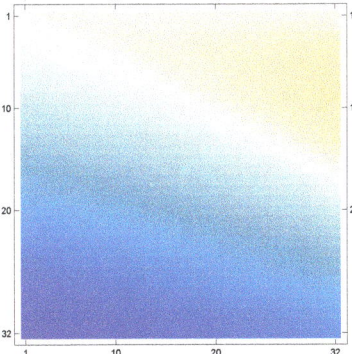

Figure 7. $\Psi^{(1)}(x,y)$.

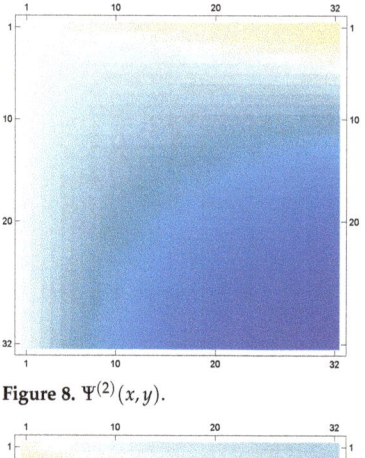

Figure 8. $\Psi^{(2)}(x,y)$.

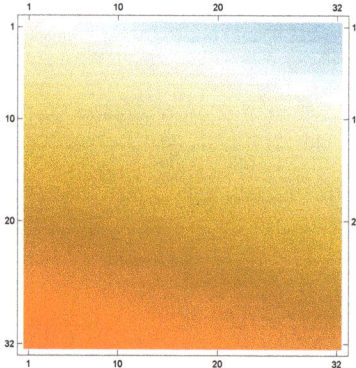

Figure 9. $\Psi^{(3)}(x,y)$.

We then solve the MK problem for the level $j - 1 = 5$. That is, we find a measure $\mu_{j-1}^* = \mu_5^*$ that is an optimal solution for the MK problem with cost function c_5. Such data can be stored in a vector of size $2^{2j-2} = 2^{10}$; see Figure 10. For each entry k, the formal application that plots this vector in a square is defined by $k \to (k_1 + 1, k_2 + 1)$, where $0 \leq k_1, k_2 < 2^{n-1}$ and $k = k_1 \cdot 2^{j-1} + k_2$.

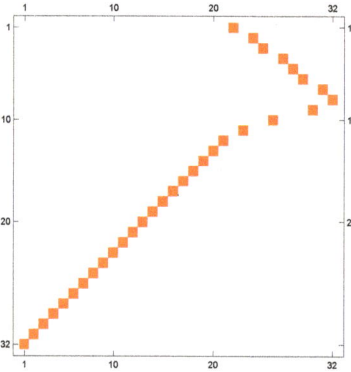

Figure 10. Step 3. We obtain a solution μ_5^* for MK^5 associated with the cost function c_5 given in Figure 6.

Since the measure $\mu_{j-1}^* = \mu_5^*$ is an optimal simple solution for the MK problem, then we can represent its support in a simple way, as we show below:

$$\text{support}(\mu_{j-1}^*) = \bigcup_{k_1,k_2} S_{k_1,k_2} \qquad (81)$$

where $S_{k_1,k_2} = S(j,k_1,k_2)$ is the square in (20). Next, we split each block $S_{k_1,k_2} \subset \text{support}(\mu_{j-1}^*)$ into four parts as in (24); see Figure 11.

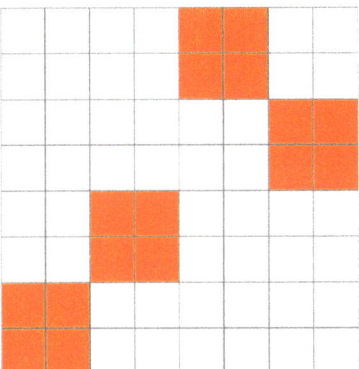

Figure 11. Division of the components of $\text{support}(\mu_{j-1}^*)$ into four parts.

From the technical point of view, in the discretization at level $j - 1 = 5$, we have a grid of $2^{j-1} \times 2^{j-1} = 32 \times 32$ squares that we call S_{k_1,k_2} and identify with the points (k_1, k_2). Thus, we refine to a grid of 64×64, splitting each square into four, which in the new grid are determined by points

$$(2k_1 - 1, 2k_2), (2k_1 - 1, 2k_2 - 1), (2k_1, 2k_2 - 1) \text{ and } (2k_1, 2k_2); \qquad (82)$$

see Figure 12.

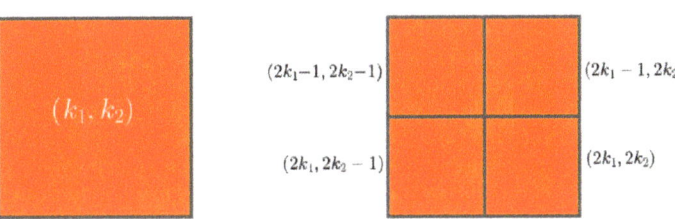

Figure 12. Refinement of grid from level $j - 1$ to j of discretization.

As we prove in Lemma 1, any feasible solution $\hat{\mu}_j = \hat{\mu}_6$ that refines μ_5^* has its support contained in $\text{support}(\mu_5^*)$. Therefore, we must only deal with the region delimited by the support of μ_5^*. By Lemma 2, in order to construct the solution $\hat{\mu}_6$, we only need to determine the values n_{k_1,k_2}^3 corresponding to the coefficients of the wavelet part ν_3; however, by (77) and (78), those values are well determined and satisfy that when added with the scaling part μ_{k_1,k_2}^*, the result is a scalar multiple of a characteristic function. For example if the square S_{k_1,k_2} has scaling part coefficient $\mu^*_{k_1,k_2} = c$, then we choose $v^3_{k_1,k_2} = -c$. Hence, by (21) and (25), we have that

$$\begin{aligned}
\hat{\mu}^6_{k_1,k_2}(x,y) &= \mu^*_{k_1,k_2}(x,y) + v^3_{k_1,k_2}(x,y) \\
&= c\chi_S(x,y) - c[\chi_{C_1 \cup C_4}(x,y) - \chi_{C_2 \cup C_3}(x,y)] \\
&= 2c\chi_{C_2 \cup C_3}(x,y).
\end{aligned} \quad (83)$$

Thus, from an operational point of view, we only need to chose between two options of supporting each division of square S_{k_1,k_2}, as we illustrate in Figures 13 and 14.

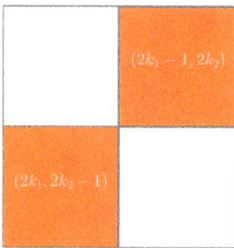

Figure 13. Supports for refinement of the element S_{k_1,k_2} corresponding to the level j: Option I.

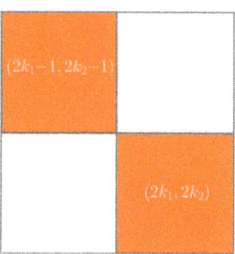

Figure 14. Supports for refinement of the element S_{k_1,k_2} corresponding to the level j: Option II.

This coincides with our geometric intuition. Hence, the resulting feasible solution $\hat{\mu}_6$ has its support contained in support(μ^*_5), and its weight within each square S_{k_1,k_2} is presented in a diagonal within that block; see Figure 15. Finally, we can improve $\hat{\mu}_6$ by observing the way the filtering process acts. To do this, we apply the proximity criteria (41) and split the support of $\hat{\mu}_6$ into points of Type I and II. In Figure 16, we identify the points of Type I and II of solution μ^*_5, whereas in Figure 15, we do the same but for $\hat{\mu}_6$.

Intuitively, the division of the support into points of Type I and II allows us to classify the points so that they have an identity function form and, consequently, that come from the discretization of a continuous function—points of Type I—and in points that come from the discretization of a discontinuous function—points of Type II. Thus, the points of Type I are located in such a way that they generate a desired solution, and therefore it is not convenient to move them, whereas Type II points are free to be changed as this does not lead to the destruction of a continuous structure in the solution. As we mentioned in the previous section, each permutation of rows or columns of one weighted element S_{k_1,k_2} with another $S_{k'_1,k'_2}$ constructs a feasible solution; see (44). Thus, as a heuristic technique to improve the solution, we check the values $\langle c_6, \mu^\sigma_6 \rangle$ associated with each solution μ^σ_6 obtained by permuting rows or columns of points of Type II of the solution $\hat{\mu}_6$. We call $\mu^{\sigma^*}_6$ the solution for which its permutation gives it the best performance. See Figure 17.

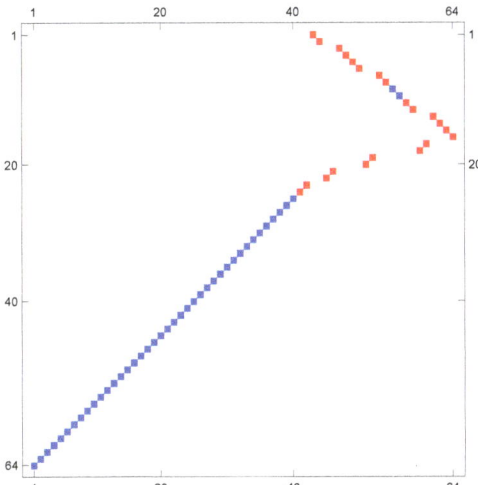

Figure 15. Step 5. Using the solution μ_5^* which is given by Figure 10, the information of the high-pass components (Figures 7, 8 and 9) and Lemma 1, we obtain a feasible solution for Level 6, which is denoted by $\hat{\mu}_6$.

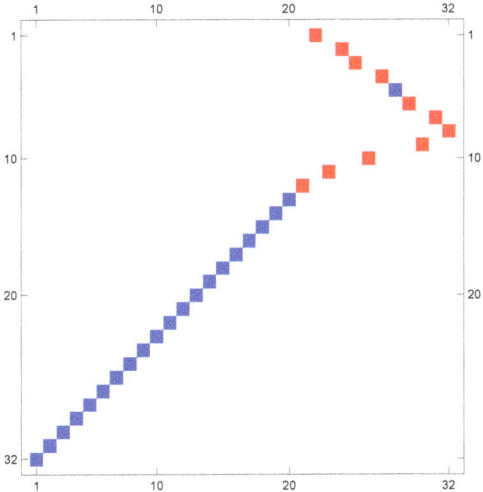

Figure 16. Step 4. We classify the points of the support of the solution μ_5^* by proximity criteria as points of Type I ■ or Type II ■ (the measure μ_5^* corresponds to Figure 10).

Finally, we present Table 1 that compare the solutions of the MK problem, in which MK^5 is the value associated with the optimal solution μ_5^* at level of discretization $j - 1 = 5$, MK_6 is the value associated with an optimal solution μ_6^* at level of discretization $j = 6$, and $MK_6^{\sigma^*}$ is the value associated with the solution $\mu_6^{\sigma^*}$ obtained by the heuristic method described in the previous paragraph.

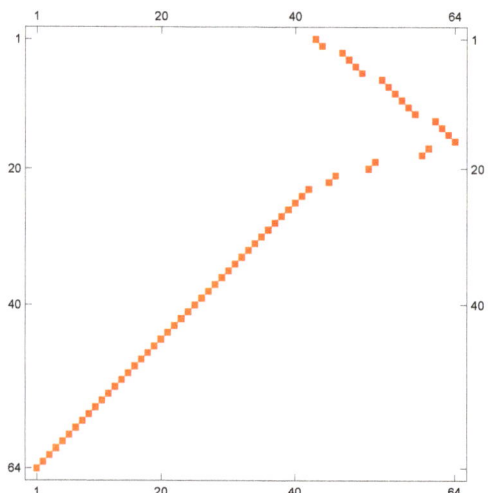

Figure 17. Step 6. Classification of the points of μ_5^* induces classification of the points in $\hat{\mu}_6$ by contention in the support. Over the points of Type I of the solution $\hat{\mu}_6$, we do not move those points. For the points of Type II, we apply a permutation to the solution over the two points that improve the solution and repeat the process with the rest of the points.

Table 1. Comparison of the values corresponding to MK_5, $MK_6^{\sigma^*}$ and MK_6.

MK_5	$MK_6^{\sigma^*}$	MK_6
0.24785	0.247738	0.247726

5. Other Examples of This Methodology

We conclude this work with a series of examples in which we apply the proposed methodology. Each of them is divided into the six-step algorithm introduced in the previous section and corresponds to a classical example existing in the literature.

5.1. Example with Cost Function $c(x,y) = x^2y - xy^2$

Let MK be the MK problem with cost function $c(x,y) = x^2y - xy^2$ and uniform restrictions η_1 and η_2 over the unitary interval $[0,1]$. In order to be more didactic, we consider the level of discretization $j = 6$. Next, we present the reduced algorithm.

Step 1. Discretize the cost function at level j—that is, over a grid of $2^j \times 2^j$. Figure 18.

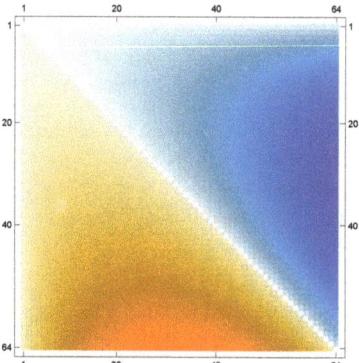

Figure 18. Discretization of the cost function $c(x,y) = x^2y - xy^2$ at level $j = 6$.

Step 2. Apply the filtering process to the cost function at level $j-1$, obtaining the filtered cost function c_5, which is plotted on a grid of $2^{j-1} \times 2^{j-1}$. Figure 19.

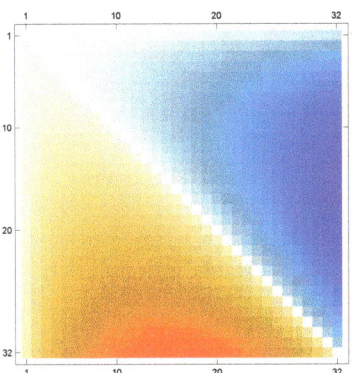

Figure 19. Filtering of the cost function c at level $j - 1 = 5$.

Step 3. Find an optimal simple solution μ_{j-1}^* for the discretized MK_j problem. That is, solve for the cost function c_5 and obtain an optimal simple solution μ_5^*. Figure 20.

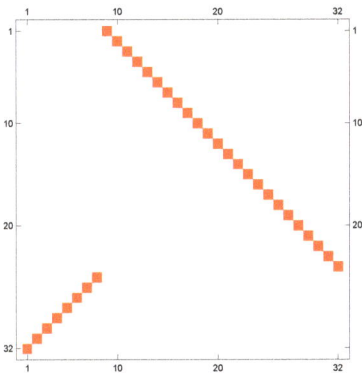

Figure 20. MK solution for the filtered function c at level $j - 1 = 5$.

Step 4. Apply the proximity criteria to the support of μ_{j-1}^*. Figure 21.

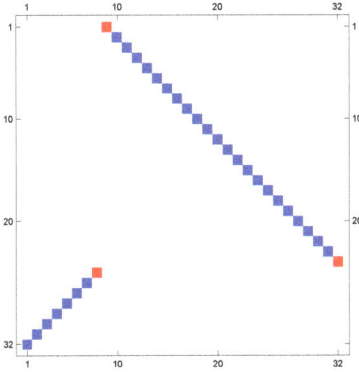

Figure 21. Classification of points of support(μ_5^*) into Type I ■ and Type II ■.

Step 5. Refine the optimal simple solution μ_{j-1}^* to a feasible solution $\hat{\mu}_j$, dividing each weighted square S_{k_1,k_2} at level $j-1$ into four squares at level j (see (82)) and place mass according to the criteria (83). Figure 22.

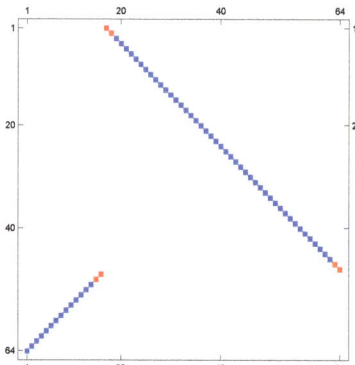

Figure 22. Solution $\hat{\mu}_6$ from refinement of μ_5^*.

Step 6. Permute the rows and columns of the points of Type II in support$(\hat{\mu}_j)$ using (44) to construct feasible solutions μ_j^σ and chose the one that has better performance. Figure 23.

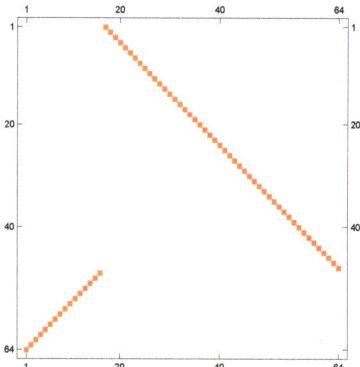

Figure 23. Final result $\mu_6^{\sigma^*}$.

The following Table 2 contains the comparison of the proposed methodology with the two immediate levels of resolution.

Table 2. Comparison of the values corresponding to MK_5, $MK_6^{\sigma^*}$ and MK_6.

MK_5	$MK_6^{\sigma^*}$	MK_6
-0.0350952	-0.035141	-0.035141

5.2. Example with Cost Function $c(x,y) = xy$

Let MK be the MK problem with cost function $c(x,y) = xy$ and uniform restrictions η_1 and η_2 over the unitary interval $[0,1]$. In order to be more didactic, we consider the level of discretization $j = 6$. Next, we present the reduced algorithm.

Step 1. Discretize the cost function at level j—that is, over a grid of $2^j \times 2^j$. Figure 24.

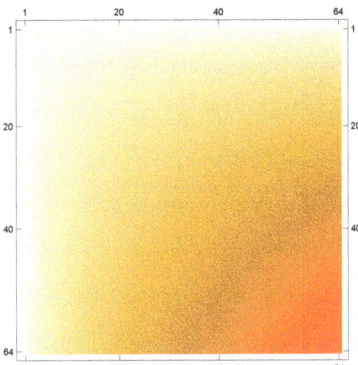

Figure 24. Discretization of the cost function $c(x,y) = xy$ at level $j = 6$.

Step 2. Apply the filtering process to the cost function at level $j - 1$, obtaining the filtered cost function c_5, which is plotted on a grid of $2^{j-1} \times 2^{j-1}$. Figure 25.

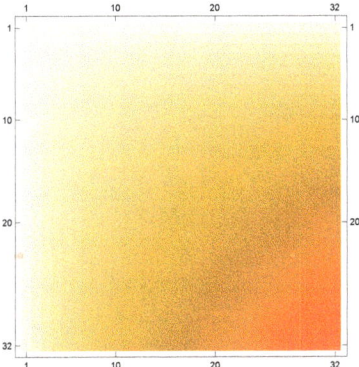

Figure 25. Apply the filter to the cost function c at level $j - 1 = 5$.

Step 3. Find an optimal simple solution μ_{j-1}^* for the discretized MK_j problem. That is, solve for the cost function c_5 and obtain an optimal simple solution μ_5^*. Figure 26.

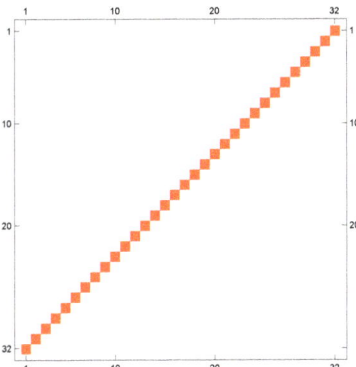

Figure 26. Solution of the MK for the function c at level $j - 1 = 5$.

Step 4. Apply the proximity criteria to the support of μ_{j-1}^*. Figure 27.

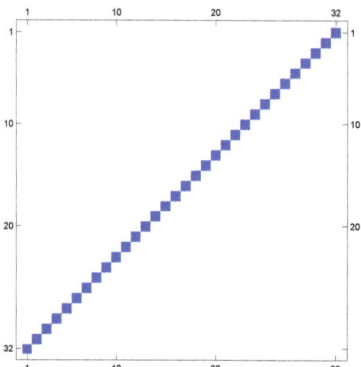

Figure 27. In this example there are only Type I points ■.

Step 5. Refine the optimal simple solution μ^*_{j-1} to a feasible solution $\hat{\mu}_j$, dividing each weighted square S_{k_1,k_2} at level $j-1$ into four squares at level j (see (82)) and placing mass according to the criteria (83). Figure 28.

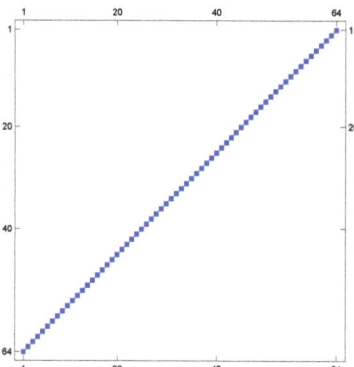

Figure 28. Solution $\hat{\mu}_6$ from refinement of μ^*_5.

Step 6. Permute the rows and columns of the points of Type II in support$(\hat{\mu}_j)$ using (44) to construct feasible solutions μ^σ_j and chose the one that has better performance. Figure 29.

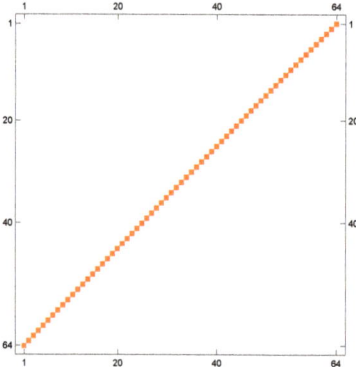

Figure 29. Final result $\mu^{\sigma*}_6$.

The following Table 3 contains the comparison of the proposed methodology with the two immediate levels of resolution.

Table 3. Comparison of the values corresponding to MK_5, $MK_6^{\sigma^*}$ and MK_6.

MK_5	$MK_6^{\sigma^*}$	MK_6
0.166748	0.166687	0.166687

5.3. Example with Cost Function $c(x,y) = (2y - x - 1)^2(2y - x)^2$

We take the MK problem with cost function $c(x,y) = (2y - x - 1)^2(2y - x)^2$ and homogeneous restrictions over the unitary interval. Again, we consider the level of discretization $j = 6$.

Step 1. Discretize the cost function at level j. Figure 30.

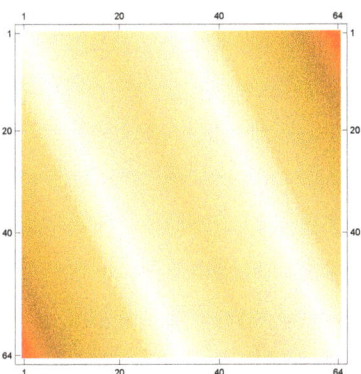

Figure 30. Discretization of cost function $c(x,y) = (2y - x - 1)^2(2y - x)^2$ for level $j = 6$.

Step 2. Apply the filtering process at level $j - 1$ to the cost function. Figure 31.

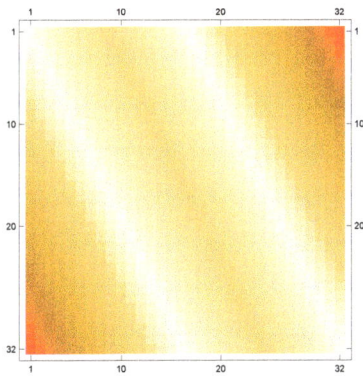

Figure 31. Filtered cost function for $j = 5$.

Step 3. Find an optimal simple solution μ_{j-1}^* for the MK_{j-1} problem. Figure 32.

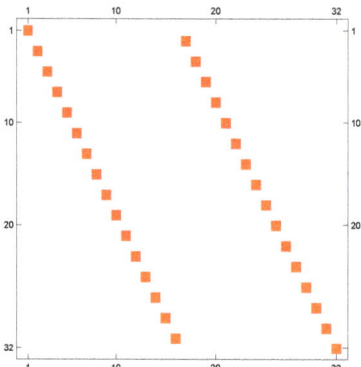

Figure 32. Solution of the MK_5 problem.

Step 4. Apply the proximity criteria to the support of μ_{j-1}^*. Figure 33.

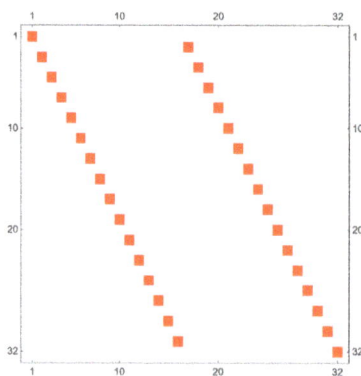

Figure 33. In this example, there are only Type II points ■.

Step 5. Refine the solution μ_{j-1}^* to a feasible solution $\hat{\mu}_6$ applying the criteria (82) and (83). Figure 34.

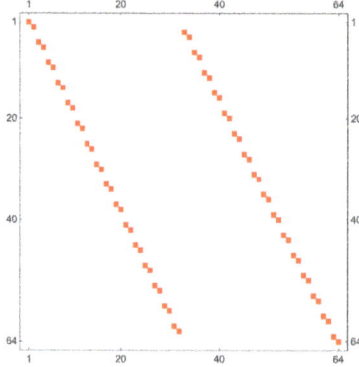

Figure 34. Feasible solution $\hat{\mu}_6$ from refinement of μ_5^*.

Step 6. Permute points of Type II of $\hat{\mu}_j$ using (44) to construct feasible solutions μ_j^σ and chose which has better performance. Figure 35.

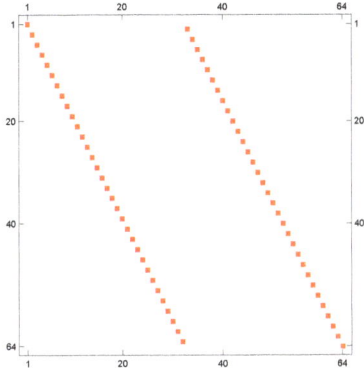

Figure 35. Final result $\mu_6^{\sigma^*}$.

The Table 4 summarizes the results obtained.

Table 4. Comparison of values MK_5, $MK_6^{\sigma^*}$ and MK_6.

MK_5	$MK_6^{\sigma^*}$	MK_6
0.000236571	0.0000600852	0.0000597889

6. Conclusions and Future Work

Note that with the methodology of [3,4,9], the authors obtain a solution of MK^j. For this, they need to resolve a transport problem with 4^j variables. We call this methodology an exhaustive method. For our methodology, in Step 3, we need to resolve a transport problem with 4^{j-1} variables, and the other steps of the methodology are methods of classification, ordering and filtering; with 2^j data for classification and ordering and 4^j data for filtering, it is clear that this method requires fewer operations to resolve transport problems.

In summary, we have the following table comparing the results of solving the examples more often used in the literature with our methodology versus the exhaustive method (using all variables).

Cost Function	MK^6	MK_6^σ	Error
xy	0.166687	0.166687	
$x^2y - xy^2$	-0.035141	-0.035141	
$4x^2y - xy^2$	0.247726	0.247738	1.52588×10^{-5}
$(2y - x - 1)^2(2y - x)^2$	0.0000600947	0.0000600947	5.31762×10^{-5}
Cost Function	MK^7	MK_7^σ	**Error**
xy	0.166672	0.166672	
$x^2y - xy^2$	-0.0351524	-0.0351524	
$4x^2y - xy^2$	0.247695	0.247698	3.8147×10^{-6}
$(2y - x - 1)^2(2y - x)^2$	0.0000600852	0.0000600852	1.24066×10^{-5}
Cost Function	MK^8	MK_8^σ	**Error**
xy	0.166668	0.166668	
$x^2y - xy^2$	-0.0351553	-0.0351553	
$4x^2y - xy^2$	0.247688	0.247688	9.53674×10^{-7}
$(2y - x - 1)^2(2y - x)^2$			3.21631×10^{-6}

Note that our method always improves the solution of the level $j - 1$ and for some examples give an exact solution; we use Mathematica© and basic computer equipment for programming this methodology, and maybe we can improve the results with software focused on numerical calculus and better computer equipment. It is also important to mention that the methodology presented in this work has some weaknesses. In our computational experiments, we noticed that if we did not start with a sufficient amount of information, then the methodology tended to give very distant results. In other words, if the initial level of discretization was not fine enough, then because the algorithm lowers the resolution level when executed, such loss of information generates poor performance. However, when starting with an adequate level of discretization, experimentally it can be observed that the distribution of the solutions for the discretized problems, as well as the respective optimal values, have stable behavior with a clear trend. The question that arises naturally is: "In practice, what are the parameters that determine good or bad behavior of the algorithm?" Clearly, if the cost function is fixed and we rule out the possible technical problems associated with programming and computing power, the only remaining parameter is the initial refinement level at which the algorithm is going to work—that is, the level j. However, if we reflect more deeply on the reasons why there is a practical threshold beyond which at a certain level of discretization the algorithm has stable behavior, we only have as a possible causes the level of information of the cost function that captures the MR analysis. In other words, if the oscillation of the cost function at a certain level of resolution is well determined by MR analysis, then the algorithm will have good performance.

The approach presented in this paper is far from exhaustive and, on the contrary, opens the possibility for a number of new proposals for approximating solutions to the MK problem. The above is due to the fact that in the work [9], it was proven that discretization of the MK problem can be performed from any MR analysis over $\mathbb{R}^2$. Therefore, the possibility of implementing other types of discretions remains open. In principle, as we mentioned in the previous paragraph, the most natural thing is to expect better performance if the nature of the cost function and the types of symmetric geometric structures that it induces in space are studied in order to use an MR analysis that fits this information and therefore has more efficient performance.

Author Contributions: Conceptualization, A.S.N. and C.G.F.; methodology, A.S.N., R.R.L.M. and C.G.F.; software, C.G.F. investigation, A.S.N. and J.R.A.P. writing—original draft preparation, A.S. N., J.R.A.P and C.G.F; writing—review and editing A.S.N. and R.R.L.M.; project administration A.S.N. All authors have read and agreed to the published version of the manuscript.

Funding: This research received no external funding.

Institutional Review Board Statement: Not applicable.

Informed Consent Statement: Not applicable.

Data Availability Statement: Not applicable.

Conflicts of Interest: The authors declare no conflict of interest.

References

1. Hernández-Lerma, O.; Lasserre, J.B. Approximation schemes for infinite linear programs. *SIAM J. Optim.* **1998**, *8*, 973–988. [CrossRef]
2. González-Hernández, J.; Gabriel-Argüelles, J.R.; Hernández-Lerma, O. On solutions to the mass transfer problem. *SIAM J. Optim.* **2006**, *17*, 485–499. [CrossRef]
3. Gabriel-Argüelles, J.R.; González-Hernández, J.; López-Martínez, R.R. Numerical approximations to the mass transfer problem on compact spaces. *IMA J. Numer. Anal.* **2010**, *30*, 1121–1136. [CrossRef]
4. Avendaño-Garrido, M.L.; Gabriel-Argüelles, J.R.; Quintana-Torres, L.; Mezura-Montes, E. A metaheuristic for a numerical approximation to the mass transfer problem. *Int. J. Appl. Math. Comput. Sci.* **2016**, *26*, 757–766. [CrossRef]
5. Avendaño-Garrido, M.L.; Gabriel-Argüelles, J.R.; Quintana-Torres, L.; Mezura-Montes, E. An Efficient Numerical Approximation for the Monge–Kantorovich Mass Transfer Problem. In *Machine Learning, Optimization, and Big Data. MOD 2015*; Lecture Notes in Computer Science; Pardalos, P., Pavone, M., Farinella, G., Cutello, V., Eds.; Springer: Cham, Switzerland, 2016; Volume 9432, pp. 233–239. [CrossRef]

6. Gröchenig, K.; Madych, W.R. Multiresolution analysis, Haar bases, and self-similar tilings of $\mathbb{R}^n$. *Inst. Electr. Electron. Eng. Trans. Inf. Theory* **1992**, *38*, 556–568. [CrossRef]
7. Liu, Y.; Xu, K.D.; Li, J.; Guo, Y.J.; Zhang, A.; Chen, Q. Millimeter-wave E-plane waveguide bandpass filters based on spoof surface plasmon polaritons. *IEEE Trans. Microw. Theory Tech.* **2022**, *70*, 4399–4409. [CrossRef]
8. Liu, K.; Yang, Z.; Wei, W.; Gao, B.; Xin, D.; Sun, C.; Gao, G.; Wu, G. Novel detection approach for thermal defects: Study on its feasibility and application to vehicle cables. *High Volt.* **2023**, *8*, 358–367. [CrossRef]
9. Sánchez-Nungaray, A.; González-Flores, C.; López-Martínez, R.R. Multiresolution Analysis Applied to the Monge–Kantorovich Problem. *Abstr. Appl. Anal.* **2018**, *2018*, 1764175. [CrossRef]
10. Haker, S.; Tannenbaum, A.; Kikinis, R. *Mass Preserving Mappings and Surface Registration*; MICCAI 2001, Lecture Notes in Computer Science; Springer: Berlin/Heidelberg, Germany, 2001; Volume 2208, pp. 120–127.
11. Zhu, L.; Yang, Y.; Haker, S.; Tannenbaum, A. Optimal mass transport for registration and warping. *Int. J. Comput. Vis.* **2004**, *60*, 225–240. .:VISI.0000036836.66311.97. [CrossRef]
12. Haber, E.; Rehman, T.; Tannenbaum, A. An efficient numerical method for the solution of the L_2 optimal mass transfer problem. *SIAM J. Sci. Comput.* **2010**, *32*, 7–211. [CrossRef] [PubMed]
13. Xie, X.; Wang, T.; Zhang, W. Existence of solutions for the (p,q)-Laplacian equation with nonlocal Choquard reaction. *Appl. Math. Lett.* **2023**, *135*, 108418. [CrossRef]
14. Peng, Z.; Hu, J.; Shi, K.; Luo, R.; Huang, R.; Ghosh, B.K.; Huang, J. A novel optimal bipartite consensus control scheme for unknown multi-agent systems via model-free reinforcement learning. *Appl. Math. Comput.* **2020**, *369*, 124821. [CrossRef]
15. Walnut, D.F. *An Introduction to Wavelet Analysis*; Birkhäuser: Boston, MA, USA, 2004; pp. 115–138.
16. Guo, K.; Labate, D.; Lim, W.Q.; Weiss, G.; Wilson, E. Wavelets with composite dilations and their MRA properties. *Appl. Comput. Harmon. Anal.* **2006**, *20*, 202–236. [CrossRef]
17. Krishtal, I.A.; Robinson, B.D.; Weiss, G.L.; Wilson, E.N. Some simple Haar-type wavelets in higher dimensions. *J. Geom. Anal.* **2007**, *17*, 87–96. [CrossRef]
18. Bazaraa-Mokhtar, S.; John, J.; Hanif, D. *Linear Programming and Network Flows*; John Wiley & Sons: Hoboken, NJ, USA, 2010; pp. 513–528.
19. Billingsley, P. *Convergence of Probability Measures*; John Wiley & Sons: New York, NY, USA, 1999; pp. 27–29.

Disclaimer/Publisher's Note: The statements, opinions and data contained in all publications are solely those of the individual author(s) and contributor(s) and not of MDPI and/or the editor(s). MDPI and/or the editor(s) disclaim responsibility for any injury to people or property resulting from any ideas, methods, instructions or products referred to in the content.

Article

A License Plate Recognition System with Robustness against Adverse Environmental Conditions Using Hopfield's Neural Network

Saman Rajebi [1], Siamak Pedrammehr [2] and Reza Mohajerpoor [3,*]

[1] Department of Electrical Engineering, Seraj University, Tabriz 5137894797, Iran
[2] Faculty of Design, Tabriz Islamic Art University, Tabriz 5164736931, Iran
[3] School of Civil Engineering, The University of Sydney, Sydney 2006, Australia
* Correspondence: reza.mohajerpoor@sydney.edu.au

Abstract: License plates typically have unique color, size, and shape characteristics in each country. This paper presents a general method for character extraction and pattern matching in license plate recognition systems. The proposed method is based on a combination of morphological operations and edge detection techniques, along with the bounding box method for identifying and revealing license plate characters while removing unwanted artifacts such as dust and fog. The mathematical model of foggy images is presented and the sum of gradients of the image, which represents the visibility of the image, is improved. Previous works on license plate recognition have utilized non-intelligent pattern matching techniques. The proposed technique can be applied in a variety of settings, including traffic monitoring, parking management, and law enforcement, among others. The applied algorithm, unlike SOTA-based methods, does not need a huge set of training data and is implemented only by applying standard templates. The main advantages of the proposed algorithm are the lack of a need for a training set, the high speed of the training process, the ability to respond to different standards, the high response speed, and higher accuracy compared to similar tasks.

Keywords: pattern recognition; image processing; independent component analysis; Hopfield's neural network; license plate; LPR

MSC: 68T07

Citation: Rajebi, S.; Pedrammehr, S.; Mohajerpoor, R. A License Plate Recognition System with Robustness against Adverse Environmental Conditions Using Hopfield's Neural Network. *Axioms* **2023**, *12*, 424. https://doi.org/10.3390/axioms12050424

Academic Editor: Palle E.T. Jorgensen

Received: 28 February 2023
Revised: 17 April 2023
Accepted: 24 April 2023
Published: 26 April 2023

Copyright: © 2023 by the authors. Licensee MDPI, Basel, Switzerland. This article is an open access article distributed under the terms and conditions of the Creative Commons Attribution (CC BY) license (https://creativecommons.org/licenses/by/4.0/).

1. Introduction

Nowadays, the use of surveillance-based security systems has become increasingly important in various applications, such as home security and traffic monitoring. Object detection is one of the fundamental building blocks of automated surveillance systems. Among the most used techniques for object recognition in surveillance systems is the recognition of vehicle license plates [1]. Automatic license plate recognition is an image-processing-based method that is used for security applications such as controlling access to restricted areas and tracking vehicles.

In real-world applications, simple License Plate Recognition (LPR) systems have low detection accuracy [2]. On the one hand, the effects of external factors such as sunlight and car headlights, license plates with inappropriate designs, the wide variety of license plates and, on the other hand, the limited quality of the software and hardware related to the camera, have reduced the accuracy of these systems. However, recent advances in software and hardware have made LPR systems much safer and more widespread [3,4]. A countless number of these systems are working around the world and are growing exponentially and can do more tasks automatically in different market segments. Even if the recognition is not 100%, a results-dependent side program can compensate for the errors and provide an almost flawless system. For example, to calculate the car's parking time, from entering to leaving the parking lot, this side program can ignore some ignorable errors in the two recognitions. This intelligent integration can overcome the shortcomings of LPR and produce reliable and fully automated systems [5–7].

Figure 1 shows a typical configuration of an LPR system. The license plate reader software is a Windows background program on a PC and an interface between a set of cameras. The program receives the images of the cameras, and by processing them it extracts the license plates of the cars in traffic. The program then displays the results, and can also send them to other parts of the system such as a camera or LED display via serial communication. It then sends this information to the local database or external databases (through the network).

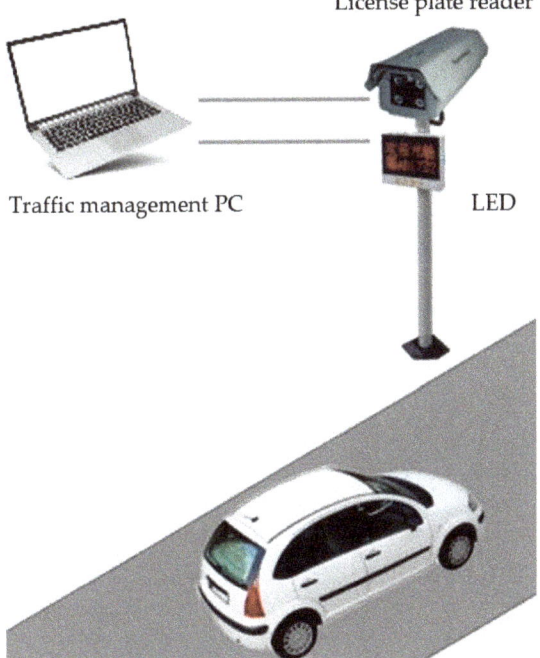

Figure 1. Typical configuration of an LPR system.

The first step in recognizing a car license plate is to distinguish the car from other objects in the image. For this, the methods presented in previous works can be used [8–12]. In similar works, the use of a convolutional neural network (CNN) replaces parts of the proposed method in this paper. Despite the ease of use of this new neural network, there are major disadvantages associated with CNNs. The main disadvantage is that CNNs take a much longer time to train. Another important disadvantage is the need for larger training datasets (i.e., hundreds or thousands of images), and for their proper annotation, which is a delicate procedure that must be performed by domain experts. Other disadvantages include problems that might occur when using pretrained models on similar and smaller datasets (i.e., of a few hundreds of images, or smaller), optimization issues due to model complexities, and hardware restrictions [13]. However, the proposed algorithm assumes there are only cars on highways or an absence of objects corresponding to license plates in non-car elements (such as humans, etc.). This contribution can overcome the burdens that were present in previous works.

In the literature, the pixel-by-pixel comparison method has been used to match the segments extracted from the image with the defined standard characters. This method, in addition to the low classification accuracy, lack of identification, and removal of noise, also requires a lot of execution time. We employed the Hopfield neural network [14] to simultaneously speed up the program's execution and increase the precision, while removing noises on the segments extracted from the image. License plate recognition systems are usually used outdoors. The presence of air pollution, fog, and other factors causes the car license plate images to become blurred. By using frequency domain techniques, it is possible to remove the side- and destructive effects of the environment on the image. In this paper, first, the location of the license plate is identified, and then the disturbing effects of the environment are removed. After extracting the license plate image's segments, the Hopfield neural network classifies these segments to corresponding defined characters.

2. Methodology and Simulation Results

Figure 2 shows the five main steps of license plate recognition. In this structure, the steps for image scheduling, camera settings, and the saving and transferring of results have been ignored. In the following, each of these five steps will be explained in full detail.

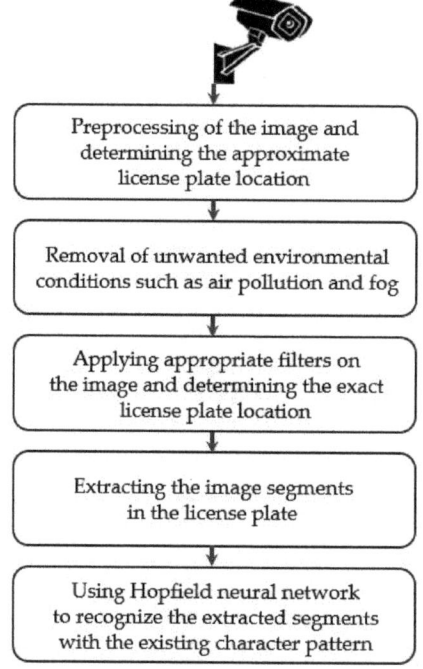

Figure 2. The proposed five main steps of license plate recognition.

2.1. Preprocessing of the Image

In tasks based on image processing, such as car license plate recognition [15–18] or eye tracking, etc., the first step is usually to determine the approximate location of the target object. For this, a large number of different cars with different license plate locations were studied. All the studied cars were photographed at the same distance and angle. In all these photos, the place of installation of the license plates was marked. Figure 3 shows the border of the area where it was possible for a license plate to exist, taking a suitable tolerance.

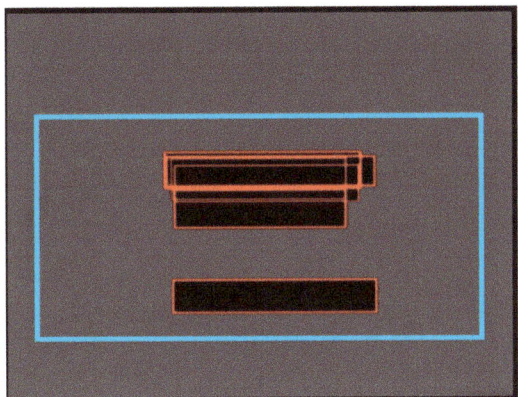

Figure 3. The border of the area where it is possible for a license plate to exist.

The area outside the border of the license plate's zone (which has non-useful information) will be affected by the Blur filter. Applying this filter reduces the calculations and the possibility of errors in future processing. Figure 4 shows a typical image affected by this filter, where non-useful areas have been blurred.

Figure 4. A typical image affected by Blur filter; non-useful areas have been blurred.

2.2. Elimination of Adverse Environmental Effects

Before determining the exact location of the license plate, and then its characters' segments, the adverse effects of the environment, such as the effects of possible fog or smoke in the space between the camera and the license plate, should be corrected as much as possible. Equation (1) shows a blurry image relation [19–24]:

$$I(x) = J(x)t(x) + A(1 - t(x)) \qquad (1)$$

where I is the intensity of the light in the image, J is the illumination of the scene, A is the general light of the environment, and t is a parameter that describes the part of the light that was not scattered and reached the camera. The elimination of adverse environmental effects means recovering J, A, and t from I. The term $J(x)t(x)$ in this equation is called direct attenuation, which describes the brightness of the scene and its decay in the environment. The term $A(1 - t(x))$ is called ambient light, which comes from the previously scattered light and leads to a change in the color of the environment. When the space is homogeneous, the transfer coefficient t is described as follows:

$$t(x) = e^{-\beta \, d(x)} \tag{2}$$

where β is the dispersion coefficient. Equation (2) clearly shows that the image brightness decreases exponentially with its depth d.

Equation (1) shows that in the RGB color space, vectors A, $I(x)$, and $J(x)$ are coplanar while their endpoints are located on a single line. The transfer coefficient t can be expressed by

$$t(x) = \frac{||A - I(x)||}{||A - J(x)||} = \frac{A^c - I^c(x)}{A^c - J^c(x)} \tag{3}$$

where c represents the index of the color channel. In blurred images, t is less than one. Thus, the resolution of the image, which is the sum of the image gradients, is low. The following illustrates this reduction:

$$\sum_t ||\nabla I(x)|| = t \sum_t ||\nabla J(x)|| < \sum_t ||\nabla J(x)|| \tag{4}$$

The transmission coefficient, t, is estimated by maximizing the image resolution, while the intensity $J(x)$ is less than the intensity A. The dark channel for a haze-free outer space image is defined as the following: in a non-sky image, at least one color channel has very low brightness in some pixels. In other words, the image brightness in these pixels is minimum. Equation (5) shows the dark channel definition:

$$J^{dark}(x) = \min_{c \in \{r,g,b\}} \left(\min_{y \in \Omega(x)} (J^c(y)) \right) \tag{5}$$

where J^c is a color channel of J and $\Omega(x)$ is a piece of the image centered at x. If the image does not include the sky and does not have fog, the intensity of J^{dark} will be almost zero. Assuming the value of A for the ambient light and the constant transmission coefficient $t(x)$ in a piece of the image, minimizing the intensity (1) gives:

$$\min_{y \in \Omega(x)} (I^c(x)) = t(x) \min_{y \in \Omega(x)} (J^c(y)) + A^c(1 - t(x)) \tag{6}$$

Dividing the sides of Equation (6) by A and minimizing again, this time among the color channels gives:

$$\min_c \left(\min_{y \in \Omega(x)} \left(\frac{I^c(x)}{A^c} \right) \right) = t(x) \min_c \left(\min_{y \in \Omega(x)} \left(\frac{J^c(y)}{A^c} \right) \right) + (1 - t(x)) \tag{7}$$

By approximating Equation (7) to zero, the transfer coefficient can be defined as Equation (8). The coefficient w is defined to adjust the blurring in the image.

$$t(x) = 1 - w \min_c \left(\min_{y \in \Omega(x)} \left(\frac{I^c(x)}{A^c} \right) \right) \tag{8}$$

By limiting the transmission coefficient on the limit of t_0, the brightness of the image is expressed as:

$$J(x) = \frac{I(x) - A}{\max(t(x), t_0)} + A \tag{9}$$

According to the above-stated contents and the presented equations, using the algorithm shown in Figure 5 it is possible to reduce the image blurring to an acceptable level.

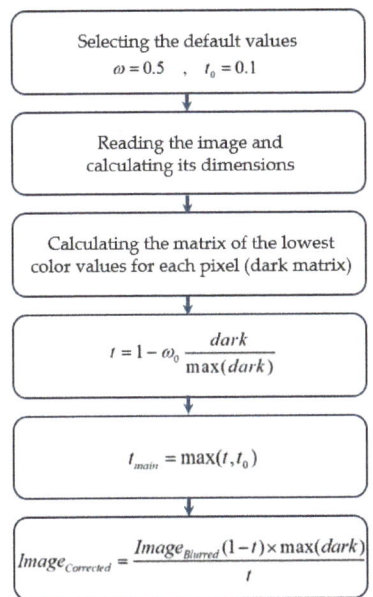

Figure 5. Implemented algorithm for removing or reducing the image blurring.

Figure 6 demonstrates the results of the algorithm in modifying an image that was artificially and exaggeratedly fogged.

Figure 6. (**a**) Artificially and exaggeratedly fogged image; (**b**) corrected version of fogged image.

2.3. Determining the Exact Location of the License Plate

After removing the adverse environmental effects, according to the following two principles, the exact location of the license plate must be determined: First, due to the difference in the colors around the license plate and its background, by using edge detection on the black–white image the edge of the license plate frame will appear as an edge and a closed path shape. Secondly, according to each country's standards, the length-to-width ratio of the license plate will be a fixed value.

According to the above content, all the edges on the image are detected. Detected edges become bolder to remove any interruptions in the closed paths. Then, by defining the closed path edges in the image as objects, the one with the standard license plate's length-to-width ratio is selected as the main object (the license plate frame). Detecting the main object's position from the initial image determines the license plate frame. Figure 7 shows all the above steps on a sample image.

Figure 7. Detecting the license plate frame: (**a**) the initial image; (**b**) edge detection for black–white mode of initial image; (**c**) filling of closed-path detected edges; (**d**) the main objects in the image and finding the object corresponding to the standard license plate; (**e**) detecting the main object's position from the initial image determined the license plate frame.

2.4. Determining the Segments inside the Plate

After cutting the image of the license plate from the original image, by applying rotation if needed, removing the unessential edges of the license plate, and turning it into the black and white mode, the segments of recognizable license plate characters are separated [25–29].

In the image shown in Figure 8, from the left side, the index of the first column has at least one white pixel, labeled as the start index of the first segment. Additionally, the index of the first column without a white pixel is labeled the final index of the first segment. This process is repeated for the whole of the plate to determine all its character segments. Figure 9 shows the cut segments separately.

Figure 8. License plate image prepared for extracting its character segments.

Figure 9. Cut segments of the license plate—black and white mode image.

2.5. Recognizing the Segments Using Hopfield's Neural Network

Determined character segments in the previous section should be recognized using standard character patterns. Diverse methods of pattern recognition include matching pixel by pixel [26], the k-nearest neighbor, and Bayesian, and various neural networks can be used [30]. The Hopfield neural network is known as the most common method for detecting patterns with binary features. Since the extracted black and white segment images have binary values (zero for black and one for white), they can be recognized using this neural network [31].

The main idea of the Hopfield neural network is based on state variables. If the new position of a system depends on its previous one, it can be written in terms of state variables in the form of the following equation [32–35]:

$$x(t+1) = f(x(t)) \qquad (10)$$

The sequence above continues until its energy is exhausted, and then remains in a balanced state. The system energy should decrease to reach this state. For this purpose, as shown in Figure 10, the Hopfield neural network is designed such that, firstly, the new position of the system is dependent on its previous one, and second, its energy equation decreases.

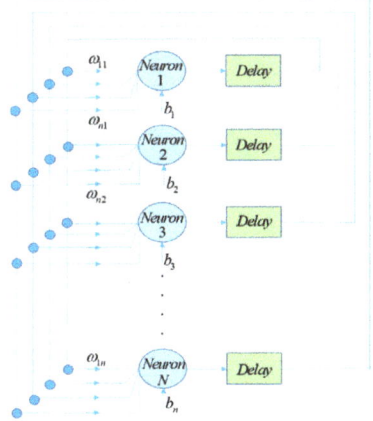

Figure 10. A typical Hopfield neural network; its position depends on the previous time's position and its energy is decreasing.

The energy function and its gradient for the system shown in Figure 10 are defined as:

$$\begin{aligned}
E &= -\tfrac{1}{2}\sum_i\sum_j \omega_{ij}x_i x_j - \sum_i b_i x_i \\
\frac{dE}{dt} &= \sum_i \frac{dE}{dx_i}\frac{dx_i}{dt} \\
&= \sum_i \frac{dE}{dx_i}\frac{dx_i}{dnet_i}\frac{dnet_i}{dt} \\
&= \sum_i \left(-\frac{dnet_i}{dt}\right)\frac{dx_i}{dnet_i}\frac{dnet_i}{dt} \\
&= -\sum_i \left(\frac{dnet_i}{dt}\right)^2 \frac{dx_i}{dnet_i} \\
&= -\sum_i \left(\frac{dnet_i}{dt}\right)^2 \varphi'(net_i)
\end{aligned} \quad (11)$$

where φ is the function of the neurons in the network and net_i is the output of the ith neuron. According to Equation (11), the energy gradient of the system decreases if the derivative of the neuron function is positive. Choosing sign function as a function of the neuron can meet this condition. When Hopfield's neural network is used as an image classifier, the two-dimensional images should be mapped to one-dimensional mode, and the black pixel values set to -1 (while the value of the white pixels are $+1$).

The segments which are in black and white format are resized to a standard size. The matrix of each segment, which is two-dimensional, is transformed into a one-column vector. The black pixels marked with 0 in this matrix are changed to -1 and then applied to the Hopfield neural network. On the other hand, in this neural network, the main characters in standard size and 0 values corresponding to black pixels, which are replaced by -1, are defined as balanced points. The Hopfield neural network moves the input matrix to the nearest balanced state. In other words, the closest standard character similar to the target segment is recognized. Figure 11 shows the noise (caused by mud) on the license plate. The designed Hopfield's neural network classified this noised license plate's character segments without error.

Figure 11. Detecting procedures of noisy license plate characters using Hopfield's neural network: (**a**) initial image; (**b**) detected license plate box; (**c**) the cut frame of the license plate; (**d**) black and white mode of cut frame; (**e**) cut noisy segments.

To determine the accuracy of Hopfield's neural network in determining numbers and letters, according to Figure 12, a set of different car license plates was considered. The graphics on these plates can play the role of noise. Hopfield's neural network classified the 253 characters on the license plates of this collection (after image processing and segmentation). Among the 253 test characters, only 6 characters were recognized wrongly, showing an accuracy of 97.6%. Using a computer with Core(TM) i7-2640 CPU and 8 GB RAM, the time spent on determining the characters of each license plate is about 0.08 s.

Figure 12. A set of selected license plates from different standards to determine the CCR of the proposed algorithm.

In addition to the 253 main characters (numbers or letters), there are also 26 special characters (such as a dash or a combination of numbers and letters). According to the different standards in these plates, all special characters were considered as a unit pattern. In addition to correctly recognizing the main characters, Hopfield's neural network could also classify special characters in this unit pattern. The updated classification rate considering the special characters was 97.1%.

The agile training capability of the Hopfield neural network has made it appropriate for application to plates with different standards, while for other neural networks, such as convolutional neural networks, a huge set of training data must be collected for each standard of the plates. Moreover, the accuracy of the proposed algorithm was higher than a number of similar ones developed on SOTA [15,16]. On the other hand, the time spent on recognizing the characters of each license plate was almost equal to the time spent on recognizing only one character in methods based on convolutional neural networks [15–18].

3. Conclusions

A new license plate pattern recognition system has been presented that is robust against adverse environmental effects such as fog or mud. Unlike previous studies that only considered a certain standard of license plates, this work evaluated all objects irrespective of their types. However, the selection of objects depends on their positions, and if the recognition of the license plate characters is unsuccessful another object enters the recognition process. Additionally, the paper has addressed the challenges posed by the presence of fog and smoke in the image by removing the matter of the image before initiating the license plate recognition process. More importantly, the use of Hopfield's neural network for license plate recognition, instead of the conventional method of pixel-to-pixel comparison of image segments with standard characters, has significantly reduced the execution time and increased the accuracy. The results pinpoint the efficacy of this approach. The neural network has shown capability in removing the noise on the license plate, making it a reliable tool for license plate recognition. The findings of this study contribute to the field of automated surveillance systems by providing an effective and efficient method for license plate recognition.

Author Contributions: All authors contributed equally to writing, editing, and reviewing the manuscript. All authors have read and agreed to the published version of the manuscript.

Funding: This research received no external funding.

Data Availability Statement: Not applicable.

Conflicts of Interest: The authors declare no conflict of interest.

References

1. Tsakanikas, V.; Dagiuklas, T. Video surveillance systems-current status and future trends. *Comput. Electr. Eng.* **2018**, *70*, 736–753. [CrossRef]
2. Sharma, S.K.; Phan, H.; Lee, J. An application study on road surface monitoring using DTW based image processing and ultrasonic sensors. *Appl. Sci.* **2020**, *10*, 4490. [CrossRef]
3. Wang, S.-Z.; Lee, H.-J. Detection and recognition of license plate characters with different appearances. *IEEE Trans. Intell. Transp. Syst.* **2003**, *2*, 979–984.
4. Radha, R.; Sumathi, C.P. A novel approach to extract text from license plate of vehicle. *Signal Process. Image Commun.* **2012**, *3*, 181–192. [CrossRef]
5. Kuo, C.Y.; Lu, Y.R.; Yang, S.M. On the image sensor processing for lane detection and control in vehicle lane keeping systems. *Sensors* **2019**, *19*, 1665. [CrossRef]
6. Zheng, K.; Wei, M.; Sun, G.; Anas, B.; Li, Y. Using vehicle synthesis generative adversarial networks to improve vehicle detection in remote sensing images. *ISPRS Int. J. Geo-Inf.* **2019**, *8*, 390. [CrossRef]
7. Sulehria, H.K.; Zhang, Y.; Irfan, D.; Sulehria, A.K. Vehicle number plate recognition using mathematical morphology and neural networks. *WSEAS Trans. Comput.* **2008**, *7*, 781–790.
8. Aggarwal, A.; Rani, A.; Kumar, M. A robust method to authenticate car license plates using segmentation and ROI based approach. *Smart Sustain. Built Environ.* **2020**, *9*, 737–747. [CrossRef]
9. Kim, T.-G.; Yun, B.-J.; Kim, T.-H.; Lee, J.-Y.; Park, K.-H.; Jeong, Y.; Kim, H.D. Recognition of vehicle license plates based on image processing. *Appl. Sci.* **2021**, *11*, 6292. [CrossRef]
10. Walia, E.; Verma, A. Vehicle number plate detection using sobel edge detection technique. *Int. J. Comput. Technol.* **2010**, *1*, 2229–4333.
11. Parasuraman, K.; Kumar, P.V. An efficient method for indian vehicle license plate extraction and character segmentation. In Proceedings of the IEEE International Conference on Computational Intelligence and Computing Research, Coimbatore, India, 28–29 December 2010.
12. Lekhana, G.C.; Srikantaswamy, R. Real time license plate recognition system. *Int. J. Eng. Res. Technol.* **2012**, *2*, 2250–3536.
13. Kamilaris, A.; Prenafeta-Boldú, F. A review of the use of convolutional neural networks in agriculture. *J. Agric. Sci.* **2018**, *156*, 312–322. [CrossRef]
14. Hopfield, J.J. Neural networks and physical systems with emergent collective computational abilities. *Proc. Natl. Acad. Sci. USA* **1982**, *79*, 2554–2558. [CrossRef]
15. Lin, C.-J.; Chuang, C.-C.; Lin, H.-Y. Edge-AI-based real-time automated license plate recognition. *System. Appl. Sci.* **2022**, *12*, 1445. [CrossRef]

16. Yousaf, U.; Khan, A.; Ali, H.; Khan, F.G.; Rehman, Z.U.; Shah, S.; Ali, F.; Pack, S.; Ali, S. A deep learning based approach for localization and recognition of Pakistani vehicle license plates. *Sensors* **2021**, *21*, 7696. [CrossRef]
17. Park, S.-H.; Yu, S.-B.; Kim, J.-A.; Yoon, H. An All-in-one vehicle type and license plate recognition system using YOLOv4. *Sensors* **2022**, *22*, 921. [CrossRef]
18. Wang, H.; Li, Y.; Dang, L.-M.; Moon, H. Robust korean license plate recognition based on deep neural networks. *Sensors* **2021**, *21*, 4140. [CrossRef]
19. Fattal, R. Single image dehazing. *ACM Trans. Graph.* **2008**, *27*, 1–9. [CrossRef]
20. Narasimhan, S.G.; Nayar, S.K. Chromatic frame work for vision in bad weather. In Proceedings of the Conference on Computer Vision and Pattern Recognition, Hilton Head, SC, USA, 13–15 June 2000; pp. 598–605.
21. Narasimhan, S.G.; Nayar, S.K. Vision and the atmosphere. *Int. J. Comput. Vis.* **2002**, *48*, 233–254. [CrossRef]
22. Tan, R.T. Visibility in bad weather from a single image. In Proceedings of the 2008 IEEE Conference on Computer Vision and Pattern Recognition, Anchorage, AK, USA, 23–28 June 2008.
23. Levin, A.; Lischinski, D.; Weiss, Y. A closed form solution to natural image matting. In Proceedings of the Conference on Computer Vision and Pattern Recognition, New York, NY, USA, 17–22 June 2006; Volume 1, pp. 61–68.
24. Wei, T.; Chen, D.; Zhou, W.; Liao, J.; Zhao, H.; Zhang, W.; Yu, N. Improved image matting via real-time user clicks and uncertainty estimation. In Proceedings of the IEEE/CVF Conference on Computer Vision and Pattern Recognition (CVPR), Nashville, TN, USA, 20–25 June 2021; pp. 15374–15383.
25. Cai, S.; Zhang, X.; Fan, H.; Huang, H.; Liu, J.; Liu, J.; Liu, J.; Wang, J.; Sun, J. Disentangled image matting. In Proceedings of the IEEE/CVF International Conference on Computer Vision (ICCV), Seoul, Republic of Korea, 27 October–2 November 2019; pp. 8819–8828.
26. Aksoy, Y.; Aydin, T.O.; Pollefeys, M. Designing effective inter-pixel information flow for natural image matting. In Proceedings of the Conference on Computer Vision and Pattern Recognition, Honolulu, HI, USA, 21–26 July 2017.
27. Xu, Z.; Yang, W.; Meng, A.; Lu, N.; Huang, H.; Ying, C.; Huang, L. Towards end-to-end license Plate detection and recognition: A large dataset and baseline. In Proceedings of the European Conference on Computer Vision (ECCV), Munich, Germany, 8–14 September 2018; pp. 255–271.
28. Menon, A.; Omman, B. Detection and recognition of multiple license plate from still images. In Proceedings of the 2018 International Conference on Circuits and Systems in Digital Enterprise Technology (ICCSDET), Kottayam, India, 21–22 December 2018.
29. Wang, W.; Yang, J.; Chen, M.; Wang, P. A light CNN for end-to-end car license plates detection and recognition. *IEEE Access* **2019**, *7*, 173875–173883. [CrossRef]
30. Murty, M.N.; Devi, V.S. *Pattern Recognition. Undergraduate Topics in Computer Science*; Springer: London, UK, 2011.
31. Fung, C.H.; Wong, M.S.; Chan, P.W. Spatio-temporal data fusion for satellite images using Hopfield neural network. *Remote Sens.* **2019**, *11*, 2077. [CrossRef]
32. Xu, X.; Chen, S. An optical image encryption method using Hopfield neural network. *Entropy* **2022**, *24*, 521. [CrossRef]
33. Yu, F.; Yu, Q.; Chen, H.; Kong, X.; Mokbel, A.A.M.; Cai, S.; Du, S. Dynamic analysis and audio encryption application in IoT of a multi-scroll fractional-order memristive Hopfield neural network. *Fractal Fract.* **2022**, *6*, 370. [CrossRef]
34. Mohd Jamaludin, S.Z.; Mohd Kasihmuddin, M.S.; Md Ismail, A.I.; Mansor, M.A.; Md Basir, M.F. Energy based logic mining analysis with Hopfield neural network for recruitment evaluation. *Entropy* **2021**, *23*, 40. [CrossRef]
35. Akhmet, M.; Aruğaslan Çinçin, D.; Tleubergenova, M.; Nugayeva, Z. Unpredictable oscillations for Hopfield-type neural networks with delayed and advanced arguments. *Mathematics* **2021**, *9*, 571. [CrossRef]

Disclaimer/Publisher's Note: The statements, opinions and data contained in all publications are solely those of the individual author(s) and contributor(s) and not of MDPI and/or the editor(s). MDPI and/or the editor(s) disclaim responsibility for any injury to people or property resulting from any ideas, methods, instructions or products referred to in the content.

Article

Application of Evolutionary Optimization Techniques in Reverse Engineering of Helical Gears: An Applied Study

Vahid Pourmostaghimi [1], Farshad Heidari [1], Saman Khalilpourazary [2] and Mohammad Reza Chalak Qazani [3,4,*]

[1] Department of Manufacturing and Production Engineering, Faculty of Mechanical Engineering, University of Tabriz, Tabriz 51666-16471, Iran
[2] Department of Renewable Energy, Faculty of Mechanical Engineering, Urmia University of Technology, Urmia 57166-93188, Iran
[3] Faculty of Computing and Information Technology, Sohar University, Sohar 311, Oman
[4] Institute for Intelligent Systems Research and Innovation, Deakin University, Geelong, VIC 3216, Australia
* Correspondence: m.r.chalakqazani@gmail.com or m.chalakqazani@deakin.edu.au; Tel.: +61-411-857009

Citation: Pourmostaghimi, V.; Heidari, F.; Khalilpourazary, S.; Qazani, M.R.C. Application of Evolutionary Optimization Techniques in Reverse Engineering of Helical Gears: An Applied Study. *Axioms* **2023**, *12*, 252. https://doi.org/10.3390/axioms12030252

Academic Editor: Behzad Djafari-Rouhani

Received: 11 January 2023
Revised: 22 February 2023
Accepted: 23 February 2023
Published: 1 March 2023

Copyright: © 2023 by the authors. Licensee MDPI, Basel, Switzerland. This article is an open access article distributed under the terms and conditions of the Creative Commons Attribution (CC BY) license (https://creativecommons.org/licenses/by/4.0/).

Abstract: Reverse engineering plays an important role in the manufacturing and automobile industries in designing complicated spare parts, reducing actual production time, and allowing for multiple redesign possibilities, including shape alterations, different materials, and changes to other significant parameters of the component. Using reverse engineering methodology, damaged gears can be identified and modeled meticulously. Influential parameters can be obtained in the shortest time. Because most of the time it is impossible to solve gear-related inverse equations mathematically, metaheuristic methods can be used to reverse-engineer gears. This paper presents a methodology based on measurement over balls and span measurement along with evolutionary optimization techniques to determine the geometry of a pure involute of a cylindrical helical gear. Advanced optimization techniques, i.e., Grey Wolf Optimization, Whale Optimization, Particle Swarm Optimization, and Genetic Algorithm, were applied for the considered reverse engineering case, and the effectiveness and accuracy of the proposed algorithms were compared. Confirmatory calculations and experiments reveal the remarkable efficiency of Grey Wolf Optimization and Particle Swarm Optimization techniques in the reverse engineering of helical gears compared to other techniques and in obtaining influential gear design parameters.

Keywords: reverse engineering; helical gear; evolutionary optimization techniques; grey wolf optimization; whale optimization; particle swarm optimization; genetic algorithm

1. Introduction

Widely exploited in almost all engineering fields, reverse engineering (RE) is an approach that consists of digitizing a real component to create a numerical or virtual model [1]. This numerical or virtual model can also be emulated in presenting a Digital Twin. The Digital Twin, which started to be used recently, is a new concept for describing a new wave in modeling and simulation. While the use of simulation tools was previously restricted to design stages, nowadays different types of simulation tools are used in testing, validation, or optimization that can be referred to as Digital Twin [2]. This technology is an emerging concept that has become the center of attention in industry, particularly in the manufacturing industry. The Digital Twin is best described as the effortless integration of data between a physical and virtual machine in either direction [3]. Digital Twin has been widely used in different industries, especially manufacturing, to monitor performance, optimize progress, simulate results, and predict potential errors. This technique also plays various roles within the whole product lifecycle from design, manufacturing, delivery, use, and end of life. With the growing demands of individualized products and implementation of Industry 4.0, Digital Twin can provide an effective solution for future product design, development, and innovation [4]. Generally, RE can be defined as a principled process that extracts design information from a product. Hence, components in various industries, including engineering, medical, defense systems, software, consumer electronics, etc., can be reverse-engineered comprehensively. Chikofsky and Cross introduced RE as "the process which analyzes a certain system to identify the systems" parts and their relationships and to create alternatives of the system in another form or at a higher level of abstraction [5]. In addition, the definition of RE in mechanical design is to "commence the redesign process where a product is observed, disassembled, analyzed, tested, and documented in terms of its functionality, form, physical principles, manufacturability, and assemble-ability.

In recent years, traditional approaches to designing, manufacturing, and constructing mechanical components and systems have been abolished. In other words, state-of-the-art methods in design and manufacturing have provided some outstanding benefits, including production preparation time decline, outstanding precision, etc., that completely change the quality of the product [6]. Nowadays, the implementation of RE is in manufacturing three-dimensional digital models of different mechanically damaged or broken components [7]. Lippmann et al. used RE for the verification of physical designs in nanoscale technologies [8]. RE is used in various fields, especially mechanics, such as composites, aerospace industries, energy plants, turbines, internal combustion components, etc.

One of the most prevalent applications of RE is redesigning and manufacturing gears with a high-precision involute widely used in the automobile industry. Modeling machine components, especially gears, with parametric or non-parametric RE methods is becoming more popular before producing samples using rapid prototype processes [9,10]. Numerous studies have been conducted on the redesign, modeling, and manufacturing of various types of gears through RE. Shamekhi et al. used RE to redesign and optimize the gear ratio and corresponding teeth number of the gears of an automatic transmission system. They proposed an accurate and efficient model to find optimum design parameters [11]. Verim et al. redesigned a damaged motor cam gear by the 3D scanning method. They evaluated the geometric values of the damaged model and the prototyped one. They reported acceptable deviations between the RE model and the actual component [12]. Dubravcik et al. made a 3D model of a damaged gear wheel using scanning and rapid prototyping. They compared and identified the new gear wheel's proportions and geometry with the original point cloud of the damaged gear. The results revealed good compliance between the original and RE-made gear [9]. Palkahas worked on the reconstruction of gears using RE and 3D printing methods. He reported that the final component's quality is highly related to the use of appropriate methods, software, hardware, and material [6]. Baehr et al. used machine learning for structural characterization in the RE domain [13].

The design of gears has a rather complex procedure involving numerous design parameters and factors. Finding an optimal or near-optimal solution for this complexity turns it into a challenging demand. There are plenty of studies in which different optimization algorithms, such as the Genetic Algorithm (GA) [14], Simulated Annealing (SA) [15], Response Surface Methodology (RSM) [16], Particle Swarm Optimization (PSO) [17], Grey Wolf Optimization (GWO), Whale Optimization Algorithm (WOA) [18], etc., have been implemented for the design optimization of gears. Xia et al. have used PSO combined with GA to optimize the operational quality of power shift transmission. The simulation and test results showed that the proposed control strategy effectively avoids the power cycle when shifting and consequently improves shift quality [19]. Artony has proposed a deterministic approach to solve simulation-based, multi-objective gear design optimization problems in the presence of general nonlinear constraints on the design variables. He has declared that, although developed with gear optimization in mind, it is broader in scope and should be tested in other computer-assisted engineering optimization problems [20]. Rai et al. used a Real-Coded Genetic Algorithm (RCGA) to achieve optimal helical gear design. They minimized the volume of a helical gear by increasing the profile shift coefficient as a design factor and other parameters such as the module, face width, and number of teeth using RCGA [21]. Mendi et al. investigated the difference between the dimensional optimization of motion and force-transmitting components of a gearbox performed by the genetic algorithm and analytical method. The results illustrated that GA is a considerably better and more reliable method to obtain minimum gear volume [22].

Because of the drawbacks of the commonly performed research in the field of RE of gears, there is an urgent demand to carry out an extensive investigation to determine accurate gear design parameters using relevant measurements such as over-ball measurements. For instance, in the reviewed case study, the matter of RE for a single gear has not been investigated. In the studies dealing with this issue, parameters such as outside diameter and root diameter are considered known input parameters in the RE process. These practices pose an excessive error in the obtained design parameters. On the other hand, current industrially applicable gear design software requires initial design parameters such as the pressure angle and module to initiate the RE process. This problem adversely affects the accuracy of calculated design parameters. In industry, to replace a damaged gear wheel, it is commonplace to get its CAD model using scanning techniques. Many factors affect 3D scanning processes. One of them is the reflective ability of the parts' surfaces. Such inaccuracies and incompetence are mainly of the tooth systems because of uncontrolled laser ray scattering and incorrect scanning [10]. Therefore, a systematic methodology is needed to solve the RE problem of gears more comprehensively. However, the major requirement that has to be satisfied for successful gear RE is the modeling of the system at hand as accurately as possible [23].

Due to the complexities governing the calculations of input gear parameters, a new methodology was proposed in the current study to reverse-engineer gears using evolutionary optimization techniques. A number of commonly used metaheuristic optimization methods with successful applications reported in engineering optimization problems, such as GWO, WOA, PSO, and GA, were applied to solve the introduced RE problem. The stability, convergence speed, and accuracy of the mentioned algorithms were compared and evaluated. The paper has the following sections. A brief theoretical background of gear calculations is presented in Section 2. The proposed methodology and optimization techniques are explained in Section 3. Section 4 describes the remarkable results of the study. The conclusion is presented in Section 5.

2. Theoretical Background of Gear Calculations

The accurate design of gears requires considerable effort in calculating the relevant gear geometry to fulfil the essential requirements of operational characteristics such as load capacity, reliability, and gear size, which directly affect the quality of power transmission. The independent variables that define a gear are the number of teeth z, normal module m_n, normal pressure angle α_n, addendum modification x, and helix angle β. Knowing the parameters mentioned, the involute form of a gear flank can be determined. The other dependent variables, including outside diameter, root diameter, and face width, are usually determined based on transmission load, which can be manipulated by the designer through design limitations and requirements [24]. The parameters that directly relate to the gear flank involute form and the parameters that do not have such a relationship are listed in Table 1.

Table 1. Division of the geometrical characteristics of gears.

	Input Parameters	Output Parameters
Direct relation with involute form	Module (m_n) Normal pressure angle (α_n) Helix angle (β) Addendum modification (x)	Span measurement (s_m) Over-ball measurement (d_m) Chordal thickness measurement (s_j)
No relation with involute form	Face width	Outside diameter Root diameter ...

One of the most important parameters that greatly impacts the gear design characteristics, load capacity of the gear, and backlash of engaged gears is tooth thickness. Normal tooth thickness can be calculated as follows:

$$TT_n = \frac{m_n \pi}{2} + 2 \times m_n \times x \times \tan(\alpha_n) \tag{1}$$

There are direct and indirect methods for measuring tooth thickness, including chordal thickness measurement (s_j), span measurement (s_m), and over-ball measurement (d_m). Among these methods, span and over-ball measurements are more industrially applicable because of their higher measurement precision and the comparatively lower equipment involved in the measurement process [25]. A schematic view of span and ball measurements is illustrated in Figure 1.

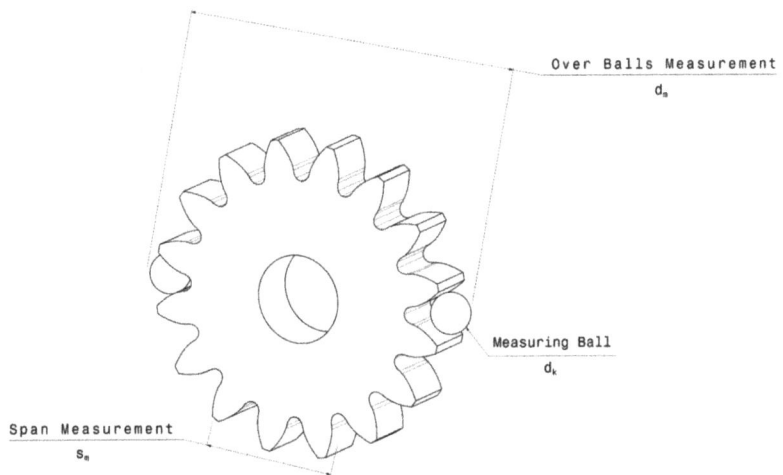

Figure 1. A schematic view of span measurement and over-balls measurement for a gear.

The value for s_m based on the aforementioned input parameters can be calculated as follows [24]:

$$s_m = m_n \times [(z_k - 0.5) \times \pi \times \cos(\alpha_n) + z \times inv(\alpha_n) \times \cos(\alpha_n) + 2 \times x \times \sin(\alpha_n)] \tag{2}$$

in which z_k is the number of spanned teeth. The function $inv(\alpha_n)$ is calculated according to Equation (3).

$$inv(\alpha_n) = \tan(\alpha_n) - (\alpha_n) \tag{3}$$

The parameter d_m is obtained as follows:

$$d_m = \begin{cases} d_k + \frac{m_n \times z \times \cos(\alpha_n)}{\cos(\varphi) \times \cos(\beta)} & z = even \\ d_k + \frac{m_n \times z \times \cos(\alpha_n)}{\cos(\varphi) \times \cos(\beta)} \times \cos(90/z) & z = odd \end{cases} \tag{4}$$

in which d_k is the diameter of the measuring ball, and φ is the pressure angle at the center of the measuring ball, which can be calculated according to Equation (5) [24].

$$inv(\varphi) = \frac{d_k}{m_n \times z \times \cos(\alpha_n)} - \frac{\pi}{2 \times z} + inv(\alpha_t) + \frac{2 \times x \times \tan \alpha_n}{z} \tag{5}$$

In Equation (5), α_t is the transverse pressure angle and is defined as below:

$$\alpha_t = \tan^{-1}\left(\frac{\tan(\alpha_n)}{\cos(\beta)}\right) \tag{6}$$

Consequently, the value of $inv(\alpha_t)$ is calculated as Equation (7) [24]:

$$\text{inv}(\alpha_t) = \tan(\alpha_t) - (\alpha_t) \tag{7}$$

3. Materials and Methods

The design of gears has become more of a necessity than ever before. In particular, gear design optimization and transmission accuracy have attracted more attention [26]. One of the most frequently used techniques in gear design is RE methods. These methods are necessary for remodeling or measuring damaged or non-damaged gears. RE also enables the design of complex mechanical components, effectively reducing production time and relevant prototyping costs. Using RE methods, damaged gear components can be calculated and modeled in a short time, and obtained models can be produced economically in a comparably short period [26].

3.1. Reverse Engineering of Cylindrical Helical Gear

When designing a new set of gears, there are many alternatives in the gear parameters selection. Therefore, the designer can freely choose among the various options. However, RE imposes a considerable challenge to the gear designer since the main problem is characterizing a previously manufactured gear whose geometry is unknown.

With a valid reference for the design, the designer must extract the exact geometry of the redesigned gear. For the completion of the RE of a cylindrical helical gear, it is obligatory to determine the number of teeth z, normal module m_n, normal pressure angle α_n, addendum modification x, and helix angle β. According to Equations (2)–(7), identifying the primary gear input parameters based on measurements obtained from s_m and d_m is impossible to solve these equations. This arises from the complex calculations governing the relations between gear input parameters and measured output characteristics. So, there is a great need to use novel methods in the RE of gears to obtain influential input parameters. Because of the inability of existing computational and mathematical methods to analytically solve these equations, it seems that applying modern evolutionary optimization algorithms can be a good choice to obtain gear design parameters in the RE process.

Inspired by natural processes, these techniques can optimize a function or find the answer to a complex equation in a logical period and with relatively high precision.

3.2. Problem Description and Solving Method

3.2.1. Objective Function

The general constrained problem considered in the present research was expressed as:

$$\begin{aligned} & minimize\ E(m_n, \alpha_n, \beta, x) \\ & subject\ to\ m_{n_{min}} \leq m_n \leq m_{n_{max}} \\ & \alpha_{n_{min}} \leq \alpha_n \leq \alpha_{n_{max}} \\ & \beta_{min} \leq \beta \leq \beta_{max} \\ & x_{n_{min}} \leq \alpha_n \leq x_{n_{max}} \end{aligned} \tag{8}$$

The objective function $E(x_1, x_2, x_3, x_4)$ to find input design parameters was set as follows:

$$E(m_n, \alpha_n, \beta, x) = \sum_{i=1}^{n} \sqrt{(Formula\ obtained\ value^i - Measured\ value^i)^2} \tag{9}$$

Since, in the present study, three values for d_m and one value for s_m are measured, Equation (9) can be rewritten as:

$$E(m_n, \alpha_n, \beta, x) = \sqrt{(s_m - S_{measured})^2} + \sum_{i=1}^{3} \sqrt{(d_m^i - D_{measured}^i)^2} \quad (10)$$

in which $S_{measured}$ and $D_{measured}$ are practically measured span and over-balls measurements, respectively. According to Equation (8), it can be concluded that the defined objective function is the resulting error of the selected design parameters and measured values. Therefore, the minimum possible value for $E(m_n, \alpha_n, \beta, x)$ can lead to the exact input gear design parameters. In this way, the present investigation strived to substitute an unsolvable series of complicated equations with an optimization problem to discover the answers by exploiting evolutionary optimization algorithms.

3.2.2. Methodology

Figure 2 presents a schematic framework that integrates the described RE technique with evolutionary optimization algorithms. The raw measured data are fed into the optimization unit to minimize the defined objective function. After the termination of the optimization algorithm, based on measured values and formulas, the optimum results are gained.

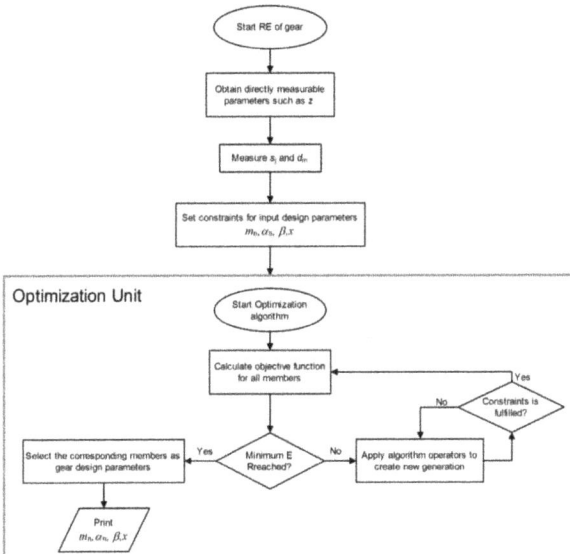

Figure 2. Flowchart of the proposed RE of gear framework.

Several termination conditions can be used to terminate the algorithm and obtain calculated optimum results. However, two are more frequently used for the problems under consideration, including the maximum number of function evaluations and minimum specific error. The former is suitable for computationally demanding problems when only a limited number of function evaluations is allowed. At the same time, the latter specifies that the optimization is terminated when the minimum desired error is reached [20].

Relatively high accuracy is required to determine the parameters in this research. Therefore, the algorithm is terminated in two modes, after a definite number of function evaluations and after reaching a predefined error. The minimum value for the cost function, ε, reflects the resolution of searching for optimum answers in the space of all possible answers. The proposed algorithmic framework is illustrated by the pseudocode in Figure 3, which summarizes the methodology discussed.

```
Input:
    • Gear formulas for s_m and d_m
    • Lower and upper bounds for m_n, α_n, β, x
    • The minimum value for cost function E(m_n, α_n, β,x) to terminate the algorithm, ε
    • Selecting proper values for z_k and d_ki for i=1:3
    • Measuring s_m and d_mi for i=1:3

1. Set i=0
2. Create objective function E(m_n, α_n, β,x)
3. do while E>ε
    3.1. Set i=i+1
    3.2. Generate initial population (m_ni, α_ni, β_i, x_i)
    3.3. Calculate s_m and d_m for members of population
    3.4. Calculate E(m_n, α_n, β,x) according to Equation 9.
    3.5. if E<ε then
            exit (leave the loop)
         else if
            Apply algorithm operators to create next population
         End
4. Return best member as gear design parameters (m_nopt, α_nopt, β_opt, x_opt)
```

Figure 3. Pseudocode of the proposed algorithmic framework.

3.2.3. Evolutionary Optimization Algorithms

Although they have been used widely in various design problems, conventional optimization methods impose some serious difficulties on the matter; accordingly, to have a slow convergence speed, these methods may be stuck in the local optimum point. Furthermore, when the objective function or constraints cannot be stated functionally explicit in the input parameters, it is hard to utilize these methods to solve the given problem. Consequently, some novel methods, quite often inspired by nature, such as GA, PSO, SA, etc., are applied to solve complex optimization problems [22]. In this research, an investigation was carried out to find the design parameters of a gear based on performed measurements. The proposed algorithms were GWO, WOA, PSO, and GA, which were used under similar conditions and objective functions. The population size was set to 40 for all of the algorithms. The primary population was created as uniformly as possible within the search space. The results of the methods above were compared, and their competencies to solve the problem were evaluated.

Metaheuristic methods have been proved to be a powerful technique to solve complex optimization problems. The majority of them consider a set of parameters that must be tuned before the triggering of the algorithm or during the process and are based on multiple runs of the metaheuristic algorithm [27]. During each iteration, significantly worse configurations are removed, and new configurations are formed through crossover and mutation. Each of the presented methods has its own features as well as advantages and disadvantages [28].

A good setup of these parameter values can result in a better and effective application of the optimization process. This job can be carried out by trial-and-error methodology [29] or by intelligent tuning methods [27]. In this regard, various tuning methods have been presented such as CRS [28], F-Race [30], Revac [31], and ParamILS [32]. Control parameters for selected optimization algorithms in this research were selected based on a trial-and-error approach.

Grey Wolf Optimization Algorithm: GWO is a metaheuristic optimization algorithm that imitates the intelligent foraging behavior of grey wolves when hunting prey. Strictly following their social hierarchy, grey wolves are divided into 4 groups from top to bottom. The top group which makes decisions during hunting is called α. The next level belongs to β wolves who help as deputy chiefs in the group. The α wolves are replaced by β ones after dying or becoming inefficient as leaders. In the third level are δ wolves, which act as hunters and scouts of the group. The last level in the established hierarchy is occupied by the weakest members, titled ω wolves. When hunting, all types of wolves are organized according to decisions made by α wolves to identify, follow the prey, encircle it, and finally attack it. In this optimization algorithm, α, β, and δ indicate the members with fitness from high to low, in that order [33].

The simulation of wolves' behavior when hunting includes encircling and catching the prey. The mathematical description of encircling the prey can be expressed as follows:

$$\vec{D} = \left| \vec{C}.\vec{X}_p(t) - \vec{X}(t) \right| \quad (11)$$

$$\vec{X}(t+1) = \vec{X}_p(t) - \vec{A}.\vec{D} \quad (12)$$

in which $\vec{A}$ and $\vec{C}$ act as coefficient vectors. $\vec{X}_p$ determines the position of the prey or global answer. The vector $\vec{X}$ describes the current position of the wolves; the new position of α, β, and δ wolves in the tth iteration would be determined by $\vec{D}$. The values for $\vec{A}$ and $\vec{C}$ can be calculated as below:

$$\vec{A} = 2.\vec{a}.\vec{r}_1 - \vec{a} \quad (13)$$

$$\vec{C} = 2.\vec{r}_2 \quad (14)$$

where $\vec{r}_1$ and $\vec{r}_2$ are random vectors varying in the range of [0, 1], and $\vec{a}$ is the convergence vector value changing linearly in [0, 2].

In the next step, the hunting process starts with α wolves as the leaders and δ wolves as the hunting contributors. Mathematically simulated hunting assumes that α, β, and δ individuals have better information about the location of prey. Therefore, all individuals update their positions according to the below equations:

$$\vec{X}_1 = \vec{X}_\alpha - A_1.\left| \vec{C}_1.\vec{X}_\alpha - \vec{X} \right| \quad (15)$$

$$\vec{X}_2 = \vec{X}_\beta - A_2.\left| \vec{C}_2.\vec{X}_\beta - \vec{X} \right| \quad (16)$$

$$\vec{X}_3 = \vec{X}_\delta - A_3.\left| \vec{C}_3.\vec{X}_\delta - \vec{X} \right| \quad (17)$$

$$\vec{X}(t+1) = \frac{\vec{X}_1 + \vec{X}_2 + \vec{X}_3}{3} \quad (18)$$

At the ones where the prey stops, the wolves attack. Mathematically, this happens when $|\vec{A}| \leq 1$. Unless the attack is delayed until finding a better position or answer [34], the schematic position update of members in the GWO algorithm is illustrated in Figure 4. The population size is set to 40.

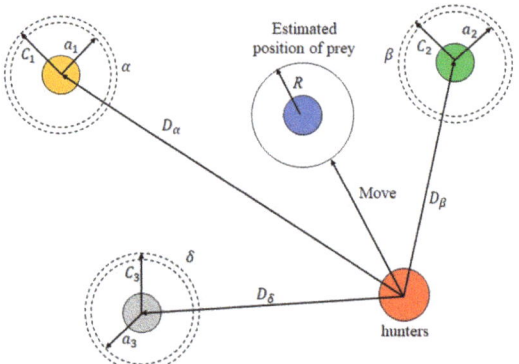

Figure 4. Position update in GWO.

Whale Optimization Algorithm: Introduced by Mirjalili et al., WOA is a swarm optimization method inspired by the hunting behavior of humpback whales. The hunting process involves searching, encircling the prey, and finally attacking to catch it [35]. The relatively easy implementation of the algorithm and its configuration with fewer parameters are the advantages of this optimization technique. The prey is the answer to the optimization problem that must be determined during the WOA process [36]. The hunting of humpback whales is illustrated in Figure 5. The movement of randomly created whales toward the prey or leader whale is shown in Figure 5a. The encircling process of the prey by the whales and their spiral movement while emitting bubbles to surround the prey is illustrated in Figure 5b,c, respectively [37].

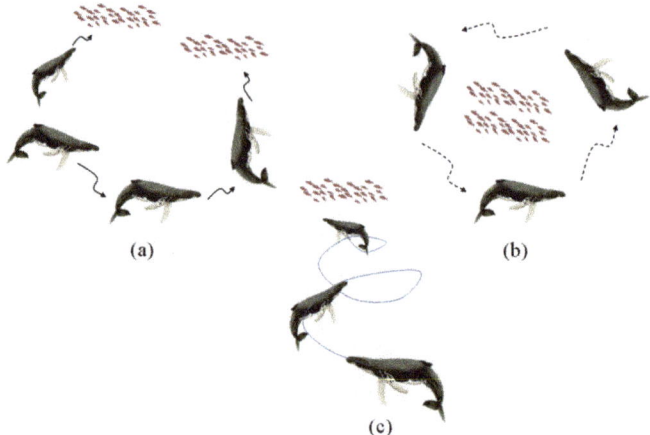

Figure 5. Hunting process of humpback whales: (**a**) movement of whales in a random direction or toward leader; (**b**) encircling process after finding the prey; (**c**) reaching the prey in spiral route.

First, a group of whales or members is created randomly to search for the prey or answer in the search space. This stage can be expressed mathematically as follows:

$$\vec{X}(t+1) = \vec{X}_{rand}(t) - \vec{A}.\left|\vec{C}.\vec{X}_{rand}(t) - \vec{X}(t)\right| \qquad (19)$$

in which $\vec{A}$ and $\vec{C}$ act as coefficient vectors. $\vec{X}_{rand}(t)$ determines the position of whales in tth iteration. The values for $\vec{A}$ and $\vec{C}$ can be obtained as follows:

$$\vec{A} = 2.\vec{a}.\vec{r} - \vec{a} \qquad (20)$$

$$\vec{C} = 2.\vec{r} \qquad (21)$$

$$a = 2 - \frac{2t}{t_{max}} \qquad (22)$$

In these equations, $\vec{r}$ is a vector selected randomly in [0,1]. The maximum number of permissible iterations is t_{max}, and $\vec{a}$ is the convergence vector value which decreases linearly from 2 to 0 by increasing the number of iterations.

After having found the prey, the whales move closer to the prey. The mathematical formula of this shrinkage mechanism can be expressed as follows:

$$\vec{X}(t+1) = \vec{X}_{g-best} - \vec{A}.\left|\vec{C}.\vec{X}_{g-best} - \vec{X}(t)\right| \qquad (23)$$

It must be added that if $|\vec{A}| \leq 1$, $\vec{X}_{g-best}$ determines the member with the best fitness value. Therefore, $\vec{X}_{g-best}$ will update the position of members automatically to encircle the prey. In the final step, the whales catch their prey, start to move in a spiral route, and simultaneously narrow the siege [38]. This process is illustrated in Figure 6.

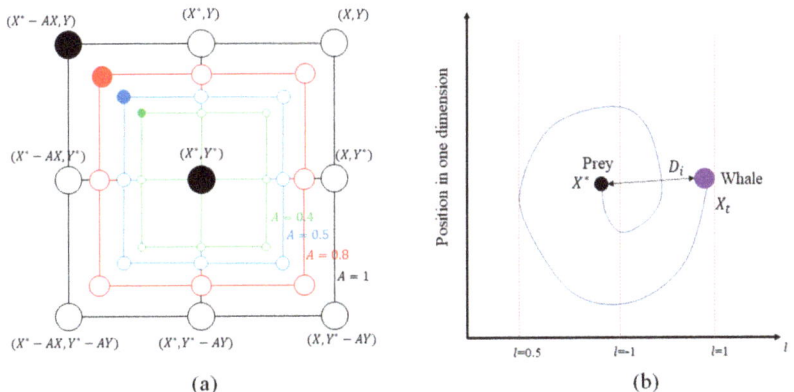

Figure 6. Search mechanism and whales' movement in WOA: (**a**) shrinking encircling process; (**b**) position update in the spiral way.

Figure 6a demonstrates a probable number of positions such as (X,Y), which can be achieved by the current global optimum (X*,Y*) in any determined way. The spiral way to narrow the encirclement is shown in Figure 6b [37]. This behavior can be mathematically expressed as below:

$$\vec{X}(t+1) = \left|\vec{X}_{g-best} - \vec{X}(t)\right|.e^{bl}.\cos(2\pi l) + \vec{X}_{g-best} \qquad (24)$$

in which b determines the shape of the spiral route, and l is a random value in the range of [0, 1] [39]. The population size is set to 40.

Particle Swarm Optimization: Nature-inspired metaheuristic optimization algorithms have recently been extensively utilized to optimize various manufacturing problems [40].

PSO has gained a special place among these algorithms because of its simplicity in programming and solving relatively complex functions [41].

Introduced by Eberhart and Kennedy in 1995 [42], PSO is a population-based optimization algorithm which comprises several particles representing a probable solution to the defined optimization problem. The goal of these particles in the algorithm is to find the answer by improving their positions [43].

Particles have a fitness factor, which determines the ability of each particle to solve the optimization problem, and a velocity factor which affects the movement direction of a particle in the course of iterations and can be mathematically obtained as follows:

$$V_{id}^{(t+1)} = wV_{id}^{(t)} + c_1 rand_1 \left(p_{best\ id}^{(t)} - X_{id}^{(t)} \right) + c_2 rand_2 \left(g_{best\ id}^{(t)} - X_{id}^{(t)} \right) \tag{25}$$

where $X_{id}^{(t)}$ and $V_{id}^{(t)}$ stand for the position and velocity of particle i in d dimensional space, respectively. $p_{best\ id}^{(t)}$ and $g_{best\ id}^{(t)}$, respectively, give the best position of particle i and other particles in the population until generation t. Inertia weight factor w adjusts the dynamic behavior of particles. Parameters rand1 and rand2 are random variables in the range of [0, 1], c1 is the determined cognitive factor, and c2 is the preferred social factor of each particle. The positions of particles are updated considering the calculated velocity:

$$X_{id}^{(t+1)} = X_{id}^{(t)} + V_{id}^{(t-1)} \tag{26}$$

in which $X_{id}^{(t+1)}$ and $X_{id}^{(t)}$ are a new position and previous position of particle i. The updating process of particles' positions is illustrated in Figure 7.

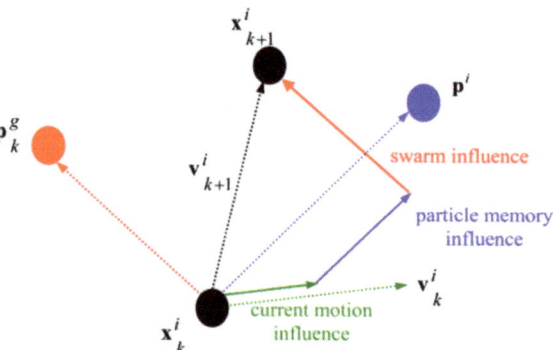

Figure 7. Updating the position of particles in PSO.

The optimization process terminates when the best answer is found, or the desired iteration is reached. The parameter configuration selected in the PSO implementation process in the research is shown in Table 2. The data were selected based on a trial-and-error method to reach the minimum possible error.

Table 2. PSO parameter configuration.

Population size	40
Range of inertia weight	0.4–0.8
Cognitive factor	1.5
Social factor	1.5
Stopping criteria	Minimum Specified Error

Genetic Algorithm: As the most recognized subset of evolutionary algorithms, it mimics the biological evolution of organisms in nature. Having been utilized in various engineering problems, GA was initially developed and characterized by John Holland [44]. This naturally inspired optimization algorithm is structured on natural genetics and selection. It allows only the solutions to survive and produce successive generations with maximum fitness according to the defined optimization problem [45].

GA deals with a set of members or solutions in the total generated population. The solutions are ranked in the population based on their fitness values. The solutions placed at the top have more chance to participate in the reproduction of the next generations, and other solutions with lower fitness must be removed from the population, and new solutions can be generated. This happens by applying crossover and mutation operators to individuals. A sample of operators applied to a pair of parents to generate new offspring is illustrated in Figure 8.

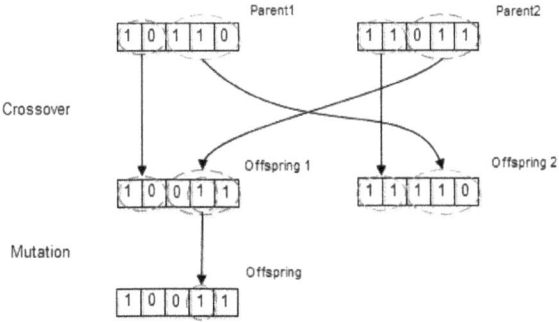

Figure 8. Crossover and mutation operators in GA.

Parameter configurations of GA in this research are given in Table 3. These parameters were obtained through the trial-and-error method.

Table 3. Parameter configuration of GA.

Population size	40
Length of chromosomes	6
Selection operator	Roulette wheel
Crossover operator	Single-point operator
Crossover probability	0.7
Mutation probability	0.15
Fitness parameter	Operation time

3.2.4. Experimental Methodology

For evaluating the proposed RE methodology of a sample gear, a helical gear related to the 1st forward movement gear of a Massey Ferguson 399 tractor's gearbox was selected. The drawing specifications, including the input-independent design parameters of the selected transmission gear, are given in Table 4.

The output measurable parameters of the gear, including values for span size and over-two-balls measurement, are listed in Table 5. The values were validated using special gear software. The measurements over two balls and span size using appropriate balls, a caliper, and a disc micrometer are demonstrated in Figure 9. To determine the form of involute, three values for d_m with different balls were obtained. The smallest one fell below the pitch diameter of the gear, the medium one was closer to the pitch diameter, and the bigger pin diameter was used to encompass the involute area of the gear over the pitch diameter. Moreover, a span measurement s_m was used to decrease the potential error of calculations and increase the precision of obtained results.

Table 4. Input-independent design parameters of the selected gear.

Input Parameter	Values of the Selected Gear Part
z	42
m_n	4.233
α_n	25
β	17° 59′ 58″
x	+0.0863

Table 5. Measurements of the selected gear.

Output Parameter	Condition of Measurement	Measured Value
d_m^1	$d_k = 6.5$	195.264
d_m^2	$d_k = 7$	196.890
d_m^3	$d_k = 7.5$	198.493
s_m	$k = 7$	87.206

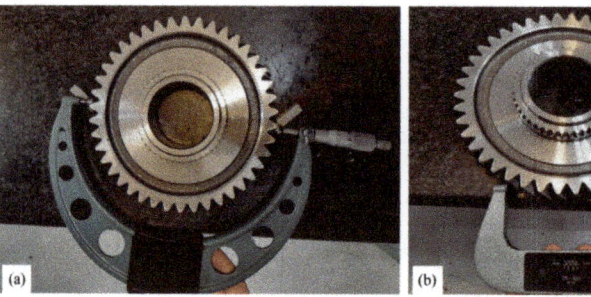

Figure 9. Measuring of over two balls and span size.

Since α_n is usually an integer value in the design process of gears, the value of this parameter is taken with no decimal while applying the optimization algorithm to find the valid answer in the search space. The rest of the parameters, including m_n, β, and x, are considered with three decimal places.

The optimization is performed in two scenarios. In the first mode, the algorithm terminates after reaching 10,000 function evaluations. The algorithms continue in the latter until the minimum desired error of 0.005 is reached. This error value guarantees that the calculated input design parameters would be obtained with the highest possible accuracy and the least deviation from actual input parameters.

All evolutionary optimization algorithms were triggered in MATLAB software. The minimum and maximum values for design parameters in search space are given in Table 6. These limits have been selected according to widespread applications observed in the power transmission mechanisms used in the automotive industry.

Table 6. The limit values of input design parameters in search space.

Parameter	Minimum	Maximum
m_n	1	5
α_n	10	30
β	0	30
x	−1	1

4. Results and Discussion

A computer equipped with Intel® core TM i7, 4.00 GHz CPU, and 16 GB RAM was selected to run algorithms in MATLAB® software, version 2020b. For optimization with the GA, function *ga* in MATLAB was used. For optimization with the PSO algorithm, Particle Swarm Optimization MATLAB Toolbox Version 1.0.0.0 was selected. For optimization with the GWO algorithm, Grey Wolf Optimizer MATLAB Toolbox Version 1.0 was utilized, and for optimization with WOA, Whale Optimization Algorithm MATLAB Toolbox Version 1.0 was applied. The population size for all algorithms was equal to perform a fair comparison of the accuracy and convergence speed of the algorithms. The performance of all optimization algorithms was submitted after 20 runs, and the run with the best result was selected in comparison with the efficiency of the algorithms. The parameter configurations for GA and PSO were discussed in the corresponding sections. GWO and WOA do not need any specific parameters [13]. As mentioned before, the RE problem was approached with two different scenarios. Concerning the first one, the efficiency of the algorithms in terms of their convergence speed was assessed by selecting a definite number of function evaluations for each algorithm to run. In the second scenario, the minimum error was selected as the final goal of optimization. Overall, the fastest algorithm to find optimum input design parameters will be determined in this case.

Scenario I: After performing 10,000 function evaluations, the algorithm's performance in finding the best solution for the problem was evaluated. The results of the optimizations and the time elapsed for each algorithm to find its best solution are given in Table 7. While the PSO method presents the best solution, other algorithms offer different values for the problem. The best result for GWO was obtained after 8824 function evaluations within 549.8 s. This means that GWO is superior to other algorithms in terms of convergence speed and proximity to the best answer. The WOA, PSO, and GA algorithms followed in obtained accuracy with elapsed times of 736.4 s, 1122.3 s, and 2364.1 s, respectively.

Table 7. Best solutions of the proposed algorithms for scenario I and relevant obtained input design parameters.

	GWO	WOA	PSO	GA
Normal module (m_n)	4.2333	4.0012	4.2122	5.2666
Normal pressure angle (α_n)	25°	25°	25°	21°
Addendum modification (x)	0.0863	−0.0128	0.0055	0.1992
Helix angle (β)	17° 59′ 58″	14° 36′ 32″	17° 02′ 11″	13° 52′ 20″
Function evaluations	8824	10,000	10,000	10,000
Elapsed time	549.8	736.4	1122.3	2364.1

The values obtained by the algorithms given in Table 7 show that the error of PSO and WOA is 2.2% and 12.3% greater than the expected value of 0.003. This value is 41.9% for GA, which indicates the weakness of this method compared to the other swarm-based optimization techniques utilized in the present research. The error was calculated based on Equation (10) for the input design parameters for each algorithm and measured values. The obtained design parameters for each algorithm are also given in Table 7.

In Table 8, the statistical results of the performance of each algorithm in all the runs are summarized. The table contains the average number of function evaluations, elapsed computation times, and the deviation of obtained results.

Table 8. Statistical results of the performance of each algorithm in all runs.

	GWO	WOA	PSO	GA
Function evaluations (ave.)	9502	10,000	10,000	10,000
Elapsed time (ave.)	601.5	751.1	1206.7	2404
Standard deviation	0.1421	4.0255	0.9054	29.1512
Function evaluations (ave.)	9502	10,000	10,000	10,000

The values given in Table 8 reveal that the repeatability of the algorithms can differ drastically. While PSO and GWO demonstrate relatively stable repeatability, the other two algorithms have negligible values, attributed to their inadequate efficiency in the optimization process in the RE of gears.

Scenario II: In this case, all algorithms were expected to fulfill predefined error criteria. The aim was to compare the efficiency of the proposed algorithms in terms of their convergence speed in finding the best solution. The results of the optimizations, including the optimum design parameter, number of function evaluations, and time elapsed for each algorithm to find its best solutions, are given in Table 9. While PSO, GWO, and WOA reached the best solution with differences in the function evaluations and consequently the computation time, the best answer was not reached by all the runs for GA. The results show the superiority of swarm-based methods in optimizing complicated problems. GWO has the highest convergence speed and lowest number of function evaluations among the proposed swarm-based optimization methods. PSO and WOA are placed in the next levels with 127.4% and 228.7% more required time and a 26.2% and 178.1% higher number of function evaluations, respectively.

Table 9. Best solutions of the proposed algorithms for scenario II and relevant obtained input design parameters.

	GWO	WOA	PSO	GA
Normal module (m_n)	4.2333	4.2333	4.2333	4.0882
Normal pressure angle (α_n)	25°	25°	25°	25°
Addendum modification (x)	0.0863	0.0863	0.0863	0.0012
Helix angle (β)	17° 59′ 58″	17° 59′ 58″	17° 59′ 58″	14° 12′ 10″
Function evaluations	8824	24,541	11,142	-
Elapsed time	549.8	1807.1	1250.5	-

The statistical results of the performance of each algorithm in all the runs are given in Table 10. In the table, each algorithm's best, mean, and worst performance; average number of function evaluations; and average elapsed time to terminate the algorithms are given.

Table 10. Statistical results of the performance of each algorithm in all runs.

	GWO	WOA	PSO	GA
Function evaluations (ave.)	9816	34,101	12,294	-
Elapsed time (ave.)	712.5	2511	1892.1	-
Standard deviation	0.1902	8.9778	0.2252	-

According to the data given in Table 10, the GWO algorithm with the lowest standard deviation is superior to the other considered algorithms in terms of stability and robustness. In all performed runs, GWO showed relatively uniform performance in reaching the best solution. Furthermore, based on Table 10, GWO, with quite a short elapsed time, is the fastest algorithm compared to the others.

The convergence graphs by the considered algorithms are shown in Figure 10. The curves are derived from the best performance of each algorithm during the optimization run.

All the methods except GA obtained the optimum input design parameters. GWO and PSO converge to the optimum values much more quickly than others without being stuck in the local minimum solution. However, the convergence speed of GWO is relatively higher than that of PSO. This method finds the optimum value in fewer function evaluations. The performance of WOA is relatively weak in this scenario. Being attached to a local minimum during the optimization progress requires more time and function evaluations for the WOA to reach the optimum value. Among the proposed optimization algorithm, GA has the lowest convergence performance. No optimum results were found in any of the runs for

GA. Therefore, it can be concluded that GA is attached to the local optimum solution and cannot be considered as an appropriate algorithm for the defined problem.

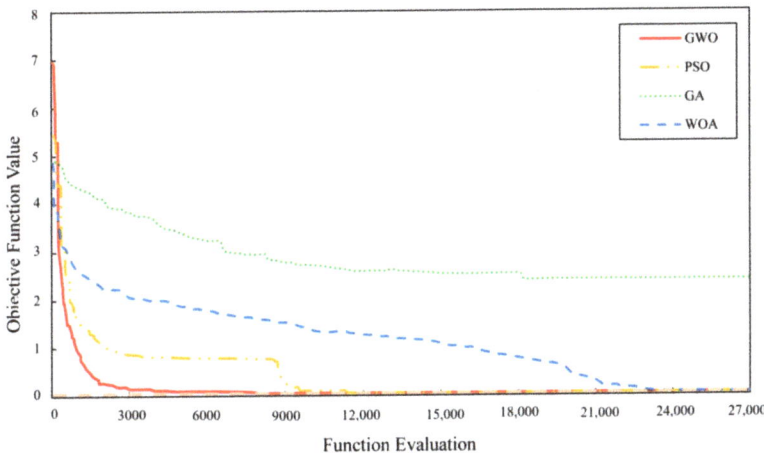

Figure 10. The algorithms' convergent curves reaching the minimum defined objective function for GWO, WOA, PSO, and GA.

To consider the average number of iterations in which the best results for each proposed algorithm are reached, boxplots for GWO, WOA, and PSO were generated and are shown in Figure 11. An illustrative comparison via the given boxplots demonstrates the superiority of GWO over the other two algorithms. Because of the poor performance of GA in finding optimum results, it has been omitted from the performance comparison.

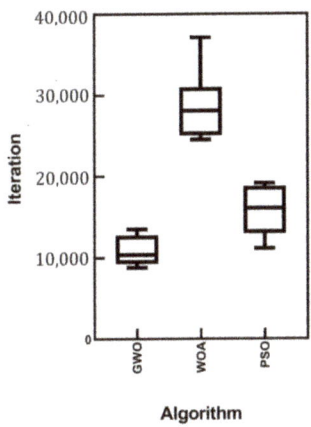

Figure 11. Boxplots of the iterations for GWO, WOA and PSO.

A two-sample unpaired t-test was performed to test the hypothesis that the mean number of iterations for GWO is lower than the same for the WOA and PSO algorithms. t-tests are divided into two groups. The first group is an unpaired t-test, which can be used when the two groups under comparison are independent of each other, and the second is a paired t-test, which can be used when the two groups under comparison are dependent on each other. As the t-test is a parametric test, samples should meet certain preconditions, such as normality and equal variances. In other words, in order to reach a statistical conclusion about a sample mean with a t-distribution, certain conditions must be satisfied: the two samples under comparison must be independently sampled from the same population, satisfying the conditions of normality and equal variance. For checking the normality and equality of variance, a Shapiro–Wilk test and Levene's test were utilized, respectively. According to the calculated Shapiro–Wilk test, the obtained p value is 0.193. Since the Shapiro–Wilk p value is greater than 0.05, it can be concluded that the samples satisfy the condition of normality. Moreover, the results of the Levene's test show that the condition of equal variance is also met.

The results for the t-test are given in Table 11. It is obvious from the test results that the zero hypothesis is rejected, and it can be concluded that there will be a meaningful difference between the effectiveness and convergence speed of the optimization algorithms in terms of the mean number of iterations, as given in Table 11.

Table 11. Two-sample t-test results for used algorithms based on iterations.

	T-Test for GWO-WOA	T-Test for GWO-PSO
p value	<0.0001	0.0005
Significant difference ($p < 0.05$)	YES	YES
t value	12.80	4.211
df	18	18
Mean iterations	10,957/28,800	10,957/15,722
Difference between mean values	17,843 ± 1394	4765 ± 1132
95% confidence interval	14,913 to 20,773	2388 to 7143

According to the performed t-tests, the hypothesis claiming the higher effectiveness of the GWO over WOA and PSO algorithms in reverse engineering using metaheuristic algorithms is confirmed.

5. Conclusions

This study proposes a new method for the RE of helical gears. This issue has been less addressed in previous studies in the literature. The main objective of the study was to find accurate gear design parameters of a helical gear, such as the normal module m_n, normal pressure angle $α_n$, addendum modification x, and helix angle $β$, using performed span and over-balls measurements. The relation between the input design parameters and relevant output measurable characteristics is obtainable with complex mathematical equations. Since it is impossible to mathematically solve the mentioned inverse equations, metaheuristic methods should be used. First, an objective function based on measurements and equations was defined. Then the defined problem was optimized by four different algorithms that have widespread use in engineering problems: GWO, WOA, PSO, and GA. The convergence speed and stability of the proposed methods were compared via statistical measures, and various indicators of the algorithms such as the convergence speed and number of function evaluations were examined. Finally, the following results were obtained:

- Based on the proposed methodology, accurate input parameters were reached. The validation of the obtained results was evaluated by the given equations.
- The performance of the algorithms was assessed in terms of the ability to reach the best solution, convergence speed, and stability. It was found that swarm-based optimization methods such as GWO and PSO are superior to the other considered algorithms such as GA.

For future work, applying the proposed methodology in the RE of other types of gears such as bevel gears and worm gears is suggested. Examining the other nature-inspired algorithms and recently published and advanced optimization methods in the RE of mechanical parts, especially gear components, is another field of research that could be considered extensively. Another vast area of research is applying the various discussed tuners in metaheuristics and their effect on the convergence speed of algorithms.

Author Contributions: Conceptualization, V.P., F.H. and S.K.; Methodology, V.P., F.H. and S.K.; Software, Validation, V.P., F.H. and S.K.; Formal Analysis, Investigation, V.P.; Data Curation, V.P.; Writing—Original Draft, V.P., F.H., S.K. and M.R.C.Q.; Writing—Review and Editing, V.P., F.H., S.K. and M.R.C.Q.; Visualization, V.P., F.H., S.K. and M.R.C.Q.; Supervising V.P. and M.R.C.Q. All authors have read and agreed to the published version of the manuscript.

Funding: This research received no external funding.

Data Availability Statement: Not applicable.

Conflicts of Interest: The authors declare no conflict of interest.

References

1. Durupt, A.; Bricogne, M.; Remy, S.; Troussier, N.; Rowson, H.; Belkadi, F. An extended framework for knowledge modelling and reuse in reverse engineering projects. *Proc. Inst. Mech. Eng. Part B J. Eng. Manuf.* **2018**, *233*, 1377–1389. [CrossRef]
2. Ayani, M.; Ganebäck, M.; Ng, A.H. Digital Twin: Applying emulation for machine reconditioning. *Procedia CIRP* **2018**, *72*, 243–248. [CrossRef]
3. Fuller, A.; Fan, Z.; Day, C.; Barlow, C. Digital twin: Enabling technologies, challenges and open research. *IEEE Access* **2020**, *8*, 108952–108971. [CrossRef]
4. Lo, C.; Chen, C.; Zhong, R.Y. A review of digital twin in product design and development. *Adv. Eng. Informatics* **2021**, *48*, 101297. [CrossRef]
5. Kirk, P.; Silk, D.; Stumpf, M.P.H. Reverse engineering under uncertainty. In *Uncertainty in Biology*; Springer: Berlin/Heidelberg, Germany, 2016; pp. 15–32. [CrossRef]
6. Palka, D. Use of Reverse Engineering and Additive Printing in the Reconstruction of Gears. *Multidiscip. Asp. Prod. Eng.* **2020**, *3*, 274–284. [CrossRef]
7. Chintala, G.; Gudimetla, P. Optimum Material Evaluation for Gas Turbine Blade Using Reverse Engineering (RE) and FEA. *Procedia Eng.* **2014**, *97*, 1332–1340. [CrossRef]
8. Lippmann, B.; Unverricht, N.; Singla, A.; Ludwig, M.; Werner, M.; Egger, P.; Kellermann, O. Verification of physical designs using an integrated reverse engineering flow for nanoscale technologies. *Integration* **2020**, *71*, 11–29. [CrossRef]
9. Dúbravčík, M.; Kender, Š. Application of Reverse Engineering Techniques in Mechanics System Services. *Procedia Eng.* **2012**, *48*, 96–104. [CrossRef]
10. Paulic, M.; Irgolic, T.; Balic, J.; Cus, F.; Cupar, A.; Brajlih, T.; Drstvensek, I. Reverse Engineering of Parts with Optical Scanning and Additive Manufacturing. *Procedia Eng.* **2014**, *69*, 795–803. [CrossRef]
11. Shamekhi, A.H.; Bidgoly, A.; Noureiny, E.N. Optimization of the gear ratios in automatic transmission systems using an artificial neural network and a genetic algorithm. *Proc. Inst. Mech. Eng. Part D J. Automob. Eng.* **2014**, *228*, 1338–1343. [CrossRef]
12. Verim, Ö; Yumurtaci, M. Application of reverse engineering approach on a damaged mechanical part. *Int. Adv. Res. Eng. J.* **2020**, *4*, 21–28. [CrossRef]
13. Baehr, J.; Bernardini, A.; Sigl, G.; Schlichtmann, U. Machine learning and structural characteristics for reverse engineering. *Integration* **2020**, *72*, 1–12. [CrossRef]
14. Jain, N.; Jain, V. Optimization of electro-chemical machining process parameters using genetic algorithms. *Mach. Sci. Technol.* **2007**, *11*, 235–258. [CrossRef]
15. Zain, A.M.; Haron, H.; Sharif, S. Simulated annealing to estimate the optimal cutting conditions for minimizing surface roughness in end milling Ti-6Al-4V. *Mach. Sci. Technol.* **2010**, *14*, 43–62. [CrossRef]
16. Kumar, A.; Kumar, V.; Kumar, J. Surface crack density and recast layer thickness analysis in WEDM process through response surface methodology. *Mach. Sci. Technol.* **2016**, *20*, 201–230. [CrossRef]
17. Savsani, V.; Rao, R.; Vakharia, D. Optimal weight design of a gear train using particle swarm optimization and simulated annealing algorithms. *Mech. Mach. Theory* **2010**, *45*, 531–541. [CrossRef]
18. Atila, Ü.; Dörterler, M.; Durgut, R.; Şahin, I. A comprehensive investigation into the performance of optimization methods in spur gear design. *Eng. Optim.* **2019**, *52*, 1052–1067. [CrossRef]
19. Xia, G.; Chen, J.; Tang, X.; Zhao, L.; Sun, B. Shift quality optimization control of power shift transmission based on particle swarm optimization–genetic algorithm. *Proc. Inst. Mech. Eng. Part D J. Automob. Eng.* **2021**, *236*, 872–892. [CrossRef]
20. Artoni, A. A methodology for simulation-based, multiobjective gear design optimization. *Mech. Mach. Theory* **2018**, *133*, 95–111. [CrossRef]
21. Rai, P.; Agrawal, A.; Saini, M.L.; Jodder, C.; Barman, A.G. Volume optimization of helical gear with profile shift using real coded genetic algorithm. *Procedia Comput. Sci.* **2018**, *133*, 718–724. [CrossRef]
22. Mendi, F.; Başkal, T.; Boran, K.; Boran, F.E. Optimization of module, shaft diameter and rolling bearing for spur gear through genetic algorithm. *Expert Syst. Appl.* **2010**, *37*, 8058–8064. [CrossRef]
23. Usman, Y.O.; Odion, P.O.; Onibere, E.O.; Egwoh, A.Y. Gear Design Optimization Algorithms: A Review. *J. Comput. Sci. Its Appl.* **2020**, *27*. [CrossRef]

24. Zhang, Q.; Kang, J.; Li, Q.; Lyu, S. The calculation and experiment for measurements over pins of the external helical gears with an odd number of teeth. *Int. J. Precis. Eng. Manuf.* **2012**, *13*, 2203–2208. [CrossRef]
25. Litvin, F.L.; Hsiao, C.L.; Ziskind, M.D. Computerized overwire (ball) measurement of tooth thickness of worms, screws and gears. *Mech. Mach. Theory* **1998**, *33*, 851–877. [CrossRef]
26. Feng, C.; Liang, J.; Gong, C.; Pai, W.; Liu, S. Repair volume extraction method for damaged parts in remanufacturing repair. *Int. J. Adv. Manuf. Technol.* **2018**, *98*, 1523–1536. [CrossRef]
27. Montero, E.; Riff, M.C.; Neveu, B. A beginner's guide to tuning methods. *Appl. Soft Comput.* **2014**, *17*, 39–51. [CrossRef]
28. Veček, N.; Mernik, M.; Filipič, B.; Črepinšek, M. Parameter tuning with Chess Rating System (CRS-Tuning) for meta-heuristic algorithms. *Inf. Sci.* **2016**, *372*, 446–469. [CrossRef]
29. Petridis, P.; Gounaris, A.; Torres, J. Spark parameter tuning via trial-and-error. In *INNS Conference on Big Data*; Springer: Berlin/Heidelberg, Germany, 2016; pp. 226–237. [CrossRef]
30. Birattari, M. F-race for tuning metaheuristics. In *Tuning Metaheuristics*; Springer: Berlin/Heidelberg, Germany, 2009; pp. 85–115.
31. Corazza, M.; di Tollo, G.; Fasano, G.; Pesenti, R. A novel hybrid PSO-based metaheuristic for costly portfolio selection problems. *Ann. Oper. Res.* **2021**, *304*, 109–137. [CrossRef]
32. Gunawan, A.; Lau, H.C.; Wong, E. Real-World Parameter Tuning Using Factorial Design with Parameter Decomposition. In *Advances in Metaheuristics*; Springer: New York, NY, USA, 2013; Volume 53, pp. 37–59. [CrossRef]
33. Qian, K.; Liu, X.; Wang, Y.; Yu, X.; Huang, B. Modified dual extended Kalman filters for SOC estimation and online parameter identification of lithium-ion battery via modified gray wolf optimizer. *Proc. Inst. Mech. Eng. Part D J. Automob. Eng.* **2021**, *236*, 1761–1774. [CrossRef]
34. Dehghani, M.; Riahi-Madvar, H.; Hooshyaripor, F.; Mosavi, A.; Shamshirband, S.; Zavadskas, E.K.; Chau, K.-W. Prediction of Hydropower Generation Using Grey Wolf Optimization Adaptive Neuro-Fuzzy Inference System. *Energies* **2019**, *12*, 289. [CrossRef]
35. Mirjalili, S.; Lewis, A. The whale optimization algorithm. *Adv. Eng. Softw.* **2016**, *95*, 51–67. [CrossRef]
36. Yang, W.; Xia, K.; Fan, S.; Wang, L.; Li, T.; Zhang, J.; Feng, Y. A Multi-Strategy Whale Optimization Algorithm and Its Application. *Eng. Appl. Artif. Intell.* **2021**, *108*, 104558. [CrossRef]
37. Wang, L.; Gu, L.; Tang, Y. Research on Alarm Reduction of Intrusion Detection System Based on Clustering and Whale Optimization Algorithm. *Appl. Sci.* **2021**, *11*, 11200. [CrossRef]
38. Ding, C.; Zhao, M.; Lin, J.; Jiao, J. Multi-objective iterative optimization algorithm based optimal wavelet filter selection for multi-fault diagnosis of rolling element bearings. *ISA Trans.* **2018**, *88*, 199–215. [CrossRef]
39. Kaveh, A.; Ghazaan, M.I. Enhanced whale optimization algorithm for sizing optimization of skeletal structures. *Mech. Based Des. Struct. Mach.* **2016**, *45*, 345–362. [CrossRef]
40. Pourmostaghimi, V.; Zadshakoyan, M.; Khalilpourazary, S.; Badamchizadeh, M.A. A hybrid particle swarm optimization and recurrent dynamic neural network for multi-performance optimization of hard turning operation. *Artif. Intell. Eng. Des. Anal. Manuf.* **2022**, *36*, e28. [CrossRef]
41. Pourmostaghimi, V.; Zadshakoyan, M. Designing and implementation of a novel online adaptive control with optimization technique in hard turning. *Proc. Inst. Mech. Eng. Part I J. Syst. Control. Eng.* **2020**, *235*, 652–663. [CrossRef]
42. Kennedy, J.; Eberhart, R. Particle swarm optimization. In Proceedings of the ICNN'95-international Conference on Neural Networks, Perth, WA, Australia, 27 November–1 December 1995; Volume 4, pp. 1942–1948.
43. Qazani, M.R.C.; Pourmostaghimi, V.; Moayyedian, M.; Pedrammehr, S. Estimation of tool–chip contact length using optimized machine learning in orthogonal cutting. *Eng. Appl. Artif. Intell.* **2022**, *114*, 105118. [CrossRef]
44. Holland, J.H. Genetic algorithms. *Sci. Am.* **1992**, *267*, 66–73. [CrossRef]
45. Zadshakoyan, M.; Pourmostaghimi, V. Metaheuristics in manufacturing: Predictive modeling of tool wear in machining using genetic programming. In *Advancements in Applied Metaheuristic Computing*; IGI Global: Hershey, PA, USA, 2018; pp. 118–142.

Disclaimer/Publisher's Note: The statements, opinions and data contained in all publications are solely those of the individual author(s) and contributor(s) and not of MDPI and/or the editor(s). MDPI and/or the editor(s) disclaim responsibility for any injury to people or property resulting from any ideas, methods, instructions or products referred to in the content.

Article

Designing a Secure Mechanism for Image Transferring System Based on Uncertain Fractional Order Chaotic Systems and NLFPID Sliding Mode Controller

Mohammad Rasouli [1,*], Assef Zare [2,3,*], Hassan Yaghoubi [4] and Roohallah Alizadehsani [5]

1. College of Skills and Entrepreneurship, Mashhad Branch, Islamic Azad University, Mashhad 9187147578, Iran
2. Faculty of Electrical Engineering, Gonabad Branch, Islamic Azad University, Gonabad 6518115743, Iran
3. Research Center of Intelligent Technologies in Electrical Industry, Islamic Azad University, Gonabad 6518115743, Iran
4. Department of Electrical and Electronic Engineering, Gonabad Branch, Islamic Azad University, Gonabad 6518115743, Iran; yaghoubihassan@yahoo.com
5. Institute for Intelligent Systems Research and Innovation (IISRI), Deakin University, Waurn Ponds, Geelong, VIC 3216, Australia; r.alizadehsani@deakin.edu.au
* Correspondence: mohamad1rasouli@gmail.com (M.R.); assefzare@gmail.com (A.Z.)

Citation: Rasouli, M.; Zare, A.; Yaghoubi, H.; Alizadehsani, R. Designing a Secure Mechanism for Image Transferring System Based on Uncertain Fractional Order Chaotic Systems and NLFPID Sliding Mode Controller. *Axioms* **2023**, *12*, 828. https://doi.org/10.3390/axioms12090828

Academic Editor: Feliz Manuel Minhós

Received: 8 June 2023
Revised: 27 July 2023
Accepted: 22 August 2023
Published: 28 August 2023

Copyright: © 2023 by the authors. Licensee MDPI, Basel, Switzerland. This article is an open access article distributed under the terms and conditions of the Creative Commons Attribution (CC BY) license (https://creativecommons.org/licenses/by/4.0/).

Abstract: A control method for the robust synchronization of a class of chaotic systems with unknown time delay, unknown uncertainty, and unknown disturbance is presented. The robust controller was designed using a nonlinear fractional order PID sliding surface. The Lyapunov method was used to determine the update laws, prove the stability of the proposed mechanism, and guarantee the convergence of the synchronization errors to zero. The simulation was performed using MATLAB software to evaluate the performance of the proposed mechanism, and the results showed that it was efficient. Finally, the proposed method was combined with a secure communication application to encrypt images, and the results obtained were favorable regarding the standard criteria of correlation, NPCR, PSNR, and information entropy.

Keywords: chaotic synchronization; fractional order sliding mode control; adaptive control; secure communication

MSC: 93D09; 93B51

1. Introduction

Chaos is a nonlinear phenomenon that appears to be random but actually follows a pattern. It was discovered about a half-century ago by Lorenz [1]. Scientists began to pay more attention to the phenomenon of chaos after that. Some systems, including the Liu system [2], the IU system [3], and the Chen system [4], have been proposed on the basis of Lorenz's ideas. About 300 years ago, fractional calculations were introduced, and more complete definitions and theorems have been introduced since then [5]. Physical systems can be represented as integer or fractional equations in this context. It is evident that modeling using fractional order systems can have more accuracy than modeling with integer order systems. Recently, the description of systems using fractional calculus has been developed in various sciences, including chemical reaction systems [6,7], biological systems [8,9], power converters [10], electrochemical processes [11], robotics [12], and others. The problem of synchronizing two chaotic systems has piqued the interest of scientists working in the field of secure communication over the past two decades. In fact, the synchronization of two chaotic systems can be described as a situation in which two or more chaotic systems coordinate their responses by the controller. As a result, two subsystems, the main or driving system and the slave or response system, constitute a coupled system. The master system's response is unconstrained and drives the slave system.

To tackle the problem, Petras et al. presented a fractional sliding surface [13]. Zare Hallaji et al. [14,15] presented research on the synchronization of positive and fractional chaotic systems with system uncertainty. They evaluated the conditions of the described problem from several perspectives, including unknown uncertainties in the system characteristics, in their research. In [16], the chaotic system was synchronized using a nonlinear observer and the benefit of adaptive control in order to determine the system's uncertainties. In this design, a sliding surface equivalent to one of the system states was provided, and its stability was demonstrated using a Lyapunov function. The authors of [17] proposed an adaptive terminal sliding mode controller (ATSMC). First, a fractional order sliding surface for the master and slave system was introduced in this article. The stability of the suggested controller was then examined, as was the ongoing convergence of the error in the synchronization problem.

A sliding surface based on the nonlinear fractional order PID was developed in this study for the synchronization of two systems with uncertainty and unknown disturbances with unknown and time-varying time delay. The following benefits might be highlighted in this research, which was conducted to synchronize two systems:

- The use of the nonlinear fractional PID (NLFOPID) sliding surface instead of typical sliding surfaces.
- The presence of unknown time delays
- The presence of uncertainty and disturbance with unknown boundaries. Then, using the suitable Lyapunov function and update laws, a control signal was extracted that could be used to overcome the chattering problem by properly adjusting the controller parameters. This is a critical issue for the suggested controller's implementation. In [10,18], a controller for the synchronization of chaotic systems in finite time was constructed utilizing a sliding surface, and the synchronization of the integer order chaotic system was investigated in [19].

The preliminary calculations of deficit accounts are reported in Section 2 of this article. Section 3 presents the equations characterizing the system as well as the set limitations for uncertainty. Section 4 introduces the sliding surface based on the proportional–integral–nonlinear fractional derivative, as well as the controller architecture. Section 5 investigates the adaptive controller's stability analysis and update laws. Section 6 presents the simulation results and visualization of the synchronized system. Section 7 discusses chaotic masking for image encryption. Finally, in the last section, conclusions and recommendations are offered.

2. Preliminary Definitions of Fractional Order Differentiation

Definition 1. *The fractional order integration and differentiation are defined as follows* [20]:

$$D_t^q = \begin{cases} \frac{d^q}{dt^q} & q > 0 \\ 1 & q = 0 \\ \int_q^t (d\tau)^{-q} & q < 0 \end{cases} \quad (1)$$

in which q is a real number.

Definition 2. *The Riemann–Liouville fractional integral of order q of the function $f(t)$ is defined as follows* [21]:

$$_{t_0}I_t^q f(t) = \frac{1}{\Gamma(q)} \int_{t_0}^t \frac{f(\tau)}{(t-\tau)^{1-q}} d\tau \quad (2)$$

in which t_0 is the initial time and $\Gamma(q)$ is the Gamma function defined as follows:

Definition 3. Suppose $n-1 < q \leq n$, $n \in N$. The fractional Riemann–Liouville differentiation of order q is defined for the function $f(t)$ below [21]:

$$_{t_0}D_t^q f(t) = \frac{d^q f(t)}{dt^q} = \frac{1}{\Gamma(n-q)} \frac{d^n}{dt^n} \int_{t_0}^{t} \frac{f(\tau)}{(t-\tau)^{q-n+1}} d\tau \quad (3)$$

Note 1: In Equation (4), the Riemann-Liouville fractional order integral is first calculated, and then differentiation is performed; thus, the derivative of a constant number in this formulation is not equal to zero.

Definition 4. In the continuous function $f(t)$, the Caputo fractional order derivative of order q is defined as follows [21]:

$$_{t_0}D_t^q f(t) = \begin{cases} \frac{1}{\Gamma(m-q)} \int_{t_0}^{t} \frac{f^{(m)}(\tau)}{(t-\tau)^{q-m+1}} d\tau & m-1 < q < m \\ \frac{d^m f(t)}{dt^m} & q = m \end{cases} \quad (4)$$

$$\Gamma(q) = \int_0^\infty e^{-t} t^{q-1} dt \quad (5)$$

Such that m is the first integer number after q.

Lemma 1. If $f(t)$ is a constant function and $q > 0$, the Caputo derivative in Equation (5) for $f(t)$ would be as follows:

$$D^q f(t) = 0 \quad (6)$$

The authors of [22] presented the stability analysis of fractional order systems using the direct Lyapunov method, as well as the determination of the necessary and sufficient conditions guaranteeing stability using the Mittag–Leffler concept, and the authors of [23] reviewed the stability analysis of nonlinear systems using convex Lyapunov functions.

Lemma 2 [23]**.** Suppose that $h(t) \in R$ is a continuous and differentiable function. Then, for $t \geq t_0$, Equation (7) is satisfied.

$$D^q h^2(t) \leq 2h(t) \cdot D^q h(t) \quad (7)$$

Lemma 3 [23]**.** Suppose that $h(t) \in R^n$ is a continuous and differentiable function. Then, for $t \geq t_0$, we have:

$$D^q h^T(t) \cdot h(t) \leq 2h^T(t) \cdot D^q h(t) \quad (8)$$

Theorem 1 [22]**.** Assume that the origin ($x = 0$) is the equilibrium point of the fractional order system (5) and that its definition domain covers the origin. Furthermore, $v(x(t), t)$ is a continuous and differentiable Lipschitz function, implying the following:

$$\begin{array}{l} D^q x(t) = f(x,t) \\ a_1 \parallel x \parallel^a \leq v(x(t), t) \leq a_2 \parallel x \parallel^{ab} \\ D^q v(x(t), t) \leq -a_3 \parallel x \parallel^{ab} \end{array} \quad (9)$$

in which $0 < q < 1$ and a, a_1, a_2, a_3, b are positive arbitrary constants. Then, the origin is stable in the Mittag–Leffler sense.

Definition 5. The continuous function $p : [0, \infty) \to [0, \infty)$ belongs to class k if its derivative is positive and $p(0) = 0$.

Theorem 2 [22]. *Assume $x = 0$ is the equilibrium point of the fractional order system (5), the Lipschitz condition for $f(x,t)$ is satisfied, and $q \in (0,1)$. If Equations (8) and (9) are satisfied for the Lyapunov function $v(x(t),t)$ and functions δ_i of class K:*

$$\begin{aligned} \delta_1(\| x \|) &\leq v(x(t),t) \leq \delta_2(\| x \|) \\ D^q v(x(t),t) &\leq -\delta_3(\| x \|) \end{aligned} \tag{10}$$

Then, system (5) is asymptotically stable in the Mittag–Leffler sense.

Theorem 3 [24]. *For the fractional order system (5) and the Lyapunov function $v(x)$, we have:*

$$D^q v(x) \leq \left(\frac{\partial v}{\partial x}\right)^T \cdot D^q x = \left(\frac{\partial v}{\partial x}\right)^T \cdot f(x,t) \tag{11}$$

Definition 6 [25]. *A continuous piecewise function $f(x,t)$ has the Lipschitz condition if:*

$$\| f(x,t) - f(z,t) \| \leq \gamma_f \| x - z \|, \ \forall \ x,z \in R^n \tag{12}$$

3. System Descriptor Equations

The equations characterizing a class of master–slave chaotic systems with uncertainty and indeterminate time delay in the presence of an unknown disturbance are introduced in this section. Following standardization, the master system dynamics in canonical form are as follows:

$$\begin{cases} D^q x_i = x_{i+1} \ 1 \leq i \leq n-1 \\ D^q x_n = \sigma_0^T x + f(x(t-\tau_1),t) + \Delta f(x(t),t) + d_1(t). \end{cases} \tag{13}$$

The slave system equations are as follows:

$$\begin{cases} D^q y_i = y_{i+1} \ 1 \leq i \leq n-1 \\ D^q y_n = \sigma_0^T y + g(y(t-\tau_2),t) + \Delta g(y(t),t) + d_2(t) + u(t). \end{cases} \tag{14}$$

The differential equations are written in the forms of well-known chaotic systems, such as the Van der Pol Oscillator, Duffing's Oscillator, the Genesio–Tesi System, Arneodo's System, and so on [26], where $x(t), y(t) \in R^n$ denote the dynamic states of the master and slave systems, σ_0^T denotes the constant coefficients in the system's linear states, and $f(x(t-\tau_1),t), g(y(t-\tau_2),t) \in R$ are nonlinear functions with an unknown delay with τ_1, τ_2 delays, and $\Delta f(x(t),t), \Delta g(x(t),t)$ represent bounded uncertainty in the master and slave systems. Furthermore, $d_1(t), d_2(t)$ indicate the external distortions applied to the master and slave systems, respectively, while $u(t)$ is the control law applied to the slave system.

Definition 7. *If the following conditions are satisfied for the systems described in Equations (13) and (14) for all the conditions governing the system, including all initial conditions, uncertainties, unknown time delay, and external disturbance, the system has robust synchronization:*

$$\lim_{t \to \infty} |y_i(t) - x_i(t)| = \lim_{t \to \infty} |e_i(t)| = 0, \ i = 1,\ldots,n. \tag{15}$$

As a result, $e_i(t)$ introduces the synchronization error of the master and slave systems.

As a result, the following are the dynamic equations describing the synchronization error for the uncertain chaotic master and slave systems with unknown time delay described in (13) and (14):

$$\begin{cases} D^q e_i = e_{i+1} \ 1 \leq i \leq n-1 \\ D^q e_n = \sigma_0^T (y-x) + g(y(t-\tau_2),t) + \Delta g(x(t),t) + d_2(t) \\ \qquad - (f(x(t-\tau_1),t) + \Delta f(x(t),t) + d_1(t)) + u(t). \end{cases} \tag{16}$$

Assumption 1. *The uncertain external disturbances $d_1(t), d_2(t)$ and the uncertain bounded nonlinear uncertainties $\Delta f(x(t).t)$ and $\Delta g(x(t).t)$ in the master and slave systems (13) and (14) meet the following conditions:*

$$\begin{aligned}\|\Delta f(x(t),t)\| &\leq \beta_1 \omega_1(x) \\ \|\Delta g(y(t),t)\| &\leq \beta_2 \omega_2(y) \\ \|d_1(t)\| &\leq \rho_1 \\ \|d_2(t)\| &\leq \rho_2 \\ \underline{\tau}_i &< \tau_i < \overline{\tau}_i\end{aligned} \quad (17)$$

Such that $\|.\|$ denotes the l_1 norm, β_2, β_1, ρ_2, ρ_1 are unknown positive real numbers, and $\omega_2(\cdot), \omega_1(\cdot)$ are positive and known functions. Also, $\rho_i < \overline{\rho}_i$, $\beta_i < \overline{\beta}_i$ where $\overline{\rho}_i, \overline{\beta}_i, \overline{\tau}_i$, and $\underline{\tau}_i$ are known values.

Assumption 2. *The nonlinear functions $f(x(t-\tau_1),t)$, $g(y(t-\tau_2),t) \in R$ satisfy the Lipschitz conditions for any $x(t), y(t) \in R$:*

$$\begin{aligned}|f(x(t-\tau_1)) - f(x(t-\hat{\tau}_1))| &\leq l_1|\tau_1 - \hat{\tau}_1| = l_1\left|\tilde{\tau}_1\right| \\ |g(y(t-\tau_2)) - g(y(t-\hat{\tau}_2))| &\leq l_2|\tau_2 - \hat{\tau}_2| = l_2\left|\tilde{\tau}_2\right|\end{aligned} \quad (18)$$

Table 1 presents the system parameters and the proposed mechanism:

Table 1. Symbols and concepts.

Symbol	Concept	Symbol	Concept
ρ_i	Disturbance bound	$\hat{\rho}_i$	Disturbance bound estimate
β_i	Uncertainty bound	$\hat{\beta}_i$	Uncertainty bound estimate
l_i	Lipschitz constant	$\hat{\tau}_i$	Time delay bound estimate
τ_i	Time delay	$\tilde{\rho}_i$	Disturbance bound estimate error
$\overline{\rho}_i$	Disturbance upper bound	$\tilde{\beta}_i$	Uncertainty bound estimate error
$\overline{\beta}_i$	Uncertainty upper bound	$\tilde{\tau}_i$	Time delay estimate error
$\overline{\tau}_i$	Time delay upper bound	b	Positive constant number
$\underline{\tau}_i$	Time delay lower bound	$\overline{\epsilon}$	Small positive constant number

In this study, all states of the system were directed to and kept on the sliding surface by designing a robust adaptive controller and introducing an integral proportional sliding surface and a fractional order nonlinear derivative. Furthermore, the system's uncertainties and unknown parameters should be estimated and updated. Then, in the robust synchronization of chaotic systems (13) and (14) in the presence of external distortions, bounded nonlinear uncertainties, and uncertain time delays, the dynamics of the slave system state must match the behavior of the master system dynamics, and the estimation error of the unknown parameters in both chaotic systems approach zero in any circumstance, ensuring the system's robust stability.

4. The Sliding Mode Control Approach Based on Fractional Order Nonlinear PID Controllers

A proportional integral sliding surface and a nonlinear fractional order derivative are presented in this section in order to synchronize chaotic systems (13) and (14) with unknown uncertainty and unknown time delay. The fractional order sliding surface is as follows, according to the nonlinear fractional order PID controller structure presented in [26], which enhances tracking:

$$s(t) = h(e) \cdot \left[k_p e_n(t) + T_I D^{-\lambda} \sum_{i=1}^{n} k_{1i} e_i + T_d D^{\delta} \sum_{i=1}^{n} k_{2i} e_i(t)\right] \quad (19)$$

Such that $h(e)$ is a nonlinear function, defined as follows:

$$h(e) = k_0 + (1-k_0)\|E(t)\|, \ k_0 \in (0,1) \tag{20}$$

where $\|E(t)\| = \sum_{i=1}^{n}|e_i|$. Coefficients T_I and T_d are time constants of integral and derivative sentences. The parameters k_{1i} and k_{2i} are positive constant values of the sliding surface such that they satisfy the stability of the desired system. If the system is in sliding mode, the following conditions must be met:

$$s(t) = 0, \ D^q s(t) = 0 \tag{21}$$

The fractional order derivative of the sliding surface in Equation (21) is as follows:

$$\begin{aligned} D^q s(t) = & \left(k_0 k_p D^q e_n(t) + k_0 T_I D^{q-\lambda} \sum_{i=1}^{n} k_{1i} e_i(t) + k_0 T_d D^{q+\delta} \sum_{i=1}^{n} k_{2i} e_i(t) + (1-k_0) k_p D^q(\|E(t)\| e_n(t))\right. \\ & \left. + (1-k_0) T_I D^q\left(\|E(t)\| D^{-\lambda} \sum_{i=1}^{n} k_{1i} e_i(t)\right) + (1-k_0) T_d D^q\left(\|E(t)\| D^{\delta} \sum_{i=1}^{n} k_{2i} e_i(t)\right)\right) = 0 \end{aligned} \tag{22}$$

Now, $D^q e_n$ is substituted into Equation (21) using Equation (16):

$$\begin{aligned} D^q s(t) = & \left(k_0 k_p\big(g(y(t-\tau_2),t) + \Delta g(x(t),t) + d_2(t) - (f(x(t-\tau_1),t) + \Delta f(x(t),t) + d_1(t)) + \sigma_0^T \cdot E(t)\right. \\ & \left. + u(t)\big) + k_0 T_I D^{1-\lambda} \sum_{i=1}^{n} k_{1i} e_i(t) + k_0 T_d D^{1+\delta} \sum_{i=1}^{n} k_{2i} e_i(t) + (1-k_0) k_p D^q(\|E(t)\| e_n(t))\right. \\ & \left. + (1-k_0) T_I D^q\left(\|E(t)\| D^{-\lambda} \sum_{i=1}^{n} k_{1i} e_i(t)\right) + (1-k_0) T_d D^q\left(\|E(t)\| D^{\delta} \sum_{i=1}^{n} k_{2i} e_i(t)\right)\right) = 0 \end{aligned} \tag{23}$$

In this case, the control signal is determined as follows:

$$\begin{aligned} u(t) = & \frac{-1}{k_0 k_p}\left(k_0 T_I D^{q-\lambda} \sum_{i=1}^{n} k_{1i} e_i(t) + k_0 T_d D^{q+\delta} \sum_{i=1}^{n} k_{2i} e_i(t) + (1-k_0) k_p D^q(\|E(t)\| e_n(t))\right. \\ & \left. + (1-k_0) T_I D^q\left(\|E(t)\| D^{-\lambda} \sum_{i=1}^{n} k_{1i} e_i(t)\right) + (1-k_0) T_d D^q\left(\|E(t)\| D^{\delta} \sum_{i=1}^{n} k_{2i} e_i(t)\right)\right) \\ & + f(x(t-\hat{\tau}_1).t) - g(y(t-\hat{\tau}_2).t) - \sigma_0^T \cdot E(t) - bs + \overline{u}(t) \end{aligned} \tag{24}$$

In Equation (25), the term $\overline{u}(t)$ comprises the terms coming from the estimation of the system's bounds of uncertainties and disturbances, which are defined using the adaptive controller, as follows:

$$\begin{aligned} \overline{u}(t) &= -\text{sgn}(s)\left[\hat{\beta}_2 \omega_2(y) + \hat{\beta}_1 \omega_1(x) + \hat{\rho}_2 + \hat{\rho}_1\right] + u_{00}(t) \\ u_{00}(t) &= \frac{-b}{k_0 k_p s} \sum_{i=1}^{2}\left[\left(|\hat{\rho}_i| + \overline{\rho}_i\right)^2 + \left(|\hat{\tau}_i| + \overline{\tau}_i\right)^2 + \left(|\hat{\beta}_i| + \overline{\beta}_i\right)^2\right] \end{aligned} \tag{25}$$

5. Stability Analysis and Determining the Update Laws

The construction of the robust adaptive controller is described in this part, employing the sliding surface based on nonlinear fractional order PID in such a way that the suggested control strategy guarantees the stability of the synchronization of chaotic systems.

Theorem 4. *The synchronization of systems (13) and (14) in the presence of disturbances d_1 and d_2 and unknown uncertainties Δf and Δg with unknown time delays τ_1 and τ_2 and the definition of the controller $u(t)$ is guaranteed as follows:*

$$\begin{aligned} u(t) = & -g(y(t-\hat{\tau}_1)) + f(x(t-\hat{\tau}_2)) \\ & -\frac{1}{k_0 k_p}\left(k_0 T_I D^{q-\lambda} \sum_{i=1}^{n} k_{1i} e_i(t) + k_0 T_d D^{q+\delta} \sum_{i=1}^{n} k_{2i} e_i(t) + (1-k_0) k_p D^q(\|E(t)\| e_n(t))\right. \\ & \left. + (1-k_0) T_I D^q\left(\|E(t)\| D^{-\lambda} \sum_{i=1}^{n} k_{1i} e_i(t)\right) + (1-k_0) T_d D^q\left(\|E(t)\| D^{\delta} \sum_{i=1}^{n} k_{2i} e_i(t)\right)\right) - \sigma_0^T \\ & \cdot E(t) - bs - \text{sgn}(s)\left(\hat{\beta}_2 \omega_2(y) + \hat{\beta}_1 \omega_1(x) + \hat{\rho}_2 + \hat{\rho}_1\right) + u_{00}(t) \end{aligned} \tag{26}$$

Such that the update laws are as follows:

$$\begin{aligned}
D^q \hat{\tau}_i &= -D^q \tilde{\tau}_i = l_i |s| sgn(\tilde{\tau}_i), \hat{\tau}_i(0) = \overline{\tau}_i \\
D^q \hat{\rho}_i &= -D^q \tilde{\rho}_i = k_0 k_p |s| \\
D^q \hat{\beta}_1 &= -D^q \tilde{\beta}_1 = -k_0 k_p |s| \omega_2(y) \\
D^q \hat{\beta}_2 &= -D^q \tilde{\beta}_2 = -k_0 k_p |s| \omega_1(x)
\end{aligned} \quad (27)$$

Thus, the convergence of the chaotic systems' synchronization error to zero is ensured.

Proof. Consider the following Lyapunov function:

$$v(t) = \frac{1}{2}\left[s^2(t) + \tilde{\beta}_1^2 + \tilde{\beta}_2^2 + l_1 \tilde{\tau}_1^2 + l_2 \tilde{\tau}_2^2 + \tilde{\rho}_1^2 + \tilde{\rho}_2^2\right] \quad (28)$$

in which the parameters' estimation error is defined as follows:

$$\tilde{\tau}_i = \tau_i - \hat{\tau}_i, \quad \tilde{\rho}_i = \rho_i - \hat{\rho}_i, \quad \tilde{\beta}_i = \beta_i - \hat{\beta}_i \quad (29)$$

Considering Equation (28), the derivative of the Lyapunov function is as follows:

$$D^q v(t) = \frac{1}{2} D^q\left(s^2 + \tilde{\beta}_1^2 + \tilde{\beta}_2^2 + l_1 \tilde{\tau}_1^2 + l_2 \tilde{\tau}_2^2 + \tilde{\rho}_1^2 + \tilde{\rho}_2^2\right) \le s \cdot D^q s + \sum_{i=1}^{2}\left(\tilde{\beta}_i D^q \tilde{\beta}_i + l_i \tilde{\tau}_i D^q \tilde{\tau}_i + \tilde{\rho}_i D^q \tilde{\rho}_i\right) \quad (30)$$

By applying Equation (23) in Equation (30), Equation (31) is determined:

$$\begin{aligned}
D^q v(t) \le \ & s \cdot [k_0 k_p (g(y(t-\tau_2),t) + \Delta g(x(t),t) + d_2(t) - (f(x(t-\tau_1),t) + \Delta f(x(t),t) + d_1(t)) + \sigma_0^T \cdot E(t) \\
& + u(t)) + k_0 T_I D^{q-\lambda} \sum_{i=1}^{n} k_{1i} e_i(t) + k_0 T_d D^{q+\delta} \sum_{i=1}^{n} k_{2i} e_i(t) + (1-k_0) k_p D^q(\|E(t)\| e_n(t)) \\
& + (1-k_0) T_I D^q(\|E(t)\| D^{-\lambda} \sum_{i=1}^{n} k_{1i} e_i(t)) + (1-k_0) T_d D^q(\|E(t)\| D^{\delta} \sum_{i=1}^{n} k_{2i} e_i(t)) + u_{00}(t)] \\
& + \sum_{i=1}^{2}\left(\tilde{\beta}_i D^q \tilde{\beta}_i + l_i \tilde{\tau}_i D^q \tilde{\tau}_i + \tilde{\rho}_i D^q \tilde{\rho}_i\right)
\end{aligned} \quad (31)$$

In this case, the Lyapunov function derivate is as follows:

$$\begin{aligned}
D^q v(t) \le \ & s \cdot [k_0 k_p (g(y(t-\tau_2),t) - g(y(t-\hat{\tau}_2),t) + \Delta g(x(t),t) + d_2(t) + f(x(t-\hat{\tau}_1),t) - f(x(t-\tau_1),t) \\
& -\Delta f(x(t),t) - d_1(t) - bs - sgn(s)[\hat{\beta}_2 \omega_2(y) + \hat{\beta}_1 \omega_1(x) + \hat{\rho}_2 + \hat{\rho}_1])] + s k_0 k_p u_{00}(t) \\
& + \sum_{i=1}^{2}\left(\tilde{\beta}_i D^q \tilde{\beta}_i + l_i \tilde{\tau}_i D^q \tilde{\tau}_i + \tilde{\rho}_i D^q \tilde{\rho}_i\right)
\end{aligned} \quad (32)$$

Thus, we have:

$$\begin{aligned}
D^q v(t) \le \ & |s| \cdot [k_0 k_p (|g(y(t-\tau_2),t) - g(y(t-\hat{\tau}_2),t)| + |\Delta g(x(t),t)| + |f(x(t-\hat{\tau}_1),t) - f(x(t-\tau_1),t)| \\
& - |\Delta f(x(t),t)| + |d_2(t) - d_1(t)|)] - k_0 k_p b s^2 \\
& + k_0 k_p s(-sgn(s)[\hat{\beta}_2 \omega_2(y) + \hat{\beta}_1 \omega_1(x) + \hat{\rho}_2 + \hat{\rho}_1]) + s k_0 k_p u_{00}(t) \\
& + \sum_{i=1}^{2}\left(\tilde{\beta}_i D^q \tilde{\beta}_i + l_i \tilde{\tau}_i D^q \tilde{\tau}_i + \tilde{\rho}_i D^q \tilde{\rho}_i\right)
\end{aligned} \quad (33)$$

On the basis of assumptions 1-2 and 2-2 presented in Equations (17) and (18) in Section 3 of the article, Equation (33) is rewritten as follows:

$$\begin{aligned}
D^q v(t) \le \ & |s| \cdot [k_0 k_p (l_2 |\tau_2 - \hat{\tau}_2| + \beta_2 \omega_2(y) + l_1 |\tau_1 - \hat{\tau}_1| + \beta_1 \omega_1(x) + \rho_1 + \rho_2)] - k_0 k_p b s^2 \\
& - k_0 k_p sgn(s) s [\hat{\beta}_2 \omega_2(y) + \hat{\beta}_1 \omega_1(x) + \hat{\rho}_2 + \hat{\rho}_1] + s k_0 k_p u_{00}(t) \\
& + \sum_{i=1}^{2}\left(\tilde{\beta}_i D^q \tilde{\beta}_i + l_i \tilde{\tau}_i D^q \tilde{\tau}_i + \tilde{\rho}_i D^q \tilde{\rho}_i\right)
\end{aligned} \quad (34)$$

The derivative of the Lyapunov function is as follows:

$$D^q v(t) \leq |s| \left[k_0 k_p \left(l_1 |\tilde{\tau}_1| + \tilde{\beta}_2 \omega_2(y) + l_2 |\tilde{\tau}_2| + \tilde{\beta}_1 \omega_1(x) + \tilde{\rho}_2 + \tilde{\rho}_1 \right) \right] - bs^2 + sk_0 k_p u_{00}(t)$$
$$+ \sum_{i=1}^{2} \left(\tilde{\beta}_i D^q \tilde{\beta}_i + l_i \tilde{\tau}_i D^q \tilde{\tau}_i + \tilde{\rho}_i D^q \tilde{\rho}_i \right) \tag{35}$$

Now, by substituting the update laws (27) into (35), the derivative of the Lyapunov function is simplified as follows:

$$\Rightarrow D^q v(t) \leq -bs^2 + sk_0 k_p u_{00}(t) \tag{36}$$

In the following, by substituting $u_{00}(t)$ from (25) into (36), Equation (37) is obtained:

$$\Rightarrow D^q v(t) \leq -bs^2 - sk_0 k_p \frac{b}{k_0 k_p s} \sum_{i=1}^{2} \left[\left(|\hat{\rho}_i| + \overline{\rho}_i \right)^2 + \left(|\hat{\tau}_i| + \overline{\tau}_i \right)^2 + \left(|\hat{\beta}_i| + \overline{\beta}_i \right)^2 \right] \tag{37}$$

On the other hand:

$$\left| \tilde{\tau}_i \right| = |\tau_i - \hat{\tau}_i| \leq |\tau_i| + |\hat{\tau}_i| \leq |\hat{\tau}_i| + \overline{\tau}_i \Rightarrow -(|\hat{\tau}_i| + \overline{\tau}_i)^2 \leq -\left| \tilde{\tau}_i \right|^2$$
$$\left| \tilde{\beta}_i \right| = |\beta_i - \hat{\beta}_i| \leq |\beta_i| + |\hat{\beta}_i| \leq |\hat{\beta}_i| + \overline{\beta}_i \Rightarrow -(|\hat{\beta}_i| + \overline{\beta}_i)^2 \leq -\left| \tilde{\beta}_i \right|^2 \tag{38}$$
$$\left| \tilde{\rho}_i \right| = |\rho_i - \hat{\rho}_i| \leq |\rho_i| + |\hat{\rho}_i| \leq |\hat{\rho}_i| + \overline{\rho}_i \Rightarrow -(|\hat{\rho}_i| + \overline{\rho}_i)^2 \leq -\left| \tilde{\rho}_i \right|^2$$

By substituting Equation (38) into Equation (35), the derivative of the Lyapunov function is simplified to Equation (39).

$$\Rightarrow D^q v(t) \leq -b \left(s^2 + \sum_{i=1}^{2} \left[\tilde{\beta}_i^2 + \tilde{\tau}_i^2 + \tilde{\rho}_i^2 \right] \right) \leq -2bv \tag{39}$$

The convergence of $v(t)$ to zero is guaranteed by Theorems (1) and (2). As a result, the sliding surface s and the estimation errors approach zero. In the following, it is proven that the synchronization errors approach zero. For this purpose, first, $\alpha_i \triangleq T_I k_{1i}$ and $\beta_i \triangleq T_d k_{2i}$ are defined. Then, by applying Equations (19)–(21), expression (40) is obtained:

$$\Rightarrow k_p e_n(t) + T_I D^{-\lambda} \sum_{i=1}^{n} k_{1i} e_i + T_d D^{\delta} \sum_{i=1}^{n} k_{2i} e_i(t) = 0 \tag{40}$$

Thus, the fractional order derivative of is obtained from both sides of Equation (37)

$$k_p D^{\lambda} e_n(t) + \sum_{i=1}^{n} \beta_i e_i(t) + \sum_{i=1}^{n} \alpha_i D^{\lambda+\delta} e_i(t) = 0, 0 < \lambda + \delta \leq 1 \tag{41}$$

The dynamics of the system error are defined as follows:

$$\begin{cases} D^q e_1 = e_2 \\ D^q e_2 = e_3 \\ \vdots \\ D^q e_{n-1} = e_n \end{cases} \Rightarrow \begin{cases} s^q E_1 = E_2 + k_2'(s) \\ s^q E_2 = E_3 + k_3'(s) \\ \vdots \\ s^q E_{n-1} = E_n + k_n'(s) \end{cases} \Rightarrow E_i = s^{(i-1)q} E_1(s) + k_i'(s) \tag{42}$$

in which $E_i(s) = \mathcal{L}(e_i)$, and $k_i'(s)$ is the effect of the initial condition of the Laplace transform. By calculating the Laplace transform using Equation (40), Equation (42) is obtained:

$$k_p s^{\lambda} E_n(s) + \sum_{i=1}^{n} \left(\alpha_i s^{q+\lambda} E_i + \beta_i E_i \right) = k_0(s) \tag{43}$$

where $k_0(s)$ is the general effect of the initial conditions. By substituting Equation (42) into Equation (43), Equation (44) is obtained:

$$\left[k_p s^\lambda s^{(n-1)q} + \sum_{i=1}^{n}\left(\alpha_i s^{\delta+\lambda} s^{(i-1)q} + \beta_i s^{(i-1)q}\right)\right] E_1(s) = k_0(s) \tag{44}$$

Therefore, the system's characteristic equation is as follows:

$$k_p s^{(n-1)q+\lambda} + \sum_{i=1}^{n}\left(\alpha_i s^{\delta+\lambda+(i-1)q} + \beta_i s^{(i-1)q}\right) = 0 \tag{45}$$

If the coefficients α_i, β_i, and k_p on the sliding surface are chosen in such a way that the roots of the above equation have a negative real part, then all e_is approach zero.

Therefore, a sufficient condition for the synchronization errors to converge to zero is that the characteristic Equation (45) is stable.

In Equation (25), if the sliding surface approaches zero, $u_{00}(t)$ will be very big; to avoid this, $u_{00}(t)$ is modified as follows:

$$u_{00}(t) = \frac{-bs}{k_0 k_p (s^2 + \bar{\epsilon})} \sum_{i=1}^{2}\left[\left(|\hat{\rho}_i| + \bar{\rho}_i\right)^2 + \left(|\hat{\tau}_i| + \bar{\tau}_i\right)^2 + \left(|\hat{\beta}_i| + \bar{\beta}_i\right)^2\right] \tag{46}$$

in which $\bar{\epsilon}$ is a small positive number.

The update laws for delays in Equation (27), which are not available, depend on the estimation error. This problem can be solved by the following:

Given that $0 < \underline{\tau_i} < \tau_i < \overline{\tau_i}$, such that $\overline{\tau_i}$ is the upper limit and $\underline{\tau_i}$ is the lower limit of the time delay, as a result of selecting $\hat{\tau}_i(0) = \overline{\tau}_i$, we have:

$$\tilde{\tau}_i(0) = \tau_i - \hat{\tau}_i(0) = \tau_i - \overline{\tau} < 0 \Rightarrow sgn\left(\tilde{\tau}_i\right) = -1$$

By defining $V_{\tilde{\tau}_i} = \frac{1}{2}\tilde{\tau}_i^{\,2}$ and calculating its derivate:

$$D^q V_{\tilde{\tau}_i} \leq \tilde{\tau}_i D^q \tilde{\tau}_i = -\tilde{\tau}_i l_i |s| sgn\left(\tilde{\tau}_i\right) = -l_i \left|\tilde{\tau}_i\right| |s| < 0 \tag{47}$$

Therefore, $V_{\tilde{\tau}_i}$ is a decreasing function that tends to zero as a result: $\forall t \geq 0 : \tilde{\tau}_i < 0 \Rightarrow sgn(\tilde{\tau}_i) = -1$.

In this way, the update laws for time delays are as follows:

$$D^q \hat{\tau}_i = l_i |s| sgn\left(\tilde{\tau}_i\right) = -l_i |s| \; i = 1.2 \tag{48}$$

Also, in order to increase the robustness of the adaptive laws against uncertainties and disturbances, the Sigma correction law was used. The behavior of the sigma function is shown in Figure 1.

The sigma function is defined as follows:

$$\sigma(t) = \begin{cases} 0 \; if \; |\hat{\theta}(t)| \leq M_0 \\ (|\hat{\theta}(t)|/M_0 - 1)^n \sigma_0 \; if \; M_0 < |\hat{\theta}(t)| \leq 2M_0 \\ \sigma_0 \; if \; |\hat{\theta}(t)| \geq 2M_0 \end{cases} \tag{49}$$

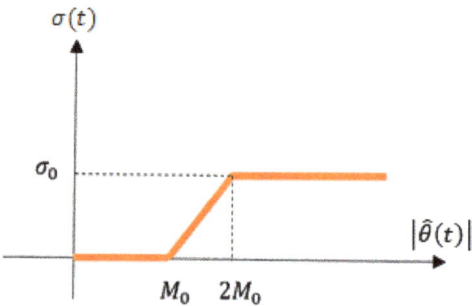

Figure 1. Sigma function behavior diagram.

Therefore, the update laws for estimations of delays, disturbance, and uncertainty bounds are as follows:

$$\begin{aligned} D^q \hat{\tau}_i &= -l_i |s| - \sigma_0(|\hat{\tau}_i|)\hat{\tau}_i, \ \hat{\tau}_i(0) = \overline{\tau}_i, \ i = 1.2 \\ D^q \hat{\rho}_i &= k_0 k_p |s| - \sigma_0(|\hat{\rho}_i|)\hat{\rho}_i, \ i = 1.2 \\ D^q \hat{\beta}_1 &= -k_0 k_p |s| \omega_1(x) - \sigma_0(|\hat{\beta}_1|)\hat{\beta}_1, \\ D^q \hat{\beta}_2 &= -k_0 k_p |s| \omega_2(y) - \sigma_0(|\hat{\beta}_2|)\hat{\beta}_2, \end{aligned} \quad (50)$$

Its stability is demonstrated for chaotic systems with unknown uncertainty, fractional order unknown time delay, and considering PI sliding surface and nonlinear fractional order derivative. □

6. Simulation Results

In this section, the process of synchronizing time-varying chaotic systems with unknown uncertainty and time delay of the fractional order using the proposed control mechanism based on the nonlinear fractional order PID and with the advantage of the adaptive controller and update laws that estimate system parameters is verified, and its accuracy is evaluated. Two modified Jerk chaotic systems with the aforementioned characteristics were utilized for this purpose. The canonical form of the master system's governing equations are as follows [15]:

$$\begin{cases} D^q x_1 = x_2 \\ D^q x_2 = x_3 \\ D^q x_3 = -\varepsilon_1 x_1(t) - x_2(t) - \varepsilon_2 x_3(t) + f_3(x_1(t - \tau_1), t) \end{cases} \quad (51)$$

In this system, $f_3(x_1(t - \tau_1), t)$ is a piecewise linear function, as follows:

$$f_3(x_1(t - \tau_1), t) = \frac{1}{2}(v_0 - v_1)[|x_1(t - \tau_1) + 1| - |x_1(t - \tau_1) - 1|] + v_1 x_1(t - \tau_1) \quad (52)$$

Such that $v_0 < -1 < v_1 < 0$, $v_0 = -2.5$, and $v_1 = -0.5$.
Also, ε_i is a time-varying function, defined as follows.

$$\begin{aligned} \varepsilon_1(t) &= 0.5 + 0.3 \sin(t) \cos(5\pi t) \\ \varepsilon_2(t) &= 0.2 + 0.15 \sin(0.5t) \cos(3\pi t) \end{aligned} \quad (53)$$

If $\varepsilon_i(t) = \varepsilon_{0i} + \Delta \varepsilon_i(t)$, $\Delta \varepsilon_i(t)$ can be considered a part of the uncertainty and summed with the general uncertainty.

Thus, Equation (49) can be rewritten as follows:

$$\begin{cases} D^q x_1 = x_2 \\ D^q x_2 = x_3 \\ D^q x_3 = -\epsilon_{10} x_1(t) - x_2(t) - \epsilon_{20} x_3(t) + f_3(x_1(t-\tau_1), t) \\ \quad\quad + \Delta f^{new}(x(t), t) + d_1(t). \end{cases} \quad (54)$$

in which $\Delta f^{new}(x(t), t) = \Delta f(x(t), t) - \Delta\epsilon_1(t)x_1(t) - \Delta\epsilon_2(t)x_3(t)$ with the previous structure. The same is carried out for the slave system.

When the initial conditions are chosen as $(x_1(0); x_2(0); x_3(0))^T = (-0.5032; 2.8545; -1.37)^T$, the chaotic behavior of the system is as shown in Figure 2.

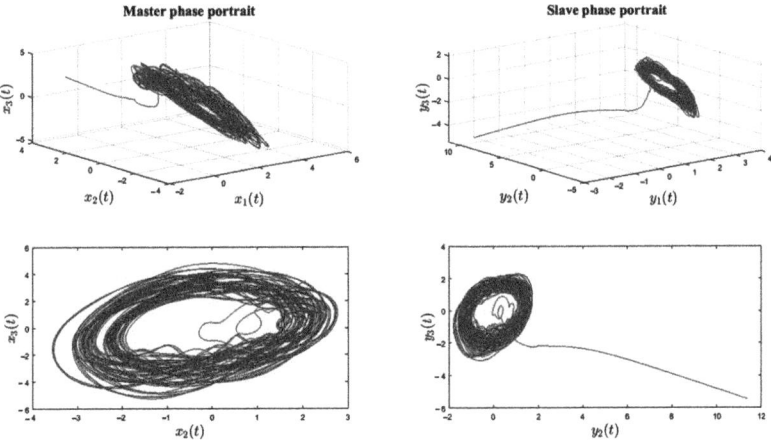

Figure 2. Chaotic behavior of the fractional order Jerk master and slave systems without applying the controller.

If the bounded uncertainty functions of the master and slave systems are as follows:

$$\begin{aligned} \Delta f(x(t), t) &= 0.3 sin(4x_1(t) + x_2(t) - x_3(t)) \\ \Delta g(x(t), t) &= 0.2 sin(y_1(t) + 2y_2(t) - y_3(t)) \end{aligned} \quad (55)$$

The dynamic equations of the master and slave system are as follows:

$$\begin{cases} D^q x_1 = x_2 \\ D^q x_2 = x_3 \\ D^q x_3 = -\epsilon_1 x_1(t) - x_2(t) - \epsilon_2 x_3(t) + f_3(x_1(t-\tau_1), t) \\ \quad\quad + \Delta f^{new}(x(t), t) + d_1(t) \end{cases} \quad (56)$$

The dynamic of the master system follows the following equations:

$$\begin{cases} D^q y_1 = y_2 \\ D^q y_2 = y_3 \\ D^q y_3 = -\epsilon_1 y_1(t) - y_2(t) - \epsilon_2 y_3(t) + g_3(y_1(t-\tau_2), t) \\ \quad\quad + \Delta g^{new}(x(t), t) + d_2(t) + u(t) \end{cases} \quad (57)$$

Such that the nonlinear terms of the slave system are as follows:

$$g_3(y_1(t-\tau_2), t) = \frac{1}{2}(v_0 - v_1)[|y_1(t-\tau_2) + 1| - |y_1(t-\tau_2) - 1|] + v_1 y_1(t-\tau_2) \quad (58)$$

According to the dynamic of the master and slave systems described in Equations (51) and (52), the synchronization error is given as follows:

$$\begin{cases} D^q e_i = e_{i+1} \ 1 \leq i \leq n-1 \\ D^q e_n = \sigma_0^T \cdot e(t) + g(y(t-\tau_2), t) + \Delta g(y(t), t) + d_2(t) \\ \quad - f(x_1(t-\tau_1)) - \Delta f^{new}(x(t), t) - d_1(t) + u(t) \end{cases} \quad (59)$$

Accordingly, the error dynamics for the chaotic Jerk system are as follows:

$$\begin{cases} D^q e_1 = e_2 \\ D^q e_2 = e_3 \\ D^q e_3 = -\varepsilon_1 e_1(t) - e_2(t) - \varepsilon_2 e_3(t) - g(y_1(t-\tau_2)) + f(x_1(t-\tau_1)) \\ \quad + \Delta g^{new}(x(t), t) - \Delta f^{new}(x(t), t) \\ \quad d_2(t) - d_1(t) + u(t) \end{cases} \quad (60)$$

At this stage, we applied the robust adaptive control signal, which is devised by combining the sliding surface based on the structure of the fractional order nonlinear PID controllers and described in Equation (26), to the slave system.

In this article, simulations were run for 100 s. Figure 2 depicts the master and slave systems in three-dimensional space. Figure 3 illustrates the behavior of the master and slave system states in the absence of any controller actions. Figure 4 shows the synchronization of the master and slave system. It is clear that after applying the control signal based on the proposed mechanism, the slave system follows the master system well. Figure 5 depicts the synchronization error of the master and slave system utilizing the proposed mechanism. Figure 6 depicts the control signal based on the proposed method. According to the range of the image's control signal (6), it is unquestionable that the proposed controller can be implemented. As this figure demonstrates, the controller signal exhibited no chattering, and a saturation limit of 24 volts was used, which is simple to implement. In this design, the controller coefficients $k_{11} = k_{22} = 9$ and $k_{12} = k_{21} = 18$ were selected. Also, the gain and time constants of the PID sliding surface are nonlinear fractional orders, as $k_p = 3$, $T_i = 0.8$, and $T_d = 0.65$. The fractional order of the integral part and the derivative of the sliding surface are defined as $\delta = 0.15$ and $\lambda = 0.75$. The parameters of the proposed robust controller are $\bar{\varepsilon} = 0.01$ and $b = 2$. The unknown time delays of the system are $\tau_1 = 0.3$ and $\tau_2 = 0.5$. The time delay of the master system changes to the value of $\tau_1 = 0.45$ at the moment $t = 40$ s, and the time delay of the follower system changes to the value of $\tau_2 = 0.58$ at the moment $t = 50$ s. The error in estimating the uncertainty, disturbance, and delay bounds is shown in Figure 7. Figure 8 shows the uncertainties and disturbances applied to the master and slave systems. The unknown disturbances are applied to both systems as follows:

$$\begin{aligned} d_1(t) &= 0.8 \sin^2 2t + 1.2 \cos 3t + 1.6 \sin 1.3t \\ d_2(t) &= \sin 1.4t + 0.3 \sin \pi t + 0.3 \cos \frac{\pi t}{2} \end{aligned} \quad (61)$$

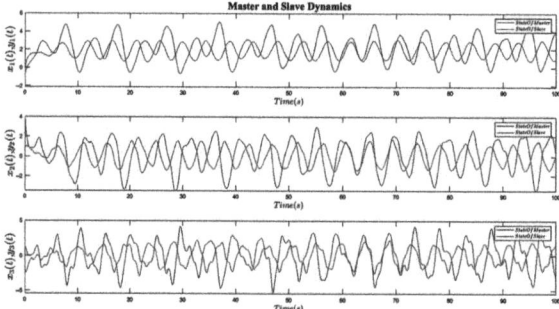

Figure 3. The behavior of the master and slave system states without applying the control signal.

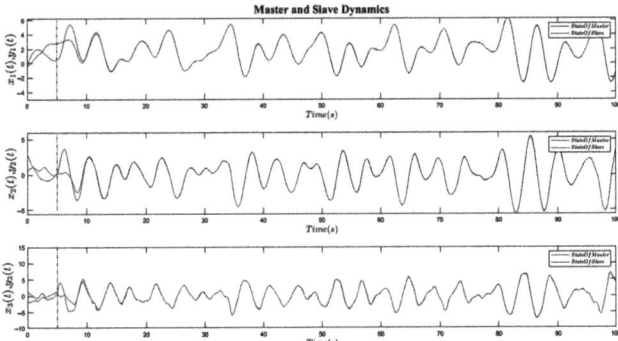

Figure 4. Synchronization of chaotic jerk systems with the help of the proposed control mechanism and application of the control signal at t = 5 s.

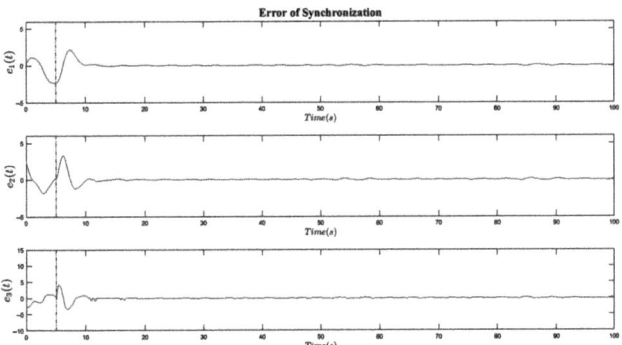

Figure 5. Synchronization error of the master and slave systems using the proposed adaptive sliding mode control mechanism.

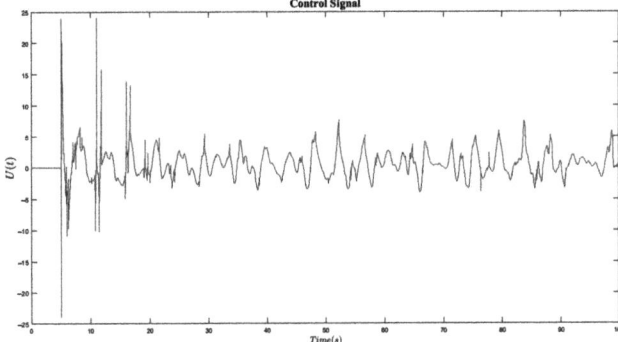

Figure 6. Control signal based on the proposed adaptive sliding mode control mechanism.

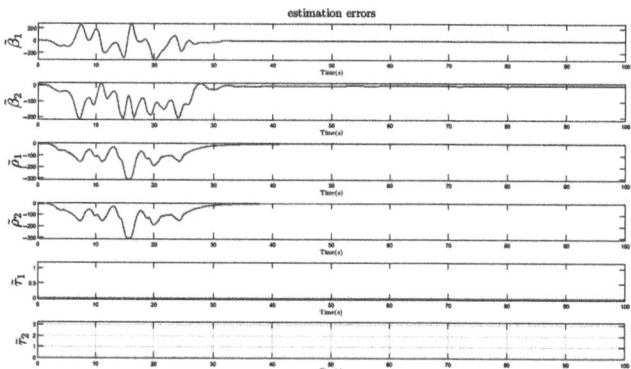

Figure 7. System parameter estimation error including time delay, disturbance bound, and uncertainty bound.

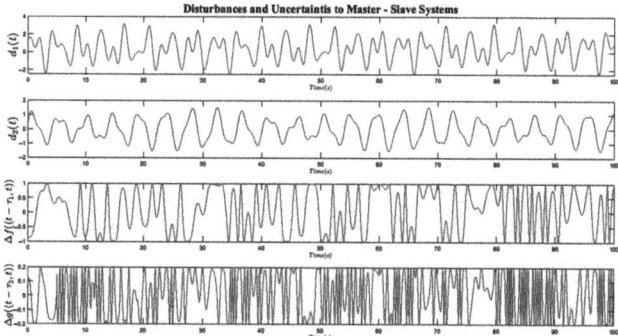

Figure 8. Uncertainties and disturbances in the master and slave systems.

7. Application of Secure Communication in Encryption and Image Retrieval

Despite the uncertainties and time delays in the system, the fractional order chaotic master and slave systems were entirely synchronized according to the proposed mechanism, the details of which were described in the previous section. Images were encrypted using the [27] algorithm in this section. The encrypted image was then transmitted using fractional order chaotic masking and received with high precision before being decoded.

Figure 9 is a block diagram detailing the encryption technique applied to the images. In this block diagram, information is exchanged via a wireless communication channel.

Various statistical parameters, including the histogram difference between the original image and the restored image, correlation, NPCR, PSNR, and information entropy, were calculated for standard color benchmark images and medical color images to demonstrate the efficacy of the proposed method. These parameters are standard criteria that have been used in numerous articles [27].

This section encrypts images for secure communication utilizing the mechanism whose efficacy was evaluated in Section 6. Figure 10 shows the result of image encryption and recovery using secure communication for the original image, and Figure 11 shows their histogram for Aletta (Isekai.Shokudou) color image.

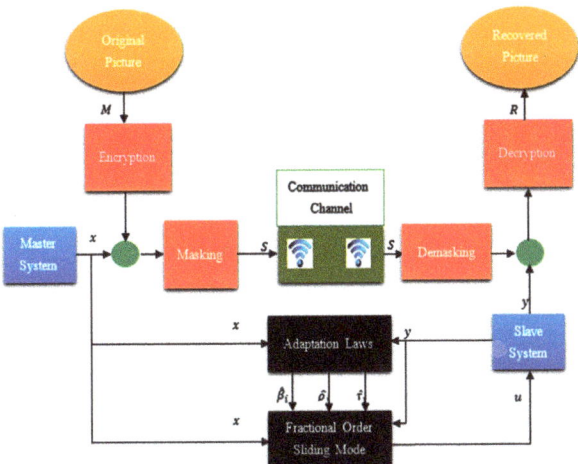

Figure 9. Block diagram of chaotic masking for image encryption.

Figure 10. The original, encrypted, and decrypted color image.

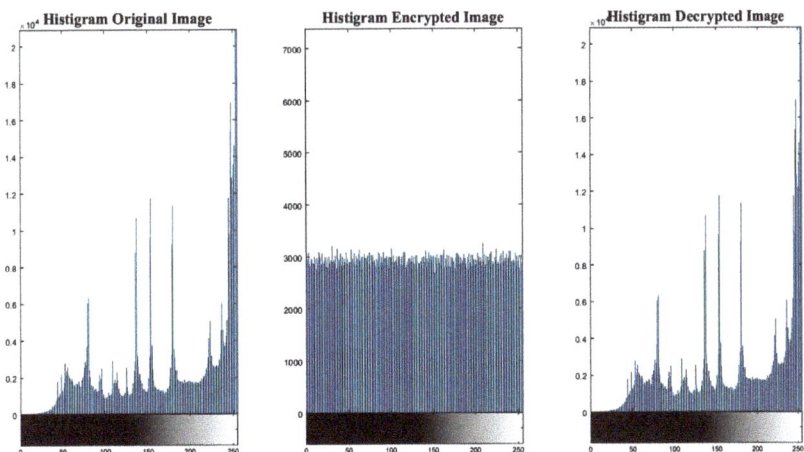

Figure 11. Histogram of the original, encrypted, and decrypted color image.

Figure 12 shows the encryption on the lena color image and Figure 13 shows its histogram.

Figure 12. Original, encrypted, and decrypted color image.

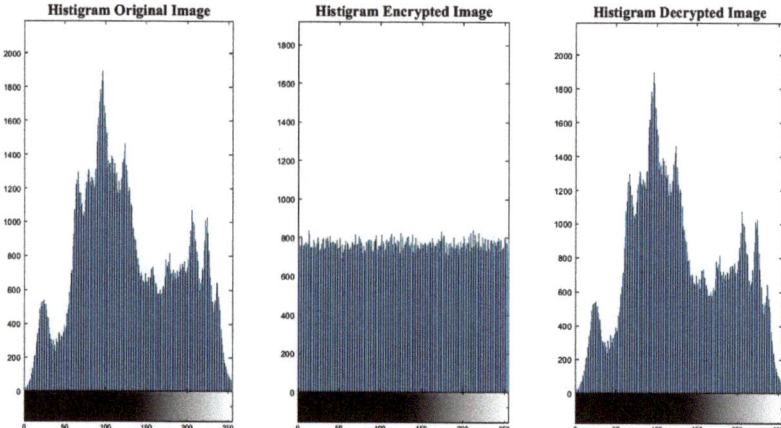

Figure 13. Histogram of the original, encrypted, and decrypted color image.

It can be seen that the decoded images were well restored using the proposed synchronization scheme.

Table 2 shows the results of the statistical criteria of Figures 10 and 12.

Table 2. Results of statistical criteria of color images.

Images	Histogram		Correlation	Differential Attack		PSNR	Information Entropy
	Standard	Encrypted		NPCR (%)	UACI (%)		
Images 10	21,153.1171	21,148.239	0.0068	99.68	33.23	8.10	7.9690
Images 12	18,144.3510	18,143.750	0.0043	99.40	33.46	8.27	7.9700

Image encryption using the above mechanism along with histogram for cameraman's black and white image is shown in Figures 14 and 15, respectively, and for panda is presented in Figures 16 and 17.

Figure 14. The original, encrypted, and decrypted black and white image.

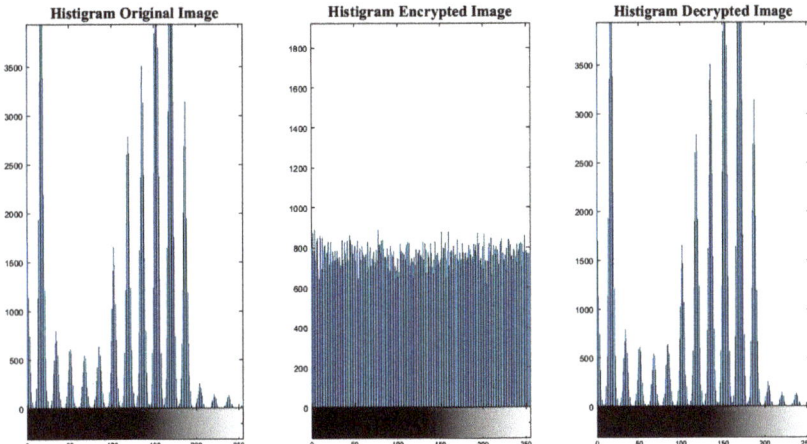

Figure 15. Histogram of the original, encrypted, and decrypted black and white image.

Figure 16. The original, encrypted, and decrypted black and white image.

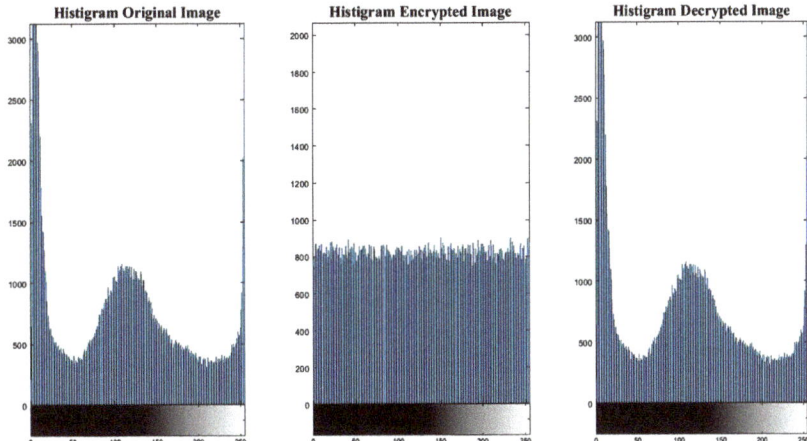

Figure 17. Histogram of the original, encrypted, and decrypted black and white image.

Table 3 shows the results of the statistical criteria of the black and white images in Figures 14 and 16.

Table 3. Results of statistical measures of black and white images.

Images	Histogram		Correlation	Differential Attack		PSNR	Information Entropy
	Main	Decoded		NPCR (%)	UACI (%)		
Images 14	398,232.09375	398,201.1053	0.9923	99.21	33.55	8.9671	7.9783
Images 16	24,466.718750	24,421.32934	0.9953	99.48	33.21	8.0221	7.9458

The encryption of the medical color image along with its histogram for the single image mode is shown in Figures 18 and 19 and for the multiple image in Figures 20 and 21, respectively.

Figure 18. Original, encrypted, and decrypted medical image.

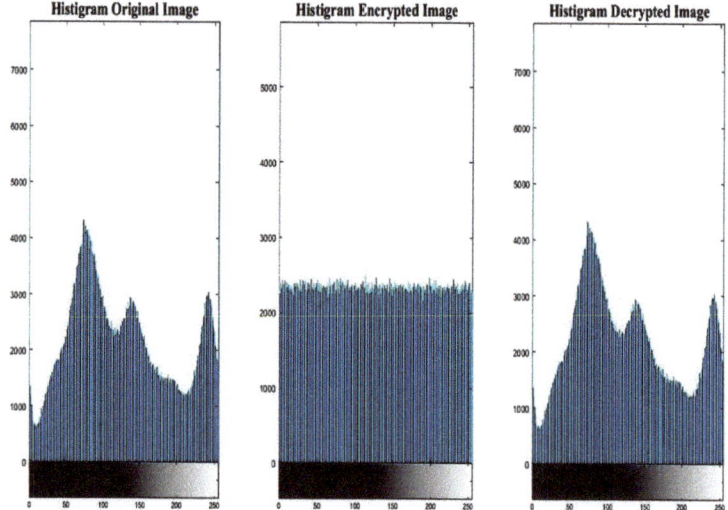

Figure 19. Histogram of the original, encrypted, and decrypted medical image.

Figure 20. The original, encrypted, and decrypted medical image.

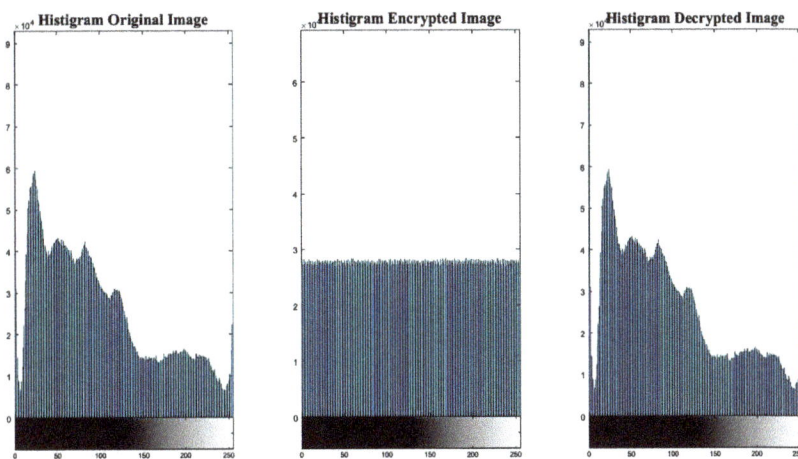

Figure 21. Histogram of the original, encrypted, and decrypted medical image.

Table 4 shows the results of the statistical criteria of the color medical images in Figures 18 and 20. The results of encryption entropy indicate excellent quality of image retrieval.

Table 4. Results of statistical measures of medical images.

Images	Histogram		Correlation	Differential Attack		PSNR	Information Entropy
	Standard	Decrypted		NPCR (%)	UACI (%)		
Images 18	65,536	65,535	0.9986	99.96	33.46	9.23	7.9627
Images 20	65,536	65,534	0.9987	99.97	33.47	9.24	7.9842

8. Conclusions

This study examined a novel adaptive sliding mode control approach for robust synchronization of a class of fractional order chaotic systems with uncertainty, external disturbance, and unknown parameters, such as unknown time delay. In the proposed robust control mechanism, a nonlinear fractional order sliding surface was first proposed based on the structure of nonlinear proportional, integral, and fractional derivative controllers. Using the Lyapunov theory and Lipschitz conditions in chaotic systems, matching criteria were established in order to estimate the unknown parameters of the system. In order to facilitate the implementation process, the control signal's saturation limit was defined, and the robust control system's stability was demonstrated. The synchronization of two fractional order Jerk chaotic systems with the stated characteristics, including uncertainties and unknown time delays, based on the proposed control mechanism was simulated using MATLAB, and the results express the capability and optimal performance of the proposed approach in the robust synchronization of the mentioned systems. In closing, the proposed adaptive sliding mode control approach was implemented in the structure of a chaotic secure communication mechanism, and the simulation results indicate a high level of quality in the secure encryption and decryption of digital images despite the presence of uncertain parameters in the master and slave systems of the communication mechanism.

Author Contributions: Conceptualization, H.Y., R.A., M.R. and A.Z.; methodology, H.Y., R.A., M.R. and A.Z.; software, M.R., H.Y. and A.Z.; validation, H.Y., R.A., M.R. and A.Z.; formal analysis, M.R., H.Y.; investigation, H.Y., R.A., M.R. and A.Z.; resources, M.R., H.Y. and A.Z.; data curation M.R., H.Y. and A.Z.; writing—original draft preparation, M.R., H.Y., R.A. and A.Z.; writing—review and editing, M.R., H.Y. and A.Z.; visualization, M.R., H.Y., R.A. and A.Z.; supervision, A.Z.; All authors have read and agreed to the published version of the manuscript.

Funding: This research received no external funding.

Data Availability Statement: Not applicable.

Conflicts of Interest: The authors declare no conflict of interest.

References

1. Lorenz, E.N. Deterministic Non-Periodic Flow. *J. Atmos. Sci.* **1963**, *20*, 130–141. [CrossRef]
2. Chen, G.R.; Ueta, T. Yet Another Chaotic Attractor. *Int. J. Bifurc. Chaos Appl. Sci. Eng.* **1999**, *9*, 1465–1466. [CrossRef]
3. Lü, J.H.; Chen, G.R. A New Chaotic Attractor Coined. *Int. J. Bifurc. Chaos Appl. Sci. Eng.* **2002**, *12*, 659–661. [CrossRef]
4. Liu, C.X.; Liu, T.; Liu, L.; Liu, K. A New Chaotic Attractor. *Chaos Solitons Fractals* **2004**, *22*, 1031–1038. [CrossRef]
5. Fernandez, A.; Baleanu, D.; Srivastava, H. Series representations for fractionalcalculus operators involving generalised Mittag-Leffler functions. *Commun. Nonlinear Sci. Numer. Simul.* **2019**, *67*, 517–527. [CrossRef]
6. Zhang, J.; Gao, F.; Chen, Y.; Zou, Y. Parameter identification of fractional-order chaotic system based on chemical reaction optimization. In Proceedings of the 2018 2nd International Conference on Management Engineering, Software Engineering and Service Sciences, New York, NY, USA, 13–15 January 2018; pp. 217–222.
7. Ionescu, C.; Lopes, A.; Copot, D.; Machado, J.T.; Bates, J. The role of fractionalcalculus in modeling biological phenomena: A review. *Commun. Nonlinear Sci. Numer. Simul.* **2017**, *51*, 141–159. [CrossRef]
8. Smida, M.B.; Sakly, A.; Vaidyanathan, S.; Azar, A.T. Control-based maximum power point tracking for a grid-connected hybrid renewable energy system optimized by particle swarm optimization. In *Advances in System Dynamics and Control*; Tomorrow's Research Today: Rochester, NY, USA, 2018; pp. 58–89.
9. Vinagre, B.; Feliu, V. Modeling and control of dynamic system using fractional calculus: Application to lectrochemical processes and flexible structures. In Proceedings of the 41st IEEE Conference on Decision and Control, Las Vegas, NV, USA, 10–13 December 2002; Volume 1, pp. 214–239.
10. Li, R.-G.; Wu, H.-N. Secure communication on fractionalorder chaotic systems via adaptive sliding mode control with teaching–learning–feedback-based optimization. *Nonlinear Dyn.* **2018**, *92*, 1221–1243.
11. Mandelbrot, B.B.; Van Ness, J.W. Fractional Brownian motions, fractional noises and applications. *SIAM Rev.* **1968**, *10*, 422–437. [CrossRef]
12. Duarte, F.B.; Machado, J.T. Chaotic phenomena and fractional-order dynamics in the trajectory control of redundant manipulators. *Nonlinear Dyn.* **2002**, *29*, 315–342. [CrossRef]
13. Petráš, I. Fractional-order nonlinear controllers: Design and implementation notes. In Proceedings of the 2016 17th International Carpathian Control Conference (ICCC), High Tatras, Slovakia, 29 May–1 June 2016; IEEE: Piscataway, NJ, USA, 2016; pp. 579–583.
14. Mirrezapour, S.Z.; Zare, A. A new fractional sliding mode controller based on nonlinear fractional-order proportional integral derivative controller structure to synchronize fractional-order chaotic systems with uncertainty and disturbances. *J. Vib. Control.* **2021**, *28*, 1–13. [CrossRef]
15. Zare, A.; Mirrezapour, S.Z.; Hallaji, M.; Shoeibi, A.; Jafari, M.; Ghassemi, N.; Alizadehsani, R.; Mosavi, A. Robust Adaptive Synchronization of a Class of Uncertain Chaotic Systems with Unknown Time-Delay. *Appl. Sci.* **2020**, *10*, 8875. [CrossRef]
16. Mohammadpour, S.; Binazadeh, T. Robust Observer-Based Synchronization of Unified Chaotic Systems in the Presence of Dead-Zone Nonlinearity Input. *J. Control Iran. Soc. Instrum. Control Eng. (ISICE)* **2018**, *11*, 25–36.
17. Modiri, A.; Mobayen, S. Adaptive terminal sliding mode control scheme for synchronization of fractional-order uncertain chaotic systems. *ISA Trans.* **2020**, *105*, 33–50. [CrossRef]
18. Mostafaee, J.; Mobayen, S.; Vaseghi, B.; Vahedi, M. Dynamical Analysis and Finite-Time Fast Synchronization of a Novel Autonomous Hyper-Chaotic System. *J. Intell. Proced. Electr. Technol.* **2021**, *12*, 47.
19. Rasouli, M.; Zare, A.; Hallaji, M.; Alizadehsani, R. The Synchronization of a Class of Time-Delayed Chaotic Systems Using Sliding Mode Control Based on a Fractional-Order Nonlinear PID Sliding Surface and Its Application in Secure Communication. *Axioms* **2022**, *11*, 738. [CrossRef]
20. Aghababa, M.P. Finite-time chaos control and synchronization of fractional order nonautonomous chaotic (hyperchaotic) systems using fractional nonsingular terminal sliding mode technique. *Nonlinear Dynam.* **2012**, *69*, 247–261. [CrossRef]
21. Balochian, S.; Sedigh, A.K.; Zare, A. Variable structure control of linear time invariant fractional order systems using a finite number of state feedback law. *Commun. Nonlinear Sci. Numer. Simul.* **2011**, *16*, 1433–1442. [CrossRef]
22. Chen, W.; Dai, H.; Song, Y.; Zhang, Z. Convex Lyapunov functions for stability analysis of fractional order systems. *IET Control Theory Appl.* **2017**, *11*, 1070–1074. [CrossRef]

23. Aguila-Camacho, N.; Duarte-Mermoud, M.A.; Gallegos, J.A. Lyapunov functions for fractional order systems. *Commun. Nonlinear Sci. Numer. Simul.* **2014**, *19*, 2951–2957. [CrossRef]
24. Chen, X.; Park, J.H.; Cao, J.; Qiu, J. Sliding mode synchronization of multiple chaotic systems with uncertainties and disturbances. *Appl. Math. Comput.* **2017**, *308*, 161–173. [CrossRef]
25. Draa, K.C.; Zemouche, A.; Alma, M.; Voos, H.; Darouach, M. *New Trends in Observer-Based Control a Practical Guide to Process and Engineering Applications*; Elsevier: Amsterdam, The Netherlands, 2019; pp. 99–135.
26. Petras, I. *Fractional-Order Nonlinear Systems: Modeling, Analysis and Simulation*; Springer Science & Business Media: Berlin/Heidelberg, Germany, 2011.
27. Kekha Javan, A.A.; Zare, A.; Alizadehsani, R. Multi-State Synchronization of Chaotic Systems with Distributed Fractional Order Derivatives and Its Application in Secure Communications. *Big Data Cogn. Comput.* **2022**, *6*, 82. [CrossRef]

Disclaimer/Publisher's Note: The statements, opinions and data contained in all publications are solely those of the individual author(s) and contributor(s) and not of MDPI and/or the editor(s). MDPI and/or the editor(s) disclaim responsibility for any injury to people or property resulting from any ideas, methods, instructions or products referred to in the content.

Article

Analysis and Design of Robust Controller for Polynomial Fractional Differential Systems Using Sum of Squares

Hassan Yaghoubi [1], Assef Zare [1,*] and Roohallah Alizadehsani [2]

1 Department of Electrical and Electronic Engineering, Gonabad Branch, Islamic Azad University, Gonabad 6518115743, Iran
2 Institute for Intelligent Systems Research and Innovation (IISRI), Deakin University, Victoria 3216, Australia
* Correspondence: assefzare@gmail.com

Abstract: This paper discusses the robust stability and stabilization of polynomial fractional differential (PFD) systems with a Caputo derivative using the sum of squares. In addition, it presents a novel method of stability and stabilization for PFD systems. It demonstrates the feasibility of designing problems that cannot be represented in LMIs (linear matrix inequalities). First, sufficient conditions of stability are expressed for the PFD equation system. Based on the results, the fractional differential system is Mittag–Leffler stable when there is a polynomial function to satisfy the inequality conditions. These functions are obtained from the sum of the square (SOS) approach. The result presents a valuable method to select the Lyapunov function for the stability of PFD systems. Then, robust Mittag–Leffler stability conditions were able to demonstrate better convergence performance compared to asymptotic stabilization and a robust controller design for a PFD equation system with unknown system parameters, and design performance based on a polynomial state feedback controller for PFD-controlled systems. Finally, simulation results indicate the effectiveness of the proposed theorems.

Keywords: polynomial fractional-order system; robust controller; stability; stabilization; Mittag–Leffler stable

MSC: 93D09; 93B51

Citation: Yaghoubi, H.; Zare, A.; Alizadehsani, R. Analysis and Design of Robust Controller for Polynomial Fractional Differential Systems Using Sum of Squares. *Axioms* **2022**, *11*, 623. https://doi.org/10.3390/axioms11110623

Academic Editor: Valery Y. Glizer

Received: 29 September 2022
Accepted: 2 November 2022
Published: 7 November 2022

Publisher's Note: MDPI stays neutral with regard to jurisdictional claims in published maps and institutional affiliations.

Copyright: © 2022 by the authors. Licensee MDPI, Basel, Switzerland. This article is an open access article distributed under the terms and conditions of the Creative Commons Attribution (CC BY) license (https://creativecommons.org/licenses/by/4.0/).

1. Introduction

Fractional calculus concerns mathematical relations about the generalizations of differentiation and integration to a noninteger order with a history of more than 300 years. Integer-order derivatives and integrals as specific cases paved the way for this mathematical branch to become very popular in fractional calculus, which resulted in many applications in engineering, physics, economics, etc. [1]. In addition, new possibilities have caused fractional calculus to model various physical systems in engineering, which have more accuracy than the classical integer system such as a robot, chaos, information science, and so on [2,3]. Moreover, new methods were proposed to solve the complexity of modeling by the fractional-order method [4]. Recently, the study of the stability and stabilization of fractional differential equations (FDEs) has attracted a lot of attention in control theory [5,6]. To this aim, many studies have focused on linear fractional differential and nonlinear fractional differential equations [7], which could conform to linear FDE systems and analyze stability based on LMI conditions.

Zhang, Tian, et al. [8] considered the stability of nonlinear FDEs, and similar stability conditions of Caputo FDEs were obtained for Riemann–Liouville FDEs. Based on the result, the stability condition of nonlinear FDEs is the same as linear FDEs if the nonlinear section follows the same conditions. Wang et al. [9] investigated the asymptotical stability of nonlinear FDEs and sufficient conditions obtained by using the state feedback stabilization controller. Furthermore, the pole replacement method was used in linear systems to design the controller gains for nonlinear FDEs [10].

Nowadays, stability analysis of nonlinear FDE systems has been considered by researchers. Thus, most of the studies are related to stability and stabilization for the fractional differential equation [11]. FDE is analyzed by Lyapunov's first and second methods. In the first method, nonlinear FDEs are converted to linear FDEs at the equilibrium point. Therefore, the nonlinear FDE is asymptotically stable if the linearization system is asymptotically stable [12,13]. In the second method, energy is decreased and allows us to evaluate the stability of the system without integrating the differential equation explicitly. The Lyapunov technique provides a sufficient condition for the asymptotic stabilization of systems. In this regard, the LMI approach can be used as a method for selecting a Lyapunov candidate. The LMI method is based on numerical solutions and optimization due to its popularity. Various studies have been conducted in the field of stability evaluation by the LMI method. In the study of Lu and Chen [14], less conservative conditions have been evaluated in terms of LMIs for robust stability and stabilization of FO dynamic interval systems. Furthermore, Li and Zhang [15] presented robust stability of the FO linear uncertain system by focusing on the observer and obtaining the necessary conditions. All of the results in some studies [14–16] were obtained based on LMI, although many design problems cannot be represented by the LMI approach. The analysis stability by using Lyapunov's method is considered an explicit way of solving the FDE in nonlinear FDE systems. Thus, Mittag–Leffler introduced stability for nonlinear fractional differential systems by the fractional Lyapunov's method [17]. Based on this method, systems are stable but have no candidate for the Lyapunov function [18]. Two theorems were proved for fractional nonlinear time-delay systems that were related to stability in the study of Badri and Tavazoei [19]. M-L stability for nonlinear FDE systems can generalize better convergence performance against asymptotic stabilization. Chen et al. [20] studied the stabilization of fractional nonautonomous systems by using the M-L function and the Lyapunov direct method. Some studies reported that it is usually difficult to find a Lyapunov candidate and calculate a fractional derivative for the FDE system (e.g., [10,18–20]). By considering all of the above-mentioned studies, a new method was presented for finding a Lyapunov candidate function. This method can help find the Lyapunov function more easily than the previous methods. The result is based on the new property of the Caputo fractional derivative, which allows the stability analysis of many FO systems to be studied [21,22].

Some studies reported that stability analysis based on M-L stability is more efficient than asymptotic stabilization [17,19–23]. In this paper, the application of the Lyapunov function method was expanded in PFD systems. To this aim, the stability of the PFD system was analyzed by using three polynomial PFD inequalities, which can be solved via the SOS toolbox in Matlab. Then, robust Mittag–Leffler stability conditions were obtained based on the SOS approach, which can exhibit better convergence. The desired robust M-L stabilization was obtained by selecting the polynomials state feedback control, which resulted in designing flexible controllers.

This paper is organized as follows. In Section 2, some definitions and lemmas are given. A sufficient condition of stability for PFD is given in Section 3. Section 4 provides sufficient conditions for robust stability and the stabilization of the PFD system. Simulation results are given in Section 5. Finally, some conclusions are made in Section 6.

2. Preliminaries

Notations and Definitions

There are several definitions of FO derivatives, among which Riemann–Liouville and Caputo's definition is considered the most common and practical definition in the literature. Thus, the Caputo definition is selected in this study.

Definition 1 ([8]). *The Caputo fractional derivative is defined as follows*

$$D_t^q f(t) = \frac{1}{\Gamma(n-q)} \int_{t_0}^t (t-\tau)^{n-q-1} f^{(n)}(\tau) d\tau. \tag{1}$$

where q is the fractional order and n shows integer.

$$n - 1 \leq q < n$$

$\Gamma(\cdot)$ represents the Euler's function

$$\Gamma(t) = \int_0^\infty x^{t-1} e^{-x} dx. \tag{2}$$

Mittag–Leffler is a function that is mostly used in solving in fractional-order systems as follows

$$E_q(z) = \sum_{k=0}^\infty \frac{z^k}{\Gamma(kq+1)}. \tag{3}$$

where $q > 0$. The M-L function with two parameters appears most frequently and has the following form

$$E_{q,\beta}(z) = \sum_{k=0}^\infty \frac{z^k}{\Gamma(kq+\beta)}. \tag{4}$$

where $q > 0, \beta > 0$.

By using the Caputo derivative, an FO system is defined by

$$D_t^q x(t) = (A(x) + \Delta A(x))x(t) + u(x). \tag{5}$$

where $x = (x_1, x_2, \ldots, x_n)^T \in R^n$ is the state vector of the state system, $A(x) \in R^{n \times n}$ defines a nonlinear matrix function field in the $n \times n$-dimensional space, and $\Delta A(x)$ represents the admissible uncertainty function. q is the order of the fractional derivative, $(0 < q \leq 1)$ $u(x)$ as the control input. Let the equilibrium point be $x = 0$ when $u(x) = 0$.

Definition 2 ([24]). *The sum of squares (SOS) approach is an important subset of the polynomials used for modeling and controlling nonlinear systems. Assume that $\sum_n$ is the set of all SOS polynomials with degree n defined as follows*

$$\sum_n = \{s \in R_n | \exists M \prec \infty, \exists \{p_i\}_{i=1}^M \subset R_n \text{ such that } s = \sum_{i=1}^M p_i^2 \}$$

where R indicates the real number. Assume that monomial $\{m_{\alpha_j}\}_{j=1}^k$ is defined as $m_\alpha(x) = x^\alpha = x_1^{\alpha_1} . x_2^{\alpha_2} . \ldots . x_n^{\alpha_n}$, $\alpha \in Z_+$. Then, polynomial p is the issue of squares if p is a monomial $\{m_{\alpha_j}\}_{j=1}^k$ linear combination.

$\{m_{\alpha_j}\}_{j=1}^k$ so that $m_\alpha : R^n \to R$ subject to

$$m_\alpha(x) = x^\alpha = x_1^{\alpha_1} . x_2^{\alpha_2} . \ldots . x_n^{\alpha_n}, \alpha \in Z_+, \{c_j\}_{j=1}^k \in R,$$
$$p = \sum_{j=1}^k c_j m_{\alpha_j}$$
$$p = \sum_{j=1}^k c_j m_{\alpha_j}, \{c_j\}_{j=1}^k \in R$$

A subset of R_n, $R_{n,d} = \{p \in R_n | \deg p \leq d\}$ is defined in such a way that n is the number of variables and d is the degree of polynomials. Based on this definition, we can define $\Sigma_{n,d}$, which can directly lead to sufficient conditions for polynomial programming. Therefore, we have $\Sigma_{n,d} = \Sigma_n \cap R_{n,d}$.

Lemma 1 ([11]). *Fix $p \in R_{n,2d}$. $p \in \Sigma_{n,2d}$ if and only if there exists a $Q \geq 0$ such that*

$$p(x) = z^*_{n,d}(x) Q z_{n,d}(x) \tag{6}$$

According to Lemma 1, polynomial p is SOS if necessary and sufficient conditions are satisfied for Lemma 1.
$z_{n,d}(x)$ is monomials with n variables of degree less than or equal to d.

Theorem 1 ([11]). *The polynomial system $\dot{x}(t) = f(x(t))$ is globally asymptotically stable about equilibrium point if there exists a positive-definite function $V : R^n \to R_+$ such that $-\dot{v}(x)$ is positive-definite.*

This theorem is important in stability, which is defined based on the following important theorem in the field of stability of polynomial systems.

Theorem 2. *Given the system $\dot{x}(t) = f(x(t))$ and fixed positive-definite functions l_1, $l_2 \in R^n$, the system is globally asymptotically stable if there exists $v(x) \in R^n$ with $v(0) = 0$ such that*

$$\begin{aligned} v(x) - l_1 &\in \Sigma_n \,. \\ -(\dot{v}(x) + l_2) &\in \Sigma_n \,. \\ \dot{v}(x) &= \Delta v(x) A(x) x \end{aligned} \tag{7}$$

Proof. Given a finite set $\{p_i\}_{i=0}^m \in R_n$, the existence of $(p_0 + \sum_{i=1}^m \alpha_i p_i) \in \Sigma_n$ is such that $\{\alpha_i\}_{i=1}^m \in R$. It is evident that the conditions $(v(x) - l_1)$ and $-(\nabla v(x) A(x) + l_2)$ are SOS polynomials if a polynomial function of $v(x)$ is found for satisfying these conditions. The positive definiteness of l_1 and l_2 is selected to satisfy the assumptions of theorem, in which both $v(x)$ and $-\dot{v}(x)$ are positive-definite. □

Definition 3 ([20]). *Assume that $v(x) : \Omega \to R$, $\Omega \in R^n$ is a convex function in Ω and $x : [t_0, \infty) \to \Omega$ is a continuous differential function. For $t \geq t_0$*

$$^c_{t_0}D^q_t v(x) \leq \left(\frac{\partial v}{\partial x}\right)^T {}^c_{t_0}D^q_t x(t). \tag{8}$$

Definition 4 ([20]). *Consider the FO nonlinear system*

$$^c_{t_0}D^q_t x(t) = A(x) x(t). \tag{9}$$

If the convex Lyapunov function $v(x)$ can satisfy the following conditions, $x = 0$ is an equilibrium point for the FO system and the system is globally Mittag–Leffler stable in equilibrium point.

$$\begin{aligned} \gamma_1 ||x||^\alpha &\leq v(x) \leq \gamma_2 ||x||^{\alpha b}. \\ {}^c_{t_0}D^q_t v(x) &\leq -\gamma_3 ||x||^{\alpha b}. \end{aligned} \tag{10}$$

3. PFDE Stability

In this section, a sufficient condition of stability is presented for the PFD equations system.

Theorem 3. *Consider the system ${}^c_{t_0}D^q_t x(t) = A(x) x(t)$. Suppose that Let $x = 0$ is an equilibrium point in the domain $D \subset R^n$ and $v(x) : [0, \infty) \times D \to R$ is a continuously differentiable* function and locally Lipschitz in x. System is M-L stable in $x = 0$ if and only if there exists $w_1(x)$, $w_2(x)$, $w_3(x) \in \sum_n$ by satisfying the following condition

$$w_1(x) \leq v(x) \leq w_2(x).$$
$$_{t_0}^{C}D_t^q v(x) \leq -w_3(x). \tag{11}$$

Proof. It follows from inequalities (11) that

$$_{t_0}^{C}D_t^q v(x) \leq -w_3(x) \leq \frac{-w_3(x)}{w_2(x)} v(x) \leq -inf_x\left(\frac{w_3(x)}{w_2(x)}\right)v(x) = -\beta v(x). \tag{12}$$

where $\beta = inf_x\left(\frac{W_3(x)}{W_2(x)}\right)$.
$w_2(x), w_3(x)$ are positive and have the same degree, therefore: $\beta > 0$.
There exists a nonnegative function $m_0(t)$ satisfying

$$_{t_0}^{C}D_t^q v(x) + m_0(t) = -\beta v(x). \tag{13}$$

By taking the Laplace transform from both sides of Equation (13)

$$v(s) = \frac{v(0)s^{q-1} - M_0(s)}{s^q + \beta}$$
$$s^q v(s) - v(0)s^{q-1} + M(s) = -\beta v(s) \tag{14}$$

Then, if $x(0) = 0$, then $v(0) = 0$, and if $x \neq 0$, then $v(0) > 0$. Applying the inverse Laplace transform to (14) and according to Definition 1 gives

$$v(t) = v(0)E_q(-\beta t^q) - M(t)\left[t^{q-1}E_q(-\beta t^q)\right]. \tag{15}$$

$t^{q-1} \geq 0, E_q \geq 0$ are nonnegative functions. It follows that

$$v(t) \leq v(0)E_q(-\beta t^q). \tag{16}$$

Substituting (16) into (11) yields

$$w_1(x) \leq v(0)E_q(-\beta t^q) = v(0)\sum_{k=0}^{\infty}\frac{(-\beta t^q)^k}{\Gamma(kq+1)}. \tag{17}$$

where $v(0) > 0$ for $x(0) \neq 0$.
Therefore $w_1(x)$ is bounded, also $v(x)$ is locally Lipschitz in x. $v(0, x(0)) = 0$ if and only if $x(0) = 0$, which guarantees the Mittag–Leffler stability of system (9). □

4. Robust Stability

In this section, a sufficient condition of robust stability is presented for the PFD equations system. The uncertain FDE system (18) is robust M-L stable if there is SOS polynomial $w_1(x), w_2(x), w_3(x)$ so that conditions (20) are satisfied.

Theorem 4. *Consider the FO nonlinear system*

$$_{t_0}^{C}D_t^q x(t) = (A(x) + \Delta A(x,t))x(t). \tag{18}$$

where $\Delta A(x, t)$ represents the admissible uncertainty function and where the following condition is satisfied

$$||\Delta A(x,t)|| \leq \gamma. \tag{19}$$

This polynomial FO system is robust Mittag–Leffler stability if and only if this condition is satisfied

$$w_1(x) \leq v(x) \leq w_2(x). \tag{20}$$

$$\left(\frac{\partial v(x)}{\partial x}\right)^T A(x)x(t) \leq -w_3(x) - \sum_{k=1}^M \alpha_k ||x||^{2k}. \tag{21}$$

$$\left\|\frac{\partial v(x)}{\partial x}\right\| \gamma ||x|| \leq w(x). \tag{22}$$

$$w(x) - \sum_{k=1}^M \alpha_k ||x||^{2k} \leq (1-\eta)w_3(x). \tag{23}$$

where: $w_1(x), w_2(x), w_3(x)$ are SOS, $\alpha_k > 0$, $M \in \mathbb{N}$ and $\eta \in (0,1)$.

Proof. The convex function $v(x) = x(t)^T p(x) x(t)$ is selected as the Lyapunov function for the PFD system ${}_{t_0}^{c}D_t^q x(t) = (A(x) + \Delta A(x,t))x(t)$. Based on Definition 3, we have

$$\begin{aligned}{}_{t_0}^{c}D_t^q v(x) &\leq \left(\frac{\partial v(x)}{\partial x}\right)^T (A(x) + \Delta A(x))x(t) = \\ \left(\frac{\partial v(x)}{\partial x}\right)^T A(x)x(t) + \left(\frac{\partial v(x)}{\partial x}\right)^T \Delta A(x)x(t) &\leq \left(\frac{\partial v(x)}{\partial x}\right)^T A(x)x(t) + \left\|\frac{\partial v(x)}{\partial x}\right\| \gamma ||x|| \\ &\leq -w_3(x) - \sum_{k=1}^M \alpha_k x^{2k} + w(x) \leq -\eta w_3(x).\end{aligned} \tag{24}$$

Therefore, according to Theorem 3, the system is Mittag–Leffler stable. □

For simplicity, we assume that

$$h(x) = (1-\eta)w_3(x) + \sum_{k=1}^M \alpha_k ||x||^{2k} - w(x). \tag{25}$$

Therefore, if conditions (20)–(23) are satisfied and $h(x) \geq 0$, the system is Mittag–Leffler stable. In this theorem, if $\Delta A(x,t) = 0$ then $\gamma = 0, \alpha = 0, \eta = 0$ and conditions of Theorem 4 are converted to Theorem 3.

5. Robust Stabilization

In this section, robust stability PFD equations are studied by designing a polynomial feedback controller.

Theorem 5. *Consider the PFDE systems*

$${}_{t_0}^{c}D_t^q x(t) = (A(x) + \Delta A(x))x(t) + u(x). \tag{26}$$

System (26) is robust Mittag–Leffler stability if and only if the condition of Theorem 4 is satisfied for $\overline{A}(x) = A(x) - k(x)$. By using state feedback controller, $u(x) = -k(x)x$, $k(x) \in R^{n \times n}$, the closed-loop system including (23) becomes as follows

$${}_{t_0}^{c}D_t^q x(t) = (A(x) - k(x))x + \Delta A(x)x = \overline{A}(x)x + \Delta A(x)x. \tag{27}$$

The main purpose is designing the controller, which ensures asymptotic stability. The flowchart of the proposed method is drawn in Figure 1.

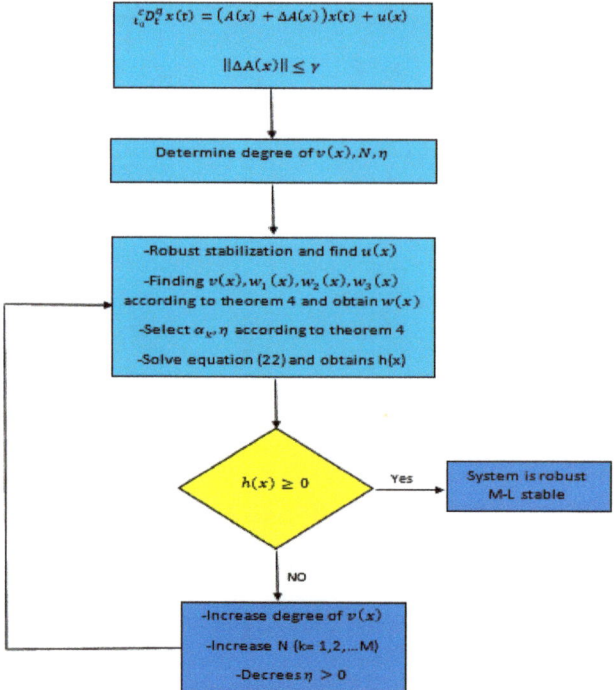

Figure 1. The proposed method.

6. Examples and Simulations

In this section, by giving examples, we show the efficiency of the methods expressed in Theorems 3–5.

Example 1. *Consider the following PFD equations system*

$$\begin{aligned}
{}_{t_0}^{c}D_t^{0.8}x_1(t) &= -x_1 - 2x_1x_2^2 - 2x_2^3. \\
{}_{t_0}^{c}D_t^{0.8}x_2(t) &= -2x_1^2x_2 - 2x_2 + 0.33x_2^3. \\
A(x) &= \begin{bmatrix} -1 & -2x_1x_2 - 2x_2^2 \\ -2x_1x_2 & 0.33x_2^2 - 2 \end{bmatrix}, \quad \Delta A(x) = 0
\end{aligned} \quad (28)$$

By using SOSTOOLS we have

$$v(x) = 0.40401x_1^4 + 0.375x_1^2x_2^2 + 0.866x_1^2 + 0.396x_2^3x_1 - 0.026x_1x_2 \\ + 0.473x_2^4 + 0.918x_2^2. \quad (29)$$

The Lyapunov function obtained is degrees four in this example, whereas no quadratic function can be found for the system.
$v(x) = z^T Q z$, where $z^T = \begin{bmatrix} x_1 & x_2 & x_1^2 & x_1x_2 & x_2^2 \end{bmatrix}$ and

$$Q = \begin{bmatrix} 0.8662 & -0.0134 & 0.0000 & 0.0000 & 0.0000 \\ -0.0134 & 0.9180 & 0.0000 & 0.0000 & 0.0000 \\ 0.0000 & 0.0000 & 0.4016 & 0.0000 & -0.1046 \\ 0.0000 & 0.0000 & 0.000 & 0.5843 & 0.1981 \\ 0.0000 & 0.0000 & -0.1046 & 0.1981 & 0.4737 \end{bmatrix} \quad (30)$$

According to Theorem 3:

$$w_1(x) = 0.246x_1^4 + 0.22875x_1^2 x_2^2 + 0.571x_1^2 + 0.1702x_2^3 x_1 - 0.026x_1 x_2 \\ + 0.010x_2^4 + 0.605x_2^2. \quad (31)$$

$$w_2(x) = 0.741x_1^8 + 0.695x_1^6 x_2^2 + 1.866x_1^6 + 0.3315x_2^3 x_1^5 - 0.0228x_1^5 x_2 \\ + 1.575x_2^4 x_1^4 + 1.683x_2^2 x_1^4 + 0.695x_1^4 x_2^6 + 1.866x_1^2 x_2^4 \quad (32) \\ + 0.3315x_2^7 x_1 - 0.0228x_2^5 x_1 + 0.875x_2^8 + 1.683x_2^6.$$

$$w_3(x) = -4.77x_1^4 x_2^2 - 1.606x_1^4 - 5.590x_1^3 x_2^3 + 0.053x_1^3 x_2 - 0.0075x_1^2 x_2^6 \\ - 5.064x_1^2 x_2^4 - 9.38x_1^2 x_2^2 - 1.73x_1^2 - 0.011x_1 x_2^7 \quad (33) \\ - 1.935x_1 x_2^5 - 6.192x_1 x_1 x_2^3 + 0.0803x_1 x_1 x_2^2 - 0.018x_2^8.$$

Then $x = 0$ is Mittag–Leffler stable.

Figure 2 is drawn for different initial conditions that show the stability of the system (25).

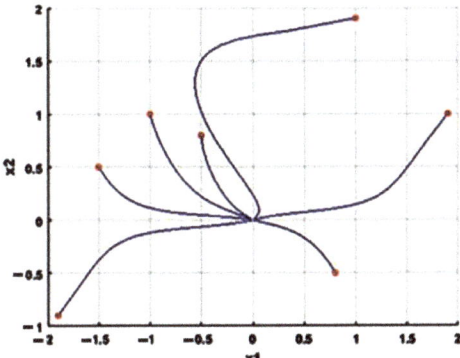

Figure 2. Phase portrait of $x_1(t), x_2(t)$ for PFDE nonlinear system (28).

Example 2. *Consider the following PFD system*

$$\begin{aligned} {}^c_{t_0}D_t^{0.8} x_1(t) &= -4x_1 + 2x_1 x_2^2 + 0.2x_1 \sin(x_1 + 2x_2). \\ {}^c_{t_0}D_t^{0.8} x_2(t) &= -x_2 - 2x_1^2 x_2 + 0.3x_2 \cos x_1. \end{aligned} \quad (34)$$

Thus $A(x) = \begin{bmatrix} -4 & 2x_1 x_2 \\ -2x_1^2 x_2 & -1 \end{bmatrix}$, $\Delta A(x(t)) = \begin{bmatrix} 0.2\sin(x_1 + 2x_2) & 0 \\ 0 & 0.3\cos x_1 \end{bmatrix}$ is the uncertainty function and $||\Delta A(x)|| \leq 0.36$. The state response of the system (34) with $q = 0.8$ demonstrate the instability of the system. According to Equation (26), we obtain polynomial controller $u_1(x) = 2.98x_1 + 4.0761x_2^2 x_1$ and obtain the condition of Theorem 4 by using SOSTOOLS.

The degree of Lyapunov function is 6 by using $\eta = 0.01$, $\alpha_1 = 3.6$ in Equations (21) and (23).

$$v(x) = 0.0328x_1^6 + 0.3831x_1^4 x_2^2 + 0.3287x_1^4 + 1.211x_1^2 x_2^4 1.512x_1^2 x_2^2 \\ + 0.9734x_1^2 + 1.285x_2^6 + 1.313x_2^4 + 1.276x_2^2. \quad (35)$$

$$w_1(x) = 0.001x_1^6 + 0.1731x_1^4 x_2^2 + 0.0187x_1^4 + 0.134x_1^2 x_2^4 + 0.414x_1^2 x_2^2 \\ + 0.253x_1^2 + 0.175x_2^6 + 0.115x_2^4 + 0.575x_2^2. \quad (36)$$

$$w_2(x) = 1.234x_1^6 + 2.485x_1^4x_2^2 + 1.52x_1^4 + 4.314x_1^2x_2^4 + 3.812x_1^2x_2^2 \\ + 0.973x_1^2 + 1.285x_2^6 + 1.313x_2^4 + 3.54x_2^2. \tag{37}$$

$$w_3(x) = 0.24x_1^4x_2^2 + 0.206x_1^4 + 0.744x_1^2x_2^4 + 1.01x_1^2x_2^2 + 2.62x_1^2 + 0.39x_2^4 \\ + 2.16x_2^2. \tag{38}$$

$w_1(x), w_2(x), w_3(x)$ are SOS and $h(x) \geq 0$. Then the closed-loop system (34) is robust M-L stable.

Figure 3 is drawn for different initial conditions that show the stability of the closed-loop system (34).

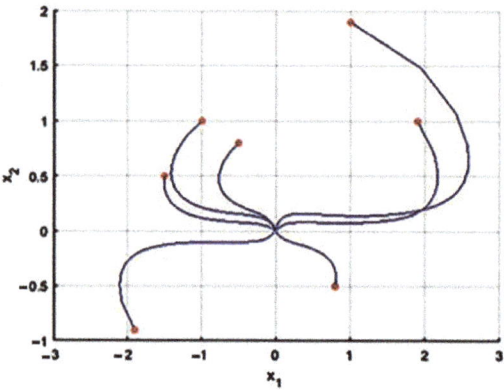

Figure 3. Phase portrait of $x_1(t), x_2(t)$ for PFDE nonlinear system (34).

Figures 4 and 5 demonstrate that Equation (25) is valid and its value is also valid for different values of $x_1(t), x_2(t)$.

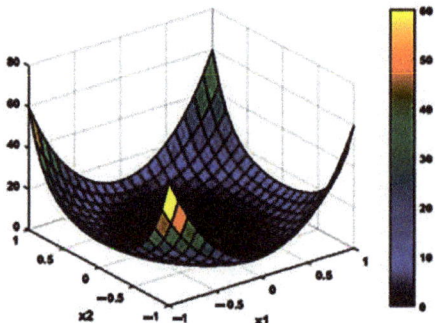

Figure 4. Surface $h(x)$ for large range of $x_1(t), x_2(t)$ and check the condition $h(x) > 0$ for stability of nonlinear system (34).

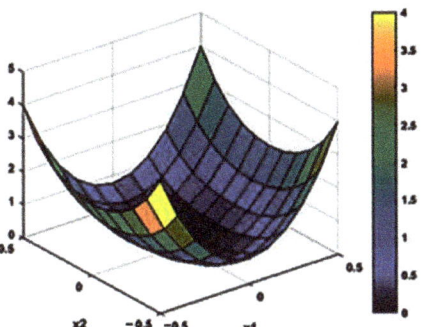

Figure 5. Surface $h(x)$ for small range of $x_1(t)$, $x_2(t)$ and check the condition $h(x) > 0$ for stability of nonlinear system (34).

Example 3. *Consider the following PFD equations system*

$$\begin{cases} {}^{C}_{t_0}D_t^{0.9}x_1(t) = -2x_1 - 4x_1x_2^2 + 0.3x_1\sin(t)\sin(x_1 - x_2). \\ {}^{C}_{t_0}D_t^{0.9}x_2(t) = -x_2 - 2x_1^2x_2 + 0.4x_2\cos x_1\cos(t) \end{cases} \quad (39)$$

where $\Delta A(x(t), t) = \begin{bmatrix} 0.3\sin(t)\sin(x_1 - x_2) & 0 \\ 0 & 0.4\cos(t)\cos x_1 \end{bmatrix}$ is the uncertainty function and $\|\Delta A(x,t)\| \leq 0.5$.

The state response of the system (39) with $q = 0.9$ demonstrates the instability of the system.

According to Equation (26), we obtain a polynomial controller

$$u_1(x) = -1.85x_1 + 7.24x_1x_2^2. \quad (40)$$

By obtaining $\eta = 0.98$, $\alpha_1 = 0.2$, then

$$\begin{aligned} w_1(x) = &\; 0.002x_1^6 + 0.218x_1^4x_2^2 + 0.224x_1^4 + 0.325x_1^2x_2^4 + 0.458x_1^2x_2^2 \\ &+ 0.281x_1^2 + 0.021x_1^6 + 0.321x_1^4x_2^2 + 0.236x_1^4 + 0.352x_1^2x_2^4 \\ &+ 0.432x_2^2 + 0.621x_1^2 + 0.321x_2^6 + 0.123x_2^4 + 0.218x_2^2. \end{aligned} \quad (41)$$

$$\begin{aligned} w_2(x) = &\; 3.78738x_1^6x_2^2 + 0.9357x_1^6 + 14.481x_1^4x_2^2 + 14.200x_1^2x_2^2 + 2.79x_1^2 \\ &+ 14.52x_1^4x_2^2 + 3.4918x_1^4 + 13.8665x_1^2x_2^6 + 14.10980x_1^2x_2^4 \\ &+ 3.5244x_2^6 + 0.89449x_2^4 + 2.2365x_2^2. \end{aligned} \quad (42)$$

$$\begin{aligned} w_3(x) = &\; 0.98x_1^6x_2^2 + 1.77x_1^6 + 2.985x_1^4x_2^4 + 7.2x_1^4x_2^2 + 6.633x_1^4 + 3.64x_1^2x_2^6 \\ &+ 7.9x_1^2x_2^4 - 7.864x_1^2x_2^2 + 5.319x_1^2 + 2.467x_2^6 + 0.626x_2^4 \\ &- 1.656x_2^2. \end{aligned} \quad (43)$$

The degree of Lyapunov function is 6 by using the conditions of Theorem 4.

$$\begin{aligned} v(x) = &\; 0.007798x_1^6 + 0.479x_1^4x_2^2 + 0.4365x_1^4 + 0.8522x_1^2x_2^4 + 0.6879x_1^2x_2^2 \\ &+ 0.741x_1^2 + 0.07798x_1^6 + 0.479x_1^4x_2^2 + 0.4365x_1^4 \\ &+ 0.8522x_1^2x_2^4 + 0.67879x_1^2x_2^2 + 0.7x_1^2 + 0.5874x_2^6 \\ &+ 0.2236x_2^4 + 1.118x_2^2. \end{aligned} \quad (44)$$

Figure 6 is drawn for different initial conditions that show the stability of the closed-loop system (39).

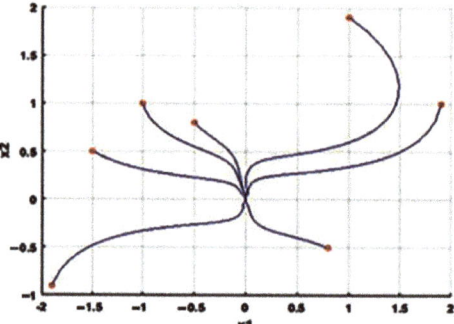

Figure 6. Phase portrait of $x_1(t)$, $x_2(t)$ for nonlinear time-variant system (39).

Figures 7 and 8 demonstrate that Equation (25) is valid and its value is also valid for different values of $x_1(t)$, $x_2(t)$.

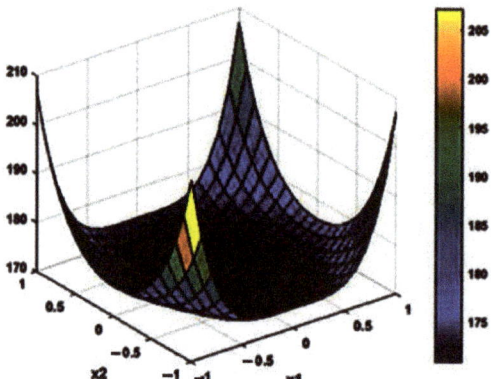

Figure 7. Surface $h(x)$ for small range of $x_1(t)$, $x_2(t)$ and check the condition $h(x) > 0$ for stability of nonlinear time-variant system (31).

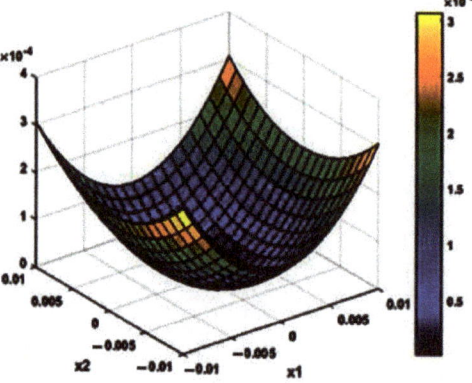

Figure 8. Surface $h(x)$ for small range of $x_1(t)$, $x_2(t)$ and check the condition $h(x) > 0$ for stability nonlinear time-variant system (39).

7. Advantages of the Proposed Approach and Suggestions for Future Research

In this paper, the method of PFD systems was highlighted. The main advantages of the proposed method are as follows.

First, the convex Lyapunov methods in the literature such as [19,21] are complicated and are not able to handle the stability and control performances. Second, although the results of some studies (e.g., [9,14,15]) are obtained based on the LMI approach, many design problems cannot be represented by the LMI inequality. This paper focused on the sum of squares approach for finding a Lyapunov candidate function for PFD systems with uncertainty.

Finally, compared with the existing studies on the stability analysis of nonlinear fractional differential systems (e.g., [14]), the results use the Lyapunov quadratic function in the stability analysis. In this paper, higher-order Lyapunov functions were used in the stability analysis of FDE systems based on the sum of squares approach. Following this, by working on PFD fuzzy systems, the stability analysis and stabilization of these systems can be obtained.

8. Conclusions

Finding a Lyapunov candidate function is difficult considering the previous methods. In this paper, the stability and stabilization of PFD systems are presently based on the Lyapunov candidate function. This method can provide the Lyapunov candidate function with a degree higher than two. Therefore, they cannot be solved with LMI techniques. Accordingly, the SOS method is used for solving. For this reason, the system (7) is Mittag–Leffler stable if the Lyapunov functional can satisfy the conditions of Theorem 3. Following this, the sufficient condition of a robust stability system (17) is expressed in Theorem (4). Finally, the polynomial Lyapunov approach is proposed using SOSTOOLS for fractional systems. This method can provide an efficient way for analyzing the stability of an uncertain polynomial fractional system.

Author Contributions: Conceptualization, H.Y., R.A. and A.Z.; methodology, H.Y., R.A. and A.Z.; software, H.Y. and A.Z.; validation, H.Y., R.A. and A.Z.; formal analysis, H.Y.; investigation, H.Y., R.A. and A.Z.; resources, H.Y. and A.Z.; data curation H.Y. and A.Z.; writing—original draft preparation, H.Y., R.A. and A.Z.; writing—review and editing, H.Y. and A.Z.; visualization, H.Y., R.A. and A.Z.; supervision, A.Z. All authors have read and agreed to the published version of the manuscript.

Funding: This research received no external funding.

Institutional Review Board Statement: Not applicable.

Informed Consent Statement: Not applicable.

Data Availability Statement: Not applicable.

Conflicts of Interest: The authors declare no conflict of interest.

References

1. Ortigueira, M.D. *Fractional Calculus for Scientists and Engineers*; Springer Science & Business Media: Berlin/Heidelberg, Germany, 2011; Volume 84.
2. Caponetto, R. *Fractional Order Systems: Modeling and Control Applications*; World Scientific: Singapore, 2010; Volume 72.
3. Mainardi, F. *Fractional Calculus and Waves in Linear Viscoelasticity: An Introduction to Mathematical Models*; World Scientific: Singapore, 2010.
4. Idiou, D.; Charef, A.; Djouambi, A. Linear fractional order system identification using adjustable fractional order differentiator. *IET Signal Process.* **2013**, *8*, 398–409. [CrossRef]
5. Balochian, S.; Sedigh, A.K.; Zare, A. Variable structure control of linear time invariant fractional order systems using a finite number of state feedback law. *Commun. Nonlinear Sci. Numer. Simul.* **2011**, *16*, 1433–1442. [CrossRef]
6. Ding, S.; Wang, Z.; Rong, N.; Zhang, H. Exponential stabilization of memristive neural networks via saturating sampled-data control. *IEEE Trans. Cybern.* **2017**, *47*, 3027–3039. [CrossRef] [PubMed]
7. Mayo-Maldonado, J.C.; Fernandez-Anaya, G.; Ruiz-Martinez, O.F. Stability of conformable linear differential systems: A behavioral framework with applications in fractional-order control. *IET Control. Theory Appl.* **2020**, *14*, 2900–2913. [CrossRef]

8. Zhang, R.; Tian, G.; Yang, S.; Cao, H. Stability analysis of a class of fractional order nonlinear systems with order lying in (0, 2). *ISA Trans.* **2015**, *56*, 102–110. [CrossRef]
9. Zhao, Y.; Wang, Y.; Li, H. State feedback control for a class of fractional order nonlinear systems. *IEEE/CAA J. Autom. Sin.* **2016**, *3*, 483–488.
10. Wen, X.-J.; Wu, Z.-M.; Lu, J.-G. Stability analysis of a class of nonlinear fractional-order systems. *IEEE Trans. Circuits Syst. II Express Briefs* **2008**, *55*, 1178–1182. [CrossRef]
11. Chen, L.; Wu, R.; Cheng, Y.; Chen, Y.Q. Delay-dependent and order-dependent stability and stabilization of fractional-order linear systems with time-varying delay. *IEEE Trans. Circuits Syst. II Express Briefs* **2019**, *67*, 1064–1068. [CrossRef]
12. Jiang, P.; Zeng, Z.; Chen, J. On the periodic dynamics of memristor-based neural networks with leakage and time-varying delays. *Neurocomputing* **2017**, *219*, 163–173. [CrossRef]
13. Wen, S.; Zeng, Z.; Huang, T. Exponential stability analysis of memristor-based recurrent neural networks with time-varying delays. *Neurocomputing* **2012**, *97*, 233–240. [CrossRef]
14. Lu, J.-G.; Chen, G. Robust stability and stabilization of fractional-order interval systems: An LMI approach. *IEEE Trans. Autom. Control* **2009**, *54*, 1294–1299.
15. Li, B.; Zhang, X. Observer-based robust control of $0 < \alpha < 1$ fractional-order linear uncertain control systems. *IET Control. Theory Appl.* **2016**, *10*, 1724–1731.
16. Lu, J.G.; Chen, Y.Q. Robust Stability and Stabilization of Fractional-Order Interval Systems with the Fractional Order α: The $0 < \alpha < 1$ Case. *IEEE Trans. Autom. Control.* **2009**, *55*, 152–158.
17. Zhao, Y.; Wang, Y.; Zhang, X.; Li, H. Feedback stabilisation control design for fractional order non-linear systems in the lower triangular form. *IET Control Theory Appl.* **2016**, *10*, 1061–1068. [CrossRef]
18. Li, Y.; Chen, Y.; Podlubny, I. Stability of fractional-order nonlinear dynamic systems: Lyapunov direct method and generalized Mittag–Leffler stability. *Comput. Math. Appl.* **2010**, *59*, 1810–1821. [CrossRef]
19. Badri, V.; Tavazoei, M.S. Stability analysis of fractional order time-delay systems: Constructing new Lyapunov functions from those of integer order counterparts. *IET Control. Theory Appl.* **2019**, *13*, 2476–2481. [CrossRef]
20. Li, Y.; Chen, Y.; Podlubny, I. Mittag-Leffler stability of fractional order nonlinear dynamic systems. *Automatica* **2009**, *45*, 1965–1969. [CrossRef]
21. Thanh, N.T.; Trinh, H.; Phat, V.N. Stability analysis of fractional differential time-delay equations. *IET Control. Theory Appl.* **2017**, *11*, 1006–1015. [CrossRef]
22. Chen, L.; Chai, Y.; Wu, R.; Yang, J. Stability and stabilization of a class of nonlinear fractional-order systems with Caputo derivative. *IEEE Trans. Circuits Syst. II Express Briefs* **2012**, *59*, 602–606. [CrossRef]
23. Xiao, Q.; Zeng, Z. Lagrange stability for T–S fuzzy memristive neural networks with time-varying delays on time scales. *IEEE Trans. Fuzzy Syst.* **2017**, *26*, 1091–1103. [CrossRef]
24. Bakule, L. Decentralized control: An overview. *Annu. Rev. Control* **2008**, *32*, 87–98. [CrossRef]

Article

On Mond–Weir-Type Robust Duality for a Class of Uncertain Fractional Optimization Problems

Xiaole Guo [1,2]

[1] School of Mathematics and Statistics, Chongqing Technology and Business University, Chongqing 400067, China; guoxiaole@ctbu.edu.cn

[2] Chongqing Key Laboratory of Social Economy and Applied Statistics, Chongqing Technology and Business University, Chongqing 400067, China

Abstract: This article is focused on the investigation of Mond–Weir-type robust duality for a class of semi-infinite multi-objective fractional optimization with uncertainty in the constraint functions. We first establish a Mond–Weir-type robust dual problem for this fractional optimization problem. Then, by combining a new robust-type subdifferential constraint qualification condition and a generalized convex-inclusion assumption, we present robust ε-quasi-weak and strong duality properties between this uncertain fractional optimization and its uncertain Mond–Weir-type robust dual problem. Moreover, we also investigate robust ε-quasi converse-like duality properties between them.

Keywords: fractional optimization; robust duality; constraint qualification condition

MSC: 90C29; 90C46

Citation: Guo, X. On Mond–Weir-Type Robust Duality for a Class of Uncertain Fractional Optimization Problems. *Axioms* 2023, 12, 1029. https://doi.org/10.3390/axioms12111029

Academic Editors: Siamak Pedrammehr and Mohammad Reza Chalak Qazani

Received: 6 October 2023
Revised: 29 October 2023
Accepted: 31 October 2023
Published: 2 Novermber 2023

Copyright: © 2023 by the author. Licensee MDPI, Basel, Switzerland. This article is an open access article distributed under the terms and conditions of the Creative Commons Attribution (CC BY) license (https:// creativecommons.org/licenses/by/ 4.0/).

1. Introduction

Let T be a nonempty infinite index set. Suppose that $f_i : \mathbb{R}^n \to \mathbb{R}$, $i = 1, \ldots, p$, and $h_t : \mathbb{R}^n \to \mathbb{R}$, $t \in T$. Let us consider the semi-infinite optimization problem:

$$(\text{MP}) \quad \begin{cases} \text{Min}_{\mathbb{R}^p_+} \ (f_1(x), \ldots, f_p(x)) \\ \text{s.t.} \ h_t(x) \leq 0, \forall t \in T, \\ x \in \mathbb{R}^n. \end{cases}$$

The study of optimization problem (MP) is a very interesting topic and has been considered extensively by many scholars from different points of view, see [1–13]. However, most semi-infinite optimization models of real-world problems are contaminated by prediction errors or asymmetry knowledge. Thus, it is necessary to consider semi-infinite optimization problems under uncertain data. This optimization problem (MP) with uncertainty can be captured by

$$(\text{UMP}) \quad \begin{cases} \text{Min}_{\mathbb{R}^p_+} \ (f_1(x), \ldots, f_p(x)) \\ \text{s.t.} \ h_t(x, v_t) \leq 0, \forall t \in T, \\ x \in \mathbb{R}^n. \end{cases}$$

Here, $h_t : \mathbb{R}^n \times \mathbb{R}^q \to \mathbb{R}$, $t \in T$, are given functions, v_t, $t \in T$, are uncertain parameters which belongs to compact sets $\mathcal{V}_t \subseteq \mathbb{R}^q$.

As we know, robust optimization [14–16] is an useful approach to solve optimization problems with uncertainty. Following robust optimization methodology, we usually associate UMP with its robust counterpart

$$(\text{RMP}) \quad \begin{cases} \text{Min}_{\mathbb{R}_+^p} \; (f_1(x), \ldots, f_p(x)) \\ \text{s.t.} \quad h_t(x, v_t) \leq 0, \forall v_t \in \mathcal{V}_t, t \in T, \\ \quad\quad x \in \mathbb{R}^n. \end{cases}$$

Recently, following robust optimization methodology, many interesting results devoted to (UMP) and its generalizations have been obtained from several different perspectives. By using scalarizing methods and robust optimization, Lee and Lee [17] establish necessary optimality theorems for robust weakly and properly efficient solutions of a multi-objective optimization problem with uncertainty. By virtue of a new concept of generalized convexity and robust type constraint qualification conditions, Chen et al. [18] give some optimality conditions and duality results for an uncertain nonconvex and nonsmooth multi-objective optimization problem. Guo and Yu [19] obtain optimality conditions for robust approximate quasi-weakly efficient solutions for uncertain multi-objective convex optimization problems. By combining robust optimization and scalarization technique, Sun et al. [20] give some new characterizations of Wolfe type robust approximate duality and saddle point theorems for a nonsmooth robust multi-objective optimization problem. Sun et al. [21] investigate optimality conditions for robust ϵ-quasi efficient solutions of a class of uncertain semi-infinite multi-objective optimization under some tools of non-smooth analysis and a new modified scalarization technique. In addition, nonsmooth robust ϵ-duality properties and ϵ-quasi saddle point theorems are also established. New results on optimality and duality results for uncertain multiobjective polynomial optimization problems are given in [22]. By using tangential subdifferential and robust optimization, Liu et al. [23] obtained some characterizations of robust optimal solution sets for nonconvex uncertain semi-infinite optimization problems.

On the other hand, the fractional multi-objective optimization problem is an important subclass of multi-objective optimization problems. In the last decades, a wide variety of interesting works devoted to fractional multi-objective optimization problems and its generalizations have been given, see, for example, [24–33]. We observe that there are some papers devoted to the study of uncertain fractional multi-objective optimization problems under a robust optimization approach. In [34], the authors study approximate optimality conditions and Wolfe-type robust approximate duality of robust approximate weakly efficient solutions for uncertain fractional multi-objective optimization problems. Li et al. [35] establish optimality theorems and robust duality properties for minimax convex–concave fractional optimization problems with uncertainty. Antczak [36] establish a new parametric approach for robust approximate quasi-efficient solutions of robust fractional multi-objective optimization problems. Feng and Sun [37] obtain some new results for robust weakly ϵ-efficient solutions for an uncertain fractional multi-objective semi-infinite optimization by employing conjugate analysis. Very recently, by employing robust limiting constraint qualification conditions and generalized convexity assumptions, Thuy and Su [38] consider optimality conditions and duality results for nonsmooth fractional multi-objective semi-infinite optimization problems with uncertain data.

In this paper, our main concern is to give new duality results of robust ϵ-quasi-efficient solutions for fractional multi-objective semi-infinite optimization problems (UFP, for brevity) with uncertainty appearing in the constraint functions. We first introduce the robust counterpart model (RFP, for brevity) for UFP. Then, with the help of a robust-type subdifferential constraint qualification, we present a necessary approximate optimality condition for robust ϵ-quasi-efficient solutions for (UFP). Subsequently, we introduce a Mond–Weir-type robust approximate dual problem of (UFP) based on the obtained necessary optimality conditions. Then, we investigate robust weak, strong and converse-like duality results between them under a new assumption of generalized convex-inclusion for Lipschitz functions.

This paper is organized as follows. In Section 2, we first recall some basic concepts in nonsmooth analysis and present approximate optimality results for robust ϵ-quasi-efficient solutions of (UFP). In Section 3, we introduce a Mond–Weir-type robust approximate dual problem for (UFP), and establish the robust ϵ-quasi duality results between them. As a special case, we also deal with robust ϵ-quasi duality results of the uncertain multi-objective optimization problem (UMP) and its robust approximate dual problem.

2. Mathematical Preliminaries

In this paper, let us recall some concepts and preliminary results [39,40]. Let $\mathbb{R}^p$ be the p-dimensional Euclidean space. We use the notation $\|\cdot\|$ for the Euclidean norm for $\mathbb{R}^p$. The nonnegative orthant of $\mathbb{R}^p$ is defined by $\mathbb{R}^p_+ := \{x = (x_1, \ldots, x_n) \mid x_k \geq 0, k = 1, \ldots, n\}$. We always use the symbol $\langle \cdot, \cdot \rangle$ for the inner product in $\mathbb{R}^p$. The closed unit ball of $\mathbb{R}^p$ is denoted by $\mathbb{B}^*$. For a nonempty infinite index set T, the linear space $\mathbb{R}^{(T)}$[41] is denoted by

$$\mathbb{R}^{(T)} := \{\gamma_T = (\gamma_t)_{t \in T} \mid \gamma_t = 0 \text{ for all } t \in T \text{ except for finitely many } \gamma_t \neq 0\}.$$

Let $\mathbb{R}^{(T)}_+$ be the nonnegative cone of $\mathbb{R}^{(T)}$, i.e.,

$$\mathbb{R}^{(T)}_+ := \{\gamma_T \in \mathbb{R}^{(T)} \mid \gamma_t \geq 0, \forall t \in T\}.$$

Let $\phi : \mathbb{R}^p \to \mathbb{R}$ be a locally Lipschitz function. The Clarke generalized directional derivative of ϕ at $x \in \mathbb{R}^p$ in the direction $d \in \mathbb{R}^p$ is defined by

$$\phi^c(x; d) := \limsup_{y \to x, t \downarrow 0} \frac{\phi(y + td) - \phi(y)}{t}.$$

The one-sided directional derivative of ϕ at $x \in \mathbb{R}^p$ in direction $d \in \mathbb{R}^p$ is defined by

$$\phi'(x; d) := \lim_{t \downarrow 0} \frac{\phi(x + td) - \phi(x)}{t}.$$

We say that ϕ is quasidifferentiable at $x \in \mathbb{R}^p$ iff, for each $d \in \mathbb{R}^n$, $\varphi'(x; d)$ exists and $\varphi'(x; d) = \varphi^c(x; d)$. The Clarke subdifferential $\partial^c \phi(x)$ of ϕ at $x \in \mathbb{R}^p$ is defined by

$$\partial^c \phi(x) := \{\zeta^* \in \mathbb{R}^p \mid \phi^c(x; d) \geq \langle \zeta^*, d \rangle, \forall d \in \mathbb{R}^p\}.$$

Obviously,

$$\phi^c(x; d) = \sup_{\zeta \in \partial^c \phi(x)} \langle \zeta, d \rangle, \ \forall d \in \mathbb{R}^n.$$

On the other hand, if $\phi : \mathbb{R}^p \to \mathbb{R}$ is a convex function, $\partial^c \phi(x)$ coincides with the convex subdifferential $\partial \phi(x)$, that is

$$\partial \phi(x) := \{\zeta^* \in \mathbb{R}^p \mid \phi(y) - \phi(x) \geq \langle \zeta^*, y - x \rangle, \forall y \in \mathbb{R}^p\}.$$

Let $\Omega \subseteq \mathbb{R}^p$ be a nonempty subset. The Clarke normal cone to Ω at $x \in \Omega$ is defined by

$$N^c(\Omega, x) := \{\zeta \in \mathbb{R}^p \mid \langle \zeta^*, w \rangle \leq 0, \forall w \in T_\Omega(x)\}.$$

Here, $T_\Omega(x)$ is the Clarke tangent cone to Ω at $x \in \Omega$. Clearly, if $\Omega \subseteq \mathbb{R}^n$ is a nonempty closed convex set, $N^c(\Omega, x)$ becomes the following normal cone:

$$N(\Omega, x) := \{\zeta^* \in \mathbb{R}^p \mid \langle \zeta^*, y - x \rangle \leq 0, \forall y \in \Omega\}.$$

In what follows, let $f_i, g_i : \mathbb{R}^n \to \mathbb{R}$, $i = 1, \ldots, p$, and $h_t : \mathbb{R}^n \to \mathbb{R}$, $t \in T$. We consider the following fractional multi-objective optimization problem

$$\text{(FP)} \quad \begin{cases} \text{Min}_{\mathbb{R}^p_+} \left(\frac{f_1(x)}{g_1(x)}, \ldots, \frac{f_p(x)}{g_p(x)} \right) \\ \text{s.t. } h_t(x) \leq 0, \forall t \in T, \\ \quad x \in \mathbb{R}^n. \end{cases}$$

The fractional optimization problem (FP) under uncertain data in the constraint functions becomes

$$\text{(UFP)} \quad \begin{cases} \text{Min}_{\mathbb{R}_+^p} \left(\frac{f_1(x)}{g_1(x)}, \ldots, \frac{f_p(x)}{g_p(x)} \right) \\ \text{s.t.} \quad h_t(x, v_t) \leq 0, \forall t \in T, \\ \quad x \in \mathbb{R}^n. \end{cases}$$

Here $h_t : \mathbb{R}^n \times \mathbb{R}^q \to \mathbb{R}$. $v_t \in \mathcal{V}_t \subseteq \mathbb{R}^q, t \in T$ are uncertain parameters. For (UFP), we consider its robust counterpart, namely

$$\text{(RFP)} \quad \begin{cases} \text{Min}_{\mathbb{R}_+^p} \left(\frac{f_1(x)}{g_1(x)}, \ldots, \frac{f_p(x)}{g_p(x)} \right) \\ \text{s.t.} \quad h_t(x, v_t) \leq 0, \forall v_t \in \mathcal{V}_t, t \in T, \\ \quad x \in \mathbb{R}^n. \end{cases}$$

In this paper, without special statements, let f_i, $i = 1, \ldots, p$, be locally Lipschitz functions with $f_i(x) \geq 0, \forall x \in \mathbb{R}^n$, and g_i, $i = 1, \ldots, p$, be locally Lipschitz functions with $g_i(x) > 0, \forall x \in \mathbb{R}^n$.

Now, we give the following important notations, which will be used later in this paper.

Definition 1. *For (UFP). We say that $\mathcal{F}$ is the robust feasible set of (UFP) iff*

$$\mathcal{F} := \{x \in \mathbb{R}^n \mid h_t(x, v_t) \leq 0, \forall v_t \in \mathcal{V}_t, t \in T\}.$$

Now, we consider the concept of robust ϵ-quasi efficient solution for (UFP). We refer the readers to [19,21,37] for other kinds of robust approximate efficient solutions.

Definition 2. *Let $\epsilon \in \mathbb{R}_+^p \setminus \{0\}$. $\bar{x} \in \mathcal{F}$ is a robust ϵ-quasi efficient solution of (UFP) if there is not $x \in \mathcal{F}$, such that*

$$\frac{f_i(x)}{g_i(x)} \leq \frac{f_i(\bar{x})}{g_i(\bar{x})} - \epsilon_i \|x - \bar{x}\|, \text{ for all } i = 1, \ldots, p,$$

and

$$\frac{f_j(x)}{g_j(x)} < \frac{f_j(\bar{x})}{g_j(\bar{x})} - \epsilon_j \|x - \bar{x}\|, \text{ for some } j \in \{1, \ldots, p\}.$$

Remark 1. *Note that $g_i \equiv 1$, the concept of robust ϵ-quasi efficient solution of (UFP) deduces to the robust ϵ-quasi efficient solution of (UMP), i.e., there is not $x \in \mathcal{F}$, such that*

$$f_i(x) \leq f_i(\bar{x}) - \epsilon_i \|x - \bar{x}\|, \text{ for all } i = 1, \ldots, p,$$

and

$$f_j(x) < f_j(\bar{x}) - \epsilon_j \|x - \bar{x}\|, \text{ for some } j \in \{1, \ldots, p\}.$$

For more details, see [20,21,42].

Definition 3 ([43] (Definition 3.2)). *Consider (UFP). We say that the robust-type subdifferential constraint qualification condition RSCQ holds at $\bar{x} \in \mathcal{F}$, iff*

$$N^c(\mathcal{F}, \bar{x}) \subseteq \bigcup_{\substack{\lambda_T \in \tilde{T}(\bar{x}), \\ v_T \in \mathcal{V}_T}} \left[\sum_{t \in T} \lambda_t \partial_x^c h_t(\bar{x}, v_t) \right],$$

where $T(\bar{x}) = \left\{ \lambda_T \in \mathbb{R}_+^{(T)} \mid \lambda_t h_t(\bar{x}, v_t) = 0, \forall v_t \in \mathcal{V}_t, t \in T \right\}$.

Next, we recall the following necessary optimality conditions for robust ϵ-quasi-efficient solutions for (UFP) under the RSCQ. For convenience, let $\epsilon := (\epsilon_1, \ldots, \epsilon_p) \in \mathbb{R}_+^p \setminus \{0\}$.

Proposition 1 ([44] (Theorem 1)). *Let $\epsilon \in \mathbb{R}_+^p \setminus \{0\}$. Assume that (RSCQ) holds at $\bar{x} \in \mathcal{F}$. If $\bar{x}$ is a robust ϵ-quasi-efficient solution of (UFP), then there exist $\bar{\eta}_t \geq 0$, and $\bar{v}_t \in \mathcal{V}_t, t \in T$, such that*

$$0 \in \sum_{i=1}^p \partial^c f_i(\bar{x}) + \sum_{i=1}^p \phi_i(\bar{x}) \partial^c(-g_i)(\bar{x}) + \sum_{t \in T} \bar{\eta}_t \partial^c h_t(\cdot, \bar{v}_t)(\bar{x}) + 2 \sum_{i=1}^p \epsilon_i g_i(\bar{x}) \mathbb{B}^*, \quad (1)$$

and

$$\bar{\eta}_t h_t(\bar{x}, \bar{v}_t) = 0, \forall t \in T. \quad (2)$$

Here, $\phi_i(\cdot) = \frac{f_i(\bar{x})}{g_i(\bar{x})} - \epsilon_i \| \cdot - \bar{x} \|, i = 1, \ldots, p$.

Remark 2. *Proposition 1 extends [45] (Theorem 3.1) from the case of scalar optimization to the multi-objective setting.*

In the case that $g_i \equiv 1$, the following result can be easily obtained by Proposition 1.

Proposition 2. *Let $\epsilon \in \mathbb{R}_+^p \setminus \{0\}$. Assume that (RSCQ) holds at $\bar{x} \in \mathcal{F}$. If $\bar{x}$ is a robust ϵ-quasi-efficient solution of (UMP), then there exist $\bar{\eta}_t \geq 0$, and $\bar{v}_t \in \mathcal{V}_t, t \in T$, such that*

$$0 \in \sum_{i=1}^p \partial^c f_i(\bar{x}) + \sum_{t \in T} \bar{\eta}_t \partial^c h_t(\cdot, \bar{v}_t)(\bar{x}) + 2 \sum_{i=1}^p \epsilon_i \mathbb{B}^*, \quad (3)$$

and

$$\bar{\eta}_t h_t(\bar{x}, \bar{v}_t) = 0, \forall t \in T. \quad (4)$$

3. Main Results

In this section, based on the optimality conditions obtained in Proposition 1, we establish a robust *Mond-Weir-type* approximate dual problem for (UMFP), and then investigate robust duality properties between them. Here, we only consider their robust ϵ-quasi-efficient solutions. For the sake of convenience in the sequel, we set $f := (f_1, \ldots, f_p), g := (g_1, \ldots, g_p), h_T := (h_t)_{t \in T}, \eta_T := (\eta_t)_t \in \mathbb{R}_+^{(T)}, \mathcal{V}_T := \prod_{t \in T} \mathcal{V}_t$, and $v_T := (v_t)_{t \in T} \in \mathcal{V}_T$.

Let $y \in \mathbb{R}^n$ and $\epsilon \in \mathbb{R}_+^p \setminus \{0\}$. For given $v_t \in \mathcal{V}_t, t \in T$, the *Mond-Weir-type* uncertain approximate dual problem (UFD) of (UFP) is

(UFD) $\begin{cases} \text{Max}_{\mathbb{R}_+^p} \left(\frac{f_1(y)}{g_1(y)}, \ldots, \frac{f_p(y)}{g_p(y)} \right) \\ \text{s.t. } 0 \in \sum_{i=1}^p \partial^c f_i(y) + \sum_{i=1}^p \frac{f_i(y)}{g_i(y)} \partial^c(-g_i)(y) + \sum_{t \in T} \eta_t \partial^c h_t(\cdot, v_t)(y) + 2 \sum_{i=1}^p \epsilon_i g_i(y) \mathbb{B}^*, \\ \eta_t h_t(y, v_t) \geq 0, t \in T, \\ y \in \mathbb{R}^n, \epsilon_i \geq 0, i = 1, \ldots, p, \eta_t \geq 0, t \in T. \end{cases}$

The optimistic counterpart of (UFD) is defined by

(OFD) $\begin{cases} \text{Max}_{\mathbb{R}_+^p} \left(\frac{f_1(y)}{g_1(y)}, \ldots, \frac{f_p(y)}{g_p(y)} \right) \\ \text{s.t. } 0 \in \sum_{i=1}^p \partial^c f_i(y) + \sum_{i=1}^p \frac{f_i(y)}{g_i(y)} \partial^c(-g_i)(y) + \sum_{t \in T} \eta_t \partial^c h_t(\cdot, v_t)(y) + 2 \sum_{i=1}^p \epsilon_i g_i(y) \mathbb{B}^*, \\ \eta_t h_t(y, v_t) \geq 0, t \in T, \\ y \in \mathbb{R}^n, \epsilon_i \geq 0, i = 1, \ldots, p, \eta_t \geq 0, v_t \in \mathcal{V}_t, t \in T. \end{cases}$

Here, the maximization is also over all the parameters $v_t \in \mathcal{V}_t, t \in T$. The feasible set of (OFD) is defined as

$$\widehat{\mathcal{F}} := \left\{ (y, \eta_T, v_T) \in \mathbb{R}^n \times \mathbb{R}_+^{(T)} \times \mathcal{V}_T \;\middle|\; 0 \in \sum_{i=1}^p \partial^c f_i(y) + \sum_{i=1}^p \frac{f_i(y)}{g_i(y)} \partial^c(-g_i)(y) + \sum_{t \in T} \eta_t \partial^c h_t(\cdot, v_t)(y) \right.$$
$$\left. + 2 \sum_{i=1}^p \epsilon_i g_i(y) \mathbb{B}^*, \eta_t h_t(y, v_t) \geq 0, t \in T \right\}.$$

Remark 3. (i) *Obviously, if $g_i(x) \equiv 1, i = 1, \ldots, p$, (UFD) becomes the following conventional Mond-Weir-type uncertain approximate dual problem of* (UMP)

(UMD) $\begin{cases} \text{Max}_{\mathbb{R}_+^p} \; (f_1(y), \ldots, f_p(y)) \\ \text{s.t.} \quad 0 \in \sum_{i=1}^p \partial^c f_i(y) + \sum_{t \in T} \eta_t \partial^c h_t(\cdot, v_t)(y) + 2 \sum_{i=1}^p \epsilon_i \mathbb{B}^*, \\ \eta_t h_t(y, v_t) \geq 0, t \in T, \\ y \in \mathbb{R}^n, \epsilon_i \geq 0, i = 1, \ldots, p, \eta_t \geq 0, t \in T. \end{cases}$

and (OFD) *becomes the following Mond-Weir-type optimistic dual problem of* (UMP)

(OMD) $\begin{cases} \text{Max}_{\mathbb{R}_+^p} \; (f_1(y), \ldots, f_p(y)) \\ \text{s.t.} \quad 0 \in \sum_{i=1}^p \partial^c f_i(y) + \sum_{t \in T} \eta_t \partial^c h_t(\cdot, v_t)(y) + 2 \sum_{i=1}^p \epsilon_i \mathbb{B}^*, \\ \eta_t h_t(y, v_t) \geq 0, t \in T, \\ y \in \mathbb{R}^n, \epsilon_i \geq 0, i = 1, \ldots, p, \eta_t \geq 0, v_t \in \mathcal{V}_t, t \in T. \end{cases}$

Here, we denote the feasible set of (OMD) by

$$\overline{\mathcal{F}} := \left\{ (y, \eta_T, v_T) \in \mathbb{R}^n \times \mathbb{R}_+^{(T)} \times \mathcal{V}_T \;\middle|\; 0 \in \sum_{i=1}^p \partial^c f_i(y) + \sum_{t \in T} \eta_t \partial^c h_t(\cdot, v_t)(y) \right.$$
$$\left. + 2 \sum_{i=1}^p \epsilon_i g_i(y) \mathbb{B}^*, \eta_t h_t(y, v_t) \geq 0, t \in T \right\}.$$

(ii) *In the case that $\epsilon = 0$ and there is no uncertainty in the constraint functions. Then, (UFP) becomes (FP), and (OMD) collapses to*

$\begin{cases} \text{Max}_{\mathbb{R}_+^p} \; \left(\frac{f_1(y)}{g_1(y)}, \ldots, \frac{f_p(y)}{g_p(y)} \right) \\ \text{s.t.} \quad 0 \in \sum_{i=1}^p \partial f_i(y) + \sum_{i=1}^p \frac{f_i(y)}{g_i(y)} \partial^c(-g_i)(y) + \sum_{t \in T} \eta_t \partial^c h_t(y), \\ \eta_t h_t(y) \geq 0, t \in T, \\ y \in \mathbb{R}^n, \eta_t \geq 0, t \in T. \end{cases}$

Now, similar to Definition 2, we introduce robust ϵ-quasi efficient solutions for (UFD).

Definition 4. *Let $\epsilon \in \mathbb{R}_+^p \setminus \{0\}$. $(\bar{y}, \bar{\eta}_T, \bar{v}_T) \in \widehat{\mathcal{F}}$ is said to be a robust ϵ-quasi efficient solution of (UFD), iff it is an ϵ-quasi efficient solution of (OFD), i.e., there is no $(y, \eta_T, v_T) \in \widehat{\mathcal{F}}$, such that*

$$\frac{f_i(y)}{g_i(y)} \geq \frac{f_i(\bar{y})}{g_i(\bar{y})} + \epsilon_i \|y - \bar{y}\|, \text{ for all } i = 1, \ldots, p,$$

and
$$\frac{f_j(y)}{g_j(y)} > \frac{f_j(\bar{y})}{g_j(\bar{y})} + \epsilon_j\|y - \bar{y}\|, \text{ for some } j \in \{1, \ldots, p\}.$$

Remark 4. *In particular, if $g_i \equiv 1$, the concept of robust ε-quasi efficient solution of (UFD) deduces to the robust ε-quasi efficient solution of (UMD), i.e., there is no $(y, \eta_T, v_T) \in \overline{\mathcal{F}}$, such that*

$$f_i(y) \geq f_i(\bar{y}) + \epsilon_i\|y - \bar{y}\|, \text{ for all } i = 1, \ldots, p,$$

and

$$f_j(y) > f_j(\bar{y}) + \epsilon_j\|y - \bar{y}\|, \text{ for some } j \in \{1, \ldots, p\}.$$

In order to give robust duality relations for (UFP) and (UFD), we introduce the new definition of generalized convex-inclusion for Lipschitz functions, which is inspired by [32] (Definition 3.4) and [21] (Definition 3.3).

Definition 5. *Let $\Omega \subseteq \mathbb{R}^n$. $(f, -g, h_T)$ is said to generalized convex-inclusion on Ω at $x \in \Omega$, iff for any $y \in \Omega$, $\xi_i^* \in \partial^c f_i(x)$, $\xi_i^{**} \in \partial^c(-g_i)(x)$, $i = 1, \ldots, p$, and $\gamma_t^* \in \partial_x^c h_t(x, v_t)$, $v_t \in \mathcal{V}_t$, $t \in T$, there exists $\omega \in \mathbb{R}^n$, such that*

$$f_i(y) - f_i(x) > \langle \xi_i^*, \omega \rangle, i = 1, \ldots, p,$$
$$-g_i(y) + g_i(x) \geq \langle \xi_i^{**}, \omega \rangle, i = 1, \ldots, p,$$
$$h_t(y, v_t) - h_t(x, v_t) \geq \langle \gamma_t^*, \omega \rangle, t \in T,$$
$$\langle b^*, \omega \rangle \leq \|y - x\|, \forall b^* \in \mathbb{B}^*,$$

and

$$0 \in \partial^c g_i(y), i = 1, \ldots, p.$$

Remark 5. (i) *In the special case that $g_i \equiv 1$, the concept of generalized convex-inclusion reduces to the concept of generalized convexity, i.e., (f, h_T) is generalized convex on Ω at $x \in \Omega$, iff for any $y \in \Omega$, $\xi_i^* \in \partial^c f_i(x)$, $i = 1, \ldots, p$, and $\gamma_t^* \in \partial_x^c g_t(x, v_t)$, $v_t \in \mathcal{V}_t$, $t \in T$, there exists $\omega \in \mathbb{R}^n$, such that*

$$f_i(y) - f_i(x) > \langle \xi_i^*, \omega \rangle, i = 1, \ldots, p,$$
$$h_t(y, v_t) - h_t(x, v_t) \geq \langle \gamma_t^*, \omega \rangle, t \in T,$$

and

$$\langle b^*, \omega \rangle \leq \|y - x\|, \forall b^* \in \mathbb{B}^*.$$

(ii) *If $g_i \equiv 1$ and there is uncertain data on f_i, $i = 1, \ldots, p$, Definition 5 reduces to [21] (Definition 3.3).*

(iii) *If $g_i \equiv 1$ and there is no uncertain data on h_t, $t \in T$, Definition 5 reduces to the concept of generalized convexity-inclusion introduced in [32] (Definition 3.4), i.e., for any $y \in \Omega$, $\xi_i^* \in \partial^c f_i(x)$, $\xi_i^{**} \in \partial^c(-g_i)(x)$, $i = 1, \ldots, p$, and $\gamma_t^* \in \partial^c h_t(x)$, $t \in T$, there exists $\omega \in \mathbb{R}^n$, such that*

$$f_i(y) - f_i(x) > \langle \xi_i^*, \omega \rangle, i = 1, \ldots, p,$$
$$-g_i(y) + g_i(x) \geq \langle \xi_i^{**}, \omega \rangle, i = 1, \ldots, p,$$
$$h_t(y) - h_t(x) \geq \langle \gamma_t^*, \omega \rangle, t \in T,$$
$$\langle b^*, \omega \rangle \leq \|y - x\|, \forall b^* \in \mathbb{B}^*,$$

and
$$0 \in \partial^c g_i(y), i = 1, \ldots, p.$$

Note that this concept has been used to establish sufficient optimality conditions for weakly ϵ-quasi-efficient solution for fractional optimization problem. For more details, please see [32] (Theorem 3.5).

Now, we show robust approximate duality properties for (UFP) and (UFD) by showing approximate duality properties between the robust counterpart (RMP) and the optimistic counterpart (OFD). In what follows, we set

$$\omega_1 \preceq \omega_2 \Leftrightarrow \omega_2 - \omega_1 \in \mathbb{R}_+^p \setminus \{0\}, \quad \forall \omega_1, \omega_2 \in \mathbb{R}^p,$$

$$\omega_1 \not\preceq \omega_2 \Leftrightarrow \omega_2 - \omega_1 \notin \mathbb{R}_+^p \setminus \{0\}, \quad \forall \omega_1, \omega_2 \in \mathbb{R}^p.$$

The following result gives robust ϵ-quasi-weak duality between (UFP) and (UFD).

Theorem 1. Let $\epsilon \in \mathbb{R}_+^p \setminus \{0\}$. Suppose that $x \in \mathcal{F}$ and $(y, \eta_T, v_T) \in \widehat{\mathcal{F}}$. If $(f, -g, h_T)$ is generalized convex-inclusion on $\mathbb{R}^n$ at $y \in \mathbb{R}^n$, then,

$$\left(\frac{f_1(x)}{g_1(x)}, \ldots, \frac{f_p(x)}{g_p(x)} \right) \not\preceq \left(\frac{f_1(y)}{g_1(y)} - 2\epsilon_1 \|x - y\|, \ldots, \frac{f_p(y)}{g_p(y)} - 2\epsilon_p \|x - y\| \right).$$

Proof. Suppose to the contrary that

$$\left(\frac{f_1(x)}{g_1(x)}, \ldots, \frac{f_p(x)}{g_p(x)} \right) \preceq \left(\frac{f_1(y)}{g_1(y)} - 2\epsilon_1 \|y - x\|, \ldots, \frac{f_p(y)}{g_p(y)} - 2\epsilon_p \|y - x\| \right).$$

Then,

$$\frac{f_i(x)}{g_i(x)} \leq \frac{f_i(y)}{g_i(y)} - 2\epsilon_i \|y - x\|, \text{ for all } i = 1, \ldots, p, \tag{5}$$

and

$$\frac{f_i(x)}{g_i(x)} < \frac{f_j(y)}{g_j(y)} - 2\epsilon_j \|y - x\|, \text{ for some } j \in \{1, \ldots, p\}. \tag{6}$$

On the other hand, note that $(y, \eta_T, v_T) \in \widehat{\mathcal{F}}$. Then, $y \in \mathbb{R}^n$, $\eta_t \geq 0$, $v_t \in \mathcal{V}_t$, $t \in T$, and

$$0 \in \sum_{i=1}^p \partial^c f_i(y) + \sum_{i=1}^p \frac{f_i(y)}{g_i(y)} \partial^c (-g_i)(y) + \sum_{t \in T} \eta_t \partial^c h_t(\cdot, v_t)(y) + 2 \sum_{i=1}^p \epsilon_i g_i(y) \mathbb{B}^*, \tag{7}$$

and

$$\eta_t h_t(y, v_t) \geq 0, t \in T. \tag{8}$$

By (5), there exist $\xi_i^* \in \partial^c f_i(y)$, $\xi_i^{**} \in \partial^c (-g_i)(y)$, $i = 1, \ldots, p$, $\zeta_t^* \in \partial^c h_t(\cdot, v_t)(y)$, $t \in T$, and $b^* \in \mathbb{B}^*$, such that

$$\sum_{i=1}^p \xi_i^* + \sum_{i=1}^p \frac{f_i(y)}{g_i(y)} \xi_i^{**} + \sum_{t \in T} \eta_t \zeta_t^* + 2 \sum_{i=1}^p \epsilon_i g_i(y) b^* = 0. \tag{9}$$

Since $(f, -g, h_T)$ is generalized convex-inclusion on $\mathbb{R}^n$ at $y \in \mathbb{R}^n$, we have for such $\xi_i^* \in \partial^c f_i(y)$, $\xi_i^{**} \in \partial^c (-g_i)(y)$, $i = 1, \ldots, p$, and $\zeta_t^* \in \partial^c h_t(\cdot, v_t)(y)$, $t \in T$, there exists $\vartheta \in \mathbb{R}^n$, such that

$$f_i(x) - f_i(y) > \langle \xi_i^*, \vartheta \rangle, \ i = 1, \ldots, p,$$

$$-g_i(x) + g_i(y) \geq \langle \xi_i^{**}, \vartheta \rangle, \ i = 1, \ldots, p,$$

$$h_t(x, v_t) - h_t(y, v_t) \geq \langle \zeta_t^*, \vartheta \rangle, \ t \in T,$$

$$\langle b^*, \vartheta \rangle \leq \|x - y\|, \forall b^* \in \mathbb{B}^*,$$

and

$$0 \in \partial^c g_i(y), i = 1, \ldots, p.$$

Together with (7)–(9), these follow that

$$\sum_{i=1}^{p} \left(f_i(x) - \frac{f_i(y)}{g_i(y)} g_i(x) + 2\epsilon_i g_i(y) \|y - x\| \right)$$

$$> \sum_{i=1}^{p} \left(f_i(y) + \langle \xi_i^*, \vartheta \rangle - \frac{f_i(y)}{g_i(y)} g_i(y) + \frac{f_i(y)}{g_i(y)} \langle \xi_i^{**}, \vartheta \rangle + 2\epsilon_i g_i(y) \langle b^*, \vartheta \rangle \right)$$

$$= \left\langle \sum_{i=1}^{p} \xi_i^* + \sum_{i=1}^{p} \frac{f_i(y)}{g_i(y)} \xi_i^{**} + 2 \sum_{i=1}^{p} \epsilon_i g_i(y) b^*, \vartheta \right\rangle$$

$$= -\left\langle \sum_{i=1}^{p} \eta_t \zeta_t^*, \vartheta \right\rangle$$

$$\geq -\sum_{t \in T} \eta_t h_t(x, v_t) + \sum_{t \in T} \eta_t h_t(y, v_t).$$

Together with $\eta_t h_t(x, v_t) \leq 0, \forall x \in F$, and $\eta_t h_t(y, v_t) \geq 0$, we have

$$\sum_{i=1}^{p} \left(f_i(x) - \frac{f_i(y)}{g_i(y)} g_i(x) + 2\epsilon_i g_i(y) \|y - x\| \right) > 0.$$

Then, there exists $i_0 \in \{1, \ldots, p\}$, such that

$$f_{i_0}(x) - \frac{f_{i_0}(y)}{g_{i_0}(y)} g_{i_0}(x) + 2\epsilon_{i_0} g_{i_0}(y) \|y - x\| > 0,$$

which follows that

$$\frac{f_{i_0}(x)}{g_{i_0}(x)} - \frac{f_{i_0}(y)}{g_{i_0}(y)} + 2\epsilon_{i_0} \frac{g_{i_0}(y)}{g_{i_0}(x)} \|y - x\| > 0. \tag{10}$$

Moreover, it follows from $0 \in \partial^c g_i(y), i = 1, \ldots, p$, that

$$g_{i_0}(x) \geq g_{i_0}(y). \tag{11}$$

Together with (10) and (11), we have

$$\frac{f_{i_0}(x)}{g_{i_0}(x)} - \frac{f_{i_0}(y)}{g_{i_0}(y)} + 2\epsilon_{i_0} \|y - x\| > 0.$$

which is a contradiction to (5) and (6). Thus, the conclusion holds. □

Now, we give the following example to justify the importance of the assumption of generalized convex-inclusion in Theorem 1.

Example 1. Let $\mathcal{V}_t := [1 - t, 1 + t], t \in T := \left[0, \frac{1}{2}\right]$. Let $f_1, f_2, g_1, g_2 : \mathbb{R} \to \mathbb{R}$ and $g_t : \mathbb{R} \times \mathbb{R} \to \mathbb{R}, t \in T$, be defined by

$$f_1(x) = f_2(x) := \frac{1}{2}|x| + \frac{1}{6}x^3, g_1(x) = g_2(x) := |x| + 1,$$

and
$$h_t(x, v_t) := tx^2 - tx - 2v_t,$$
where $x \in \mathbb{R}$ and $v_t \in \mathcal{V}_t, t \in T$. Then, (UFP) becomes

$$\begin{cases} \text{Min}_{\mathbb{R}^2_+} \left(\frac{\frac{1}{2}|x|+\frac{1}{6}x^3}{|x|+1}, \frac{\frac{1}{2}|x|+\frac{1}{6}x^3}{|x|+1} \right) \\ \text{s.t.} \quad tx^2 - tx - 2v_t \leq 0, \forall t \in \left[0, \frac{1}{2}\right], \\ \quad x \in \mathbb{R}, \end{cases}$$

and (RFP) becomes

$$\begin{cases} \text{Min}_{\mathbb{R}^2_+} \left(\frac{\frac{1}{2}|x|+\frac{1}{6}x^3}{|x|+1}, \frac{\frac{1}{2}|x|+\frac{1}{6}x^3}{|x|+1} \right) \\ \text{s.t.} \quad tx^2 - tx - 2v_t \leq 0, \forall v_t \in [1-t, 1+t], t \in \left[0, \frac{1}{2}\right], \\ \quad x \in \mathbb{R}. \end{cases}$$

Obviously, $\mathcal{F} = [-1, 2]$. Let us consider $\bar{x} := -1 \in \mathcal{F}$. Then,

$$\left(\frac{f_1(\bar{x})}{g_1(\bar{x})}, \frac{f_2(\bar{x})}{g_2(\bar{x})} \right) = \left(\frac{1}{6}, \frac{1}{6} \right).$$

Now, consider the dual problem (UFD). In this setting, (OFD) becomes

$$\begin{cases} \text{Max}_{\mathbb{R}^2_+} \left(\frac{f_1(y)}{g_1(y)}, \frac{f_2(y)}{g_2(y)} \right) \\ \text{s.t.} \quad 0 \in \partial^c f_1(y) + \partial^c f_2(y) + \frac{f_1(y)}{g_1(y)} \partial^c(-g_1)(y) + \frac{f_2(y)}{g_2(y)} \partial^c(-g_2)(y) \\ \quad + \sum_{t \in T} \eta_t \partial^c h_t(\cdot, v_t)(y) + 2\epsilon_1 g_1(y) \mathbb{B}^* + 2\epsilon_2 g_2(y) \mathbb{B}^*, \\ \eta_t h_t(y, v_t) \geq 0, t \in \left[0, \frac{1}{2}\right], \\ y \in \mathbb{R}, \epsilon_1 \geq 0, \epsilon_2 \geq 0, \eta_t \geq 0, v_t \in [1-t, 1+t], t \in \left[0, \frac{1}{2}\right]. \end{cases}$$

Clearly, for any $y \in \mathbb{R}$ and $v_T \in \mathcal{V}_T$, we have

$$\partial^c f_1(y) = \partial^c f_2(y) = \left[\frac{1}{2}y^2 - \frac{1}{2}, \frac{1}{2}y^2 + \frac{1}{2} \right],$$

$$\partial^c(-g_1)(y) = \partial^c(-g_2)(y) = [-1, 1],$$

and

$$\partial^c h_t(\cdot, v_t)(y) = \{2ty - t\}, \forall t \in T.$$

By selecting $\bar{y} := 1, \bar{\eta}_t := 0$, and $\bar{v}_t := -t$, we have

$$\partial^c f_1(\bar{y}) + \partial^c f_2(\bar{y}) + \frac{f_1(\bar{y})}{g_1(\bar{y})} \partial^c(-g_1)(\bar{y}) + \frac{f_2(\bar{y})}{g_2(\bar{y})} \partial^c(-g_2)(\bar{y})$$
$$+ \sum_{t \in T} \bar{\eta}_t \partial^c h_t(\cdot, \bar{v}_t)(\bar{y}) + 2\epsilon_1 g_1(\bar{y}) \mathbb{B}^* + 2\epsilon_2 g_2(\bar{y}) \mathbb{B}^*$$
$$= \left[-4\epsilon_1 - 4\epsilon_2 - \frac{1}{3}, 4\epsilon_1 + 4\epsilon_2 + \frac{7}{3} \right],$$

and

$$\bar{\eta}_t h_t(\bar{y}, \bar{v}_t) \geq 0, t \in \left[0, \frac{1}{2}\right].$$

These mean that $(\bar{y}, \bar{\eta}_T, \bar{v}_T) \in \widehat{\mathcal{F}}$.

Now, take an arbitrarily $\epsilon = (\epsilon_1, \epsilon_2) \in \mathbb{R}_+^2 \setminus \{0\}$ such that $\epsilon_i < \frac{1}{12}, i = 1, 2$. Clearly,

$$\left(\frac{f_1(\bar{y})}{g_1(\bar{y})} - 2\epsilon_1 \|\bar{x} - \bar{y}\|, \frac{f_2(\bar{y})}{g_2(\bar{y})} - 2\epsilon_2 \|\bar{x} - \bar{y}\| \right) = \left(\frac{1}{3} - 2\epsilon_1, \frac{1}{3} - 2\epsilon_2 \right)$$
$$\succ \left(\frac{1}{6}, \frac{1}{6} \right) = \left(\frac{f_1(\bar{x})}{g_1(\bar{x})}, \frac{f_2(\bar{x})}{g_2(\bar{x})} \right).$$

Thus, Theorem 1 is not applicable since $(f, -g, h_T)$ is not generalized convex-inclusion at $\bar{y}$. To do this, by choosing $\bar{\xi}_i := 0 \in \partial^c f_i(\bar{y}), i = 1, 2$, we have

$$f_i(\bar{x}) - f_i(\bar{y}) = -\frac{2}{3} < 0 = \langle \bar{\xi}_k, \omega \rangle, \forall \omega \in \mathbb{R}.$$

Similarly, we obtain the following robust weak duality between (UMP) and (UMD).

Corollary 1. *Let $\epsilon \in \mathbb{R}_+^p \setminus \{0\}$. Suppose that $x \in \mathcal{F}$ and $(y, \eta_T, v_T) \in \overline{\mathcal{F}}$. If (f, h_T) is generalized convex on $\mathbb{R}^n$ at $y \in \mathbb{R}^n$, then,*

$$(f_1(x), \ldots, f_p(x)) \not\preceq (f_1(y) - 2\epsilon_1 \|x - y\|, \ldots, f_p(y) - 2\epsilon_p \|x - y\|).$$

Remark 6. *Clearly, by virtue of Example 1, we can also illustrate that the assumption of generalized convexity imposed in Corollary 1 is indispensable.*

Now, we give robust strong duality results between (UFP) and (UFD).

Theorem 2. *Let $\epsilon \in \mathbb{R}_+^p \setminus \{0\}$. Assume that (RSCQ) holds at $\bar{x} \in \mathcal{F}$. Suppose that $(f, -g, h_T)$ is generalized convex-inclusion on $\mathbb{R}^n$ at $y \in \mathbb{R}^n$. If $\bar{x}$ is a robust ϵ-quasi-efficient solution of (UFP), then there exist $\bar{\eta}_T \in \mathbb{R}_+^{(T)}$ and $\bar{v}_T \in \mathcal{V}_T$, such that $(\bar{x}, \bar{\eta}_T, \bar{v}_T) \in \widehat{\mathcal{F}}$ is a robust 2ϵ-quasi-efficient solution of (UFD).*

Proof. Assume that $\bar{x} \in \mathcal{F}$ is a robust ϵ-quasi-efficient solution of (UFP). By Theorem 1, there exist $\bar{\eta}_t \geq 0$, and $\bar{v}_t \in \mathcal{V}_t, t \in T$, such that

$$0 \in \sum_{i=1}^{p} \partial f_i(\bar{x}) - \sum_{i=1}^{p} \phi_i(\bar{x}) \partial g_i(\bar{x}) + \sum_{t \in T} \bar{\eta}_t \partial h_t(\cdot, \bar{v}_t)(\bar{x}) + 2 \sum_{i=1}^{p} \epsilon_i g_i(\bar{x}) \mathbb{B}^*, \quad (12)$$

and

$$\bar{\eta}_t h_t(\bar{x}, \bar{v}_t) = 0, \forall t \in T. \quad (13)$$

From (12), (13) and $\phi_i(\bar{x}) = \frac{f_i(\bar{x})}{g_i(\bar{x})}$, we have

$$(\bar{x}, \bar{\eta}_T, \bar{v}_T) \in \widehat{\mathcal{F}}.$$

By Theorem 1, for all $(y, \eta_T, v_T) \in \widehat{\mathcal{F}}$, we have

$$\left(\frac{f_1(\bar{x})}{g_1(\bar{x})}, \ldots, \frac{f_p(\bar{x})}{g_p(\bar{x})} \right) \not\preceq \left(\frac{f_1(y)}{g_1(y)} - 2\epsilon_1 \|\bar{x} - y\|, \ldots, \frac{f_p(y)}{g_p(y)} - 2\epsilon_p \|\bar{x} - y\| \right).$$

Thus, $(\bar{x}, \bar{\eta}_T, \bar{v}_T)$ is a robust 2ϵ-quasi-efficient solutions of (UFD). Thus, the conclusion holds. □

Remark 7. *In [32] (Theorem 4.2), the authors established duality properties for ϵ-quasi-weakly efficient solutions between (FP) and its Mond Weir-type dual problem. Therefore, Theorem 2 encompasses [32] (Theorem 4.2), where the corresponding results were given in terms of the similar methods.*

Similarly, we give robust strong duality properties for robust ϵ-quasi efficient solutions between (UMP) and (UMD).

Corollary 2. *Let* $\epsilon \in \mathbb{R}_+^p \setminus \{0\}$. *Assume that* (RSCQ) *holds at* $\bar{x} \in \mathcal{F}$. *Suppose that* (f, h_T) *is generalized convex on* $\mathbb{R}^n$ *at* $y \in \mathbb{R}^n$. *If* $\bar{x}$ *is a robust ϵ-quasi-efficient solution of* (UMP), *then there exist* $\bar{\eta}_T \in \mathbb{R}_+^{(T)}$ *and* $\bar{v}_T \in \mathcal{V}_T$, *such that* $(\bar{x}, \bar{\eta}_T, \bar{v}_T) \in \overline{\mathcal{F}}$ *is a robust 2ϵ-quasi-efficient solution of* (UMD).

Now, we give a robust converse-like duality property between (UFP) and (UFD).

Theorem 3. *Let* $\epsilon \in \mathbb{R}_+^p \setminus \{0\}$ *and* $(\bar{x}, \bar{\eta}_T, \bar{v}_T) \in \widehat{\mathcal{F}}$. *If* $(f, -g, h_T)$ *is generalized convex-inclusion on* $\mathbb{R}^n$ *at* $\bar{x} \in \mathcal{F}$, *then*, $\bar{x} \in \mathcal{F}$ *is a robust 2ϵ-quasi efficient solution of* (UMP).

Proof. Sine $(\bar{x}, \bar{\eta}_T, \bar{v}_T) \in \widehat{\mathcal{F}}$ and $(f, -g, h_T)$ is generalized convex-inclusion on $\mathbb{R}^n$ at $\bar{x}$, it follows from Theorem 1 that

$$\left(\frac{f_1(x)}{g_1(x)}, \ldots, \frac{f_p(x)}{g_p(x)}\right) \not\preceq \left(\frac{f_1(\bar{x})}{g_1(\bar{x})} - 2\epsilon_1 \|x - \bar{x}\|, \ldots, \frac{f_p(\bar{x})}{g_p(\bar{x})} - 2\epsilon_p \|x - \bar{x}|\right), \forall x \in \mathcal{F}.$$

Therefore, $\bar{x} \in \mathcal{F}$ is a robust 2ϵ-quasi efficient solution of (UFP) and the proof is complete. □

Remark 8. *Note that the converse-like duality result obtained in Theorem 3 extends* [32] *(Theorem 4.4) from the deterministic (i.e., with singleton uncertainty sets) to the robust setting. Moreover, Theorem 3 extends* [43] *(Theorem 4.3) from the scalar case to the multi-objective setting.*

Similarly, we have the following results for (UMP) and (UMD), which has been considered in [21] (Theorem 4.3).

Corollary 3. *Let* $\epsilon \in \mathbb{R}_+^p \setminus \{0\}$ *and* $(\bar{x}, \bar{\eta}_T, \bar{v}_T) \in \overline{\mathcal{F}}$. *If* (f, h_T) *is generalized convex on* $\mathbb{R}^n$ *at* $\bar{x} \in \mathcal{F}$, *then,* $\bar{x} \in \mathcal{F}$ *is a robust ϵ-quasi efficient solution of* (UMP).

4. Conclusions

In this paper, we consider robust ϵ-quasi-efficient solutions for a class of uncertain fractional optimization problems. By employing robust optimization and the obtained optimality conditions, a Mond–Weir-type robust dual problem for the fractional optimization problem is established. Then, we give robust ϵ-quasi-weak, strong and converse duality properties between them in terms of generalized convex-inclusion assumptions. We also show that the obtained results extend the corresponding results obtained in [21,32,37].

In the future, similar to [21,43], it is of interest to formulate *Mixed-type* robust approximate dual problem of uncertain fractional optimization problems, and study robust ϵ-quasi-weak, strong, and converse duality properties between them.

Funding: This research was supported by the Natural Science Foundation of Chongqing (Grant no.: cstc2021jcyj-msxmX1191) and the Research Fund of Chongqing Technology and Business University (Grant no.: 2156011).

Data Availability Statement: Not applicable.

Conflicts of Interest: The author declares no conflict of interest.

References

1. Chankong, V.; Haimes, Y.Y. *Multiobjective Decision Making: Theory and Methodology*; North-Holland: New York, NY, USA, 1983.
2. Liu, J. ϵ-duality theorem of nondifferentiable nonconvex multiobjective programming. *J. Optim. Theory Appl.* **1991**, *69*, 153–167. [CrossRef]

3. Caristi, G.; Ferrara, M.; Stefanescu, A. Semi-infinite multiobjective programming with generalized invexity. *Math. Rep.* **2010**, *12*, 217–233.
4. Fan, X.; Cheng, C.; Wang, H. Density of stable convex semi-infinite vector optimization problems. *Oper. Res. Lett.* **2012**, *40*, 140–143. [CrossRef]
5. Huy, N.Q.; Kim, D.S. Lipschitz behavior of solutions to nonconvex semi-infinite vector optimization problems. *J. Glob. Optim.* **2013**, *56*, 431–448. [CrossRef]
6. Verma, R.U. Weak ε-efficiency conditions for multiobjective fractional programming. *Appl. Math. Comput.* **2013**, *219*, 6819–6827. [CrossRef]
7. Chuong, T.D.; Kim, D.S. Approximate solutions of multiobjective optimization problems. *Positivity* **2016**, *20*, 187–207. [CrossRef]
8. Kim, D.S.; Son, T.Q. An approach to ε-duality theorems for nonconvex semi-infinite multiobjective optimization problems. *Taiwan J. Math.* **2018**, *22*, 1261–1287. [CrossRef]
9. Peng, Z.Y.; Peng, J.W.; Long, X.J.; Yao, J.C. On the stability of solutions for semi-infinite vector optimization problems. *J. Glob. Optim.* **2018**, *70*, 55–69. [CrossRef]
10. Peng, Z.Y.; Wang, X.; Yang, X.M. Connectedness of approximate efficient solutions for generalized semi-infinite vector optimization problems. *Set-Valued Var. Anal.* **2019**, *27*, 103–118. [CrossRef]
11. Son, T.Q.; Tuyen, N.V.; Wen, C.F. Optimality conditions for approximate Pareto solutions of a nonsmooth vector optimization problem with an infinite number of constraints. *Acta Math. Vietnam* **2020**, *45*, 435–448. [CrossRef]
12. Long, X.J.; Liu, J.; Huang, N.J. Characterizing the solution set for nonconvex semi-infinite programs involving tangential subdifferentials. *Numer. Funct. Anal. Optim.* **2021**, *42*, 279–297. [CrossRef]
13. Sun, X.K.; Mo, X.Q.; Teo, K.L. On weighted robust approximate solutions for semi-infinite optimization with uncertain data. *J. Nonlinear Convex Anal.* **2021**, *22*, 2507–2524.
14. Ben-Tal, A.; Nemirovski, A. Robust optimization-methodology and applications. *Math. Program.* **2002**, *92*, 453–480. [CrossRef]
15. Ben-Tal, A.; Ghaoui, L.E.; Nemirovski, A. *Robust Optimization*; Princeton University Press: Princeton, NJ, USA, 2009.
16. Bertsimas, D.; Brown, D.B.; Caramanis, C. Theory and applications of robust optimization. *SIAM Rev.* **2011**, *53*, 464–501. [CrossRef]
17. Lee, G.M.; Lee, J.H. On nonsmooth optimality theorems for robust multiobjective optimization problems. *J. Nonlinear Convex Anal.* **2015**, *16*, 2039–2052.
18. Chen, J.W.; Köbis, E.; Yao, J.C. Optimality conditions and duality for robust nonsmooth multiobjective optimization problems with constraints. *J. Optim. Theory Appl.* **2019**, *181*, 411–436. [CrossRef]
19. Guo, T.T.; Yu, G.L. Optimality conditions of the approximate quasi-weak robust efficiency for uncertain multi-objective convex optimization. *Pac. J. Optim.* **2019**, *15*, 623–638.
20. Sun, X.K.; Tang, L.P.; Zeng, J. Characterizations of approximate duality and saddle point theorems for nonsmooth robust vector optimization. *Numer. Funct. Anal. Optim.* **2020**, *41*, 462–482. [CrossRef]
21. Sun, X.K.; Teo, K.L.; Long, X.J. Some characterizations of approximate solutions for robust semi-infinite optimization problems. *J. Optim. Theory Appl.* **2021**, *191*, 281–310. [CrossRef]
22. Sun, X.K.; Tan, W.; Teo, K.L. Characterizing a class of robust vector polynomial optimization via sum of squares conditions. *J. Optim. Theory Appl.* **2023**, *197*, 737–764. [CrossRef]
23. Liu, J.; Long, X.J.; Sun, X.K. Characterizing robust optimal solution sets for nonconvex uncertain semi-infinite programming problems involving tangential subdifferential. *J. Glob. Optim.* **2023**, *87*, 481–501 [CrossRef]
24. Egudo, R. Multiobjective fractional duality. *Bull. Austral. Math. Soc.* **1988**, *37*, 367–378. [CrossRef]
25. Liu, J.C.; Yokoyama, K. ε-Optimality and duality for multiobjective fractional programming. *Comput. Math. Appl.* **1999**, *37*, 119–128. [CrossRef]
26. Long, X.J.; Huang, N.J.; Liu, Z.B. Optimality conditions, duality and saddle points for nondifferentiable multiobjective fractional programs. *J. Ind. Manag. Optim.* **2008**, *4*, 287–298. [CrossRef]
27. Long, X.J. Optimality conditions and duality for nondifferentiable multiobjective fractional programming problems with (C, α, ρ, d)-convexity. *J. Optim. Theory Appl.* **2011**, *148*, 197–208. [CrossRef]
28. Khanh, P.Q.; Tung, L.T. First- and second-order optimality conditions for multiobjective fractional programming. *Top* **2015**, *23*, 419–440. [CrossRef]
29. Chuong, T.D. Nondifferentiable fractional semi-infinite multiobjective optimization problems. *Oper. Res. Lett.* **2016**, *44*, 260–266. [CrossRef]
30. Stancu-Minasian, I.M. A ninth bibliography of fractional programming. *Optimization* **2019**, *68*, 2125–2169. [CrossRef]
31. Shitkovskaya, T.; Hong, Z.; Kim, D.S.; Piao, G.R. Approximate necessary optimality in fractional semi-infinite multiobjective optimization. *J. Nonlinear Convex Anal.* **2020**, *21*, 195–204.
32. Shitkovskaya, T.; Jiao, L.; Kim, D.S. Multi-criteria optimization problems with fractional objectives: Approximate optimality and approximate duality. *J. Nonlinear Convex Anal.* **2021**, *22*, 1117–1131.
33. Su, T.V.; Hang, D.D. Optimality and duality in nonsmooth multiobjective fractional programming problem with constraints. *4OR-Q. J. Oper. Res.* **2022**, *20*, 105–137.
34. Sun, X.K.; Long, X.J.; Fu, H.Y.; Li, X.B. Some characterizations of robust optimal solutions for uncertain fractional optimization and applications. *J. Ind. Manag. Optim.* **2017**, *13*, 803–824. [CrossRef]

35. Li, X.B.; Wang, Q.L.; Lin, Z. Optimality conditions and duality for minimax fractional programming problems with data uncertainty. *J. Ind. Manag. Optim.* **2019**, *15*, 1133–1151. [CrossRef]
36. Antczak, T. Parametric approach for approximate efficiency of robust multiobjective fractional programming problems. *Math. Methods Appl. Sci.* **2021**, *44*, 11211–11230. [CrossRef]
37. Sun, X.K.; Feng, X.Y.; Teo, K.L. Robust optimality, duality and saddle points for multiobjective fractional semi-infinite optimization with uncertain data. *Optim. Lett.* **2022**, *16*, 1457–1476. [CrossRef]
38. Thuy, N.T.T.; Su, T.V. Robust optimality conditions and duality for nonsmooth multiobjective fractional semi-infinite programming problems with uncertain data. *Optimization* **2023**, *72*, 1745–1775. [CrossRef]
39. Rockafellar, R.T. *Convex Analysis*; Princeton University Press: Princeton, NJ, USA, 1970.
40. Clarke, F.H. *Optimization and Nonsmooth Analysis*; Willey: New York, NY, USA, 1983.
41. Goberna, M.; López, M.A. *Linear Semi-Infinite Optimization*; Wiley: Chichester, UK, 1998.
42. Sun, X.K.; Teo, K.L.; Long, X.J. Characterizations of robust ε-quasi optimal solutions for nonsmooth optimization problems with uncertain data. *Optimization* **2021**, *70*, 847–870. [CrossRef]
43. Sun, X.K.; Teo, K.L.; Zeng, J.; Liu, L.Y. Robust approximate optimal solutions for nonlinear semi-infinite programming with uncertainty. *Optimization* **2020**, *69*, 2109–2129. [CrossRef]
44. Feng, X.Y.; Sun, X.K. Characterizations of approximate optimality conditions for fractional semi-infinite optimization problems with uncertainty. *Appl. Math. Mech.* **2022**, *43*, 682–689.
45. Zeng, J.; Xu, P.; Fu, H.Y. On robust approximate optimal solutions for fractional semi-infinite optimization with uncertainty data. *J. Inequal. Appl.* **2019**, *2019*, 45. [CrossRef]

Disclaimer/Publisher's Note: The statements, opinions and data contained in all publications are solely those of the individual author(s) and contributor(s) and not of MDPI and/or the editor(s). MDPI and/or the editor(s) disclaim responsibility for any injury to people or property resulting from any ideas, methods, instructions or products referred to in the content.

MDPI
St. Alban-Anlage 66
4052 Basel
Switzerland
www.mdpi.com

Axioms Editorial Office
E-mail: axioms@mdpi.com
www.mdpi.com/journal/axioms

Disclaimer/Publisher's Note: The statements, opinions and data contained in all publications are solely those of the individual author(s) and contributor(s) and not of MDPI and/or the editor(s). MDPI and/or the editor(s) disclaim responsibility for any injury to people or property resulting from any ideas, methods, instructions or products referred to in the content.

www.ingramcontent.com/pod-product-compliance
Lightning Source LLC
LaVergne TN
LVHW070401100526
838202LV00014B/1360